ELIZABETH'S
SPY MASTER

FRANCIS WALSINGHAM AND THE
SECRET WAR THAT SAVED ENGLAND

ROBERT HUTCHINSON

PHOENIX

To my mother,
who gave me the precious gift
of a love of history

A PHOENIX PAPERBACK

First published in Great Britain in 2006
by Weidenfeld & Nicolson
This paperback edition published in 2007 by Phoenix,
an imprint of Orion Books Ltd,
Orion House, 5 Upper St Martin's Lane,
London WC2H 9EA

1 3 5 7 9 10 8 6 4 2

A CIP catalogue record for this book
is available from the British Library.

ISBN-13 978-0-7538-2248-7

Printed and bound in Great Britain by
Mackays of Chatham plc, Chatham, Kent

The Orion Publishing Group's policy is to use papers that are natural,
renewable and recyclable products and made from wood grown in sustainable
forests. The logging and manufacturing processes are expected to conform
to the environmental regulations of the country of origin.

www.orionbooks.co.uk

Robert Hutchinson is a fellow of the Society of Antiquaries in London and an expert on the Reformation in England. He is a tutor in church archaelology for the University of Sussex Centre for Continuing Education, and the consultant on church monuments to the Diocese of Chichester Advisory Committee. He was a contributing author to *The Archaeology of the Reformation* and has written numerous papers on ecclesiology and church monuments. His acclaimed account of intrigues and conspiracies at the court of Elizabeth's father, *The Last Days of Henry VIII*, was published in 2004 by Weidenfeld & Nicolson.

Shall Honour, Fame and Titles of Renown
In Clods of Clay be thus enclosed still?
Rather will I, though wiser Wits may frown,
For to enlarge his Fame extend my Skill.
Right gentle Reader, be it known to thee,
A famous knight doth here interred lye,
Noble by Birth, renown'd for Policy
Confounding Foes, which wrought our Jeopardy.
In Foreign Countries their intents he knew
Such was his Zeal to do his Country good,
When dangers would by Enemies ensue,
As well as they themselves he understood.
Launch forth ye Muses into Streams of Praise,
Sing and sound forth praiseworthy harmony;
In England Death cut off his dismal days,
Not wronged by Death but by false Treachery:
Grudge not at this imperfect Epitaph
Herein I have expressed my simple skill,
As the First fruits proceeding from a Graft
Make then a better whosoever will.

An acrostic poem – the initial letter of each line spelling out Sir
Francis Walsingham's name. Written by 'E. W.' – probably his
grand-daughter, the poet Elizabeth Walsingham – and placed
over his tomb in Old St Paul's Cathedral, London. It was lost in
the Great Fire of London in 1666.

Contents

Author's Note

Sir Francis Walsingham is one of the great unknown heroes of English history. By right, he should rank with Horatio Nelson, the Duke of Wellington and even Sir Winston Churchill as one of the great patriotic defenders, against all-comers, of this island state, its monarchs, governments, beliefs and creeds. But as befits a man very much of the shadows, his star has traditionally been eclipsed by many, not least by William Cecil, Baron Burghley, his fellow Minister in Elizabeth's government.

It is time to redress that imbalance and recount how one man's single-minded, ruthless campaign to protect his sovereign and state, in truth, changed the course of European history.

This is a grim, dramatic tale of subversion, cruelty, greed, disloyalty and deception. If those human failings seem familiar to us in the twenty-first century, it is because four hundred years on, they are still very much with us in the realms of international politics, diplomacy and espionage.

Walsingham would not have felt uncomfortable with the draconian Prevention of Terrorism Acts that have passed onto Western nations' statute books in recent years. Indeed, he would have felt thwarted and handicapped by the modern notion of the importance of human rights and the restrictions on harsh methods of questioning imposed by Western societies. In the 1585 *Act for the Surety of the Queen's Person*, he and Burghley produced a startling example of counter-terrorist legislation that was tantamount to lynch law: empowering ordinary citizens to hunt down and kill on sight any successful conspirator against Elizabeth I's life. The measure also extended to such conspirators' associates and descendants, if claimants to the throne.

Today's dictum that 'One man's terrorist is another man's freedom fighter' was just as true in the 1580s. To Walsingham, faced with a succession of plots against his queen and state, the many English Catholics covertly practising their religion were potential terrorists and assassins. Most of his suspects were therefore subjects of his own queen – individuals driven by a breathtakingly strong religious faith into becoming the enemy within. Their courage and fortitude, however misguided and dangerous their aims in the eyes of those in authority at the time, still have the power to astonish and fill us with wonder today.

In Walsingham's time, dealing with the enemies of the state was much more straightforward than it is in the twenty-first century. The critical path to the neutralisation of the threat they posed was frequently taken and brutally simple: betrayal; arrest; imprisonment; interrogation, often under torture; confession; the semblance of a legal trial; and finally a horrific, barbarous execution. Walsingham's weapons against them were his spies and informers – mostly motivated by the prospect of hard cash rewards, some drawn from the dregs of Tudor society – the insidious arts of state propaganda and a raft of punitive penal legislation.

For all his considerable erudition and culture, Walsingham did not hesitate to employ torture to extract the information he sought from a prisoner. In 1575, whilst investigating allegations of secret channels of communication between the sequestered Mary Queen of Scots and the outside world, Walsingham told Burghley darkly, 'Without torture I know we shall not prevail.' He employed all the black instruments of the police state at his disposal to crush the treason and sedition he saw around him, including the establishment of the first internment camp in England – he sent obdurate Catholics to Wisbech Castle in Cambridgeshire. Walsingham, ever a man with wide vision, even had a plan to exile obstinate recusants to a new colony in North America.

After the close-run defeat of the Spanish Armada, England's most famous sea captain, Sir Francis Drake, paid this tribute to Walsingham's role in the defence of the realm:

> I will not flatter you, but you have fought more with your pen than many in our English navy fought with their enemies . . . But that your place and most necessary attendance about her majesty [could not] be spared, your valour and desserts in such place opposite to the enemy [would have] showed itself.

Largely unrecognised by Elizabeth, his parsimonious and havering sovereign, it is time to award Walsingham his proper place in English history by shining a light into the dark corners of the murky world he inhabited – a realm of deceit, deception and betrayal. Even as a man of high moral principles, he would have firmly believed that his game was worth the candle.

Robert Hutchinson

WEST SUSSEX AUGUST 2005

Acknowledgements

This book could not have been written without the help and active support of many friends and colleagues, not least my dear wife Sally, who has lived with the dour persona of Francis Walsingham for more time than she cares to remember. Anyone who writes about this statesman and spy master will inevitably be greatly in the debt of Conyers Read, who produced the magisterial three-volume biography of him in 1925. Research has moved on considerably since then and perceptions of the reality of Elizabethan governance have changed, but his work retains enormous perception and value.

Much of the material for this book has been drawn from contemporary sources and my grateful thanks are due to all those whose patience and kindness have assisted me in tracking down documents and rare books. In particular, I would like to thank Robin Harcourt Williams, Librarian and Archivist to the Marquis of Salisbury at Hatfield House; Bernard Nurse, Librarian, and Adrian James, Assistant Librarian, of the Society of Antiquaries of London; the ever-willing and helpful staff at the former Public Record Office (now the National Archives) at Kew; the Manuscripts and Rare-Book Departments at the British Library; Kay Walters at the incomparable library at the Athenæum Club; the Revd Father Jerome Bertram for much help, as always, with Latin translations; Sister Mary Joseph OSB, Librarian of the Venerable English College in Rome; Alison Waggitt for the index; Ian Drury of Weidenfeld & Nicolson for all his encouragement; to Ilona Jasiewicz, managing editor, for her manifold kindnesses and patient assistance; Lisa Rogers for her painstaking care and considerable editing skills; and finally Marcel Hoad and his team at Fowlers for their invaluable support in so many ways.

To all these kind people, I would like to pass on my grateful thanks. I must point out, however, that any errors or omissions are entirely my own responsibility.

Prologue

'My mind is far from malice. I call God to record that as a private person, I have done nothing [unbecoming to] an honest man. Nor, as I bear the place of a public man, have I done anything unworthy . . . I confess that being very careful for the safety of the Queen and realm, I have curiously searched out practices against the same.'

SIR FRANCIS WALSINGHAM, AT THE TRIAL OF MARY QUEEN OF SCOTS, 14 OCTOBER, 1586.[1]

It is his dark, deepset eyes that immediately arrest your attention. Staring out of the painting, they seem hooded, thoughtful, even quizzical, as if they seek to peer directly into the viewer's mind, mercilessly probing and exploring one's most private thoughts and innermost emotions. The portrait of Sir Francis Walsingham, Queen Elizabeth I's principal Secretary of State, painted around 1587 probably by the fashionable artist John De Critz the Elder,[2] is an uncompromising study of an equally uncompromising man. More than four centuries later, the authority and intense energy of his personality, captured by this stark, dour likeness, remain wholly undiminished.

That finely chiselled face with its prominent aquiline nose and receding hairline appears to us cold, cruel and calculating – suggesting a man not to be trifled with. The heavily starched white ruff beneath his neatly trimmed beard is the single gesture from this brooding, fanatical Protestant towards the glamorous chic of the Elizabethan court's opulent and extravagant costume. The background of the picture, which hangs now in London's National Portrait Gallery, is dark and mysterious, providing few clues or hints about the man or his life. Many visitors idly pass by, eager to get to the familiar portraits of Tudor royalty half-remembered from their school lessons or, more likely, from a recent history programme on television.

In doing so, they miss the chance of confronting, face to face, the enigmatic image of one of the great, powerful engines of state who drove, shaped and, above all, safeguarded the late-sixteenth-century English fledgling Protestant nation.

Walsingham was far more than a mere pen-pushing bureaucrat, a ministerial apparatchik of Elizabeth's autocratic government. True, he was heavily involved in forging and implementing England's foreign policy during the two turbulent and bloody decades from 1570 onwards – acting as the equivalent, perhaps, of a modern Foreign Secretary or the US Secretary of State. But his other, more sinister responsibilities profoundly touched the lives of almost every one of his queen's 3.5 million subjects. For Walsingham was also Elizabeth's spy master, secret policeman and de facto propaganda chief.

During his single-minded mission both to protect Elizabeth's sacred person from the continual threat of assassination and to defeat the many Catholic enemies of *Gloriana*'s government domestically and overseas, he constantly deployed all those devious and underhand techniques now known by the intelligence community's disarming sobriquet of 'tradecraft'. His dire, black methods would be familiar to any aficionado of today's espionage thrillers: the perfidious paraphernalia of dead letter boxes, complex ciphers, secret writing, bribery, extortion, blackmail, forgery, double – sometimes triple – agents, and yes, even torture to brutally extract timely and incriminating information from his helpless prisoners.

Walsingham's clandestine activities combined the roles fulfilled in modern British society by the Secret Intelligence Service (better known as MI6), the Security Service (or MI5) and the Special Branch of the Police. He was concerned not only with gathering and analysing vital military and diplomatic intelligence, but also with entrapping and ruthlessly destroying those subversives plotting the downfall of Elizabeth's government. At its peak, his extensive espionage network is said to have numbered fifty-three spies and eighteen agents in foreign courts, as well as a host of informers within the English realm itself, some of them turncoats, others from the detritus of Tudor society. One of his spies was probably the playwright Christopher Marlowe, who almost certainly worked for him in return for escaping state prosecution for the blasphemy contained in his drama *Tamburlaine*, first produced in 1587.[3] Walsingham also employed a range of technical experts, from his codebreakers, who swiftly deciphered the secret messages sent by Elizabeth's enemies, to one Arthur Gregory, who was skilled in opening letters and then resealing them – without trace, as far as the addressee was concerned.

Walsingham's methods brought many from the highest born to the most lowly to the executioner's scaffold, including an anointed monarch, Mary Queen of Scots, in February 1587. His intelligence network and international financial machinations were major factors in the defeat of the Spanish Armada just over a year later in 1588. But his most chilling duty was masterminding the government's intensive campaign, at home and abroad, against the Catholic missions sent to England – viewed by those in power as rebellious, seditious and traitorous – and those who harboured them.

A disturbing flavour of life as a fugitive priest in Elizabeth's police state is provided in a letter to Alfonso Agazzari, Rector of the English College in Rome, from the Jesuit Robert Persons, then living undercover in England. The missionary wrote in August 1581 of the dreadful, numbing fear of that sudden Gestapo-like knock on the door from Walsingham's questing pursuivants:

It is the custom of the Catholics themselves to take to the woods and thickets, to ditches and holes even, for concealment, when their houses are broken into [at] night.

Sometimes when we are sitting at table quite cheerfully, conversing familiarly about matters of faith or piety . . . it happens that someone rings at the front door a little more insistently than usual, so he can be put down as an official.

Immediately, like deer that have heard the voice of hunters and prick their ears and become alert, all stand to attention, stop eating and commend themselves to God in the briefest of prayers; no word or sound of any sort is heard until the servants report what is the matter . . .

It can be truly said of them that they carry their lives always in their hands.[4]

Walsingham sat spider-like at the centre of his carefully constructed web of deceit and deception, gathering information about the Catholic seminaries and their recusant[5] supporters in England from battalions of spies and informers. One, the young Charles Sledd, was employed as a servant at that same English College in Rome in 1579–80. He provided many physical descriptions of those priests and Jesuits who had secretly departed for England, to facilitate their arrests. For example:

John Neale, sometime rector of Exeter College in Oxford. Was made priest in Rome and sang his first Mass [on] 8 September 1579. About fifty years of age, tall and slender in body, a brownish grey beard, lean and slender faced [with] little eyes and fast of speech.

Thomas Hide, priest, about thirty years of age. The hair of his head and beard milk white and to look at, a simple man and of a mean stature. A Berkshire man born.

Thomas Worthington, priest, [ordained] at Rheims or Douai, about thirty-four years of age. Of a reasonable stature, the hair of his beard of a brown colour cut short and rather thick, the tip of his nose somewhat red. A simple man to look at, slender of body. A Lancashire man.[6]

On arrival in England, if they eluded the government's watchful customs 'searchers' based at the ports, the priests were ruthlessly hunted, always having to be ready to move at a moment's notice from safe house to safe house, constantly trying to keep one step ahead of Walsingham's hunters. The prisons in London and elsewhere were soon full. The terrifying fate for many was execution for treason: hanging by the neck until half-dead, their genitals cut off and organs ripped out, these then burnt before the victim's eyes and then the final beheading and quartering of the corpse. The mangled body parts were then displayed in public places as a warning and deterrent to any who dared conspire against the English crown. Such gruesome deaths became regular grim spectacles on scaffolds throughout the land. The tragic list of Catholic martyrs, dying horribly for their faith, grew inexorably year on year.

The root causes of Elizabeth's draconian penal policy were not only religious, but also dynastic. The virulent persecution of the Catholics in England by Elizabeth's government was a direct legacy of her father Henry VIII's turbulent reign. He had assumed the title of Supreme Head of the Church of England after his break with Rome over the messy divorce from his Spanish first wife, Catherine of Aragon.

Henry's last Act of Succession in 1544[7] and his controversial will[8] firmly laid down the Tudor line of succession: firstly to Edward, his son and heir by Jane Seymour; secondly to Mary, his daughter by Catherine of Aragon; and thirdly to Elizabeth, his daughter by Anne Boleyn. If none of this was applicable or went unfulfilled, the succession would be settled on the heirs of Lady Frances (eldest daughter of the king's late younger sister, Mary) or her sister, Lady Eleanor.

Henry VIII died, to all intents and purposes, a good, devout Catholic, although still defiantly denying the Pope's supremacy over religion in England. Edward VI, who came to the throne as a precocious nine-year-old in January 1547, presided wanly over a militant Protestant government that callously cleansed England's churches and cathedrals of their pious riches in a quest for cash to fill his painfully bare exchequer, as well as dramatically sweeping away the last familiar and much-loved rites of the Catholic liturgy. Edward's successor, his half-sister Mary, swiftly returned the realm to the religious jurisdiction of Rome after 1553, amid a ferocious repression of the new beliefs: 280 Protestant heretics died piteously at the stake during her five-year reign.

Thus, when Henry's last daughter, the Protestant Elizabeth, finally ascended the throne in 1558, the vast majority of her subjects still remained Catholic. The veteran Privy Councillor Sir Ralph Sadler wrote tellingly in 1569 that in his area, there was

> not in all this country ten gentlemen that do favour and allow of her majesty's proceedings in the cause of religion and the common people are ignorant, full of superstition and altogether blinded with the old popish doctrine.[9]

He warned that adherence to the Protestant creed was only skin deep, and added graphically, 'The ancient faith still lay like lees[10] at the bottoms of men's hearts and if the vessel was ever so little stirred, [it] comes to the top.'

Moreover, for Elizabeth's government and England's Protestant minority, the continuing, dreadful sufferings of the Netherlands were never far from the forefront of their minds. In 1559, Philip of Spain had re-enacted a draconian edict against Protestant thought, word and deed within his possessions in the Low Countries. Those found guilty of such heresy must always die: the men by the sword and the women by being buried alive. Unrepentant heretics were burnt at the stake and those who failed to inform on their neighbours were adjudged heretics themselves and faced the same fate of torture and execution. Philip took great pride in the horrific activities of the Inquisition against his Dutch Protestant subjects: 'Why introduce the Spanish inquisition,' he wrote in 1562, '[when] the inquisition of the Netherlands is much more pitiless than that of Spain?'[11]

When the Low Countries rose in revolt against this violent religious repression, Fernando Alvarez de Toledo, Duke of Alva, was dispatched with a hand-picked army of veterans to put it down ruthlessly with fire and sword. Alva set about his task with a burning conviction that he was engaged in a personal crusade against infidel forces and planned to plant his banner of the Holy Cross on the blackened and bloody battlements of three hundred Protestant towns. In September 1567, Alva set up his Council of Troubles to administer harsh justice on the insurgents. It soon became known as the 'Blood Council' for the thousands upon thousands who died at its merciless hands.

Across the southern North Sea in London, the lessons were written starkly in Protestant blood in the decades that followed for Walsingham and his fellow Ministers. They believed that a new Catholic regime in England would wreak genocidal vengeance in the same terrible way, almost certainly supported by Spanish pikes and artillery called in to help suppress the inevitable civil war. Would such trappings of terror as the grim, gaudy spectacle of the Inquisition's auto-da-fé – the march to the scaffold – become a regular occurrence in the streets and squares of England's towns and cities?

The worst fears of Elizabeth's government were quickly realised.

In November 1569, the always restive and conservative North of England was electrified by open rebellion breaking out with the twin aims of overthrowing Elizabeth's rule and re-establishing the Catholic religion. On 14 November, the Earls of Northumberland and Westmorland, escorted by 300 armed horsemen, broke into Durham Cathedral, destroyed the English Bibles and prayer books within and banned further Protestant services there. They then marched south, and as with any marauding army, looting and destruction went unchecked. Sir George Bowes, later Provost Marshal of Elizabeth's avenging army, complained bitterly that the rebels had

> ... spoiled and taken all my goods and cattle ... with all my household stuff and all manner of provision for maintenance of a house and have threshed and carried away all my corn from all places to the value of £3,000.[12]
>
> They have utterly defaced my principal house, pulling down and carrying away the glass and iron of the windows and ... doors and some of the [roof] covering, being lead.
>
> They have carried away from my house all my evidence,

charters, leases and writings that concerned all my lands, to the extreme prejudice of me and my heirs for ever.[13]

Unfortunately for the rebel leaders, however, their 7,500-strong insurrection, drawn from their tenantry who were mostly poor and unschooled in war, became a military farce. Even the strongest faith may falter for want of money and grievous shortages of food, as well as constant exhaustion and cold. The Northern Rebellion swiftly turned into a hopeless cause in the teeth of the growing numbers of well-armed royal troops being mobilised to destroy it. After inconclusive military manoeuvrings, the rebel army hesitated, retreated and then quietly melted away as government forces marched to defeat them. Tudor mercilessness now flowing strongly through her veins, Elizabeth wrote crisply to her field commanders in January 1570:

> We marvel that we have heard of no execution by martial law, as was appointed, of the meaner sort of rebels in the north. If the same be not already done, you are to proceed thereunto, for the terror of others, with expedition.[14]

Around 750 insurgents were executed to satisfy her increasingly strident calls for vengeance. The queen's General, Thomas Radcliffe, Third Earl of Sussex, ordered that in Richmondshire, part of Yorkshire, a total of 231 were to be hanged out of the 1,241 in the neighbourhood who had joined the rebellion.[15] One commander, Sir Thomas Gargrave, wrote to Bowes on 4 February objecting to the scale of reprisals, which would leave many villages bare of male inhabitants, and recommended that

> some select number may be chosen of the least and meanest sorts and chiefly the papists and these to be attainted as well here [York] as at Durham, and all the rest would I wish to be pardoned, except certain chosen persons that be abroad, for in my opinion, the poor husband man and mean subject (if he be not a great papist) will become good subjects.[16]

Those tardy unfortunates who did not quickly rally to Elizabeth's flag against the rebels were also not allowed to escape her ruthless retribution. She ordered: 'Spare no offenders in that case – but let them come to trial and receive due punishment.'[17]

Of the rebellion leaders, Sir Thomas Percy, Seventh Earl of Northumberland, took refuge in Scotland but was handed over to the English authorities by the Scottish Regent James Stewart, Earl of Moray, and beheaded in August 1572 at York.[18] His severed head was stuck on top of the city's Micklegate Bar (or gate) to pointedly exemplify the inevitable grim fate of traitors. Percy's partner in rebellion Charles Neville, Sixth Earl of Westmorland, fled for his life to Flanders.[19] On 13 March 1570, Elizabeth's government issued a proclamation demanding that the rebels must swear an oath of allegiance, confess to their crimes and hear sermons on the evil of rebellion.[20] Religious homilies written later by Matthew Parker, Archbishop of Canterbury, firmly stressed that obedience to the queen was a duty to God for all within the realm of England.

But other, still powerful voices had very different ideas.

On 25 February 1570, Pope Pius V[21] published the bull *Regnans in Excelsis* which excommunicated Elizabeth and deprived this 'pretended' English queen of her throne – as well as absolving her subjects of any allegiance or loyalty to her. It claimed she had usurped the place of Supreme Head of the Church and returned the English nation to 'miserable destruction' after Mary I had brought it back 'to the Catholic faith and good fruits'.[22] A few months later, the bull was cheekily nailed to the garden gate of the Bishop of London's home in St Paul's churchyard for all to see and wonder at.[23]

It was a grave tactical mistake by the Vatican in its campaign against Protestant England, for it instantly transformed each of Elizabeth's Catholic subjects into an individual and palpable threat to her life. Pius V had given his blessing – his permission – for their treason against both state and monarch. As far as Elizabeth and her ministers were concerned, so soon after the scare of the Northern Rebellion, all English Catholics were now potential enemies within.

In addition, there were numerous Catholic missions being dispatched to England to support the covert celebration of the Mass and to institute large-scale conversions. Always present, always threatening, were the wild and impractical conspiracies hatched by English Catholic exiles to invade England, topple Elizabeth off the throne and throw her Ministers and advisers into prison. In the Pope, the Catholic states in Europe and the Catholic population at home, her government and the state religion now faced what they saw as a clear and present danger to their survival.

The campaign against Elizabeth was personal, motivated by a very real hatred. Many Catholics regarded her as an illegitimate heretic, the bastard daughter of Anne Boleyn, who had secretly married Henry before the death of his wife Catherine of Aragon. A dark, embittered memorandum, the frustration virulently scorching off the pages, written in September 1570 probably by an English Catholic exile in Brussels, discusses the 'condition of England'. It says of Elizabeth:

> Verily she is the whore depicted in the Apocalypse with the wine of whose prostitution the kings of the earth are drunk.
>
> Seeing that meanwhile she is drunk with the blood of the martyrs of Jesus, significant indeed is the figure of that whore and yet more confirmed in that belief would they be who knew that in the time of Queen Mary[24] of happy memory, she would have lost her life for complicity of treason, but that one of the chief nobles of the land intervened to save it.[25]
>
> Therefore, seeing that Elizabeth is now of evil odour not only with God but also with men, we demand . . . that Catholic Princes cease to accord her regal honour.[26]

What many English Catholics fervently desired was the replacement of Elizabeth by Mary Queen of Scots, widow of first Francis II of France and then of Henry, Lord Darnley and latterly the wife of the dashing James Hepburn, Fourth Earl of Bothwell. For her personal heraldry, she had unwisely quartered the arms of England with those of Scotland and France, in what was tantamount to a none-too-subtle claim to the throne of England. She steadfastly maintained that she was the strongest heir presumptive to the English crown because of her direct descent from

Henry VIII's elder sister, Margaret.[27] Such claims, regularly and loudly professed, do not endear one to the sitting occupant of the throne, nor to those whose continued status and prosperity depend on that incumbent remaining in power.

Mary had fled to England from Scotland after her defeat in a brief civil war in Scotland in 1568 and spent the remainder of her life to all intents and purposes a prisoner of Elizabeth I, closely watched over in a variety of five-star jails in the Midlands and the North in an attempt to quarantine her from the pestilence of English politics.

To Walsingham, she was always a grave threat – to his queen and her crown, to his state and to his beloved religion. He called her 'that devilish woman' as early as 1572, when he maintained that as long as she lived, Elizabeth would not enjoy a quiet reign 'nor could her faithful servants assure themselves of the safety of their lives'.[28] Always calculating, always cautious, eventually, by deciphering her letters and indulging in a little light forgery to produce incriminating evidence, he entrapped the Scottish queen.

Today, the spy master's role in Elizabethan England is little appreciated, almost completely overshadowed by the authority and presence of that giant of the Tudor world, Sir William Cecil, Baron Burghley, the Chief Minister of the realm.

But Walsingham's name still pops up in unexpected places. The surreal 'Kids' Page' of the website of the National Security Agency – the US Government agency that eavesdrops on your international telephone calls, faxes and e-mails – features Walsingham, together with a game involving a cipher that substitutes letters of the standard alphabet for others to form a simple code. 'The word "hello",' says the website, cheerfully providing the solution, 'could be encrypted ITSSG.' Good fun for those crowded around a computer screen on a long, dark winter evening. Educational, perhaps, certainly an innocent enough pastime.

But in Walsingham's day, the game would have been far more deadly, and participants would have been playing for the highest stakes. In those days, torture and the scaffold were the grim penalty for getting the answer wrong.

CHAPTER ONE

'Serviceable to Our Age'

'Especially have regard . . . chiefly of the nobility
[and] gentry . . . that you see the inclination
of each man, which way he is bent, whether it be
a marshal or counsellor, a plain open nature,
[or] dissembling or counterfeit and what
pension[1] he has from abroad . . . '

ADVICE FROM SIR FRANCIS WALSINGHAM TO ONE OF HIS NEPHEWS,
PROBABLY WRITTEN IN THE LATE 1570s.[2]

Francis Walsingham was born around 1532,[3] the only son of William, a London lawyer with extensive estates in Kent, and his wife Joyce, the daughter of Sir Edmund Denny of Cheshunt in Hertfordshire. She was sister to Sir Anthony Denny, Chief Gentleman of the Privy Chamber to Henry VIII and the real unseen power behind the throne during the ailing monarch's last months.[4] Politics, particularly Protestant politics, therefore ran vigorously through Walsingham's veins. Francis' uncle was Sir Edmund Walsingham, a gallant soldier who fought against the Scots in the crushing English victory at Flodden Field in 1513 and who later became the Lieutenant of the Tower of London,[5] being rewarded with grants of property by Henry VIII for his 'good, true and faithful service'.[6]

Some confusion surrounds the Walsingham family's ancestry. Several pedigrees exist that seek to prove their gentle blood – a direct lineage from the lords of the manor of Walsingham in north Norfolk. One of these – drawn up by a fawning Robert Glover, the *Somerset Herald*, sometime during 1570–88 – lists a host of Walsinghams, some knighted, beginning with a Thomas who died in 1337.[7] This genealogy is largely fictitious, indeed is an Elizabethan fake, and is wholly unsupported by history. The harsh truth is that the Walsinghams came from trade.

The family was hardly 'in every way splendidly conspicuous', as Walsingham's epitaph later gushingly claimed. Their lowly origins lie in Alan Walsingham, a humble cordwainer – in other words, a shoemaker – who purchased tenements in the parish of St Benet's, Gracechurch Street, in London in 1403. His prosperity grew and he bought up a number of valuable properties elsewhere in the city, including a 'mansion house' in Eastcheap and a brewery and alehouse, called the Cock and Hoop, in Cripplegate. By 1412, his property holdings were incurring sizeable taxes totalling £17 11s a year, or just over £7,000 in today's money. His son Thomas became a wine merchant and also dabbled in other profitable trades, such as the export of fish and cloth from London. In terms of city hierarchy, Thomas married well – to Margaret Bamme, daughter of the goldsmith Henry Bamme, whose influential family included two former Lord Mayors of London in 1390 and 1396. In 1424, he purchased, as his country house, the manor of Scadbury in Chislehurst, Kent, which was to become a seat of the Walsinghams in succeeding generations. His descendants remained in the lucrative vintner trade until James, Francis Walsingham's grandfather, made the final triumphant transition from merchant to gentleman, signing himself 'esquire' and being granted the socially all-important coat of arms. It was a saga typical of many in England during the fifteenth century, of a family successfully clambering their way up the ladder of society.

Francis' father William was the younger of James's two sons, and trained as a lawyer at Gray's Inn. In 1524, he was appointed a Commissioner of the Peace in Kent, and again in 1526 and 1532, and was recommended by both Henry VIII and his queen, Catherine of Aragon, to fill the post of Common Serjeant for London in 1526.[8] Three years later, he may be the William Walsingham who appears on a long list of debtors, owing a total of £330 in sealed bonds to the rapacious Thomas Cromwell, who became Henry's Chief Minister. In 1530, William was one of three commissioners appointed to investigate the possessions of the disgraced Cardinal Wolsey and two years later became one of the two Under-Sheriffs of London. He prospered as a lawyer, purchasing considerable new property including the manors of Foots Cray, Rokesly and Chelsfield in Kent and in the parish of St Mary Aldermanbury, where he maintained his London home. He died in 1534, seeking in his will to reserve Chelsfield to fund the marriage of his five daughters, and 'if Joyce, my wife [dies] before Francis my son be twenty-one, my said manors of Foots Cray to be used as payment of my debts and for the advancement of my daughters'.[9] His twenty-seven-year-old widow was left with Francis, now a two-year-old infant, and all those daughters to marry off into good families. She remarried herself in 1538 to the courtier Sir John Carey of Plashy[10] in Hertfordshire, a match probably mooted and arranged by her own family, the Dennys, who held property in that county.

Walsingham's early life is frustratingly short on detail, as perhaps befits the man of the shadows he was later to become as head of Queen Elizabeth's secret service.

At the age of sixteen he went to the then notoriously Protestant King's College, Cambridge,[11] where John Cheke, Edward VI's reformist tutor, was then provost. Walsingham's tutor was Thomas Gardiner, another keen adherent of the new religion. He matriculated as a fellow commoner on 12 November 1548 and probably went down, seemingly without taking a degree, sometime before 1551. Walsingham then travelled in Europe, visiting 'many foreign countries whose manners, laws, languages and policies he accurately studied and critically understood',[12] before returning to London a year later, a confirmed and devout Protestant. He enrolled as a student at Gray's Inn, clearly intending to follow his father into the legal profession. But his ambitions and dreams in the staid and stuffy world of the law were not to be fulfilled.

Edward VI died 'thin and wasted' in his sixteenth year on 6 July 1553, from a suppurating pulmonary infection, septicaemia and renal failure. As planned, the leaders of his Protestant government immediately proclaimed the teenage Lady Jane Grey, grand-daughter of Mary, one of Henry VIII's sisters, his lawful successor. Edward's elder half-sister, Princess Mary, fled London for the safety of East Anglia. There she mustered forces loyal to her Catholic cause and, gathering more troops en route, marched on the capital where the chastened Privy Council hastily named her queen on 19 July. Catholicism had returned to England.

Around 1,000 Protestant reformers fled England for safety, particularly after the Kent-based rebellion launched by Sir Thomas Wyatt in 1554 in protest against Mary's marriage to Philip of Spain was finally defeated at the western gates of the City of London. It may be that some relatives of the Walsingham family were caught up in that abortive uprising and were closely involved in the attempt to maintain a Protestant royal line via that tragic and misused figure of English history, Lady Jane Grey.[13] Certainly, by the time the fearsome torchings of heretics began in London's Smithfield and the market squares of many English towns as Mary sought to cauterise the fervour of the new religion, Walsingham had departed the shores of England for Europe once again, youthful discretion overcoming his gamecock valour.

After some journeying in Europe, he reappears at the University of Padua in Italy on 29 December 1555, where he was elected *Consularius* or representative of the English students studying in the faculty of civil law, with an influential seat on the university's governing senate. But his time at this liberal and tolerant seat of learning was strangely brief, as Walsingham left there in 1556 and travelled on to France, Switzerland and probably Frankfurt in Germany. He returned from exile sometime after Mary's death in 1558 and the accession of the Protestant Elizabeth, the last of Henry's turbulent brood to come to the throne of England.

Walsingham was probably in England when his mother died in 1560; she was buried next to her first husband in St Mary Aldermanbury Church.[14] Despite Walsingham's now fervent Protestant beliefs, a Mass was said during the funeral and communion was taken by at least some of the mourners. Four of his sisters had married during his exile,[15] the youngest, Mary, to Walter Mildmay, later to become Chancellor of the Exchequer in Elizabeth's government, the founder of Emmanuel College in Cambridge[16] and a staunch friend. Walsingham was by this time aged twenty-eight, fluent in French, Italian and Latin – indeed, he was later reckoned to be 'the best linguist' of the period.[17] He had his own complex coat of arms, recording the Walsingham family marriages, with the motto *Auspicante Deo* – 'With God being propitious'.[18] It was high time he found himself a wife and made something of his life.

During this period he met Anne Carleill, or Carlyle, the widow of a London wine merchant and the daughter of the haberdasher Sir George Barnes, who was Lord Mayor of London in 1552. She already had a young son, Christopher, by her dead husband. Walsingham married her in 1562 and sold his property at Foots Cray in Kent to John Gillibrand in April that year. He leased the manor at Parkebury in Hertfordshire, where the family lived quietly as country gentle folk for several years, with members of the Denny family and Sir William Cecil, Elizabeth's Chief Minister, as near neighbours.

Walsingham was a good catch for the widow – he was well off and, having some influential relations and friends, looked to have excellent prospects. Utilising that patronage, he had already been elected to the second parliament of Elizabeth's reign[19] as the pluralist member for both the Dorset port of Lyme Regis and also the Oxfordshire market town of Banbury, although he appeared to play no active role in its legislative proceedings.

Sadly, Anne died in 1564, just two years after the wedding. There were no children of the marriage. Her will, dated 29 July of that year, leaves £100 (just over £20,000 in today's money) to her husband. 'By his consent' she made a host of small legacies to her friends and family. These included £10 to her friend Christopher Robinson, the public notary living in Paternoster Row, near Old St Paul's, who witnessed and subsequently proved her will, and a 'purse of silk and gold' to her brother-in-law William Dodington, an officer at the Mint. A bequest of £2 also went to the sister of her first husband, Cicely Hastenden, née Carleill.

Most importantly, for her, there remained the issue of the wellbeing and education of her son by her previous marriage:

> My husband to have custody of my son Christopher Carleill, to be by him virtuously brought up and to pay him when twenty-one all money and goods remaining out and besides my said son's exhibition.[20]

This Walsingham faithfully fulfilled, even after his second marriage, probably in August of 1566, to Ursula,[21] the comfortably-off widow of Sir Richard Worsley of Appuldurcombe[22] on the Isle of Wight, who had died a few months before. She was left with two young sons, John and George, as well as ample financial provision through the manor, the estates of the former Benedictine priory at Carisbrooke and the manors of Godshill and Freshwater on that garden isle. Appuldurcombe was a handsome property in the parish of Godshill, consisting of a large house with extensive grounds, including a bowling green, which had come into the Worsley family by marriage in 1511.

The following year, tragedy struck Walsingham's new family. His two stepsons

> being in the lodge or gatehouse at Appledurcombe, where they went to school, the servants were drying of [gun] powder there against [before] the general muster [of the local militia].
>
> A spark flew into the dish, that set fire to a barrel which stood by, blew up a side of the gatehouse, killed the two children and some others [and] hurt one James Worsley, a youth, their kinsman, that went to school there with them.[23]

This heartbreak was not the only calamity that came with Ursula's hand in wedlock to Walsingham, for the violent death of the two boys spawned a bitter legal dispute over the terms and intentions of her first husband's will.[24] Her brother-in-law John Worsley, the executor, amongst other contentious issues, maintained that various moveable goods and chattels left to her sons when they came of age now belonged to him, as they had both been killed. The lengthy suit was finally decided in favour of Walsingham and his wife in June 1571.[25]

Despite this annoying distraction, the added wealth brought by his second marriage enabled Walsingham to quit the leased manor at Parkebury. He purchased a house in the parish of St Giles Cripplegate in London on 5 March 1568, as well as maintaining a fine, if somewhat remote, country home at Appuldurcombe. He later bought a new town residence, 'The Papey',[26] a substantial building across the street from the church of St Mary Axe,[27] next door to the Fletchers' Hall and hard up against the north-eastern section of the city walls. Next door was the newly built house of Walsingham's brother-in-law Robert Beale, then one of the clerks of the Privy Council, who had married Ursula's sister Edith.[28]

Little is known of Ursula, but her formidable likeness, painted in 1583 by an unknown artist, probably when she was in her early forties, is still preserved in London's National Portrait Gallery.[29] The painting shows an elegant red-haired lady wearing a tight-fitting black 'Paris' cap, a starched white ruff and a long, heavy and obviously expensive gold chain hanging around her neck. Her face is oval with a pointed chin, pursed lips and an angular, almost beak-like nose. There is something about her expression and that thin, disapproving mouth that strongly suggests this was not a wife whose feelings or views could be taken for granted, and it is easy to imagine that Ursula would not have tolerated any kind of nonsense from her husband. Some clues to Walsingham's relationship with Ursula emerge from his surviving correspondence, containing broad hints that Walsingham's second marriage suffered not a few tempestuous moments. Writing from Paris to Thomas Heneage, Treasurer of the queen's Privy Chamber, in June 1571 regarding the marriage then being brokered between Elizabeth and the Duke of Anjou, Walsingham described the French suitor as:

> choleric, yet he lacks not reason to govern and bridle [the queen]. And you know that these natures are the best . . . and commonly prove the best husbands. Or else should not you and I be in the highest degree in such perfection as we are. Yet in this matter, we shall well not to be judged, neither by Mrs Heneage nor Mrs Walsingham, because they are parties.[30]

And in January 1574, he told his friend William More:

> Bear, sir, with my earnestness, in recommending my wife's causes.
> You are yourself a married man. You know, therefore, what force
> Mrs More's commandments are to you.[31]

Despite these tell-tale suggestions of marital tension or discord, Walsingham warmly describes Ursula as 'my well-beloved wife' in his will, written in December 1589, in which she was appointed sole executor.[32] Throughout the twenty-four years of their marriage, perhaps Walsingham was a generous husband, attempting to compensate her for his constant overwork and distraction, at all hours, with the complexities and secrecy of state business. In contrast to her husband's rather dour, puritanical outlook on life, it seems likely that Ursula had a penchant for expensive and pretty things, having an account with a goldsmith.[33]

She bore him two daughters: the first, called Frances, was probably born in October 1567, and the second, Mary, in early January 1573,[34] but she died seven years later.[35]

We come now to the defining moment in Walsingham's career, and like much of his early life, it is shrouded in tantalising mystery. He first appears in the State Papers in a cryptic comment scribbled hastily in September 1566 by Elizabeth's Chief Minister Cecil. The brief note is contained in a memorandum concerning issues to be discussed by Parliament: Mr Walsingham, he instructed, 'to be of the House.'[36] His attendance at Westminster was therefore required. What role he was to play there remains obscure, like an actor caught dimly in the footlights. There is no doubt that his presence in the Parliament House was important to the political objectives of Elizabeth's government at the time, possibly with him acting as a lobbyist, or perhaps whipping the members into voting for a specific piece of legislation. The issue and its outcome remain unknown. Two years later, he makes another brief but significant appearance. Walsingham was now aged thirty-six and a letter from him to Cecil on 18 August 1568 may well signal the beginning of his distinguished, arduous and generally thankless career in the queen's service.

Walsingham wrote on behalf of Sir Nicholas Throgmorton,[37] whom he had replaced as MP for Lyme Regis a few years before and who was now a close friend. Throgmorton, a former ambassador in Paris and subsequently a supporter of the French Huguenots, had fallen ill, and therefore asked Walsingham to contact Cecil about one Robert Stewart, an emissary who had come to England to seek the queen's support for their cause in the French civil wars. Walsingham urged the Chief Minister to arrange an audience with Elizabeth for Stewart, as he had much important information to impart only 'by mouth' on this sensitive matter, and asked that Cecil should organise lodgings for him and see him 'properly attended'. Walsingham added as a postscript:

> Touching these matters wherein you appointed me to deal, I will tomorrow, in the morning, attend upon your lordship to advertise [tell] you what I have done therein.[38]

These last few words are telling. They indicate that Walsingham was now engaged in secret work for Cecil, who already operated an active intelligence service for Elizabeth.

Amongst those on the state payroll was one Rooksby, at that time living undercover in Edinburgh to spy on the intrigues of the court of Mary Queen of Scots,[39] who had fled to England and Elizabeth's unwilling protection in the middle of May 1568. In September of that year, King Philip II of Spain replaced his ambassador to London, Diego de Guzman de Silva, with the aggressive and conspiring Don Guerau de Spes, who described Cecil as 'that astute and false liar and old heretic'. Fernando Alvarez de Toledo, Duke of Alva and the Spanish commander in the Netherlands, was forced to admonish de Spes to end his conspiracies 'for a meddling fool!' Alvarez had heard from reports in France how Mary 'was being utterly ruined by the plotting of her servants with you, for they never enter your house without being watched'.[40] Allington, one of Cecil's private secretaries, was also arrested after receiving bribes from de Spes to murder the Chief Minister. The Spanish envoy's correspondence was quickly intercepted and deciphered by a government cryptographer called Somers.[41] This was the dark, dangerous world into which Walsingham – armed only with his linguistic skills and the 'knowledge how best to use his tongue'[42] – patriotically stepped that summer of 1568.

Two days after delivery of his letter concerning the Huguenot messenger Stewart, Walsingham wrote again to warn Cecil of a plot to poison the queen by contaminating her bedding and furniture with some toxic substance. This startling intelligence was based on a tip-off passed to Walsingham by 'Franchiotto, the Italian' – alias Captain Tomaso Franchiotto of the ancient walled city of Lucca in Tuscany, a Protestant who had spied for the French crown for forty years.[43] Franchiotto was well known to Cecil: another of his pseudonyms was 'Captain François', a codename under which the Chief Minister had employed him to uncover French agents in England.[44]

With Mary Queen of Scots now the focal point of burgeoning Catholic plots, both at home and overseas, to put her on the throne in place of Elizabeth, the need to monitor subversion and espionage in England became ever more pressing. On 7 September, Walsingham supplied information about 'a Frenchman and an Italian secretly lodged in London' and asked for the assistance of the city authorities to immediately search their houses. He also suggested that taverns and inns should report on foreigners staying with them – an early version of today's familiar hotel register.[45] A week later, Walsingham told Cecil that he had arranged with Sir Thomas Row, then Lord Mayor of London, to draw up weekly lists of all strangers who took up lodgings within the square mile of the city. He also reported information, imparted 'from a friend', about two suspects 'with a loathsome disease' who had just left Southwark, across on the South Bank of the River Thames. In addition, he helpfully enclosed physical descriptions of the secret agents employed in London by Charles de Guise, Cardinal of Lorraine and uncle of Mary Queen of Scots.[46]

The following month, Walsingham passed on intelligence about preparations in Marseilles to transport soldiers to the North of England, using twelve galleys then in readiness, 'for the better execution of some conspiracy'.[47] This report proved to be unfounded. The subsequent embarrassment may have taught Walsingham a hard lesson in the world of espionage – both the importance of evaluating or analysing raw information and knowing the reliability of one's sources. Perhaps as a result of this, in late December he was sceptical about more reports from Paris he had submitted, warning that France and Spain were working closely together 'for the alteration of religion and the advancement of Mary Queen of Scots' in England. He explained his doubts to Cecil:

> For that this advertisement [news] is so general and descends to no particulars, I thought to have [not] troubled your honour with [it] at present.
>
> But, weighing [the] earnest protestations of the credibility of the party it came from, the nature of the matter as of the greatest importance, the malice of this present time, the allegiance and particular goodwill I owe her majesty and the danger that might come to me by the concealing thereof, if any such thing (which God defend) thereafter should happen, I saw it in duty [that] I could not forbear to write.[48]

Here lies the eternal dilemma in espionage – can you afford *not* to pass on intelligence of possibly vital importance because of any doubts, however small, you may harbour about its veracity or credibility? Nothing changes: no doubt today's MI6 and CIA officers frequently suffer the same testing quandary, as emerged over the issue of weapons of mass destruction in Saddam Hussein's Iraq in 2003. Back in 1568, Walsingham sought to explain his perplexity:

> I beseech your honour that I may without offence conclude that in this division that reigns among us [the Catholic plots] there is less danger in fearing too much than too little and there is nothing more dangerous than security.[49]

Guard against complacency! This was to become one of his key beliefs when he later took over Elizabeth's secret service from Cecil and completely reorganised England's spy network at home and overseas. For Walsingham, this letter and this intelligence also marked the genesis of the major *bête noire* of his career – the striking, sensuous figure of Mary Queen of Scots and the constant plotting that surrounded her.

The acrid stench of conspiracy was in the very air of England that autumn. The premier peer of the realm Thomas Howard, Fourth Duke of Norfolk, Earl Marshal of England and a Privy Councillor, had tragically lost his third wife Elizabeth[50] and their child during her confinement the previous year. The son of the wild and arrogant Earl of Surrey – the 'poet earl' executed for treason in the dying hours of Henry VIII's reign – Norfolk had been a loyal Protestant all his life. However, he lacked foresight,[51] was politically naïve and, fatally, remained ever ambitious for greater power and influence, despite already being the richest man in England. Now he was one of the commissioners[52] appointed to head north to investigate allegations of Mary Queen of Scots' complicity in the murder, in December 1567, of her husband, the distinctly unattractive, hard-drinking and syphilitic Henry Stuart, Earl of Darnley.[53]

Whilst taking a break from the deliberations, Norfolk went hawking on 16 October with the Scottish Secretary of State William Maitland, on the banks of the River Ouse near Cawood, eight miles south-west of York. During a pleasant day's sport, the Scot suddenly suggested to the duke that he should marry the Scottish queen as a convenient way of bringing the two nations into a powerful alliance, as well as securing Mary's claim as heir to the throne of England. After much pondering, Norfolk found himself sorely tempted by the marriage plan.

The murder investigation was inevitably adjourned without result and Elizabeth called a full Privy Council meeting in London to continue the inquiries away from the machinations of the Scottish delegation.[54] The queen was now becoming suspicious about her cousin Norfolk[55] and she suddenly asked him point-blank whether he intended to marry Mary Queen of Scots, a match that in her eyes threatened both her person and her crown. Disingenuously, the duke replied that

> no reason could move him to like of her that has been a competitor
> to the crown and if her majesty would move him thereto, he will
> rather be committed to the Tower, for he meant never to marry with
> such a person, where he could not be sure of his pillow.[56]

He would come to bitterly regret those rash words. Foolishly, he became more set on the enterprise of marriage with Mary. The Scottish queen, seeing a chance both of freedom from virtual imprisonment at the hands of Elizabeth and leapfrogging all the objections to her claim to the English throne, enthusiastically pledged her love for the duke.[57] At the same time, Mary did not hesitate to hedge her bets and secretly contacted the Catholic Earls of Northumberland and Westmorland to seek their help in releasing her, by force of arms if necessary.

By the middle of the following year, 1569, the proposed match between Mary and Norfolk was taking on its own momentum, and Elizabeth, still harbouring dark suspicions fuelled by the whispering in the corridors of her court, was becoming exasperated. She gave Norfolk three separate opportunities that summer to confirm that he sought to marry the Scottish queen. Three times, he could not find the courage in his heart to reveal his plans to Elizabeth and on 6 September, when he finally did tell the queen of his intentions on his sickbed while visiting Titchfield in Hampshire, he was treated to a vintage Tudor tantrum. She angrily forbade any notion of such a marriage and solemnly charged him, on his allegiance to her, 'to deal no further with the Scottish cause'. He hastily assured Elizabeth that he had 'a very slight regard' for Mary and that her rank and fortunes meant little to him. Norfolk, with the fatal, foolish pride that afflicted the house of Howard in the Tudor period, boasted that his own revenues 'were not much less than those of the kingdom of Scotland . . . and that when he was in his tennis court at Norwich, he thought himself in a manner equal with some kings'.[58] It was not a statement to calm the proud, prickly queen.

On 26 September, the duke arrived, still unwell with an ague (an attack of malaria), at Kenninghall, his opulent country estate in Norfolk, hoping that his departure might help to cool tempers at court. Even he had noticed his social ostracism and he wrote to the queen that his enemies found 'such comfort of your majesty's heavy displeasure that they began to make of me a common table talk [and] my friends were afraid of my company'.

In this case, Norfolk's absence did not make Elizabeth's heart grow fonder. She feared that his sudden, unexplained disappearance could be the prelude to a rebellion by her Catholic subjects, with him in the vanguard, marching as their figurehead. The painful memories of the 1549 'Prayer Book' insurrections against her half-brother Edward VI in the West, the Midlands and in East Anglia must have loomed large in her thoughts. She closed the main English ports as a security measure and put the militia on full alert. She had issued a peremptory summons on 25 September to Norfolk to attend upon her, now safely ensconced within the protective walls of Windsor Castle, but as ill-luck for the house of Howard would have it, the duke somehow failed to receive the royal charge.

A second, more pressing royal command eventually reached him and Norfolk set off for Windsor on 1 October with a thirty-strong escort. He was arrested on suspicion of treason and taken by Sir Francis Knollys to the Tower of London. He was confined in the Constable's Lodgings, ironically in the very same rooms that had been occupied by his grandfather Thomas, Third Duke of Norfolk, for six years after his own arrest for treason in December 1546 on the orders of Henry VIII.

A pamphlet virulently attacking Norfolk's marriage plans was swiftly published in London. There seems little doubt that Walsingham wrote the polemic *Discourse Touching the Pretended Match between the Duke of Norfolk and the Queen of Scots*, probably at Cecil's prompting,[59] and it demonstrates an early talent for producing the rawest of propaganda, aimed principally at the enthusiastic and willing audience of England's Protestants.[60] The author minces few words, nor wastes any opportunity to blacken the character of his targets, and like all effective disinformation or today's 'spin', utilises a number of truths and half-truths to provide veracity. Centuries later, little limping Josef Goebbels, Hitler's *Reichsminister* for National Enlightenment, would have glowed with pride if he had produced it himself.

The Queen of Scots, claimed the document, was 'either a Papist, which is evil, or else an atheist which is worse'. She was in league

> with the confederate enemies of the Gospel by the name of the holy league, to root out all such princes and magistrates as are professors of the same. A thing well known, though not generally.

Of nation, she is a Scot, of which nation I forebear to say what may be said, in a reverend respect of a few godly of that nation. Of inclination . . . let her own horrible acts[61] publicly known to the whole world witness, though now of late seduced by practice [to] seek to cloak and hide the same.

Of alliance on her mother's side, how she is descended of a race that is both enemy to God and the common quiet of Europe,[62] [as] every man knows, but, alas, too many have felt.

In goodwill towards our sovereign, she has showed herself [in] sundry ways very evil affected, whose ambition has drawn her by bearing the arms of England, to decipher herself a competitor of the crown, a thing publicly known.

Norfolk is then rolled out to be roundly abused. His religious beliefs are left to 'God and his own conscience'. But, says this poisonous pamphlet, he is clearly inconstant in his supposedly Protestant beliefs, for five reasons:

First, his education of his son under the government of a Papist [shows] it.

Secondly, the corruption of his house, his chief men of trust being Papists.

Thirdly, the reposed trust and confidence he has in the chief Papists in this realm.

Fourthly, his last marriage with a Papist and lastly, this pretended match.

Was it likely, asks Walsingham, raising the spectre of the murdered Darnley, that any man who professes some religious belief, or respects worldly honour, 'or regards his own safety, would match with one detected of so horrible crimes in respect of love?' Mary could solemnly swear by oath that she posed no threat to Elizabeth, or 'confirm anything that may tend to the queen's safety', but, adds the pamphlet bleakly, 'If she [falsifies] her faith, no pleading will serve. The sword must be the remedy.'

Regarding the alliance between England and Scotland that such a marriage could bring, Walsingham is scathing:

If we look well upon the uniters with a single eye that loves the continuance of God's glory and the safety of our sovereign and the quietness of this state, we shall see more profit in division than in union.

Mary's son by Darnley, the three-year-old James VI, had a Protestant 'governor' and was being brought up 'faithfully inclining' to England and Elizabeth

whereby during his government she may assure herself of most perfect union. Thus, you see the queen in safety, the two realms united and this remedy [the marriage] needless.[63]

After speedily producing this propaganda, Walsingham was asked to take on a new role – that of secret policeman, for a conspiracy against the crown had been discovered.

A curious and sinister figure now steps into the ring of intrigue – the Italian banker Roberto Ridolphi. He was born in November 1531 into a family connected with the nobility of Florence – the Ridolphi di Piazza. His parents were amongst the directors of prominent banking and commercial concerns in that city[64] and he too entered the business. He came to London in 1561 and within five years had been tasked to channel the secret funds provided by Pope Pius V to the English Catholics to help overthrow Elizabeth and her government in a conspiracy that came to be called 'the Enterprise of England'. The French and Spanish ambassadors were both involved in the plot, as were some of Elizabeth's Catholic nobles (with whom Ridolphi had business dealings) and Mary's special envoy in London, John Leslie, Bishop of Ross.[65] Ridolphi's visits to the home of the Spanish ambassador and to Norfolk's London base, Howard House, had been closely monitored by Cecil's agents. On 7 October, Robert Dudley, Earl of Leicester, wrote to the Chief Minister and Walsingham informing them that orders had been issued to the Lord Mayor of London Alexander Auenon to immediately arrest Ridolphi. He was to be confined in Walsingham's home at The Papey and there questioned by him in several sessions.[66]

It was Walsingham's first experience of the interrogation of a suspect.

Under close questioning in fluent Italian over many days, Ridolphi admitted dealing with the Bishop of Ross and giving both him and Norfolk cash from overseas. Elizabeth was puzzled by some of the Florentine's answers, which seemed 'very different from the truth'. She asked for copies of Walsingham's questions about issues on which Ridolphi was to be further examined. Four days later, there were more instructions on the interrogation, specifically on the banker's dealings with Mary Queen of Scots.[67] Walsingham also searched Ridolphi's home for incriminating papers and submitted all the evidence to Cecil. Suddenly, on 11 November, Leicester and Cecil wrote to Walsingham ordering Ridolphi's release from his custody and into house arrest at his own lodgings. Their letter said that the queen, now 'disposed to act with clemency', was pleased

> to give Ridolphi his liberty on certain conditions. Say to him that he has misused his privileges, seeing he is but [allowed] to live here as a merchant and has interfered in affairs of state. These he has confessed in part. Her majesty, if she were disposed to be severe, might force him to confess more. Nevertheless, she will grant him liberty if that he shall be bound by writing by you to the sum of £1,000, with securities besides, not to deal directly or indirectly in any matters concerning her majesty or the state of this realm, except by her consent.[68]

The following January, his bond for good behaviour was returned. He was completely free.[69] What on earth had happened? In modern espionage parlance, Walsingham had probably 'turned' Ridolphi – persuaded him to become a double agent in the pay of the crown. The herald and antiquary William Camden, who probably knew Walsingham well, said he was 'a most subtle searcher of hidden secrets, who knew excellently well how to win men's minds unto him and apply them to his own use'.[70] Here, then, were these talents brought to play, and their full value was to be demonstrated later, in bringing down the house of Howard. Cecil may also have hoped that Ridolphi, now at liberty, might flush out other traitorous members of the conspiracy.

The government's concerns about the security of queen and state were amply justified. Ridolphi's plot may have been nipped in the bud and the Pope's agent in London removed from circulation at a crucial time; and the Duke of Norfolk may have been safely incarcerated in the Tower. But overarching all were continuing fears about a potential Catholic insurgency coupled with possible attempts to free Mary Queen of Scots.

Their worst-case predictions became true.

In November 1569, the Catholic magnates in the North – Thomas Percy, Seventh Earl of Northumberland, and Charles Neville, Sixth Earl of Westmorland – gathered together, armed their tenantry and marched on Durham. Then they headed south, planning to free Mary Queen of Scots from her confinement at Tutbury Castle in Staffordshire.[71] Although poorly equipped and possessing little military training, the rebels managed to eject the royalist forces from Barnard's Castle before suddenly withdrawing back in the direction of Durham, fearing the advance of troops hastily levied by the government, 265 miles (425 km) away in London. Elizabeth's retribution was terrible: as well as the executions, the destruction wreaked by her forces on the homes and properties of the insurgents meant that the economy of the North of England would not fully recover for almost two centuries.

Norfolk was eventually released from the Tower after ten months, in early August 1570, but kept under close surveillance and house arrest at his London home under the charge of Sir Henry Neville.

Walsingham meanwhile had risen steadily in the estimation of both Cecil and the queen. In the same month as Norfolk's release, he was instructed to go on a diplomatic mission to the French court, charged with winning justice and security for the Huguenot Protestants in France after the bloody civil wars in that country. However, Bertrand de Salignac de la Mothe Fénelon, the French envoy in London, believed Walsingham's task was more about discovering his master King Charles IX's attitude towards Mary Queen of Scots and his policy on Scotland than merely reassuring the Huguenot party.

The presentation of diplomatic credentials is normally a staid, formal occasion, clothed in grandeur. When Walsingham and the English ambassador Sir Henry Norris arrived at the French court on 28 August, the

French king's mother, Catherine de Médici, threw aside any subtle niceties and went straight for the jugular. She asked Walsingham outright if the harsh treatment accorded to Mary Queen of Scots in England was caused by Elizabeth's Ministers' hatred of her. The envoy was equally direct in his reply. His royal mistress, he said, would not be diverted from an honourable course by any Minister and, moreover, she could and would justify her actions to anyone in the world.

A forthright reply – but the English delegation apparently made another kind of impression on the French royal family. Francés de Alava, the Spanish ambassador in Paris, reported that the

> English nobleman at his audience was clothed entirely in black. He entered haughtily and spoke with the king and queen in a blunt and uncourtly fashion. At his dismissal, both he and Norris were so ill-mannered that I hear that both of them did not escape censure as they passed out [of] the doors. They did not bestow upon [Henry] Duke of Anjou [one of the king's brothers] so much as a salutation or even a glance, nor for that matter, upon any other of the great personages present.[72]

Walsingham's version of the meeting was different – he reported the discussions as cordial. His diplomatic work in Paris, moreover, led to his appointment as Norris's successor as English ambassador there. He did not want the job. Back temporarily in London, he wrote to a lady – probably his wife – of his hopes that Elizabeth would find

> so small taste in this my present service that she will forbear to employ me any further by making choice of some other of more sufficiency. Thus madam, you see in what doubtful terms [I] stand whereby I cannot dispose of myself.

His Puritanism shines through his comment that he would rather stay in England 'with a piece of bread and cheese' than be based in France with all 'their best [delicacies] and entertainments'. Haplessly, he realistically conceded that 'seeing I am born a subject and not a prince, I am tied to the condition of obedience and commandment'.[73]

At the heart of his objections to taking up the job was probably the notorious personal cost of being a resident ambassador overseas, serving a queen known to loathe parting with any cash to repay expenses outlaid on her behalf. He was therefore unwilling to bankrupt himself to further her interests in France. Walsingham told Cecil that if Elizabeth decided to appoint

> any of my mean calling and ability, she must also resolve to enable them some way whereby they may bear the [financial] burden. Sir Henry Norris, whose living is known to be great, has found the charge very heavy and therefore unfit for the shoulders of any other of my mean calling . . .[74]

Eventually, doubtless after much debate, the queen agreed on a daily allowance of £3 6s 8d (£657 in today's monetary values). Parsimoniously, it was the same amount she had allowed her ambassador in Paris in the 1560s – but at least the sum was payable three months in advance. In addition, he was allowed his costs of travel and for transporting ten horses and his belongings to France, amounting to £84 9s 11d.[75] On 23 December 1570, he received his instructions from Elizabeth for his embassy: to obey her commands and pass on her messages; to keep her informed about political events in France; and to promote and protect the interests of English merchants in that country.

The Spanish ambassador in London, de Spes, told Philip II of Spain: 'The queen is shortly sending Walsingham as her new ambassador . . . as she thinks he is more likely to raise dissensions there than any other man.'[76] Walsingham left England five days later, with his brother-in-law Robert Beale as his secretary.

His partial journal for this period of his life survives,[77] but is sadly short on detail, merely recounting whom he met or dined with. On 14 February 1571, he had an audience with the French king to discuss complaints made by English cloth merchants about their treatment in trade matters, an issue constantly to be raised with the French authorities. A few weeks later, on 2 March, he records the removal of a copy of the papal bull excommunicating Elizabeth, issued thirteen months before, from a Parisian gate,[78] clearly pasted up by a mischievous Catholic. He also tackled the Spanish ambassador de Alava about reports that Irish rebels had been received at Philip II's court in Madrid. De Alava refused to converse in any language but Spanish (which Walsingham did not speak) and afterwards Walshingham told Cecil that 'he seems to be no better affected towards me than I am towards him . . . Never spake I with a prouder man or with one more disdainful in countenance or speech. I mean to have little else to do with him'.[79] Just over a fortnight later, Walsingham travelled to Clermont to meet his wife Ursula, who had been in the Auvergne region. She arrived in Paris 'about two of the clock in the afternoon' of Sunday 19 March.[80]

The remainder of the diary entries reflect very much the daily round, the common task of an ambassador hard at work protecting his nation's interests. He was already receiving secret intelligence – part and parcel of any diplomatic work: his journal records the arrival of 'Jacomo, [who] came out of England with letters' on 8 June 1571. This was almost certainly Jacomo Manucci, a Florentine, who was later to control a number of agents inside Walsingham's spy network and was a trusted confidant, capable of handling very sensitive matters. Walsingham's old Italian contact 'Captain Tomaso' Franchiotto also sent him letters on 26 June and visited him twice in Paris in November and December.

Walsingham's major diplomatic mission in Paris was handling the protracted discussions over plans for Elizabeth, now aged thirty-seven, to wed Henry, Duke of Anjou, the French king's younger brother, and seventeen years her junior. Elizabeth's suitor, Walsingham told Leicester, was

> three fingers taller than myself, in complexion somewhat sallow, his body of very good shape, his leg long and small but reasonably well proportioned. Touching the health of his person, I find the opinion [so] diverse, as I know not what to credit.[81]

As a devout Protestant, he could not have approved of any marriage between Elizabeth and a Catholic, but he was careful to hide his personal feelings in the snake pit of diplomatic life in Paris. He emphasised to Leicester that he had left his 'private passions behind me and do here submit myself to the passions of my prince, to execute whatsoever she shall command me as precisely as I may'.[82]

His professed attitude seemed to satisfy the supporters of the marriage, even though he had been 'adjudged to be a very passionate enemy' of the project by some within Elizabeth's government. England's adversaries naturally sought to block the Anjou marriage plan, fearing the strength of the Anglo-French political alliance that it would bring. The Papal Nuncio in Paris told Anjou dismissively that Elizabeth was old, probably barren and, moreover, a heretic. The powerful Guise faction at the French court did all they could to derail the marriage plans. They mounted a whispering campaign against Elizabeth and her government to sour attitudes in the Valois court, and Charles de Guise, Cardinal of Lorraine, even bribed one of Anjou's favourites to persuade the duke to drop Elizabeth as a prospective bride and marry Mary Queen of Scots instead. As ever, the issue of religion was the stumbling block in the Anglo-French marriage negotiations. When the special English envoys Henry Killigrew[83] and Sir Thomas Smith[84] eventually met the French queen mother in her private chamber in early January 1572, she told them that her son had become so devout a Catholic that he began to be 'lean and evil coloured' from his constant vigils and fasts. Secret, closet worship in England would not satisfy the duke, said his mother, and nothing less than the celebration of very public high Masses would be required. Smith replied sarcastically: 'Why, madam, then he may require also the four orders of friars, monks, canons, pilgrimages, pardons, oils, creams, relics and all such trumperies. That in no way can be agreed.'[85] It was obvious that, to all intents and purposes, the marriage plans were dead and buried.

Walsingham by now had other preoccupations that realised his worst fears: an acute shortage of money. His ambassadorial duties had incurred considerable expense and he had been forced reluctantly into debt. He reported to Burghley on 3 March 1572 that he had spent £1,600 more than his income and had been forced to sell his own land, which yielded

£60 a year, as his debts now totalled more than £730. Perhaps unwisely, later in July he borrowed money in anticipation of his salary from Guido Cavalcanti, an agent of Catherine de Médici, and now owed him many thousands of pounds.[86]

But Walsingham's duties as royal matchmaker had not ended. Astonishingly, attention turned to Anjou's younger brother, the seventeen-year-old Francis, Duke of Alençon, as a possible substitute candidate for Elizabeth's hand in marriage. He was no great catch: he had a callow, pock-marked face – the result of a bad attack of smallpox – and a puny, undersized body. Walsingham had grave doubts about how his vain royal mistress would view the lad's physical suitability. He told Cecil, now created Lord Burghley for services rendered in one of his queen's rare gestures of generosity, of his frank concerns over the possible match:

> The great impediment I find . . . is the contentment of the eye. The gentleman is void of a good humour, besides the blemish of the smallpox. When I weigh the same with the delicacy of her majesty's eye, I hardly think there will grow any liking.[87]

Even Elizabeth ignored the diplomatic blandishments about Alençon's age and appearance and became worried over 'the absurdity that in general opinion of the world might grow' if she entered into matrimony with an immature youth with only a stubble of beard first appearing on his chin.

Worse was to come for the chances of any meaningful political alliance between England and France against Spain. The French Huguenot leader Admiral Gaspard de Coligny had been urging war against Philip II's Spanish forces in the Low Countries. This augured ill for Elizabeth's government, anxious over what French control of Flanders would mean for English maritime power and trade. Burghley wrote to Walsingham in June 1572 warning that French control of the Low Countries' ports would restrict shipping movements and regulate their merchants, and 'our sovereignty upon the narrow seas will be abridged with danger and dishonour'.[88] The following month, Elizabeth, concerned over French territorial ambitions, sent Sir Humphrey Gilbert[89] (who had savagely repressed the Fitzmaurice Rebellion in Southern Ireland in 1569) with more than 1,000 volunteer soldiers to occupy the Zeeland coastal towns of Flushing and Sluys against the Spanish, to prevent their occupation by French troops. The expedition was strictly unofficial and Gilbert knew the queen would quickly disown him if disaster struck and his force was defeated.

In Paris, Catherine de Medici became alarmed that Coligny's policy would suck France into a dangerous and potentially disastrous war with Spain, possibly on two fronts. Something dramatic had to be done to dilute or dissipate the Huguenot influence on French foreign policy.

At around eleven o'clock on the morning of 22 August 1572, four days after the marriage of the French king's daughter Marguerite of Valois to the Protestant Prince Henry of Navarre, Coligny was walking along the rue de Béthisy after meeting the Duke of Anjou at the Louvre. He bent down to adjust his overshoe, which he wore as protection from the filthy, muddy roadways, and this sudden action saved his life, for a shot fired by Maurevel, alias Maurevert, an assassin hired by the Guises, injured rather than killed him. The shot was fired from an arquebus[90] through an iron grille in the window of a house owned by Canon Pierre de Pille, former preceptor to the Duke of Guise. The would-be assassin fled through the cloister of a nearby church to a horse, waiting already saddled on the banks of the River Seine, and made his escape.

Coligny was carried home, bleeding from a shattered left elbow and hand. The king, playing a game of tennis in the Louvre, heard the shot, and when told of the attempt on Coligny's life seemed beside himself with anger. He immediately sent his own physician, Ambrose Paré, to tend the wounded man. The admiral's right index finger had to be amputated.

The royal outrage and concern were all a sham, however. In the early hours of St Bartholomew's Day, 24 August, a hastily but well-constructed plan to murder all the Huguenot leaders was put into action. The wounded Coligny was amongst the first to die, stabbed in the chest in his bedroom even though his house was guarded by royal troops. His murderer was

Besme, a Bohemian also known as Vanovitch, who was a Guise follower. Coligny's body was hurled out of the window and down into the street, where the Duke of Guise himself and the Duke of Angoulême, the bastard brother of the king, were waiting. Coligny's head was hacked off and his gore-soaked body dragged away to be hung in chains from the public gibbet at Montfaucon. Another dozen Huguenot leaders were killed soon afterwards: La Rochefoucauld, who had been joking with Charles IX only hours earlier, was stabbed by a masked servant; the Seigneur de la Force and one of his sons had their throats slashed.

In their home on the quai des Bernardins in Faubourg St Germain,[91] Walsingham, his wife and their four-year-old daughter Frances heard the bells of the Church of St Germain l'Auxerrois, up the River Seine, ring out at midnight. Unknown to them and their house guest Philip Sidney, who was visiting France, it was a pious signal for bloody genocide. The homes of known Protestants in Paris had been quickly identified and their doors daubed with a white cross, indicating them as targets for the coming bloodbath.

As the sun rose that morning, a Sunday, there were more bells ringing and gunfire could be heard from the direction of the Louvre, across the water. By mid-afternoon, some of the terrified English in the city had sought shelter in Walsingham's house and told the stark, terrible story: a concerted massacre of Huguenots had been carried out by a Catholic mob and disciplined troops of soldiers. Three Englishmen had already been killed. No doubt Walsingham led their prayers for survival within the locked and barred embassy. The Spanish ambassador in Paris maintained that the mob attacked Walsingham's home and he was forced to cravenly conceal himself, but this claim is likely to be disinformation. Charles IX certainly sent a guard, under the command of the Duke de Nevers, to protect Walsingham and his family and their growing band of refugees from the continuing bloodshed.[92] The Huguenot General François de Beauvais, Sieur de Briquemault, also hid in the ambassador's house, but was dragged out by royal troops and later hanged.[93]

Over the next few days, more than 3,000 Huguenots were slaughtered in Paris, and the massacre spread like a red stain of terror across the rest of France. An estimated 70,000 Protestants died horribly in Toulouse, Bordeaux, Lyons,[94] Rouen and Orléans as the carnage carried on into October, despite belated royal orders to cease and desist.[95]

Walsingham managed to smuggle his wife and daughter out of the city and back to England. He was granted royal protection for his coach as he moved around Paris but was subjected to abuse and insults hurled by the still rampaging mob.[96] Fearing that his letters to London were being intercepted, his frank account of the St Bartholomew's Day massacre was committed to his diplomatic messenger's memory,[97] probably the trusty Welshman Walter Williams who was to be employed by Walsingham in this role and others over the next fifteen years.[98]

On 1 September, Walsingham had an audience with Catherine de Medici. She told him that her son King Charles IX would now only allow one religion to be practised in France: Catholicism.

Five days later, John Facchinetti, Bishop of Nicastro and Papal Legate in Venice, wrote to Ptolemy Galli, Cardinal of Como, congratulating him on the

> good news from France of the death of the admiral and the great slaughter of the Huguenots and their chiefs . . . The king [Charles IX] speaking of the [Protestant] princes of Navarre and Condé said: 'Let these poltroons be forthwith shut up.' And . . . he caused all the gentlemen and servants of the count of Navarre to be killed.[99]

In Rome, Pope Gregory XIII ordered a *Te Deum* to be sung to celebrate the signal victory over Protestantism and for a medal to be struck to mark the event, with an image on its reverse of an angel with a cross and drawn sword, killing the Huguenots. Irrevocably, perhaps unintentionally, the international battle lines against England were being drawn up.

The horrors of the St Bartholomew's Day slaughter scarred Walsingham for the remainder of his life. A numbed and terrified eyewitness to the bloody, state-sponsored repression of his fellow Protestants, he had seen the pools of congealing blood on the streets and smelt the smoke of the raging fires lit by blind hatred and prejudice across Paris. His memory was seared by the sight of the naked fear in the faces of his fellow Englishmen as, day after day, the Catholic mob clamoured and bayed for their deaths outside the walls of his ambassadorial home, a tiny, frail bastion of Protestant safety amid the noisy carnage around them.

For Walsingham, and indeed for Elizabeth's government, the French massacre was a stunning, horrific reminder of the brutal, genocidal anti-Protestant Spanish campaign in the Low Countries and a warning of what might follow in England if the realm was ever returned to Catholicism.

The grim-faced ambassador must have sworn to move heaven and earth to ensure the survival of his precious Protestant state, clearly now dangerously beset on every side by powerful, determined and devout enemies.

CHAPTER TWO

'The Poison Against This Estate'

'. . . If they should show themselves obstinate and perverse, as they have done before, they should carry them to the Tower, there to be kept close prisoners and to be put to the Rack and torture, to compel them to utter their innermost knowledge in all matters they dealt in or are privy to.'

PRIVY COUNCIL INSTRUCTIONS ON THE FATE OF CATHOLIC PRISONERS, JANUARY 1587.[1]

Out of the windblown embers of the fires that brutally destroyed 280 heretics during Queen Mary I's reign was born the fervency of England's new state religion under her half-sister Elizabeth, after she came to the throne in November 1558. The problem the queen and her government faced was that while the law of the land may have firmly established the Protestant Anglican church, a majority of her subjects, particularly in North and North-West England, remained staunchly Catholic. At various times during her reign, they were seen as representing grave threats to her crown and state and Francis Walsingham, a few months after his return from France in April 1573,[2] was tasked to bring to bear the repressive measures of the police state to neutralise them. Around 125 Catholic priests and sixty recusants, including three women, were to be hunted down and cruelly executed as traitors during Elizabeth's reign, mainly during the 1580s when Walsingham directed the security of the realm.[3]

A plot to overthrow the queen had already galvanised England in 1571–2, centred yet again on that arch-conspirator Roberto Ridolphi. Within days of the Duke of Norfolk's release from the Tower in August 1570 and into confinement at Howard House in London, the audacious Florentine had visited him secretly. A visitor with such a poor sense of timing could hardly have been less welcome. Ridolphi asked the apprehensive Norfolk to write to the Duke of Alva, the Spanish captain-general in the Netherlands, seeking funds for the imprisoned Mary Queen of Scots. Wisely, Norfolk shunned him – 'I began to mislike him,' he said much later, and 'sought ways to shift me from him.'

It was a rare moment of perception, for this double agent was eventually the deceitful means used to bring Norfolk to the scaffold. Despite all that he had suffered, Norfolk's other nemesis, Mary Queen of Scots, was still keen to marry him and to embroil him in a new, dangerous conspiracy. She wrote to him on 31 January 1571, encouraging his escape from house arrest – 'as she would do [herself], notwithstanding any danger' – in order that they could be married.[4] One can imagine Norfolk's incredulous expression when he read her wholly unrealistic letter, its contents, if not the stuff of daydreams, certainly of rampant self-deception.

The Scottish queen's fantasies aside, the duke's final downfall was triggered by the arrest of Charles Bailly, a young Fleming who had entered Mary's service in 1564 and later worked for John Leslie, Bishop of Ross, her agent in London. Burghley's agents in Dover had detained him in early April 1571 after discovering he was carrying books and letters from English exiles and had no valid passport. Two of the communications, 'hid behind his back secretly', were addressed to the bishop and had been dictated to Bailly by the ubiquitous Ridolphi in Brussels.[5] The prisoner was brought to London and held in the Beauchamp Tower in the Tower of London, where grim inscriptions on the walls of a second-floor room, carved by him in the utter despair of imprisonment, survive to this day.[6] They include some painfully true words, and Bailly's woeful sentiments are justified by the treatment he received at the hands of his torturers in the Tower. A brief session on the rack – a fiendish machine that stretched the body and agonisingly dislocated the joints[7] – plus the threat of further such treatment to come compelled the prisoner to make some startling admissions. He admitted that Ridolphi had left England on 25 March with personal appeals from Mary to the Duke of Alva in the Low Countries, his master – King Philip II – and the Pope to organise and fund an invasion of England. The aim was to overthrow Elizabeth, crown the Scottish queen and re-establish Catholicism as the state religion. Earlier that month, Ridolphi had revisited Norfolk at Howard House in Charterhouse Square, leaving a document with him that outlined the invasion plans and listed some forty luminaries in England who secretly supported Mary, each name identified by a number for use in ciphered correspondence.[8]

Over in Paris, Walsingham, still Elizabeth's ambassador to the Valois court, quickly received wind of the plot. He wrote to Burghley on 14 May:

> I am given secretly to understand that Ridolfi has letters of credit given him by the Spanish ambassador unto the duke of Alva; where upon he had [a] long conference with the duke and was dispatched to Rome with letters of credit to the King of Spain promising to be in Madrid the 20th of this month.
>
> Touching the matter of secrecy committed unto him, I can learn nothing as yet, notwithstanding, I thought it my part to advertise [tell] your Lordship of this much which perhaps by other advertisements can give some guess what the same imports.[9]

But the Florentine banker failed to make a good impression upon the Spanish general. During their meeting, he enthusiastically described how Spain could generously supply 6,000 harquebusiers for the invasion along with military equipment, including twenty-five artillery pieces, to augment a popularist English Catholic army, led by Norfolk, which would free Mary and seize Elizabeth. The reliability of his information was somewhat damaged by urging a landing at the port of Harwich, which he claimed was in Norfolk rather than in Essex. His credibility quickly sank and the canny Alva was hardly convinced of the wisdom of the plan. He later told Philip II that Ridolphi was a 'great babbler' and had 'learned his lessons parrot fashion'. Instead, the general urged the king that Spain should provide military assistance only after the English Catholics had risen up in rebellion and Elizabeth was already 'dead . . . or else a prisoner'. Then there would be an opportunity 'which we must not allow to escape'. Alva added: 'We may tell [Norfolk] that these conditions being fulfilled, he shall have what he wants.'[10] Such requirements were virtually impossible to achieve, given the brutal suppression of the Northern Rebellion in 1569, and the Spanish general must have known that. Ridolphi, unaware of Alva's cynical dismissal of his plans, hastened on to the Vatican and Madrid, but by then Philip already knew that the conspiracy had been uncovered through the arrest of Bailly and had received Alva's adverse military advice.

Back in London, Bailly was moved to the Marshalsea Prison in Southwark, where Burghley inserted one of his stool pigeons, the linguist William Herle, disguised as an Irish priest, to extract more information from him.[11] Slowly, piece by piece, the details of the conspiracy were teased out by the queen's investigators and fitted together like a giant, sinister jigsaw. Then the moment came for action.

Betrayed by his servants under interrogation, Norfolk was arrested again on 7 September 1571 and taken to the Tower as a close prisoner. Three days later, he wrote a pathetic letter of submission to Elizabeth, seeking her pardon 'with an overwhelmed heart and watery cheek'. He rued the day when he had first considered marrying Mary Queen of Scots – as he always 'coveted nothing but a quiet life'.[12] So do we all, even those of us not regularly accused of treason. He stumbled and excused his way through several painful examinations by members of the Privy Council,[13] but in his heart, he now knew it was his own stupidity, his own vanity, that had caused his ruin.

Ridolphi, safely in Paris, wrote to Mary Queen of Scots on 30

September reporting the results of his negotiations with the Pope and the king of Spain, adding that he would now judiciously 'retire into privacy that he may not give umbrage to Queen Elizabeth'.[14] Mary's reaction to his letter is not recorded, but may be imagined.

The Spanish ambassador de Spes was expelled from England after Elizabeth told him bluntly that he would 'secretly seek to inflame our realm with firebrands'. .

Excited rumours reverberated throughout Europe. A newsletter received in Rome in early January 1572 reported wrongly that Mary had been convicted of complicity in the plot and was now 'so straitly confined that no one may speak with her and [her] food is conveyed to her through a window'.[15]

Archbishop John Baptista Castagna, the Papal Nuncio in Madrid, observed that the Ridolphi affair was 'a matter of importance and substance, had it not been discovered, which causes the king [Philip II] infinite mortification'. If Norfolk and the other conspirators should be put to death, as was expected, there was no more to be done but to be patient, because to make war

> and attack those realms deliberately without a rising of the [Catholic] magnates of the said kingdom is no enterprise for these times, nor would the king so much as think of it at present and this is the answer to the two ciphered [letters] received touching this matter.[16]

Norfolk was tried for his life in Westminster Hall on 16 January 1572. None of the witnesses against him were allowed to appear, to prevent them from facing questions posed by the prisoner. The duke cut a figure that was haughty at times, redolent of that old Howard dynastic arrogance, but pathetic at others, claiming that his memory was 'too weak to answer a heap of matters huddled up'. It came as no surprise that his peers unanimously found him guilty and the Tower axe was ominously turned towards him as sentence of death was pronounced by the Earl of Shrewsbury, the Lord High Steward.[17]

Norfolk was an unlikely traitor. He was more guilty of foolishly concealing information than of planning the downfall of Elizabeth and her government. He complained that he was 'betrayed and undone by my own, while I knew not how to mistrust'.[18]

The duke climbed the Tower Hill scaffold at eight o'clock on the morning of 2 June. He told the crowd that he only talked with Ridolphi – a 'stranger, a naughty man' – but once and

> not to the prejudice of the queen, for many men know I had dealings with him for money matters, upon bills and bonds. I found him to be a man that enjoyed the tranquillity of England and of a prompt and ready wit for any wicked design.[19]

Norfolk also stressed that he remained a good Protestant to the end: 'I take God to witness, I am not, nor never was, a Papist, since I knew what religion meant.' His head was then cut off with a single blow of the executioner's axe. He was aged thirty-four. His body was buried in the Chapel of St Peter ad Vincula within the Tower's walls.

Ridolphi had heard that the conspiracy had been discovered when he visited Paris the previous October. He eventually returned to Rome where Pope Pius V gratefully made him a papal senator, and he lived on for another four decades in Florence, fat and prosperous from his lucrative financial transactions. He died there peacefully in his bed on 18 February 1612. What his precise role in the affair amounted to is difficult to discern, more than four centuries later. After his season as an unwilling guest in Walsingham's London home during the winter of 1569, he almost certainly had become a double agent for the English government. It is tempting to imagine that Ridolphi was also an agent provocateur, part of an elaborate and cunning plot by Burghley to finally neutralise any remaining threat posed by Norfolk and the disaffected Catholic nobility after the Northern Rebellion a few years earlier. In this shadowy world of intrigue and double-dealing, the conspiracy theorist is in his element: the crafty Chief Minister was surely capable of such Byzantine trickery. It is perhaps significant that years later, in 1600, Sir Walter Raleigh wrote to Burghley's son, Sir Robert Cecil, pointing out a belief prevalent at the time that 'your own father . . . was esteemed to be the contriver of Norfolk's ruin'.[20]

Elizabeth's government may have chopped off one head of the hydra of conspiracy, but in the months and years to come, there were many others to combat.

Walsingham was named a Privy Councillor and one of Elizabeth's two Principal Secretaries of State on 20 December 1573. The following day, he swore to be a 'true and faithful councillor to the queen's majesty' as one of the notionally seventeen-strong Privy Council. In many ways, all this merely formalised his duties, as he had already been acting as a trusted unofficial adviser to the queen since before his return from France the previous April. Leicester told him just before his departure for London:

> You know what opinion is here of you and to what place all men
> would have you unto, even for her majesty's sake. Besides that, the
> place you already hold is a councillor's place and more than [that] . . .
> for oft-times, councillors are not made [privy to] such matters as you
> are acquainted withal.[21]

Between his arrival back in England and his appointment as Secretary of State, Walsingham had probably been convalescing from bouts of ill health suffered in France. He was still, however, receiving intelligence from abroad. In August, he forwarded on to Burghley a letter from an Italian agent about the activities of the Dutch Protestant leader, the Prince of Orange, and the attempt on his life.[22] A brief insight into Walsingham's domestic life during this period is provided by the plea from Richard Arnold of Churcham in Gloucestershire that 'his extreme sickness' had prevented him from sending 'the brace of greyhounds', which he now begged Walsingham to accept.

Aside from the joys of hunting hares with his dogs, it was time to return to the service of Elizabeth. The post of Secretary of State involved handling practically every paper concerned with international affairs, embarking on various foreign embassies and tackling the humdrum administration of the realm such as construction projects, cleansing the coasts of rampant piracy, royal patronage appointments and the regulation of trade.

In addition, Walsingham became Elizabeth's secret policeman, utilising a host of informers to root out treason, using torture to extract incriminating information and hunting down fugitive priests from house to house, county to county, after their missions to England began in 1574. His workload must have been an immense and heavy burden to carry for a man frequently afflicted by bad health.

A description of the duties of a Principal Secretary of State under Elizabeth survives, written in 1592 probably by Robert Beale, Walsingham's brother-in-law and one-time secretary, for Sir Edward Wotton.[23] The thirteen-page document contains some sound, sensible advice for any official dealing with the feisty queen, as well as providing a flavour of Walsingham's working practices. For example, when there was some unpleasant matter to be discussed with Elizabeth 'or other matters to be done of great importance, let not the burden be laid on you alone, but let the rest join with you'. Safety in numbers, then, was a good idea. When 'her highness is angry, or not well disposed, trouble her not with any matter which you desire to have done, unless extreme necessity urges it'. When the queen was finally persuaded to sign some state papers, the Secretary should 'entertain her with some relation in speech, whereat she may take some pleasure'. Unfortunately, there is no advice regarding her sense of humour or, just as pertinently, what precisely pleased her. (Walsingham did his best, always joining in the custom of giving New Year's presents to the sovereign. One gift, in January 1578, of a quantity of French satin appears to have particularly delighted Elizabeth.)[24]

The guidance document also pointed out that too many clerks or servants could become a burden to administration. Most importantly, 'Let your secret services be known [only] to a few. The Lord Treasurer [Burghley] had not above two or three [having this knowledge].' Security, then as now, was everything:

> The secretary must have a special cabinet whereof he is himself to keep the key for his signets, ciphers and secret intelligence, distinguishing the boxes or tills rather by letters than by the names of countries or places, keeping that only unto himself.

And as for spies:

Mr Secretary Walsingham with her majesty's allowance and his own purse entertained [employed spies in more than] forty places. In the time of Mr la Mott and Mr Mauvesier[25] he had some of his secretaries that betrayed the secrets of both the French and Scottish dealings. In Scotland he was well beloved of many of the nobility, ministers and others whom he relieved when they were banished into England. With money, he corrupted priests, Jesuits and traitors to betray the practices against this realm.

But, seeing how much his liberality was misliked[26] I do not think that you can follow the like example.[27]

For Walsingham, stamping down on Catholic subversion and conspiracy was a very personal mission, verging on religious devotion. He was, at heart, a radical Protestant. Indeed, Elizabeth regarded him as a 'rank Puritan' and sometimes unjustly castigated him for caring more for his fellow believers than he did for England, but she may have been overly harsh in her assessment of his religious beliefs. Walsingham did provide Thomas Cartwright, then leader of the Puritans, with £100 as financial assistance to counter the Catholic version of the New Testament produced at Rheims, but this could be said to fall within his propaganda remit. Later, he funded a lectureship at Oxford for the Puritan John Reynolds. With his deep strategic vision of the European political scene, Walsingham saw a desperate need for Protestants to unite internationally against the potent threat posed by the Catholic powers and was prepared to deploy devious methods to protect England's tender young religion against all-comers. It was probably in 1583 that King James VI of Scotland commented that he was 'very Machiavel[lian]' in his religious fervour.[28]

In 1582, Richard Hopkins, a former ambassador in Paris, wrote to Walsingham of the

fervency of zeal which your honour has against our ancient Catholic religion and the professors thereof. So should you be noted among the chiefest of our religion to be one of the most severe persecutors we have in our realm.[29]

An example of his determination that Protestantism should ultimately prevail and of the interrogatory techniques he may have employed is provided by an admittedly subjective source: Bernardino de Mendoza, the new Spanish ambassador in London. The envoy reported in June 1578 that he had been told some months earlier that Walsingham had questioned a Catholic prisoner and asked him if he believed that Elizabeth was excommunicated. The prisoner claimed he did not know, but the Secretary

> put down that [the prisoner] held her to be excommunicated. He then asked him if, the queen being excommunicated . . . she ought to be obeyed as sovereign or not and the prisoner answered the same way as before. Walsingham put down that he said that being excommunicated, she could not be queen.
>
> He then went to the queen with the so-called confession and told her that this was proof of what Catholics in general thought, for which she could see what was desirable to do with them.[30]

Later, on 30 January 1584, Walsingham wrote to Sir Christopher Hatton about the interrogation of a priest:

> I doubt not that you will have care, both that he may be forthcoming [and] also that he may be kept from intelligence [any contact with the outside world].
>
> They that have given [information] that he is a priest do take upon them to be most assured of it . . . Therefore I find it strange that his answers should be so pre-emptive. It may be when pressed with [swearing an] oath, he will yield another answer.
>
> If he proves to be a priest (as is reported) then will he not greatly weigh his allegiance, having, as the rest of his associates have, a very irreverent opinion of her majesty's authority.[31]

In 1592, the Jesuit Robert Persons published a pamphlet, *Response to the Unjust and Bloody Edict of Elizabeth against the Catholics*, in which he attacked Walsingham for maintaining the reputation of an honest man if such can be called who was cruel and inhumane, who was not content with mocking and bullying and insulting the confessors of the faith of Jesus Christ, but even went so far as to beat them and kick them, so violently was he moved to the defence of his sect against the truth of our religion.[32]

Given his position within the government, it is inevitable that Catholics and their sympathisers alike have vilified Walsingham. One later writer castigated him for his

unmistakable marks of brutality and fanaticism. Blinded by religious passion, he honestly believed every Roman priest was deceitful and dangerous to the state and he presided in person at their examination.[33]

Walsingham probably would not have disagreed with that viewpoint.

Yet this was not one man fulfilling a personal vendetta or crusade. Indeed, he was probably opposed to the wholesale slaughter of captured missionary priests – although he called them the 'poison of the estate' – save for 'a few, for example's sake'. A paper written by him in December 1586 distinguishes between two types of seminary priest: some were 'learned and politic', the others 'simple, having more zeal than wit or learning'. The first group, he urged, should be held 'under honest keepers and be restrained from access and intelligence, for that, being banished, might do a great deal of harm'. As for the second, they 'may be banished as others before, upon penalty to be executed if they return, and for the more terror, such as were banished and are returned, to be presently executed'.[34] Four years earlier, there was even a plan, probably conceived by Walsingham, to exile some of the English Catholics to North America, where the problems of mere survival in an alien hostile environment could well subsume the importance of treasonable conspiracies. Transporting undesirables to the colonies is an older idea than we perhaps imagined.

No, for all his Protestant fervency, all his diligence in hunting down Catholic fugitives, Walsingham was merely prosecuting government policy to the best of his ability. After his death in 1590, the state campaign against Catholic recusancy and the Jesuit missionaries continued just as fiercely as it had under his supervision.

There is little doubt that Elizabeth's life was frequently in real danger from Catholic fanatics, particularly after Pope Pius V denounced her as a heretic and absolved her subjects from any allegiance to her and her government by publication of the bull *Regnans in Excelsis* in 1570. Plot after plot followed, all aimed at violently removing her from the throne and restoring England to Catholicism. In October 1583, a number of prisoners in the Tower of London were interrogated about 'certain speeches against the queen's majesty supposed to have been spoken by John Somerfield', alias John Holland, a gentleman from Edneston, Warwickshire, when he protested against the persecution of English Catholics. He said he 'meant to shoot her through with his dagg [pistol] and hoped to see her head set on a pole [because] she was a serpent and a viper'.[35] Somerfield was later found hanged 'with his own garters' in his cell in Newgate Prison the day before his execution, and one of Walsingham's agents, operating undercover in Exeter Jail, claimed Somerfield was 'hanged to avoid a greater evil' by supporters of the Catholic cause.[36] Somerfield was clearly mentally unstable – even the Spanish ambassador Mendoza described him as 'the lunatic'. At Somerfield's trial, to judge whether he was insane, 'they brought into court a letter signed by five [privy] councillors, certifying that he was not – but there are proofs to the contrary'.[37]

The ambassador also reported that only days after Somerfield's arrest, an English sailor went to court

> with such boldness that he found his way to the place where the queen was with two other ladies. She . . . cried out angrily for him to be seized and carried to the chamber of the earl of Leicester, where he was asked whether I sent him to kill the queen and if he bore arms, though he had nothing but a blunt knife.

The sailor said his visit was aimed at irritating the people against Mendoza and to 'make them cry out that it was by my intervention that the lunatic desired to kill the Queen'. Mendoza said the interloper had told the French ambassador that there were 300 Catholics who had sworn to kill Elizabeth.[38] The episode has all the hallmarks of a state-inspired propaganda exercise.

The threats of invasion and rebellion were also ever present. In July 1572, the adventurer Sir Thomas Stucley[39] suggested to King Philip II of Spain his hare-brained plan to overthrow Elizabeth. He wrote that

> My lord [Sir Leonard] Dacres offers for the hire of 6,000 soldiers, 1,000 being foreign arquebusiers, in six months to wrest the kingdom [of England] from the pretended [queen], or at least to wrest from her . . . Cumberland, Westmorland, Northumberland, Durham, Yorkshire and Lancashire, and make of them a safe refuge and, as it were, a realm free and independent, whither all the Catholics of England may repair.[40]

Alternatively, he suggested, Philip's forces could occupy the Isle of Wight, Portsmouth and Southampton 'because these places are in that part of England where there are many Catholics'. Recklessly optimistic, he offered to capture all three objectives 'at a stroke, in a single night and in less than twelve hours and from thence to London is not a two days' journey and one can march straight upon the city'.

Three months later, Stucley, then in Louvain in present-day Belgium, jotted down the broad headings of an outline agreement on papal policy towards England for the new Pope Gregory XIII, again urging the invasion of England, when, he promised, a 'vast number [of Catholics] will join the invader and very few will oppose him'. Furthermore 'His Holiness should not desert the cause of the Queen of Scots, who after suffering much and sorely for so many years for the Catholic faith ought not now [to] be deprived of her realm'.[41] It was the cause, the 'Good Old Cause', all over again.

The following year, 1573, the new Papal Nuncio in Madrid, Bishop Nicholas Ormanetto, was almost beside himself at the slowness of events to destroy the Protestant government in London.

> Secretary Cecil, who may be called king of England in order to maintain his greatness and authority, seeks by all manner of ways

and means to extirpate the Catholic faith in that realm and to foster heresies in the neighbouring realms . . .

And then there is our queen [Mary Queen of Scots], who for all the persuasions of the pretended queen, and all the wiles of that secretary, has refused to follow the Huguenot sect; nay, rather woman though she be, and alone amid so many enemies, oppressed and defamed in the eyes of the world . . . remains constant and steadfast in the Catholic faith and deserted and disparaged though she be, in defiance of all the dictates of humanity by Christian princes . . .

What were the praise, how great were the merits of his Catholic majesty [Philip II] if by his aid, the holy faith were restored in the realms of England and Scotland! Especially since, as the Saviour say, a single soul is worth more than all the world, and so many would be gained thereby.[42]

Amid all this sound and fury, doubts must have existed in the Vatican about the practicality, never mind legality, of removing Elizabeth from the throne of England. The papal archives contain a curious memorandum, drawn up around 1573–4, that raised various unpleasant questions stemming from Pope Pius V's bull excommunicating the English queen. It acknowledges, frankly, arguments that the bull was 'no longer binding upon Catholics because it has failed of its purpose, since instead of helping the Catholic cause, it has damaged it'. The document added:

Catholics may, with a clear conscience, obey [Elizabeth] in civil matters.

They may even, with a mental reservation, acknowledge her as head of the Anglican church.

They may defend her against those who attack her unlawfully.

Then the author, perhaps remembering the opinions of his readership, makes a sudden swerve back to orthodoxy:

They may not, however, defend her against those who attack her *vi bullæ* [in pursuance of the bull] or *studio religionis* [in religious zeal] and with reasonable hope of victory, but in such a case, are bound to co-operate against her.

The queen, though the bull had not been published [in England] might lawfully be dethroned as a perturber of the peace of the universal church.

In 1575–6, yet another scheme for the invasion of England was proposed by an odd assembly of English exiles in Rome, amongst them Stucley, Sir Richard Shelley – Prior of the Order of Jerusalem in England – and Sir Francis Englefield, and submitted to Pope Gregory XIII for his blessing and support. The Pope gave them special crucifixes for the enterprise, and after a request by Stucley granted ten separate indulgences to those who 'regarded [the conspirators] with reverence or devotion'. These graces included:

For each time that prayer is made before any one of them for the prosperity of Holy Mother Church and the exaltation of the Holy Catholic Faith and the preservation and liberation of Mary Queen of Scotland, and the reduction of the realms of England, Scotland and Ireland, and the extirpation of the heretics, another fifty days, and on feast [days] 100 days' indulgence.[43]

There was another theological weapon in the papal arsenal aimed at England: the missionary priests now being trained in the new English seminaries founded in Europe. Three were dispatched in 1574, and four years later there were more than fifty in the realm, mainly English-born, administering to a Catholic community feeling oppressed and threatened, as well as energetically converting new adherents to the faith.

The Privy Council in London seemed unaware of the growing danger to their Protestant policies until the capture and execution of a priest named Cuthbert Mayne in June 1577 in Cornwall. Mayne, 'a reverend and learned bachelor of divinity', had been trained in Douai and, disguised as a steward, had become chaplain to a member of the local gentry, Francis Tregian,[44] in whose house he was arrested.[45] He was eventually executed by hanging, drawing and quartering in Launceston marketplace on 30 November 1577. In being cut down from the gallows, still alive, he fell against the upright beam and horrifically knocked one of his eyes out of its socket. His head was placed above the town's castle gate and his body quarters were sent to Barnstaple, Bodmin, Wadebridge and Tregony, near Tregian's house, as a deterrent to further Catholic recusancy.

Mayne's arrest was closely followed by a dire official warning of the spread of Catholicism. On 21 June, the new Bishop of London John Aylmer wrote to Walsingham, thoroughly alarmed at the activities of the Catholic missions and their secret congregations:

> I have had conference with the archbishop of Canterbury and we have received from diverse of our brethren, bishops of this realm, news that the papists marvellously increase both in numbers and in obstinate withdrawing of themselves from the church and the service of God.[46]

The Privy Council was goaded into urgent action and sought reports from all dioceses of the local levels of recusancy in order to evaluate the scale of the problem. They also proposed to collect the more obdurate and lock them up in what today would be seen as internment camps. A document from this period, in Walsingham's handwriting, lists ten castles to be used for this purpose – Wisbech and Kimbolton (Cambridgeshire); Banbury (Oxfordshire); Framlingham (Suffolk); Portchester (Hampshire); The Vize (Wiltshire); Melborne (Derbyshire); Hatton (Cheshire); Wigmore (Herefordshire); and Barnard Castle (Durham). The plan was never fully carried out, but several castles were commandeered as prisons for Catholics.[47] Of these, Wisbech became the most notorious.[48]

The first prisoners were sent there in October 1580 after the Bishop of Ely, Richard Cox, was asked to put the castle 'in order and strength'. Catholic priests were to be confined at Wisbech and Banbury and laymen in the many London jails. Eight priests, including Thomas Watson, the Marian Bishop of Lincoln,[49] and Abbot John Feckenham[50] of Westminster Abbey became inmates, held under a strict regime. The prisoners were locked in separate rooms and only released for meals and thirty minutes' exercise before dinner and supper every day. Discipline and confinement were relaxed following the defeat of the Spanish Armada in 1588, when there were about thirty-five prisoners held there. Visitors were permitted, as were servants, and the priests were allowed out to stroll around the town surrounding the castle.

The community held loosely within the walls of Wisbech became a kind of ecclesiastical college, a forum for debating theological issues and a place of pilgrimage for Catholic laity from far and wide,[51] particularly for the sons of the gentry, who arrived disguised as servants. One Catholic prisoner recounted how he secretly celebrated Mass at the castle:

> In the dead of night, we were enabled to obtain vestments by a rope, which was let down from [a] window [above] and in the early morning, before the wardens and other prisoners were awake, we returned them in the same manner.[52]

Discipline became so lax that in 1590, allegations of slackness were made against the prisoners' keeper, Thomas Gray, and a commission was appointed to investigate conditions there. Matters had truly got out of hand at Wisbech: the priests could unlock each other's doors, they interrupted Gray's Puritan prayers by whistling and stamping on the floorboards of the room above and even his daughter Ursula had become a Catholic convert. The inquiry recommended that 'trustworthy townsmen' should be chosen to assist the keeper, who was not allowed to absent himself from the castle without permission; visits were stopped; letters were to be censored; and no communication between prisoners permitted except at meal times.[53]

Elsewhere, overly optimistic attempts were made to persuade recusant prisoners of the errors of their religious ways. A group was taken to York Cathedral in August 1580 for indoctrination, where they were exhorted to 'forsake your vain and erroneous opinions of Popery and conform yourselves with all dutiful obedience to [the] true religion now established'. These earnest pleas were rudely ignored and the prisoners tried to drown them out by loudly coughing and holding their hands over their ears. After refusing to recite the Lord's Prayer in English, they were sent packing back to York Castle.[54]

Enough was enough. Elizabeth's government began to tighten its grip on recusants in the spring of 1580. Bernardino de Mendoza, the Spanish ambassador, reported to his master King Philip II in June that 'For the past three weeks they have proceeded with much more rigour than formerly against the Catholics. Those of them who had been released on bail [are now] sent back to prison again'.[55]

William Herle, Burghley's old stool pigeon in the Marshalsea, wrote to the military and naval commander Sir Edward Horsey[56] in December that year that Elizabeth was 'sharper bent against the papists and is resolved that the oath [of allegiance] shall be ministered to the recusants'. He warned that a first refusal would be deemed an act of praemunire (the crime of asserting papal jurisdiction over England) and a second would be 'treason to those that persist'. This, insisted Herle, 'will gall them indeed and is the direct way to meet with their seditions and practices at home and to discourage [them] abroad'.[57]

A raft of penal measures was introduced by Burghley to hone the sharp edge of the law in countering the Catholic threat. The Parliament of 1580–1 passed, without opposition, new legislation that increased fines for non-attendance at Church of England services from one shilling per Sunday to a punitive £20 per month. These fines appear to have only been patchily imposed, as in the five years that followed, only sixty-nine recusants paid fines totalling £8,938 1s 11d, or nearly £1.5 million in today's monetary values. More importantly, the act declared high traitors all those priests who entered England to convert Protestants.[58] Five years later, another new law[59] enabled the crown to confiscate Catholic lands and property for non-payment of fines and gave 'Jesuits, seminary priests and other priests in England' just forty days to quit the country on pain of being declared a traitor and facing the death penalty. Income from these fines totalled £3,332 9s in the next five years, or £500,000 in modern prices, which must have pleased the parsimonious Elizabeth.

Bolstered by this new legislation, in July 1581 she ordered Walsingham to examine various individuals accused of conspiring against her, including the 'runnagate priests' Thomas Cottam[60] and Luke Kirby,[61] Jesuit seminarists from Douai[62] and the English College in Rome. Walsingham's questions focused on who they had been in contact with since arriving in England, what they knew of papal plans for an invasion and if they had any links with Mary Queen of Scots.

These unfortunates were probably swept up in Walsingham's hunt for the two Jesuits Robert Persons and Edmund Campion, who had entered England in June 1580. Persons had arrived ahead of Campion and after evading the searchers at the ports of Dover and Gravesend had boarded a small boat to travel up the River Thames to London by night. He found himself in the company of 'the queen's musicians that returned from Kent which imported [for] him extreme danger if God's holy hand had not kept them off for a time'. Moving through London on foot, Persons could get no lodgings and was

> forced to go up and down half a day from place to place . . . until
> noon, [when] he resolved to adventure into the prison at the
> Marshalsea and to ask for a gentleman prisoner there named
> Thomas Pound[63] in whose chamber he dined and was singularly
> comforted at the sight not only of him but of many confessors of
> Christ that had suffered there for His cause and religion.[64]

Meanwhile, Campion was also now in London, hiding for ten days in a house in Chancery Lane on the western outskirts of the city. At Pound's suggestion, Campion wrote a letter to the Privy Council explaining the reasons why both priests had come to England – to preach and comfort the Catholic population and, he emphasised, avoiding all politics. This communication was to be kept secret and only released when one or other was captured, but Pound stupidly circulated the document and a copy fell into Walsingham's hands. The hunt for the priests was now on.

Campion was active in Lancashire and in the Midland counties, but on 17 July 1581 he was arrested at the house of a Mr Yates[65] at Lyford Grange, near Wantage in Berkshire, hidden in a secret room above the gatehouse, after the authorities were tipped off by an informer called George Eliot, who was already under suspicion of murder. The priest was taken under escort to London, bound hand and foot and riding backwards with a paper prominently marked 'seditious Jesuit' stuck in his hat.[66] On his arrival in London, he was quickly interviewed at the home of the Earl of Leicester. Walsingham was probably one of the group who interrogated him before dashing off later that day to attend to diplomatic duties in Paris.[67] He wrote to Burghley from France, hoping that the queen 'may take profit of Campion's discovery by severely punishing the offenders, for nothing has done more harm than the overmuch lenity that has been used in that behalf'.

In the Tower, Campion was tortured three times on the rack in attempts to force him to divulge the names of those who had helped him, the whereabouts of Persons and the details of a plot to murder the queen, believed by the government to have been hatched at the seminary college at Rheims. He was so badly injured that at his trial on 14 November he was unable, as was the custom, to raise his right hand to plead 'not guilty'. Inevitably, he was condemned and on 1 December was dragged on a hurdle to a traitor's hideous death at Tyburn, on the site of today's Marble Arch in London. On the scaffold, Campion told the crowd that if 'our religion do make us traitors, we are worthy to be condemned but . . . [we] are and have been as true subjects as ever the queen ever had'. Moreover, he prayed for Elizabeth, 'your queen and my queen, unto whom I wish a long quiet reign with all prosperity' and acknowledged to the spectators that 'if you esteem my religion [as] treason, then I am guilty'. He was beatified in December 1886 and canonised by Pope Paul VI in 1970.

Throughout the sixteenth century, the rack was the instrument of first choice used to persuade prisoners to talk. In 1575, whilst investigating allegations of secret channels of communication between Mary Queen of Scots and the outside world, Walsingham told Burghley darkly: 'Without torture I know we shall not prevail.'[68] There were other instruments of violent persuasion available. These included the 'Scavenger's Daughter',[69] an iron band that compressed the head whilst the body was locked in a crouching position, and the metal gauntlets fitted with screws that crushed the hands. The hapless prisoner could also be confined in the 'Little Ease', a cell in the Tower so small that it was impossible to stand upright or lie down, a forerunner of the modern technique of sleep deprivation to reduce resistance to interrogation. Campion was one of its occupants, spending an agonising four days within its cramped walls. Another place of special confinement was 'The Pit', an oubliette twenty feet deep, and totally dark. Other cells were said to be full of vermin, especially rats, which at high water were driven up in shoals from the River Thames.

If prisoners refused to talk or to enter a plea even under such extremes they could face the ordeal of 'pressing'. This involved the placing of rocks or other heavy objects on their bodies until their resistance collapsed or they were crushed to death. That grim fate befell the butcher's wife and schoolmistress Margaret Clitherow in York in 1586, after she was accused of harbouring priests.[70] She died rather than speak. Such strong faith posed real problems for the interrogators. The Privy Councillor and evangelical Protestant Sir Francis Knollys drew up a list of questions to put to prisoners 'in the examination of Papists' and the 'prevarication and pleas of Popish recusants' were described, the better to counter them.[71]

The first notorious 'rackmaster' was Thomas Norton, the lawyer-turned-printer, playwright and poet, based at London's Guildhall. After a period of imprisonment in the Tower, he became an enthusiastic hunter of Papists,[72] writing to Walsingham enquiring how he could best serve the queen. After becoming an interrogator and torturer, in March 1582 he wrote to Walsingham angrily complaining about a seditious book that claimed that he had racked the Jesuit Alexander Briant so fearfully that he left him 'one foot longer than ever God made him'.[73] The following month, Briant's name appears amongst a list of tortured priests contained in a letter, written in Latin by a priest held in the Tower to other Catholics, complaining at the 'cruelty and severity with which they were being treated'.[74]

Norton died in 1585, but not before the crowning moment of his extraordinarily varied career: the racking and interrogation of Francis Throgmorton, involved in yet another plot to murder Elizabeth in November 1583. Walsingham ordered Thomas Wilkes, clerk to the Privy

Council, to bring Throgmorton to the Tower 'tomorrow morning early [and] to be present at [his] racking'.[75] Throgmorton refused to talk after his first session strapped to the fiendish device. Walsingham was sanguine that Norton would break the prisoner's resistance:

> I have seen as resolute men as Throgmorton stoop, notwithstanding the great show he has made of Roman resolution.
>
> I suppose the grief of the last torture will suffice without any extremity of racking to make him more comfortable than he has hitherto shown himself.[76]

His optimism and confidence in Norton's skills were fully justified. On 19 November, Throgmorton was placed on the rack again, but confessed 'before he was strained to any purpose'.

Like so many other distinguished civil servants down the years, Norton believed his experiences and political insight were worthy of a larger audience. He later wrote the polemic *Chain of Treasons*,[77] containing graphic details of a number of Catholic plots against the state during 1583–5, for both public education and entertainment and containing a number of verses praising Elizabeth in Latin. He also left manuscript notes: *Mr Norton's Devices*, containing information on the oath of allegiance to be administered to suspects and a scheme for reforming the church, courts, universities and schools 'for keeping out of Jesuits and seminarians from infecting the realm'.[78] His last appearance in the State Papers is as a witness to an affray between the Venetian Mark Anthony Bassano, one of the queen's musicians, and 'certain soldiers, then on the point of departure for Flanders', just outside Aldgate on the eastern edge of London, on 16 August 1585.[79]

An especially potent propaganda weapon against the Catholics was Norton's successor, the notorious and odious Richard Topcliffe (1532–1604), self-appointed priest-finder general and expert torturer, frequently used by Walsingham to extract information from his luckless detainees. He was a loathsome figure, feared and hated amongst England's recusant families with some justification for the obvious relish with which he turned the windlasses of the rack, or taunted and tormented his victims, agonisingly suspended by their arms against the dripping walls of the Tower of London's cells.

Today, Topcliffe would be labelled an out and out certifiable sadist, possessing unhealthy sexual fantasies. In the 1580–90s, the authorities regarded him as a determined hunter of fugitive priests, whom he pursued with a grim, paranoid persistence verging on obsession. He sought them out like a circling jackal that never deviates from its quarry, always sensing and seeking out their weaknesses and vulnerabilities. Pity the poor priest or recusant who fell into his merciless clutches. And many did, en route to the inevitable scaffold and a barbaric death. Take for example poor Richard Tankard. A Privy Council order of 24 May 1589 to Sir Owen Hopton, Lieutenant of the Tower, authorised him

> to receive into his custody Richard Tankard, alias Yaxley, a seminary priest, at the hands of the beadle of Bridewell [Jail] and to commit [him as] a close prisoner . . . under sure and safe custody, permitting only Mr Topcliffe at usual times to have access to him.[80]

Topcliffe was the eldest son of Robert Topcliffe of Somerby, Lincolnshire, and his wife Margaret, the daughter of Thomas, Third Baron Burgh of Gainsborough, but he was orphaned at the age of twelve. Although admitted to Gray's Inn in London to train as a lawyer, he does not appear to have pursued any career other than looking after his estates in the North Riding of Yorkshire and elsewhere in Nottinghamshire and Lincolnshire. In his early forties he took an active role against Catholics both inside and out of Parliament. During one Royal Progress in the late 1570s, he personally warned Elizabeth of 'sundry lewd Popish beasts' who were gathering at Buxton in Derbyshire.[81] In a letter to the Earl of Shrewsbury on 30 August 1578, Topcliffe recounted his conversation with the queen:

> Amongst [the papists] there is a detestable Popish priest, one Dyrham or Durande, as I remember at the bath or lurking in those parts after the ladies. Mr Secretary [Walsingham] has written to your Lord[ship] . . . herein enclosed, to wish your Lord[ship] to apprehend

him [and] to examine him of his coming to the church and upon the least or lightest occasion, to commit him . . .

[This letter would] have come to your Lord[ship] ere now, but that my best nag, by chance, did break his leg, wherefore I trust you pardon.[82]

It seems clear that Topcliffe was very happy in his work and derived immense satisfaction from his cruel interrogation of helplessly manacled Catholic prisoners. The Jesuit John Gerard, who thought him 'old and hoary and a veteran in evil' and a 'cruel creature who thirsted for the blood of Catholics', fell into Topcliffe's power whilst confined in the Poultry, one of London's jails, in 1594. The torturer told him: 'You know who I am, I am Topcliffe! No doubt, you have often heard people talk about me.' To make his point, he 'slapped his sword on the table close at hand, as if he intended to use it, if occasion arose'.[83]

Several of the Englishmen captured in the defeat of the Spanish Armada also fell into Topcliffe's hands. A order from St James's Palace, London, on 8 September 1588 to Topcliffe and the Lieutenant of the Tower concerned Tristram Winslade, then held in Newgate Prison,

heretofore taken in one of the Spanish ships, their lordships' pleasure is that he be conveyed to the Tower . . . and to appoint a time of meeting for the examination of the said Winslade upon the Rack, using torture [on] him at their pleasure.'[84]

No doubt Topcliffe had his pleasure. Satisfaction of another more fetid kind may also have come his way. During the interrogations, Topcliffe may also have indulged in bizarre sexual fantasies. Testimony from the captured priest Thomas Pormont,[85] later executed, describes Topcliffe's lascivious boastings as he questioned him in the comfort of his own home, alongside the churchyard of St Margaret's Church, Westminster. He told Pormont:

that he was to [MS torn] familiar with her majesty; that he many times put [MS torn] between her breasts and paps and in her neck.

That he has not only seen her legs and knees [words missing] with his hands above her knees.

That her felt her belly and said unto her majesty that she [had] the softest belly of any womankind.

That she said to him: 'Be not these the arms, legs and body of King Henry?' To which, he answered: 'Yes.'

That she gave him for a favour, a white linen hose, wrought with white silk.

That he is so familiar with her that when he pleases to speak with her, he may take her away from any company and she [was] not as pleasant with everyone that she did not love.[86]

There seems little doubt that Topcliffe was seeking to impress his prisoner by demonstrating his power at court, in a clumsy and egocentric attempt to persuade him that he alone could win the priest a pardon in exchange for information. Moreover, he emphasised that his position was unassailable: he did not care a jot for those government apparatchiks on the Privy Council, as he believed he held his authority directly and personally from Elizabeth herself. Perhaps, if one were to be generous, by gloating over his supposed intimate relationship with the Virgin Queen he was trying to shock the other-worldly Pormont into submission. But his breathless prurience goes far beyond mere boasting and strays into the unreal world of sexual fantasy. Certainly, Topcliffe had obscure obsessions. He was convinced that the priest was the bastard son of John Whitgift, Elizabeth's Archbishop of Canterbury, for whom he had little respect: 'The archbishop . . . was a fitter counsellor [in] the kitchen, among the wenches, than in a prince's court,' he told the wretched and frightened Pormont, who must, by that point, have been questioning, in his mind at least, the sanity of his captor and inquisitor. Topcliffe, still rambling on, then turned his ire to a rival pursuer of Catholic fugitives: 'and to Justice [Richard] Young, he [Topcliffe] would hang the archbishop and 500 more if they were in his hands'.

In June 1592, in an extraordinary letter to Elizabeth seeking her permission to apply his own violent methods of extracting information, Topcliffe recommends that a Catholic

> prisoner should be manacled at the wrists with his feet upon the ground and his hands [stretched up] as high as he was [able to] reach against the wall.[87]

He used such methods against the Jesuit priest Robert Southwell[88] in Newgate, who was 'hanged by the hands, put in irons [manacles], kept from sleep and such like devices to men usual.'[89] Few could withstand his tortures. Anne Bellamy, imprisoned in the gatehouse at Westminster, betrayed twenty-six people, including her parents, friends and relations after a session with Topcliffe. He then raped her and after she became pregnant she was forced to marry his servant Nicholas Jones in 1592 to cover up the scandal.[90]

Topcliffe also believed firmly in the biblical tenet that the labourer was worthy of his hire: he required rewards and honours for his gruesome work. In October 1584, he petitioned Elizabeth over a dispute he was involved in with Lord Chief Justice Sir Christopher Wray for the profitable lease of the parsonages at Corringham and Stow, both in Lincolnshire. He bitterly complained of the judge's 'corrupt attempt' to try the case himself, and nimbly slipped in the knife about Wray's family, pointing out that 'his lordship's grandfather served the Lord Conyers as a morrow Mass priest and vicar of East Witton [Yorkshire]'.[91]

After the fear and agony of the interrogation came the travesty of trial and the horrors of execution. Let there be no lingering doubts about the stark and dreadful nature of the judicial murder of these priests as traitors. The state's lawful methodology deliberately carried heavy biblical symbolism, used coldly and calculatedly. A few decades later in 1606, after the Gunpowder Plot against James I, the distinguished judge Sir Edward Coke claimed that such 'Godly butchery' indicated to all and sundry that the victim was dying for committing treason against the realm rather than for their religion. Ripping out their organs whilst they were still alive showed that the miscreant was unworthy to 'tread upon the face of the earth whereof he was made'. As he 'has been retrograde to nature, therefore, is he drawn backward at a horse's tail' on the hurdle on the way to the scaffold. The victim was first hanged because 'being hanged up by the neck between heaven and earth' demonstrated the individual's unworthiness to be part of either place, and the head was lopped off because it had 'imagined the mischief'. Castration was inflicted to demonstrate that the victim was 'unfit to leave any generation behind' and the heart was removed because it had 'harboured such horrible treason'. Displaying the body parts in public places evoked shame and infamy. The bloodthirsty old jurist added: 'Their carcase will I give to be meat for the fowls of the heavens and for the beasts of the earth.' He then quoted the Bible – the Book of Jeremiah, chapter eight, verse two: their bones were to 'be spread before the sun and the moon and all the host of heaven . . . They shall not be gathered or be buried; they shall be dung upon the face of the earth'.[92]

His words would have been meat and drink to Topcliffe. His self-appointed role in carrying out the executions is well exemplified by the death of Edmund Jennings,[93] slaughtered at the upper end of Holborn on the eastern edge of the City of London on 10 December 1591. Standing on the scaffold, a gloating Topcliffe urged his victim to confess his treason to secure a pardon from Elizabeth. Jennings, with the noose already around his neck, calmly replied: 'I know not ever to have offended her. If to say Mass be treason, I confess to have done and glory in it.' His words sent his tormentor into a fury and, leaving him scarce time 'to recite the *Pater Noster*',[94] Topcliffe kicked him off the ladder and left him hanging, half-strangled and gasping desperately for breath. Cruelly, the rope was immediately cut and Jennings landed heavily on his feet. The executioner tripped him up and, wielding a sharp butcher's knife, sliced off his genitalia, disembowelled him and ripped out his living organs, holding them up for the crowd to see. Jennings cried out, calling upon his patron Saint Gregory to help him, and the astonished blood-soaked hangman shouted: 'God's wounds! His heart is in my hand – and yet Gregory is in his mouth.'[95]

Another priest, Anthony Middleton,[96] was arrested in mid-1590 by Topcliffe, disguised as a Catholic, in a grocer's shop in Fleet Street,

London, together with Edward Jones.[97] When Jones was told to address the Old Bailey jury trying him, he claimed that during the reign of Edward VI, a statute was passed that forbade indictments for treasonable offences unless the crimes were proved by the testimony of two 'lawful witnesses' or admitted by voluntary confession. In his case, he claimed, there was neither a confession nor two witnesses involved. An enraged Topcliffe jumped to his feet and waved a slip of parchment at the prisoner. He snapped: 'No! Will you deny this to be your confession?' Jones replied: 'It was done by torture, for I was hanged by [the] arms and therefore, it was not voluntary.'

At Middleton's execution in Fleet Street, a gloating Topcliffe banned the priest from speaking 'except you [can] speak to the glory of God [and] the honour of your prince and country'. Middleton replied:

> You know, Mr Topcliffe, I never approached any man, nor confessed in any place. Therefore you wrong me. But if I had 10,000 deaths to suffer, I would suffer them for the Roman Catholic faith and I hope my death shall confirm many Catholics in their faith which are present.

Topcliffe, stung by the priest's defiance, told him to hold his peace, and the crowd thronging round the scaffold cried: 'Away with him!'

Middleton was still alive when the executioner threw his heart into the brazier on the scaffold.

The task of hunting down Catholic priests was much aided by a network of spies and informers. One of the most useful was Charles Sledd, who, masquerading as a Catholic, infiltrated the English College in Rome in 1579 and stayed at the home of the tailor Solomon Aldred, who later became another of Walsingham's agents. On Sledd's return to England in May 1580, he wrote out long lists of Catholic exiles and priests, some with physical descriptions, all of whom he had met on his travels in France and Italy. These he supplied to Walsingham, together with a curious diary of his time in Rome that still exists, bound in a vellum folio volume in the British Library.[98] When he arrived at the English College on Saturday 11 July 1579, he was shown around by Luke Kirby –

a priest who fell into Walsingham's hands in 1581 and was later executed. Sledd saw

> all the scholars in their several chambers, placed three or four . . .
> very finely decked and everyman his bed appointed . . . Last of all
> Kirby brought me into the chamber of John Pasquall, gentleman,
> accompanied by three others, George Martin, George Birke and
> Edward Ristone, priests

who questioned him closely regarding his reasons for coming to Rome – clearly fearing he was a spy.

On the Monday he confessed his sins to the Jesuit Thomas Derbyshire, was absolved and was given a certificate in Latin demonstrating that he was a good Catholic – although, as he assured Walsingham later, 'I never consented to it in [my] heart.' That certificate was an 'open sesame' to the heady world of the English Catholic exiles in Rome:

> Every man which [was] in doubt before he speak to me or be seen
> [with] me was afterwards familiar with me . . . they all assure them-
> selves that I am of the same faction and belief as they are [and are]
> read[y] to pleasure me in anything they may . . . [and] with many
> friendly preservations wish me to be a priest.

He attended an after-dinner meeting of English Catholics on 29 November when plans for the invasion of England were discussed:

> They appointed their landing place . . . to be Milford Haven [in
> Wales] where they estimated that there might be three or four
> hundred sailors [on] ships [lying] at [anchor].

Then they looked at what forces could be mustered to oppose them:

> The able and warlike men . . . in the city of London, which they all
> agreed could not exceed twelve or twenty thousand men at the most
> . . . and of all the land else could not make sixty thousand able men
> more.

The Tower of London held munitions for 30,000 men and as regards gunpowder 'they were certain of no great store to be in England and daily sent out of the land into Flanders'. The conspirators also decided that their supporters amongst the nobility were 'more in number than the queen's majesty had on her side' and very well 'furnished with horses and armour'.[99]

It was pure, self-deluding cloud-cuckoo-land.

Sledd also passed on useful tactical intelligence gleaned from the English College, such as the 'watch-' or passwords used between missionary priests – including the rather obvious '*Jesus Marie*' – and the means by which secret letters were smuggled into England: pasted between the covers of books that could be lawfully imported, mainly through Dover.

He arrived back in London on the morning of 17 May 1580 and wasted no time in seeking an interview with Walsingham. That afternoon Sledd went to court, and through the good offices of Francis Milles, one of the Secretary's officials, saw the spy master. Nine days later he had another interview, arranged by the London magistrate Richard Young, and he passed over his treacherous notes and various letters he had acquired or copied.

His career as one of Walsingham's best informers had been launched.

CHAPTER THREE

Her Majesty's Secret Service

*'Advice from Rome says the Pope has got fourteen
or sixteen Jesuits to go [to] England and has
hallowed and charmed their persons so that no
harm can come to them. They should be looked
for in time, before they do any mischief.'*

INTELLIGENCE SENT TO WALSINGHAM FROM NUREMBURG,

17 JULY 1582.[1]

On his appointment as a Principal Secretary of State in December 1573,
Sir Francis Walsingham became responsible for the government's intelligence-gathering operations in a number of areas: the growing Catholic
threat, both internally and externally; the religiously inspired plans to
invade England; and the intentions and policies of the governments of the
major players on the European political stage. His appetite for information was voracious. Eighty years after his death, his reputation as a clever
and devious spy master lived on: 'He outdid the Jesuits in their own bow
[at their own game] and over-reached them in their own equivocation,'
David Lloyd wrote admiringly in his *State Worthies*.[2]

The loosely organised intelligence network he inherited from Lord
Burghley was only patchily effective. John Lee, one of Burghley's agents
who had been shadowing the fugitives from the 1569 Northern Rebellion,
was caught in Antwerp in November 1572 where he was spying on the

Spanish forces in the Low Countries. Two years later, Burghley asked Walsingham to intercede on behalf of the spy Thomas Bath, alias Tomazo, who had been arrested in Flanders and now was 'in danger of death'.[3]

Such casualties in the field – by capture, assassination or subornation into treachery – were almost inevitable, and consequently greater depth of coverage was required in the number of active agents available. It was also clear that Walsingham needed to insert more spies in the areas of specific danger to his sovereign and state: the new English seminary colleges in France and Rome; the Vatican; the Netherlands; the French court; Spain; and the Baltic. He also required agents who would be ready to be deployed on an ad hoc basis to root out information on various issues and events – what today's CIA euphemistically calls 'episodic employment'.

International intelligence was already flowing into London through normal diplomatic channels and domestically from the Lord Lieutenants of the counties and from the bishops, who employed spies against the Catholic recusants. Some of Walsingham's fellow Privy Councillors, like Leicester, also operated their own small private groups of 'intelligencers'. The system of customs searchers at the major English ports was very much in the front line. They were responsible for stopping and questioning travellers from abroad and searching them for hidden messages and letters. By and large, this system worked well, although there were sometimes accusations of corruption levelled against them. Indeed, the English ambassador in Paris Sir Edward Stafford complained that his personal correspondence was being intercepted and read by the searchers at the Sussex port of Rye. Walsingham told him that in order to avoid 'such inconvenience' he should put his private letters in an official packet – the equivalent of today's diplomatic bag.

The Secretary of State began to build an overseas network using, initially, the tried and trusted Italian agents he had employed when he was ambassador in Paris. He must also have built up many personal contacts during his earlier travels in Europe who now became useful in his new role. On 4 March 1571, he had told Burghley of information 'a spy of his had obtained from one Darbyshire, an English Jesuit, of a plot contrived against Elizabeth'.[4] Just before his appointment as Elizabeth's Secretary of State, he wrote again to Burghley recommending two of his men for intelligence work:

If your lordship has any suspicion of any unsound meaning in the Low Countries towards her majesty, I think [Captain] Sassetti[5] would be a very good instrument to decipher the same, having as he has, great familiarity with Chiapin Vitelli.

Vitelli, Marquis of Cetona, was a Spanish general and Sassetti would have been aware of the military and political personalities and issues involved in the Low Countries. This type of knowledge is vital in deciphering, when it can be used to identify frequently mentioned places or names as clues to cracking codes. In addition, Walsingham offered up for secret work another of his favourite Italians, Jacomo Manucci:

Your lordship wrote unto me to find out one to be employed in Spain. If you think such employment presently necessary, I think I could find the means to place my old servant Jacomo in the French king's ambassador's resident's house in Spain.[6]

This Florentine worked for Walsingham in Lyons and elsewhere in France in 1573–4 – his letters written in Italian – but he was later imprisoned by Catherine de Médici. He eventually returned to London, living in the parish of St Andrew Undershaft, controlling part of the English network of agents in Europe and acting for Walsingham on particularly delicate missions, often passing on the Secretary's instructions verbally rather than in writing.

At home, much information about covert Catholics and sedition was casually supplied by the busybodies present in any society: the nosy neighbour, the man living around the corner nursing a grudge against you. From such a source we have the examination and confession of Alice Lake, wife of the vicar of Ringwood in Hampshire, who was interrogated in late December 1586 after Edmund Eaton reported her declaration that the queen's 'days should not be long'.[7] There was also the Welshman named Griffiths who knew of a cave 'three fathoms deep' used to hide missionary priests who had just landed from the sea. Alexander Barry saw William Edmonds reading out of his 'Papistical catechism' along the pew from where he was kneeling to pray in the church at Great Torrington in Devon.[8] In the disaffected county of Westmorland, the 'substantial' yeoman John Warrender reported 'the great increase of seminary priests and Jesuits' and attached a list of names to be apprehended. He added: 'The only means to take the Papists and priests must be by parish search, under a commission [by] one or two trusty gentlemen.'[9] Walsingham noted passages of importance in these documents by inking his private mark in the margin: a trefoil or cloverleaf device.

Walsingham also utilised the good offices of English merchants abroad, often in return for his diplomatic favours in resolving local trade disputes. One example was the cloth and kersey[10] trader Thomas Beckner, whom the spy master helped in Rouen over legal disputes 'that have been a great burden to me these twelve years'. In 1584, he wrote to Walsingham promising that 'for your friendly remembrance of my suit, I and mine shall ever be bound to you'. He thereafter regularly sent intelligence to London about what he saw or heard. In August that year, Beckner reported the activities of

> James Penson . . . who haunts the company of Papists and has been seen at Eu and other suspicious places, transporting money to and fro. There are to go from hence for England and Scotland, English seminary [priests] daily. There is now a son of Sir John Sotherhet of Lancashire, going over with a priest.[11]

The following year, he wrote regarding unusual security measures at Rouen and added:

> It is also said that the king will have all strangers void this town and that diverse noblemen levy forces at sundry places and mean this summer to besiege Geneva . . . It is said the king has determined to have but one religion in his realm.[12]

In addition to this gossip, patriotic Englishmen overseas contacted

Walsingham with snippets of information, such as Richard Stallynge in February 1584, again from Rouen in France:

> I pray you pardon my boldness, as one unknown to your honour . . .
> but I cannot tell of what effect this letter I have received from my
> friend . . . from the straits in the furthest part of Spain [may be] . . .
> My friend writes that there is coming [to] Flanders a great number
> of soldiers . . .[13]

Others wrote to him to volunteer for 'gentlemanlike service that may be grateful to her majesty', such as Humfrey Jenney in August 1583 from Milan:

> You are thought in Spain, France and Italy to govern that noble ship
> [the queen] and guard her from danger of shipwreck, which
> navigation may God maintain and prosper. Although your honour
> knows me not, I am bold to pray you to accept me for your poor friend
> and servant.[14]

Further profitable sources of potential agents were disaffected Catholics and especially captured priests, who faced the lonely duress of solitary confinement in a stinking prison, the agonies of torture and almost certain death. An example from December 1581 concerns the priest John Hart, then held in the Tower, who wrote to Walsingham offering his services as a spy in return for a pardon. Hart pleaded that he enjoyed 'intimacy with Dr Allen [the de facto leader of the English Catholic exiles] . . . [which would enable him] to discover all his designs and to know the very secrets of his whole heart'.[15] There were others whose previously steadfast faith was broken by fear and pain.

Walsingham's chief concern now was the threat posed by Mary Queen of Scots, that 'bosom serpent', as he graphically described her. Therefore, his most urgent task was to discover the secret means she used to communicate with the world outside her various prisons, so that he could tap into her correspondence and monitor what he saw as treasonous machinations.

In May 1574, the Scottish government detained an eighteen-year-old boy called Steward who turned out to be a carrier of Mary's letters to her supporters in Scotland. The youth had received the packages from the Scotsman Alexander Hamilton at Doncaster. Hamilton was tutor to the children of George Talbot, Sixth Earl of Shrewsbury, then 'keeper' or jailer of the Scottish queen at Sheffield.

Hamilton was dispatched, under guard, to London and interrogated personally by Walsingham. He vehemently denied any involvement in handling Mary's clandestine messages. Eventually, more information arrived from Scotland and the trail led to a London bookseller, Henry Cockyn. He was immediately arrested on suspicion of being a go-between for Mary with some of the greatest in the realm of England. On 5 February 1575, Walsingham wrote despondently to Burghley about the progress of his investigation:

> This day we examined Cockyn from whom we can draw nothing. He has been three times imprisoned before and always so mildly dealt with as he takes no account of [threats]. I think the show of torture (the fellow being so resolute as he is) will little prevail, but rather make him more obstinate – seeing himself but dallied with.[16]

Walsingham tried another tactic – secretly offering Cockyn both a royal pardon and a bribe in return for his full confession. Most importantly, he guaranteed his anonymity as a source. He grimly assured the bookseller that if he refused the deal 'he would be made to confess the bottom of the matter by torture'.

The ploy worked. Cockyn duly wrote out his confession, admitting that he had agreed to a request from Mary's London representative John Leslie, Bishop of Ross, to deliver his letters to the Scottish queen, and that he had regularly supplied her with information about events at court. Cockyn further acknowledged that he had carried messages from Mary to Lord Henry Howard, the younger brother of the executed Duke of Norfolk, and his nephew Philip (later Earl of Arundel), and implicated five of Shrewsbury's servants and one of those working for the French ambassador Michel de Castelnau, Seigneur de la Mauvissière, in handling the Queen of Scots' letters. He also mentioned the name of Lady Cobham, one of Elizabeth's own ladies-in-waiting, as being part of the chain of treachery.[17] Although shocked by the startling disclosures of disloyalty so close to home, the cautious queen predictably hesitated, prevaricated and finally did very little, apart from what any government does when faced by such a quandary – appoint a commission of inquiry. Exasperated, Walsingham told Leicester:

> Her majesty's strange dealings in this case will discourage all honest ministers that are careful for her safety to deal in the discovery of the sores of this diseased state, seeing her majesty bent [inclined] rather than cover [disregard] them than to cure them.[18]

It was not the first time his patience was sorely tried by Elizabeth and it would not be the last. But he remained resolved to be ever vigilant for conspiracies against her life and her state.

In 1579 Walsingham purchased the manor of Barn Elms in Barnes, Surrey, close to the River Thames. He spent much of his last decade there, when he needed to be removed from the noise and gossip of court, although he could reach the Palaces of Whitehall or Greenwich relatively quickly by boat if the tide was in his favour. He maintained close contact with his office in London at such times, however, through a system of mounted couriers. His stables at his country home accommodated sixty-eight horses for such a purpose and he maintained another twenty-three elsewhere around London.

His new network of 'intelligencers' was nearing full operational capability by 1580. He now had agents based in twelve towns or cities in France, nine in Germany, four in Italy, three in the Low Countries, four in Spain and others within the huge Turkish Empire in Algiers, Tripoli and Constantinople.

Anxious to flex his muscles overseas, Walsingham conceived an audacious project early that year that not even the modern CIA, in its wildest flights of fantasy, would dare to consider today, let alone implement. Walsingham planned to boldly kidnap the Papal Legate to France, Cardinal Alexander Riario, whilst he was en route to Paris. Huguenot pirates from La Rochelle were to be paid to seize the Legate, so that he could be questioned about the Vatican's scheme for a possible military expedition against Ireland involving Spanish troops. Although some planning was put in place, the daring abduction was never mounted, for reasons that remain unclear. Perhaps Burghley stymied the plot – or it may have been vetoed by the always cautious Elizabeth.

Undeterred, Walsingham employed an agent called Best in France to masquerade as a disaffected Englishman in order to discover the extent of the papal plans. Best's source was the secretary of the Spanish ambassador in Paris, but before he was up and running in the role, he was brutally killed in July 1580 in a suspiciously convenient street brawl in the French capital.

As so often happens in intelligence-gathering, one door opens as another closes. The spy master was told that a papal agent in Bologna was willing to sell information to the English government. Walsingham immediately sent one of his private secretaries – Lawrence Tomson[19] – to the northern Italian city, who, after handing over the requisite bribe, was told that Pope Gregory XIII intended to raise an army under Jacomo Bonacampanini. This general, with the assistance of Henry, Duke of Guise, was to invade England and dethrone Elizabeth. Frustratingly, the informant refused to part with any details about the all-important dates, timings, places and numbers of troops.

Most of Walsingham's agents were motivated purely by money. They had a commodity to sell – information – and the spy master was only too ready to purchase it, despite the hardly generous budgets allocated to espionage by Elizabeth. As Sir Edward Stafford perceptively told him in 1581: 'If there were no knaves, honest men should hardly come by the truth of any enterprise against them.'

By July 1574, Walsingham was employing a David Jones in London to seek out information about priests hiding in the capital. It was a short-term employment, as it was for many of his spies – either because their cover was soon blown or he harboured doubts about their honesty or reliability. Many were hard up, like the Magdalene College scholar James Welsh who became a spy for the Bishop of London because he could not find work as a schoolmaster. Such situations often led to exaggerated or distorted intelligence being supplied in the hope of greater reward, and Walsingham must always have been fully aware of this danger.

Jones had acknowledged to Francis Milles, one of the spy master's confidential secretaries, that he had made confession to a priest in the Marshalsea Prison 'with two other persons, Mr Blewitt of the Hanging Sword [tavern] in Fleet Street and David Sadler'. Jones's career as an informant seems to have lasted just over a month; his third letter to Milles reported him being saved from starvation by a Mrs Cawkins, 'a notorious Papist', and the stonehearted and rapacious Jones requested: 'I pray you [to] desire my master that I may have the benefit of what she [will] lose by statute, even if it be [only] the chain she wears.'[20] So much for Christian charity. The informant's last letter, a month later, pathetically sought a loan of two shillings 'to be left at the George' tavern.

Robert Barnard, alias Robert Woodward, was a man of some education who became a very active agent in rooting out fugitive priests and recusants. He submitted reports – always signed with the codename or pseudonym 'P. H.' – for more than three years, beginning on 5 January 1581 with a letter, as an aperitif for his talents, providing full details of the fugitive Earl of Westmorland's movements in Europe and his receipt of 500 crowns from the Pope. He went on to supply more meaty information about a Mr Gardiner and his wife of Uxbridge, Middlesex, who were sheltering a priest called Gimlet.

That October, Barnard was working in London and was desperately short of cash. He begged Walsingham:

> I must humbly beseech you to consider of me. I owe my host above £4, who threatens to have me in prison for the same. I have not received anything from you in three months past. I beseech you to give me order whereby I may, with less trouble to your honour, receive monthly that which it may seem good to you to bestow upon me.
>
> I was never in better credit with the papists, nor of some great acquaintance among them, for I have attained the means to have access to all the prisons in London, the Tower only excepted, whereby there is nothing that comes over or goes over, nor anything be done here within our country but I am assured to hear thereof.[21]

No doubt the spy master had heard such boasts before from others anxious to tap into his secret-service funds. But Barnard produced a stream of reports that helped Walsingham keep his finger on the ever faster-beating pulse of English recusancy. Here are two from 1582:

19 April: There is no probability of rebellion this spring or summer. The Papists have no hope of aid from the Pope and the King of Spain. [The Jesuit] Persons is at present in Rouen to write a book in answer to the one against Campion.

Very few priests in London now. One, Mr Vaine, a priest at the Temple. One other in Gray's Inn named Lyell. Another, a Mr March, at the sign of the White Swan in High Holborn.[22]

17 November: Information sent of a letter from Dr Henshawe,[23] a seminary priest to a friend, stating that he, with Father Holt[24] and Father Heywood,[25] the Jesuits, had spent three months in Staffordshire and had converted 228 persons to the Catholic faith. If it please your honour, that I may go down, I doubt not to meet them all, for my acquaintance there is such as I shall have access among them all.[26]

Walsingham will have swooped on these priests and in at least one instance he may have been successful: John March is recorded as a seminary priest still being held in a London prison in September 1588. In July 1582, Barnard exposed John, First Baron Lumley, who had been caught up in the original plot involving the Florentine banker Ridolphi and imprisoned in 1569–73. The spy told Walsingham that he had been talking with the wife of a man called Carter[27] who had been jailed several times for distributing Catholic pamphlets. Now he had been rearrested that day in a raid on his home in the parish of St Olave's Hart Street and taken to the Tower. His wife, walking along a road in Lambeth with Barnard, confided to him that she was going to talk to Lumley 'whom I wished to God I had never known . . . to tell him that all in our house is taken away' – books, vestments, crosses, chalices and other accoutrements of the Mass. These belonged to Lumley 'and by the means and entreaty of Mr Smith and Mr Caines, two of my lord's gentlemen, my husband was made to take them in'. Barnard suggests to Walsingham:

> If it please your honour to cause both Smith and Caines to be apprehended forthwith and these being led to their charge as confessed by Carter and Carter's wife to be taken who knows as much as her husband, not only in this but in all other affairs and causes concerning the dealing of the Papists ...
>
> If this be ripped to the bottom, there will be such matter revealed as [has] long been full secret ... [28]

Carter was 'nearly killed on the rack, but nothing could be drawn from [him] but the name of "Jesus"'.[29] Lumley escaped the state's retribution and led a curiously charmed life, blatantly holding regular Catholic Masses at his huge and grand mansion Nonsuch, between Cheam and Ewell in Surrey,[30] complete with his own choir to sing sacred music especially written for him by the composer William Byrd.[31]

Later, Barnard became a kind of roving double agent, using his contacts to uncover priests. He regularly sent in details of obdurate Catholics he had discovered while travelling up and down the realm. In December 1584, he sent a list entitled 'secret advertisements touching Mass priests' covering suspects in the counties of Cheshire, Lancashire, Westmorland, Northumberland and Yorkshire, listing nearly 100 recusants and priests in this still disaffected region of England. He begins with:

> The Lady Warberton at Congleton [Cheshire] keeps an old priest who calls himself Walkens but his name is William Worthington. He is her butler when he is there [but] at times he goes abroad for a month or six weeks and he has been at Rome.

Then, near York:

> Mr Gail at Acame Grange. His wife had the resolution of me.[32] He has been eight years married and yet never come [to] the church. He was married at a Mass. He has six children who were all christened by the old law. She is Sir Richard Stapleton's daughter. Mr Graves, a

notary at Tickell. His house was searched by Cootes, an officer of the town and certain books with other things were found but he remains yet without further trouble.

Barnard also informed on corrupt officials:

There is one Gilpin, who is [an] official for Derbyshire, who refuses no bribe and [nor] does his man who has to deal for him, whose name is Lye . . . In like case, has Munday, who has been in [many] places where I have passed, whose dealing[s] have been very rigorous and yet very small [in effect] . . . but [has caused] much hurt, or in one place . . . under pretence to seek [for an] Agnus Dei . . . he carried from a widow £40 [which he] took from a chest. A few of these . . . [?incidents may] either raise a rebellion, or cause your officers to [be] murdered.

He ends with an assurance of the veracity of his information:

Most [of] these places I have been at since I was last with [your] honour: for the rest, I am most assured to be most certain of and for my service to be to your content.[33]

Walsingham's agents and pursuivants were remarkably effective, particularly in the teeming, stinking streets and alleys of London. The Jesuit priest Robert Persons reported that in July 1580 'the searches grew so eager and frequent . . . and the spies so many and diligent as every hour almost we heard of some [priests] taken, either on suspicion or detection against them'. That month, five or six of the newly arrived priests had already been arrested. The Jesuits daringly held a synod at St Mary Overy in Southwark to plan their missionary campaign. Shortly before the meeting's close, Henry Orton,[34] a former lay student of the English College, was on his way to the safe house when he was unluckily recognised in the street by Walsingham's spy Charles Sledd, who had known him in Rome. Sledd followed him to discover his hiding place, but grew tired of the chase and arrested him. A priest in the hand is worth two hidden in a secret chamber. A little more patience and he would have captured the entire Jesuit leadership in England.[35] Persons commented: 'It was a marvel that . . . we all together had not been taken.' However, that same day Sledd also captured another priest, Robert Johnson,[36] 'as he was walking about the streets'.

> Sledd was an assiduous priest-hunter. According to Persons, he was on our track more than [the] others for he has authority from the royal council to break into all men's houses as he will and to search all places which he does diligently whenever there is a gleam of booty.[37]

The priest later wrote to Alfonso Agazzari, Rector of the English College in Rome, that 'false brethren' now working for Walsingham were 'the most troublesome to us and more deadly than anything else'. Another time, he complained of being unable to write a long letter 'because I cannot, without difficulty, stop anywhere long enough to finish writing one page'.[38] His hunters must have been pressing hard on his heels. From the other side, the paranoid torturer Richard Topcliffe complained bitterly to the Privy Council in 1586 that about twenty seminary priests of

> reputation and best learning [are] now in London. They walk auda-ciously, disguised, in the streets of London. Their wonted fears and timorousness is turned into mirth and solace among themselves, as though the day of their expectation were not past . . .[39]

The oddly named Maliverny Catlyn was another of Walsingham's agents directly tasked with spying on covert Catholics. The spy master seemingly already knew him, for when Catlyn wrote from Rouen on 22 April 1586 to offer his services, he mentioned opening 'the way for a *further* [author's italics] entrance into matters needful to be discovered for her majesty's surety'. A former soldier in the Low Countries, he was something of a sober-sides Puritan with a burning moral hatred for actors and stage plays.[40] He had wormed his way into the confidence of English Catholics exiled in France and reported 'secret intelligence of a most dangerous person who brought Adams the priest into England [with] three Agnus Dei and certain jewels of Edmund Campion'.[41]

Two months later, Catlyn was languishing in a Portsmouth prison after being detained by the searchers at that port. Clearly an opportunist, Catlyn saw his inconvenient imprisonment as an excellent cover story to use in his later efforts to gather information. He asked Walsingham to arrange for him to be transferred to the Marshalsea Prison in Southwark and, once there, ingratiated himself with the priest Edward Jackson and another prisoner. Poor innocent priest! Believing Catlyn to 'be participant to his estate', Jackson hinted at the plans for invasion being drawn up by the Pope and Philip II of Spain. The spy immediately sent the intelligence to Walsingham, urging that the other (unnamed) prisoner be summoned and interrogated:

> No doubt being either terrified or gently entreated, he will declare to you the circumstance thereof, by which means this wicked instrument may presently be called into question and the matter avouched before his face, and yet I may still remain without suspicion.

Catlyn suggests that he should be summoned by Walsingham, in order that he might impart further information more discreetly:

> Besides the inconvenience of the place is such as I can hardly be suffered to have paper, pen or ink, except I will impart to my keeper what I write. [He] in truth, uses me like a prisoner committed for high treason, so that I was forced to charge him, in her majesty's name, to deliver this to your honour with speed, as [a] confession touching the suspicion ... against me.[42]

The spy walked out of the gates of the Marshalsea in August 1586 and headed to the North of England on Walsingham's orders to investigate Catholic disaffection there. After his experiences in jail, Catlyn had no doubts about the tide of subversion created by locking up priests. He told his master:

> If you mean to stop the stream, choke the spring. Believe me, the prisons of England are [the] very nourishers of papists. Banish them, for God's sake, or let them remain close prisoners, so that they may not daily poison others.[43]

Ironically, the spy's viewpoint was unconsciously echoed by the Jesuit Robert Persons, but naturally from an opposite perspective. Persons maintained that jailed priests

> are sometimes of more use to us there than if they were at liberty. For these men, being always definitely in the same place, make possible the visits of many people who are unable to discover the whereabouts of other priests.[44]

Catlyn returned to London in the early autumn and was then employed to spy on a number of the great and good who had come under suspicion in the spy master's mind of harbouring Catholic sympathies. Catlyn reported in November:

> Yesterday, I spied the Earl of Worcester[45] and Lord Mordaunt[46] go off on a clandestine journey on a wherry[47] to an obscure inn [the Red Lion] and have conference with a third man whom I knew not. I have within these four or five weeks used my best endeavour to pierce into the mind of a very great one of this realm and have been with him these few hours, not doubting but to find [out] his affections thoroughly and then I will advertise [tell] you.[48]

The spy continued to work for Walsingham in London and the North until at least June 1587, but annoyingly there are no more clues or hints in the State Papers as to the identity of this mysterious great personage. Catlyn must have possessed the manners and bearing of a gentleman to be able to circulate freely within the higher echelons of society. Despite this, he suffered periods of poverty and at one point, in December 1586, appealed to Walsingham for funds as 'I and mine are like to keep the coldest Christmastide that hitherto we ever tasted'.[49] He received £5 as a stop-gap payment for his pains.

Within his personal secretariat, Walsingham assembled a group of experts to organise and process his intelligence work, unobtrusively based at his new London home, an impressive house in Seething Lane in the parish of St Olave, Hart Street.[50] It was also handily located for the great fortress and prison of the Tower, a few hundred yards away to the south. Some of his agents wrote directly to Walsingham; others were handled by his assistants, acting as 'case officers', in modern intelligence parlance.

Of course, the best method of thwarting conspiracy was by interception of the communications necessary for the planning and execution of the plot. Signals intelligence was as important in the sixteenth century as it remains in the twenty-first. Aside from the developing science of cryptography, which is discussed in detail in Chapter 4, the government's counter-intelligence resources had to detect a huge range of methods utilised to covertly transmit messages. Secret inks were widely used at that time – a dilute solution of alum[51] or a thin mixture of milk and lemon juice – which needed the application of warmth to reveal the handwriting. If these ingredients were unavailable, the hard-pressed agent could resort to using his own urine, if watered down.[52] Seemingly innocuous books were employed by both sides to disseminate instructions by using one or more words on pages indicated by a separately issued cipher. Alternatively, messages could be hidden inside a bound book's leather cover. Letters were also concealed in wine bottles, in the linings of luggage, or, in Mary Queen of Scots' case, the fashionably high heels of ladies' shoes. Dead letter boxes were employed, whereby messages were hidden at a pre-arranged location to be safely retrieved later by another agent. The greatest prize of all was the discovery of the key to a cipher – the ill-fated Duke of Norfolk hid his codes beneath two roof tiles at his London home in the Charterhouse.

In all this, the overriding imperative was not to allow your adversary to learn that his correspondence had been compromised. Walsingham employed Arthur Gregory who was adept at opening and resealing intercepted letters in such a way that the addressee would be unaware they had been tampered with. His specific skill was in forging seals, so he may have had some training in engraving precious metals. After Walsingham's death, Gregory was employed for similar work by Sir Robert Cecil, Burghley's son, who acted informally as Principal Secretary of State until his official appointment in 1596. Gregory remains a mysterious figure, but at the end of his life he not unreasonably expected some reward. The Cecil Papers contain his suit, made early in the reign of James I:

> In consideration of my services done and which I shall be able ever
> to do during my life, to grant me the two-thirds of recusant lands ...
> and to receive good assurance for the payment of £20 by the month.

Gregory adds, very frankly: 'His majesty by this grant gains nothing. And I will accept it for recompense for my services and never crave another suit.'[53]

Walsingham's trusted chief assistant was the code-breaker Thomas Phelippes, the son of William, a London customs officer. He was a Cambridge Master of Arts who lodged in Leadenhall Market, an easy 500-yard walk from Seething Lane. He was fluent in French, Italian and Latin but less skilled in Spanish. Phelippes was described by Mary Queen of Scots as being 'of low stature, slender every way, dark yellow hair on the head, [eaten] in the face with small pocks [scars of smallpox], of short sight, thirty years of age by appearance'.[54] He may have been ugly but his skills as a decipherer and a forger were to become the instrument of her destruction.

He first appears in 1578 when Walsingham sent him on temporary attachment to the staff of Sir Amyas Paulet, then Elizabeth's ambassador in Paris, to decode correspondence intercepted there. Subsequently he controlled spies in France and carried the cash that Elizabeth secretly supplied to the French Huguenots during the religious civil wars. At various times he used the pseudonyms 'John Morice' and 'Peter Halins, merchant'. His servant Casey was often employed for delicate missions.

In his heyday, his services were greatly valued. In May 1586, Walsingham told Phelippes 'that the queen has signed his bill for a pension of 100 marks[55] and takes his services in good part'.[56] Six months later, Walsingham reported his conversation with Elizabeth when she said that Phelippes 'was greatly beholden to the Lord Treasurer for his good report of him to her'.[57] Always venal, the codebreaker complained to Walsingham in August 1589 that he had heard of the death of his good friend Paulet and 'that Mr Middlemore had obtained a grant of his office of clerk of the Duchy [?of Lancaster] but which had been promised to himself by her majesty'.[58]

Edward Burnham, another of Walsingham's servants, was used for sensitive diplomatic missions as well as intelligence-gathering forays overseas. In 1577 he was sent to Picardy and elsewhere in northern France to 'see and learn what French forces were levied there to enter the Low Countries' as well as holding discussions with military governors. Surprisingly for a spy master obsessed with secrecy, Burnham was allowed to write an account of his mission – '*Special Services . . . performed . . . at the commandment and appointment of Sir Francis Walsingham, her majesty's principal secretary and my honourable master*'.[59] This was presumably for the queen's eyes only – and was probably written in the hope of soliciting some mark of royal favour.

Six years later, in 1583, Burnham was dispatched to the Netherlands to assure the Dutch Protestant government of Elizabeth's goodwill and to assess how much reliance they were placing on France for assistance in their campaign against the Spanish forces in the Low Countries. In 1585, he carried letters and verbal instructions to William Davison, the queen's envoy in Holland, and to George Gilpin, the Merchant Adventurers' company representative in Zeeland (who was also Walsingham's agent), to tell the Dutch unofficially that Elizabeth was prepared to protect them if they handed over the towns of Flushing, Enkhuizen and Briel to England as financial security. A more dangerous assignment followed for Burnham: he was detailed to keep watch on the headquarters of Spanish forces in the run-up to the Armada invasion in 1588 and warn of the movement of troops towards embarkation in the Channel ports.

Estimates of exactly how much Walsingham's espionage operations cost Elizabeth's always hard-pressed exchequer vary wildly. The cash was paid out by warrants of the Privy Seal 'for such purposes as the queen shall appoint'. The earliest surviving record of payments is for July 1582, when he was paid £750 for secret services for the year (£120,000 in today's money), remitted in quarterly payments. More detailed records survive from 1585 onwards, citing £800 for that year and £1,100 for 1586.

Thereafter, with the Catholic sedition and the emerging threat of the Spanish Armada, payments increased to at least £2,000 per annum, although some calculations put the total received by Walsingham as high as £30,000 (or £4,800,000 at current prices) for 1588–9.[60] Perhaps a better indication of the steadily growing funds available for the queen's secret services are the estimates prepared in 1610 by one of Walsingham's successors, Sir Robert Cecil, another royal civil servant. In modern spending equivalents, these show payments of £946,502 for 1583–4; £1,646,171 for 1584–5; £1,357,883 for 1585–6 and £1,825,915 in 1586–7.[61] One thing is certain: the budget was never enough, as it had to cover the costs of both overseas and domestic intelligence-gathering. And Walsingham was never afraid to spend money if the necessity arose. In 1580, faced with a potential threat in Scotland, Walsingham instructed Sir Robert Bowes, the English agent in Scotland, and Sir Henry Cobham, then English envoy in Paris, to 'spare no cost' to gather information. Typically, after the threat from the Armada was lifted, Elizabeth quickly reduced the secret-service budget down to £1,200 in 1589. No wonder the spy master frequently had to dip into his own purse.

Indications of a new international plot against England emerged in May 1582 when retainers of Sir John Forster, Warden of the Middle Marches of the border with Scotland, stopped and detained a man disguised as a dentist, or less exaltedly, a tooth-puller. He carried all the gruesome instruments of his trade, including a small looking glass. The man was released, but in making a hasty departure he left his mirror behind. Concealed beneath its silvered glass was a batch of folded documents from Bernardino de Mendoza, the Spanish ambassador in London, to a Jesuit priest, Father William Creighton, based in Scotland. The tooth-puller was, in reality, using this cover to conceal his role as a secret messenger.

Walsingham received the documents in London the following month and, to his delight, they clearly indicated a conspiracy involving Mendoza, his master Philip II of Spain, Mary Queen of Scots and Esmé Stuart – Seigneur d'Aubigny, Earl of Lennox and a favourite of the young Scottish king, James VI. New intelligence from Scotland indicated that Castelnau, the French ambassador in London, was the clearing house for all communications with the Scottish queen.

Now everything that went on at the French ambassador's home in Salisbury Court, a few yards south of bustling Fleet Street on the western edge of the City of London, was of interest to Walsingham. In February 1583, there was a curious attack on Castelnau's reputation that smacks of an officially inspired whispering campaign against the envoy, perhaps instigated by the spy master himself.

Spluttering with indignation at being so assailed, Castelnau wrote to Walsingham angrily complaining that

> several in your court and throughout the kingdom who would like, in attacking my honour, to charge the French in general; [have] incited a good-for-nothing hussy of a woman to make wicked statements about me and of my actions, [which are] highly honourable and God-fearing.
>
> I have had her forbidden my house, not wishing to hear the thousand slanderous lies which she told [to] everyone and in recompense, they take pleasure at your court and elsewhere in using her as a trumpeter to accuse all France under my name . .
>
> It seems to me that the least that can be done is to put a stop to these rumours and give the hussy the whip and pierce her tongue with a hot iron; first making her declare who had incited her and taken pleasure in making her utter such slanders, as she would not otherwise have done for the sake of the alms she has received at my house.[62]

Black propaganda aside, the spy master searched around for an agent to insert into the French embassy. He found his man in the Scottish theologian William Fowler, who arrived in England after being expelled from his studies in France that autumn and was immediately imprisoned. In return for his freedom, Fowler agreed to spy for Walsingham. He persuaded the French envoy that he could supply intelligence on Scottish affairs and, in turn, told the English government about Castelnau's dealings with the Scots.

The French ambassador was having a torrid time. In March 1583, another Jesuit, Father William Holt, alias Brereton, was detained as he was boarding a ship for France at Edinburgh's port of Leith,[63] after being betrayed by another of Walsingham's agents, Roger Almond, alias William Vavasour, described as a 'renegade papist'.[64] A number of letters in cipher were found on the priest, which were speedily and covertly copied. When interrogated by the Scots, Holt acknowledged that there was 'a purpose in hand by the Pope and diverse Catholic Princes to make war on England in the cause of religion and for the benefit of the Queen of Scots'.[65] It was clear that he was an agent working for Mendoza. Walsingham chafed at the slowness of the Scottish investigation of the conspiracy and wrote to Bowes on 16 April that Elizabeth earnestly desired that Holt might be 'substantially examined and forced by torture to deliver what he knows'. But before any more information could be extracted, Holt had escaped and gone to ground.

Fowler had also reported that Castelnau was sending some letters via a 'gentlewoman' who was about to sail to Scotland. As soon as he received the report, Walsingham ordered the ship to be detained at Gravesend in the Thames Estuary and searched. Three letters from the French envoy to François de Roncherolles, Seigneur de Mainville, his opposite number in Scotland, were found and forwarded on to the spy master. No doubt the skills of Arthur Gregory were deployed to open them, record their contents and reseal the packages. Mainville received an apology for the delay in his mail and was earnestly assured that the letters had not been tampered with. Bowes, the English agent in Edinburgh, said the Frenchman was 'partly satisfied' with the apology, because 'he found the seals of the letters unbroken'.

The true extent of the plot and the means to prove Mary's involvement in it continued to elude Walsingham. A month later, in April, he managed to insert a second spy into the French embassy in London, known by the alias Henry Fagot. As recent research conclusively demonstrates, he was an Italian house guest there called Giordano Bruno.[66] The garrulous after-dinner conversation at the genial Castelnau's table was a rich source of intelligence, worthy of the risks. Bruno told of a letter from the Duke of Guise encouraging the ambassador to continue his clandestine activities on behalf of Mary Queen of Scots. On 28 April he even mentioned the arrival of the double agent William Fowler 'who haunts the ambassador's house practically every day . . . whence the ambassador knows everything that goes on in Scotland'.[67]

The following night, Bruno reported that a Monsieur Throgmorton had dined with Castlenau, who had 'recently sent the Queen of Scots 1,500 *écus sol* [golden crowns] which is on the ambassador's account'.[68] Walsingham's eyes must have gleamed when he read this. He immediately put twenty-nine-year-old Francis Throgmorton under close surveillance by his agents in London. His target was a known Catholic zealot and a nephew of the spy master's one-time friend Sir Nicholas Throgmorton, who had died in 1571.

Still the spy hidden within the embassy churned out his messages – all written in French and all carrying a sign, used as a symbol in astronomy or astrology to denote the planet Jupiter, to establish their authenticity. Fowler reappeared on 4 May and

> dined at the ambassador's house. He brought two gold rings, set [with jewels] but I do not know the stones. They went to the Queen of Scots by the Duke of Lennox and the ambassador has charge to convey them to her. This day the ambassador received letters from [his wife] in which she mentions that she hopes to return to this realm shortly and she strongly begs that [he] will be as secret as possible in these matters. Today I heard the ambassador say that he was almost afraid to be in this realm as he saw some things which are making ready in Scotland. Some marvellous things would be seen before very long . . . as there are several lords who are at great enmity and that the Duke of Guise and the Duke of Lennox have the password (*mot de guet*) of all this. This story passed between him and an English lord whose name I could not get.[69]

Walsingham's agent also suborned the ambassador's secretary Nicholas Leclerc, Seigneur de Courcelles, into becoming a mole for the English government. Probably sometime in early June 1583, Bruno told Walsingham:

> If your excellency wishes, I have made the ambassador's secretary
> so much my friend, that if he is given a certain amount of money,
> he will let me know everything he does – including everything to do
> with the Queen of Scots and the cipher which is used with her.[70]

Walsingham jumped at the opportunity and made the funds immediately available. Courcelles began passing copies of correspondence to Bruno the following month. The spy's message ends with another intelligence *coup de théâtre*:

> The chief agents for the Queen of Scots are Monsieur Throgmorton
> and Lord Henry Howard.[71] They never come to bring things from
> her except at night and the ambassador does the same (when he is
> sending to her).

His postscript must have made Walsingham smile: 'Keep a close eye, I beg you, on a Scot called Fowler: he is extremely treacherous. The ambassador's secretary told me to tell you this.'

The spy master diligently collected evidence against Throgmorton and pounced early on 4 November: two gentlemen of 'no mean credit and reputation' were sent to arrest him at his house near Paul's Wharf on the banks of the Thames, just east of Baynards Castle. As he was carried off to the Tower, his home was searched and papers discovered that named a number of Catholic noblemen, as well as plans of harbours ideal for use by invading foreign forces. There were also twelve copies of an illegal pedigree of the descent of the crown of England, demonstrating the justice of Mary's claim to the throne. Lord Henry Howard was arrested at the same time.

Throgmorton's second spell on the rack was enough to persuade him to talk, despite his earlier oath that he would 'endure a thousand deaths rather than accuse anyone'.[72] The Duke of Guise, he blurted out through the cold sweat of pain and fear, was to command the invasion, planned to come ashore at the port of Arundel in Sussex, which would liberate Mary Queen of Scots and reintroduce Catholicism to England. It had been held up by lack of finance, despite the promises of the Pope and Philip II of Spain to underwrite the costs of the expedition. His confession made it obvious that the real centre of the web of conspiracy was the cunning and devious Spanish ambassador in London, Bernardino de Mendoza.

On 19 January 1584, the Spanish envoy was summoned to meet a committee of Privy Councillors at the London home of the Lord Chancellor, Sir Thomas Bromley, amongst them Walsingham. After all had assembled, the dour Secretary of State stood up, his face grim and determined. He clutched a piece of paper in his hand containing six accusations against the ambassador, which he listed in turn in his fluent Italian whilst Mendoza, his face darkening with rage, was forced to listen:

1. That he had secret intelligence with the Scots Queen.
2. That he conspired with certain of her majesty's subjects for her delivery [rescue].
3. That he sought to [sound out] the Catholics in this realm whether they would join with foreign forces if the Catholic Princes should send any.
4. That he put them in comfort that the king [of Spain] would assist them and contribute half the charges.
5. That he was privy to the coming into this realm of Charles Paget,[73] a fugitive out of this realm and a servant to the Scots Queen who was sent hither, both to [sound out] the Catholics' minds and to view the ports and landing places.
6. That he received a [green velvet] casket containing the plans and papers of the conspiracies . . . sent to him by Francis Throgmorton.[74]

The queen, said Walsingham pointedly, preferred his room to his company and was graciously pleased to give him fifteen days to depart the realm.

Blustering under the accusations, Mendoza angrily challenged Walsingham to support his claims with some proof. He arrogantly thundered: 'Don Bernardino Mendoza was born not to disturb kingdoms but to conquer them.'[75] Nonetheless, he quietly departed England within a few days, closely shadowed by Walsingham's agents,[76] and became Spanish ambassador in Paris the following November.

In London, fears of conspiracies and assassination attempts upon Elizabeth's life were heightened by the murder of the Dutch Protestant leader William of Orange in Middleburg in early July 1584. Walsingham wrote to Stafford in Paris:

> The Prince of Orange was murdered by a Burgonian . . . [Balthazar Serack, who] pretending, as the Prince was going out of his dining room, that he had a letter and some further matter to deliver to him, shot him through with a pistol under the breast, whereof he presently fell down dead, without uttering any speech at all. How nearly this touches us, I leave you to judge.[77]

The murder reinforced the reality of the ever-present threat to the queen's person and stiffened the English government's resolve to stamp out subversion. Those associated with the Throgmorton plot suffered accordingly. Throgmorton was executed as a traitor at Tyburn on 10 July 1584. Lord Henry Howard found himself in prison again[78] and a further casualty was Henry Percy, Eighth Earl of Northumberland and brother of the leader of the 1569 Northern Rebellion, who committed suicide in the Tower on 20 June 1585 after being arrested for complicity in the plot. He shot himself in the chest with a pistol loaded with three lead bullets.[79]

Another of Walsingham's most effective agents was Nicholas Berden, alias Thomas Rogers. He was the servant of a prominent Catholic layman, George Gilbert, and travelled with him to Rome. His first contact as a spy was a note to Walsingham concerning 'the proceedings there, touching the Queen of Scotland' in 1583. But he was quickly suspected of treachery by the Catholic exiles and was imprisoned in the papal castle of St Angelo, high above the River Tiber, for a time. On swearing an oath of loyalty to Catholicism, Berden was freed and he returned to England. His oath and fidelity all swiftly forgotten, he was soon spying again for Walsingham. He wrote to Thomas Phelippes on 1 January 1584 in terms fully redolent of a patriotic Victorian high melodrama:

> I profess myself a spy, but I am not one for gain, but to serve my country . . . When any occasion shall be offered, wherein I may

adventure some rare and desperate exploit, such as may be for the honour of my country and my own credit. You shall always find me resolute and ready to perform the same.[80]

In March 1585 he was operating in London, tasked with watching the activities of Philip Howard, Earl of Arundel, who was coming under suspicion of conspiracy. With his knowledge of the recusants, Berden was quickly assimilated into the Catholic community and soon had a cosy dinner with a priest, William Weston, alias Edmonds. As far as the spy was concerned, it was a productive meal. Afterwards he supplied Walsingham with the addresses of four or five houses the Jesuit had hidden in and, in addition, the names of eleven Catholic gentlemen and the same number of priests they were harbouring. He added:

> Also, the Papists expect forty or fifty priests from Rome and Rheims to arrive here in London . . . Thus, according to my duty, I have advertised your honour of the premises and for my further service and duty to be done, I rest both night and day at your honourable commandment.[81]

Early in April, Berden investigated the secret communications between Catholic prisoners in the Tower of London. He informed Walsingham:

> I had conference with Gervais Pierrepoint[82] late prisoner in the Tower concerning [Father William] Creighton, the Scottish Jesuit there, [on] whether he had any means to confer with his friends. He answered me that when Creighton was first committed, he was lodged in the Martin Tower, right over the lodging [cell] of Nicholas Roscarrock,[83] [and] Nicholas did often times by some device, open two doors which were between their lodgings and so they conferred at pleasure . . . Also, such letters as Creighton did write were by Nicholas conveyed out of his chamber window, which was near the ground, to a little maiden, which was sent often to him by [Father Henry] Orton[84] and so by him further conveyed out of the Tower . . .[85]

A week later, Berden reported to Walsingham regarding supplies of

Catholic books smuggled into England and of his conversation with Richard, the servant to Dr (later Cardinal) William Allen. Allen was to leave London the following night for France

> with a pair of oars to Tilbury Fort[86] where . . . Nicholas de Hew, a Frenchman of Calais will attend him and . . . convey him to Dieppe or some such place near to it.

By way of a bonus, Berden tipped off Walsingham that two academics, Barker of Oxford and Moore of Cambridge (both Masters of Arts), would be on the same ship, intending to be ordained priests at the college in Rheims. The spy asked Allen's servant about how the missionary priests currently entered England.

> Dr Allen . . . deliver[s] to every priest for his journey . . . £6 or £8 in money and a new suit of apparel to wear . . . The priests most commonly do come over to England in French boats that come to Newcastle for coal . . . They make choice of that place [because] Robert Highcliffe, her majesty's officer at Newcastle, is a papist at heart and made acquainted with their coming and that his wife is and has been a papist these three or four years and that by her directions the priests with their books do pass in security . . .

Walsingham had clearly briefed Berden on the questions he should ask and the spy master was particularly interested in three seditious books then in circulation – Allen's *True, Sincere and Modest Defence of Catholics*, printed in 1585; *Leicester's Commonwealth*, which appeared anonymously in Paris or Rouen in September 1584 and contained a number of libels about the queen's favourite; and finally John Leslie, Bishop of Ross's *A Treatise touching the Right, Title and Interest of the most Excellent Princess Mary, Queen of Scotland*, published the same year. Berden discovered that William Bray and one Rogers, alias Bruerton, servants to his late master George Gilbert 'brought over the greatest part of them'. There remained at Rouen 'in the custody of one Flynton 1,000 of Allen's book; 1,000 of Leicester's book and 500 of the Bishop of Ross's book, which the same Richard should have brought over but he dared not'.

In the margin of his letter, Berden scribbled:

This Rogers was lately taken [arrested] by the Sheriff of Hampshire
at Winchester and sent up to Bishop Cooper and by him committed
to the Clink [jail] where he did break prison and remains at a
widow's house, a farm between Portsmouth and Petersfield
[Hampshire], where he [awaits] William Bray coming to him for . . .
they are to pass in one ship from some creek near to Arundel.[87]

In a postscript, Berden describes a chance meeting with Bray at the Bell
public house in London's Aldersgate Street. Bray was 'ready to ride
onward of his voyage to Rouen . . . for he referred me to Tremayne, his
brother for [Catholic] *New Testaments* if I need, in whose custody there
remains ninety unsold'.

Later Berden went to France to spy on the English Catholic community
there. In March 1586 he wrote to Walsingham offering his services to
spy on the exiles in France and Italy. He was, in effect, a double agent,
as he was being used to receive and deliver letters for them and also to
circulate intelligence gathered in England amongst them. He proposed
'to keep an entire correspondence with all the parties for the avowed
purpose of communicating it to Walsingham'. Thomas Phelippes
endorsed the letter: 'From Berden to Mr Secretary Walsingham, the
account of his employment put upon him by them beyond the sea.'
Berden repeats his unctuous, self-deprecating views about his profession in a letter to Phelippes, probably written in July 1586:

Though I am a spy (which is a profession odious though necessary)
I prosecute the same not for gain but for the safety of my native
country . . .
    It grieves me much to have to draw on his honour's treasure,
and if he would yield to some suits now and then at my request, I
might be served out of the store of those traitors . . .[88]

His first request was not long in coming. On 11 June, now back in
London, he asked Phelippes to

procure me the liberty of Ralph Bickley, seminary priest in the Gatehouse [Prison, Westminster] at his honour's hands, it will be worth £20 to me; and the liberty also of Richard Sherwood, alias Carleton, prisoner in the Counter in Wood Street [City of London] will be worth £30. The money will do me great pleasure being now in extreme need thereof, neither do I know how to shift [manage] any longer without it.[89]

Eventually, in 1588, Berden decided to quit the exciting world of spying and adopt a 'more public course of life'. He wrote to Walsingham seeking the post of Royal Purveyor of Poultry that he had performed for three years in 'my father's lifetime'. It was granted to him within a month, upon the Secretary's recommendation. It was a remarkable metamorphosis: one moment he was a spy, the next he was respectably selling dead chickens.

Walsingham employed double agents and knew that some of his own spies would be easily diverted by offers of money from the Spanish. One such was Antony Poyntz, the brother-in-law of Sir Thomas Heneage, Treasurer of the Privy Chamber and an old friend. Poyntz was a law student at the Inner Temple but had been in and out of trouble for some years. He was sent to Paris in December 1586 to spy on Mendoza, but he immediately revealed his true role to the ambassador, apparently flourishing a royal letter of credit as proof of his story.[90] Later he was sent by Walsingham to Spain to gather information about the threat posed by the Spanish Armada, but how effective he was there remains unknown.

Amongst this crew of grubby, venal and dissolute agents, one name stands out today. The most famous spy in Walsingham's network was the dramatist Christopher Marlowe, who worked for him as a student in Paris and Rheims in 1586. As a result of this activity, the award of his Master of Arts degree was placed in jeopardy, but the Privy Council came swiftly to his aid with the Cambridge authorities, stating in June 1587 that 'he had done her majesty good service and deserved to be rewarded for his faithful dealing'. He almost certainly continued as an agent working against Catholic intrigues in London in return for escaping state prosecution for the blasphemy contained in his drama *Tamburlaine*, first produced in 1587.[91]

A vivid picture of the instructions provided to one of Walsingham's spies before his mission is portrayed in a letter signed by Phelippes, addressed to 'a person going to Scotland' in February 1587, immediately after the death of Mary Queen of Scots. The unknown spy is told

That he shall presently repair to Scotland, addressing himself to such persons as are known or suspected to be enemies to this state.

That he shall principally observe what alteration the death of the king's mother works either in the said king or in any person of quality in that realm.

To learn how the boroughs stand affected which heretofore have been noted to be enemies to the said queen [Mary].

To seek very carefully what English Catholics resort into that realm, by whom and for whom they are sent and to whom they repair and what is the end of their employment

To learn how the king stands affected to the [Protestant] religion and whether he be disposed to [listen] either to Spain or to France.

To seek out who be the harbourers of such instruments [agents] as are employed by the Catholics between the two realms of Scotland and England.

To advertise [report] weekly what he can learn.

That he address [send] his servant to Mr Anderson, [the] sheriff of Northumberland, to whom he shall have letters of credit, with order to send up his letters hither in post.

That he shall in no sort discover [reveal] himself to Mr Anderson.

To procure letters of credit from the Catholics here.

Beware of David Inglebye.[92]

In the fevered atmosphere of distrust and suspicion in London in 1584–5, the slightly insane figure of Dr William Parry emerges to become another central, if not bizarre, character in this continuing drama of intrigue and conspiracy. Parry, described by the chronicler Camden as 'passing proud, neat and spruce', came from a Northrop, Flintshire, family[93] and had managed to spend his way through the fortunes of the two rich widows[94] he had married, one after the other.

During the 1570s, Parry spied on the English Catholics resident in Rome, Paris and Siena for Burghley. In 1580, he escaped the death sentence for assaulting and badly wounding one of his creditors, Hugh Hare (whom he owed £600), after breaking into his room in the Temple in London. Parry spent more than a year inside the Poultry Prison before being bound over to keep the peace on a surety of £1,000.[95] In return for his freedom, he was instructed to spy on English Catholics abroad once again for Burghley and Walsingham, firstly in Paris, then in Venice and finally in Milan and Lyons. He boastfully told Burghley on 10 May 1583: 'If I am not deceived, I have shaken the foundation of the English seminary at Rheims and utterly overthrown the credit of the English pensioners at Rome.'

The following January, Parry returned to London and told the queen frankly that he had been involved in dealings with Pope Gregory XIII and Thomas Morgan, Mary Queen of Scots' agent in Paris, in planning an attempt on her life. His involvement, he maintained, was merely to unmask the plans of 'malicious persons' at home and overseas, and to prove his story's veracity he produced a letter written to him by Ptolomy Galli, Cardinal of Como, which contained a papal blessing upon him and absolution for his sins. Elizabeth was initially unimpressed by his tale: 'She took it doubtfully [and] I departed with fear,' Parry commented. She later changed her mind about his loyalty and in May 1584 he wrote to Burghley seeking the Mastership of St Katherine's Hospital in London;[96] thwarted in this, in September he sought a 'deanery, provostship or mastership of requests' which 'is all I crave'. He ended up with the Queenborough Seat in the Commons in the Parliament of 1584.

In mid-December of that year, new legislation against Jesuits and seminary priests was debated in the House of Commons. Parry was the only member to speak against it, saying it was 'cruel and bloody, full of desperation and hurtful to the English nation'. These were rash, imprudent words at such a tense time, and it was no surprise that Parry quickly found himself in the custody of the serjeant of arms, before being freed by Sir Christopher Hatton, on Elizabeth's orders, the following day. Still short of funds, Parry returned to spying to augment his income, and sought the role of freelance agent provocateur in concocting a new plot against the queen. He suggested to Edmund Neville, cousin of the exiled rebel Westmorland, during a meeting at St Giles in the Fields that Elizabeth should be murdered. The assassination would be attempted on horseback

> with eight or ten horsemen, when she should ride abroad at St James. It was once thought fit [to be attempted] in a garden and the escape would be easiest by water to [the Isle of] Sheppey [in Kent] but we resolved upon the first [plan].[97]

Neville promptly betrayed Parry and he was arrested and taken to Walsingham's home in Seething Lane for interrogation, sleeping there that night but later taken to the Tower. Neville was also imprisoned (and released a decade later), but for the unpredictable and mercurial Parry there was only the march to the scaffold, in Great Palace Yard, Westminster, on 2 March 1585.

A special prayer of thanksgiving for the deliverance of Elizabeth was promulgated which castigated Parry as a

> miserable, wretched, natural-born subject, a man of no religion, [who] under colour seeking to be a diligent and most careful servant to our gracious queen and pretending to discover . . . how her own person was in danger . . . determined very often most desperately to have with his own cursed hand destroyed her majesty's sacred person . . .

Fortunately, God was on her side, and had 'diverted [Parry's] desperate heart and bloody hand'.[98] Propaganda and religion sometimes cannot be separated.

No one within the London-based nobility with the merest hint of Catholic sympathies was now immune from suspicion. Philip, Earl of Arundel, was detained off the coast of Hampshire after sailing out of the small port of Lymington in April 1585 and taken to the Tower. During interrogation the following month, he was taxed about a three-page letter allegedly written by him that was said to hold 'great danger to the queen and state'. Addressed to William Dix, one of his estate officials in Norfolk, it began: 'Sir – This letter contains such matter as is fitter for the fire to consume, than to be laid up in your study.' The contents included specific issues relating to his Norfolk lands – such as recent sales of timber – and appeared to be in handwriting 'very much resembling his'. Howard denied all knowledge of it, and Catholic sources at the time maintained it was a complete forgery. The letter was first brought to light by Walsingham's agents and 'was pretended to have been intercepted at the very time of his going to sea'. It was claimed to have been 'forged by some who had notice beforehand of his going, as the secretary and some of his greatest enemies had . . .'[99]

Can one detect here the clever hand of Thomas Phelippes, that shortsighted wizard of forgery? His skills were to become crucial in removing the greatest threat to the Protestant throne and state – Mary Queen of Scots.

CHAPTER FOUR

The Babington Plot

'Is it like our Sovereign's safety should be grounded and depend upon her who has deciphered herself to be a competitor of this crown? I speak of things publicly known. I leave other secret practices tending to the same end . . . If she falsify her faith, no pleading will serve – the sword must be the remedy.'

SIR FRANCIS WALSINGHAM, *A DISCOURSE TOUCHING THE PRETENDED MATCH BETWEEN THE DUKE OF NORFOLK AND THE QUEEN OF SCOTS*, 1569.[1]

After the thwarted Throgmorton Plot, there were very real fears that an assassin would succeed in his attempts to kill Elizabeth. The murder of the Prince of Orange in the Netherlands was on everyone's lips. Burghley and Walsingham needed once and for all to neutralise the threat of Mary Queen of Scots as a successor to the throne in order to defuse the powder keg of conspiracy they believed was threatening the survival of the Protestant realm of England.

The so-called 'Bond of Association' was their adroit solution.

In anyone's language, it was little more than lynch law.

The idea, probably the product of Burghley's devious ingenuity, had initially been very simple. It proclaimed that any wicked person who caused the death of Elizabeth would be ineligible to succeed her as ruler of England. Its objective was thus very clear: at a stroke, it removed Mary as the focal point of any Catholic conspiracy. Then came a series of more hard-line revisions, probably drawn up by Walsingham, and the final version, tabled at a Privy Council meeting at Hampton Court on 19 October 1584, went much further than the original concept.[2] This decreed that the procurer of the assassination of Elizabeth would be put to death *whether or not they were aware of the conspiracy* to take the queen's life. Moreover, the Bond was also to be signed by loyal subjects who pledged themselves to 'act [with] the utmost revenge' on any heirs to the pretender to the throne for 'their utter overthrow and extirpation'.[3] Its propaganda value was incalculable amongst Elizabeth's loyal Protestant subjects, as it reinforced their belief that their religious creed and way of life were grievously threatened.

The Privy Councillors signed it 'voluntarily and most willingly', thereby solemnly binding themselves to

> withstand, pursue and offend . . . by force of arms, as by all other means of revenge, all manner of persons . . . and their abettors that shall attempt any act, or counsel or consent to any thing that shall tend to the harm of her majesty's royal person and will never desist from all manner of forcible pursuit against such persons, to the utter extermination of them, their counsellors, aiders and abettors.[4]

These were harsh, unambiguous words, a manifest symptom of just how endangered the state felt itself to be. Walsingham later circulated copies of the document to the nobility and leading gentry, pointedly suggesting that true patriots would feel impelled to sign such a 'necessary and dutiful' instrument for the protection of the queen.[5] Despite some strong misgivings within the legal classes – lawyers and magistrates – men and women in their thousands did sign copies of the Bond, the illiterate simply with a cross as their personal mark. They pledged themselves before God to take the law into their own hands and to ruthlessly hunt down and destroy anyone associated with a plot to kill Elizabeth. There were even special church services to further sanctify the process of oath-taking. As the signatures were being collected in Flintshire, a Catholic

Welsh schoolmaster called Richard White was quartered alive in Wrexham for composing a song in praise of the death of William of Orange.[6]

Walsingham ordered that Mary Queen of Scots should be shown the document and careful note taken 'of her countenance and speech' after she had read it.[7] If he hoped she would be disconcerted by this very public vow of vengeance, Mary did not display it. Indeed, she happily signed the paper herself on 5 January 1585.[8]

The Bond was enshrined in law in an 'Act for the Surety of the Queen's Person'[9] passed by Parliament in March 1585, which introduced a new legal dimension to any popular movement for revenge. Now a commission of Privy Councillors and judges would sit to hear evidence of the guilt of a claimant to the throne alleged to be involved in a conspiracy or plans for a rebellion or foreign invasion of England.

If found guilty, they would still die.

In the event of Elizabeth's assassination, if the commissioners again came up with a guilty verdict, those involved could be 'by all forcible and possible means prosecuted to death' by loyal subjects.[10]

Burghley also sought to introduce a Parliamentary Bill to authorise the creation of an interregnum government led by a 'Great Council' in the event of Elizabeth's murder. However, this impinged too closely on the queen's private definition, indeed, ownership of the divine right of princes and she firmly vetoed her Chief Minister's prudent proposals, much to his chagrin.[11]

Mary Queen of Scots was meanwhile placed into the strict custody of the dour Puritan Sir Amyas Paulet, a close friend of Walsingham's, in April that year at Tutbury Castle, Staffordshire, where she had been transferred for greater security.[12] It was a dark, unhealthy, dank-moated building, permeated with the stench from its crude latrines.

Paulet was a very different jailer from her former easy-going custodians, the Earl of Shrewsbury and the veteran Sir Ralph Sadler. Paulet was under strict instructions from Walsingham to halt Mary's unauthorised communications with the outside world.[13] The Secretary told Paulet to ban all contact between his servants and those of the Scottish queen; to forbid Mary's servants from leaving the castle; to admit no stranger to its precincts; and especially to watch Mary's 'laundresses and coachmen' as they were suspected of carrying her clandestine letters in the past.[14] The strait-laced custodian had doubts on whether he could, with decency, institute all the strict security measures. He fretted about searching the laundresses by 'stripping them down to their smocks [underclothes]' as, with so many uncouth soldiers about, this 'cannot be comely'.[15]

Across the English Channel, Thomas Morgan, Mary's agent in France, had been imprisoned in the Bastille in Paris on 1 March 1585,[16] but was still able to write letters to his mistress at Tutbury. This Welsh former servant to the Earl of Shrewsbury had fled England a decade earlier in the wake of Walsingham's investigations into Henry Cockyn's letter-carrying for Mary and had remained close to the vortex of Catholic conspiracy in France, being involved in both the Throgmorton and Parry plots. After Walsingham instructed Stafford, the English envoy in Paris, to protest about his activities, Morgan was jailed, but the French steadfastly refused to extradite him to England and delivered up his papers only after the compromising or incriminating material had been carefully weeded out.[17] Perfidious Gaul! A furious Elizabeth wrote to the French king:

> I swear to you that if he is denied me, I shall conclude that I have
> joined a league not with a king, but with a Papal legate or the
> president of a seminary. I shall be as much ashamed at yours as I
> should be at their bad company.[18]

However, her protests came to nought and Morgan remained in comfortable quarters in the Bastille, his incarceration merely token.

Back in England, in May Walsingham ordered Paulet to open the letters sent to Mary by Castelnau, the French ambassador in London, to read them and deliver them opened to his prisoner. There was now no need for secrecy, as those involved knew full well that their correspondence was being intercepted. Moreover, he had heard from his spy Nicholas Berden that the Scottish queen was receiving secret correspondence via Ralph Elwes, a servant to 'Mr Fenton of Derbyshire'. But Walsingham's efforts to track down this messenger failed totally. By now he was less concerned with detecting her methods of communication and much more anxious to establish hard evidence of her treachery and treason.

Mary had been complaining about the living conditions at Tutbury and on 13 September, the Secretary told Paulet to examine Chartley, a manor house in the same county, as a possible new place of confinement for her. Elizabeth, he said

> doubting [not] that the coldness of Tutbury Castle may increase [Mary's] sickness, thinks it right she should be removed to some other place, and hearing that Chartley, the Earl of Essex's house, is both large and strong, in respect that it is environed with water, she would have you to see it and certify how you like it.[19]

Mary and her household were duly moved there on Christmas Eve, 1585.

Castelnau had been replaced as French ambassador in London in September by Claude de l'Aubespine de Châteauneuf, a well-known fervent sympathiser of the Scottish queen. Mary urged him to be cautious about his secretaries' loyalties, instinctively fearing that Walsingham had subverted them, and she asked the envoy to avoid using an alum solution as a secret ink as this was too easily detected. Secret messages, she said, could be hidden in new books, 'writing always on the fourth, eight, twelfth and sixteenth leaf and so continuing from four to four [pages] . . . and [to] cause green ribbons to be attached to all the books that you have written [in] in this way'.[20]

Thomas Morgan also cast around for more secure methods of secretly communicating with Mary. He could send packets to the French embassy in London through normal diplomatic channels, but getting them to Chartley without them being intercepted was a more intractable problem. Fatefully, he decided to employ Gilbert Gifford, a member of a Catholic family with a somewhat chequered career as a trainee priest. He had been expelled from the English College in Rome but had been allowed to join the Rheims establishment in 1582. After three years there, he became a deacon and a reader in philosophy. He left France for England in early December 1585 with letters for Mary from the

Archbishop of Glasgow, Morgan and the fugitive Catholic Charles Paget.

Gifford, described as 'young and without any beard', was immediately stopped at Rye, arrested and sent to London, escorted by Richard Daniel, one of the port searchers. He met Walsingham at Greenwich Palace and lodged for a time with Thomas Phelippes so that he could be kept under close surveillance. After a number of interviews with the grim-faced Minister, it did not take much to subvert him. Gifford agreed that in return for suitable remuneration, all Mary's secret letters and those she received would pass through the spy master's hands. With £20 of Walsingham's secret service funds in his purse, he was sent to see Châteauneuf, who appointed one of his secretaries, Cordaillot, to handle the Scottish queen's correspondence.

All that now remained was to arrange for a method of getting the correspondence in and out of Chartley that would not arouse the suspicions of Mary or her household there. Walsingham dispatched Phelippes to Staffordshire to find a suitable covert means.

Phelippes spent four or five days at the manor house and met Mary there. She apparently sounded him out on his susceptibility to bribery, which must have caused him some amusement but at least indicated that she did not harbour any suspicions about his presence. After some investigation, the method of communication was fixed. The household received their supplies of beer from a brewer in the nearby town of Burton, delivered once a week to Chartley in small wooden casks or kegs. It was decided that the secret letters would be held in a waterproof wooden canister small enough to slip into the keg via the hole used for its bung. The brewer – referred to as 'the honest man' by Paulet – was told to transport the letters by this method and when the process was reversed, to hand over Mary's letters to Gifford.

The plan was swiftly put into operation and on the evening of 16 January 1586, the Scottish queen was delighted to receive her first secret message for almost a year. Ironically, it was a letter from Morgan in Paris, recommending the services of Gilbert Gifford. She immediately dashed off a reply, which spoke of her concern for her new messenger's safety: 'I fear his danger of sudden discovery, my keeper [Paulet] having settled such an exact and rigorous order in all places.'[21] This letter quickly found its way to Walsingham, who handed it over to Phelippes for deciphering and copying and then to Arthur Gregory for resealing. It was conveyed to the French ambassador and eventually reached Morgan on 15 March. The system had worked and both sides were delighted by its success – but for very different reasons.

The next few weeks were occupied with Mary dictating letters to catch up on the long gap in her correspondence. They were duly inserted into the empty beer keg and Gifford handed them over to Paulet late on 5 February. Mary's custodian wrote to Walsingham:

> [Gifford] desired that these packets might be sent to you with speed and that his father might be advised by Mr Phelippes to call him to London as soon as . . . possible, to the end that he might deliver these letters to the French ambassador in convenient time for the better conservation of his credit that way.

The suspicious Paulet retained doubts about the honesty and loyalty of Gifford: 'I will hope the best of your friend but I may not hide from you that he doubled in his speech [contradicted himself] once or twice . . .'[22] He also had fears about the Burton brewer: 'God knows if under the cloak of this trifle, greater treacheries may be contrived.'

Mary's correspondence included letters to the Duke of Guise, the Archbishop of Glasgow and another to Morgan. Again they were intercepted, decoded, resealed and delivered to Châteauneuf on 19 February. The French envoy then handed over all the secret letters that had been held for her for so long in the embassy. Gifford immediately delivered them to Phelippes, who reported to Walsingham:

> The party [Gifford] has brought one and twenty packets great and small but not so soon as I looked for and himself thought. I find them of very old dates, which I impute, considering the number also, to the stay of intelligence . . .[23]

Phelippes also returned one 'alphabet' – the key to a cipher – that he had taken away by mistake. Although now very dated, the letters – from

Morgan, the Catholic fugitive Charles Paget, Father Persons, Sir Francis Englefield in Spain, Mendoza in Paris and from the Duke of Guise and the Prince of Parma – must have been an intelligence treasure trove to Walsingham and read eagerly by him. Gifford departed for France in April and a substitute messenger was found, one Thomas Barnes. The packets from the embassy were too bulky to squeeze through the bung hole of the beer cask, so the pages were divided up into smaller rolls, which at least removed the need for Gregory to reseal them. Such a huge volume of correspondence must have taken both Phelippes and Gilbert Curle, one of Mary's confidential secretaries, much time to decode and transcribe.

A number of types of cryptography were used by both Mary and Walsingham in their letters. In the National Archives at the Public Record Office at Kew in Surrey are preserved two small blue leather folio volumes of ciphers and decodes used by Walsingham in the final entrapment of Mary Queen of Scots.[24] The first volume alone contains fifty-five separate codes, or alphabets, some later seized by Paulet in his search of her rooms at Chartley. All are simple substitution ciphers: using a mix of numbers, letters and symbols as substitutes for names, places and words in English or in French.

In its least sophisticated form, both receiver and sender would have a copy of the cipher to decode messages. The more frequently such codes are changed, the greater the security of the messages. Hence, today, 'one-time-only' ciphers pose real problems for those attempting to crack them. Here is an example of a simple substitution cipher of the type used in the late sixteenth century:

a	b	c	d	e	f	g	h	i	j	k	l	m
P	K	G	B	C	I	A	R	Q	Z	D	N	T

n	o	p	q	r	s	t	u	v	w	x	y	z
E	Y	X	M	F	W	O	J	H	L	U	S	V

Thus, the coded message T P F S F C W G J C B Y E T Y E B P S could be read off the cipher as 'Mary rescued on Monday'. To disguise the message further, the words would be run together with the breaks between them removed to avoid offering up clues from the use of short words containing vowels.

In the code used by Gilbert Gifford and Mary at Chartley, the symbols '#', 'X/', 'V' and 'Z' represent the king of France, the king of Spain, Elizabeth and Mary herself, respectively.[25] In another code, 'X.' represents the Pope; 'Ø' the word 'intelligence'; '8', packet; 'y', letter; 'e', secret; and '_', Francis Walsingham.[26] Interestingly, a very similar cipher system was used in mobile telephone text messages by al Qaeda agents in Pakistan in 2005 to disguise rendezvous locations and individuals' identities.

The use of ciphers and the methods employed to decode them had come to the attention of Burghley in the 1560s when the mathematician, astrologer and magician John Dee returned to England with a copy of a book entitled *Stenographia*, written by Trithemius, Abbot of Spandheim, in the late fifteenth century. Dee adapted the ideas in the book and made them available to Walsingham, who visited him several times from January 1583 and with whom he was an irregular correspondent.[27]

Deciphering substitution codes is based on the frequency of use of letters of the alphabet. This method had been known for a long time, using techniques evolved by the ninth-century Arab codebreaker al-Kindi. In English, the letter 'e' accounts for thirteen per cent of all letters used in any kind of prose – whereas 'z' is used less than one per cent of the time. Whatever letter, number or symbol is substituted, it retains its original frequency of use. Thus by analysing the frequency of the different letters used in a code, it is possible to work out which consonant or vowel each substituted letter represents. However, in the sixteenth century, to confuse and complicate the work of the decipherer, some codes included 'nulls' – letters that were fakes and represented nothing, or, as Thomas Phelippes sometimes noted, 'doubles the precedent' – thereby changing the rules of the code. Naturally, the work is made immeasurably easier if a copy of the cipher falls into the decipherer's hands – which Mary fatally facilitated in March 1586 when she sent a new code to Châteauneuf, which was intercepted and copied by Walsingham.

The key figure in all this movement of secret correspondence to and from Chartley was, of course, the brewer in Burton. Without his co-

operation, the whole elaborate scheme would have collapsed. Although
he was reputedly a good Catholic, he was not ashamed to receive bountiful
bribes from both Walsingham and Mary Queen of Scots. With an eye
on market forces, he also put up the price of his beer, comfortable in the
knowledge that Paulet could not now go elsewhere for his supplies of
ale. Gifford in turn extorted money from Morgan by pretending that he
was paying the brewer.[28] Paulet was disgusted.

> The 'honest man' plays the harlot with this people egregiously,
> preferring his particular profit and commodity before their service .
> . . The house where he dwells is distant from here only ten miles
> and yet, I do not remember that he has delivered at any time any
> packet to this queen until six or seven days after the receipt . . .
>
> He appoints all places of meeting at his pleasure, wherein he
> must be obeyed, and has no other respect that he may not ride out
> of his way, or at the least, that his travel for his cause may not hinder
> his own particular business.[29]

Regardless of these various machinations, Walsingham's trap had
been baited: he only needed to wait for the jaws to snap shut upon Mary.

The genesis of that much-sought evidence lay in the person of John
Ballard, who had been ordained priest at Châlons in France on 4 March
1581 and secretly entered England later that month. He was quickly
arrested and imprisoned in the Gatehouse Jail at Westminster, where
he met another priest called Anthony Tyrrell. They both escaped and left
the country, returning on Boxing Day 1584 at Southampton. Sometime
during Lent in 1586, Ballard had supper at the Plough Inn, just outside
Temple Bar on the western fringe of the City of London. Present were a
number of young Catholic gentlemen, including one Anthony Babington
and Bernard Maude.

Babington, twenty-five years old and married with a young daughter,[30]
had been a page to the Earl of Shrewsbury when he was Mary's keeper in
1579. He had delivered five packets of letters to the Scottish queen during
1583–4 and had then ducked out of this dangerous duty. The Jesuit Father
William Weston described him as 'attractive in face and form, quick of

intelligence, agreeable and facetious'.[31] But he was inexperienced in the ways of the world and an unlikely man of action.

Maude was formerly a member of the household of Edwin Sandys, the Archbishop of York, and had falsely accused the prelate of religious unorthodoxy. Sandys had handed over cash to Maude and his friends in an optimistic attempt to keep them quiet. But Maude's sins had found him out and he was forced to repay the archbishop the money, as well as a £300 'fine' to the queen, and served three years in the Fleet Prison in London for his blackmail. If he had not confessed, 'his ears would have been slit' as a common offender.[32] He was another miscreant who had been freed early in return for agreeing to undertake clandestine work for Elizabeth's government. As Maude sat, laughing and joking with his Catholic colleagues over their wine and ale in the Plough, they did not guess that he was another of Walsingham's spies.

Ballard was completely taken in. He travelled to Rouen with Maude in May and on to Paris where he met Charles Paget, leader of the English Catholic laity in the French capital. There, Ballard told his receptive audience that the Catholic population of England were willing to take up arms against Elizabeth and that this was an opportune time, as most of the best Protestant military leaders and soldiers were away fighting in the Low Countries with Leicester's expeditionary force. An excited Paget took Ballard to Mendoza, the Spanish ambassador in Paris, and he repeated his views. Paget told Mary in a letter dated 19 May 1586 (and later read by Walsingham):

> [Mendoza] heard him very well and made him set down in number how many in every shire would be contented to take arms and what number of men armed and unarmed they could provide . . . He likewise gave him information of the ports with many other things fit to be known.[33]

All this must have been drearily familiar to the canny Mendoza: the eternal mirage of an English Catholic uprising, merely requiring a foreign invasion to ensure a total victory over the heretic forces of Protestantism. He and the Spanish government had heard it all before: more wishful thinking than the hard reality of military capability. But this time there was more, which must have made the Spanish envoy prick up his ears. Afterwards, he carefully wrote out an account for King Philip II in Madrid and encoded the dispatch himself:

> I am advised from England by four men of position who have the entry into the queen's house, that they have discussed for at least three months the intention of killing her. They have at last agreed and the four have mutually sworn to do it.
>
> They will, on the first opportunity, advise me when it is to be done and whether by poison or steel, in order that I may send the intelligence to your majesty, supplicating you to be pleased to help them after the business is effected.[34]

Maude and Ballard returned to England on 22 May. The priest immediately looked up Babington in his lodgings in London at Herne's Rents in Holborn. He told him that a grand conspiracy against Elizabeth was now in play, supported by Pope Sixtus V, and that the king of Spain and an army of 60,000 foreign troops, possibly led by the Duke of Guise, would be invading England. Mendoza had sworn, said Ballard, that September would not pass without a powerful landing on the English coast.

Unbeknown to Babington, this stunning news bore no resemblance whatsoever to the priest's conversations in Paris, but had been fermented in Ballard's fevered fanatic's mind. Babington promised to discuss the plan with his immediate friends – Thomas Salisbury of Denbighshire, Chidiock Tichbourne of Portchester, Hampshire, and Robert Barnwell of London, thus sucking them into the spiral of conspiracy. They too were seduced by the excitement and religious righteousness of the cause, and by early June, after a number of meetings in Babington's rooms, the number of conspirators had increased to thirteen. Ballard meanwhile had travelled north to gauge the level of support amongst the Catholic gentry for an uprising. The spy Bernard Maude rode with him, thereby enabling Walsingham to monitor his movements and receive intelligence on how rampant the disease of sedition had become in England's body politic.

On 6 July 1586, Babington wrote to Mary Queen of Scots, talking of this great and honourable action, upon the issue of which depend not only the life of your most excellent majesty . . . and the lives of all us actors herein, but also the honour and wealth of our country . . . and the last hope ever to recover the faith of our forefathers and to redeem ourselves from the servitude and bondage which has [been] imposed upon us with the loss of thousands of souls.

Six separate actions or factors needed to be implemented or assured, he told her. First, an invasion of England was necessary, and second, this had to be in sufficient strength to guarantee a military victory. Third, the ports where the invading forces would come ashore or be resupplied should be chosen. Fourth, there must be 'a strong party at every place to join with them and warrant [guarantee] their [successful] landing'. Fifth, Mary herself had to be freed from her imprisonment. And last, Elizabeth had to be finally dispatched into oblivion and eternal damnation.

Babington would recommend those 'fittest in my knowledge to be your lieutenants in the West, in the north, South Wales, North Wales and the counties of Lancaster, Derby and Stafford'. He would lead Mary's rescue party himself: 'Myself, with ten gentlemen and a hundred of our followers, will undertake the delivery of your royal person from the hands of your enemies.'

And what of Elizabeth?

For the dispatch of the usurper, from the obedience of whom we are by excommunication made free,[35] there be six gentlemen, all my private friends, who for the zeal they bear to the Catholic cause and your majesty's service, will undertake that tragic execution [sic].

He was also seeking ample reward for the assassins:

It rests that according to their infinite good deserts and your majesty's bounty, their heroic attempt may be honourably rewarded . . . if they escape with [their lives] or in their posterity and so much I may be able by your majesty's authority to assure them.

In a postscript addressed to Claude Nau, one of Mary's private secretaries, Babington made enquiries about a Robert Pooley 'whom I find to have intelligence with her majesty [on] occasions. I am private with the man and by means thereof know somewhat but suspect more. I pray you deliver your opinion of him'.[36] Poor gullible, innocent Babington! Pooley was another of Walsingham's double agents – indeed, he was a member of the household of his daughter Frances, who had married the soldier-poet Sir Philip Sidney in September 1583. Morgan had earlier told the Scottish queen on 11 March that on his advice, Pooley was 'placed with the Lady Sidney, the daughter of Secretary Walsingham, and by that means ordinarily in his house and thereby able to pick out many things to the information of your majesty'. His words have a triumphant tone, as he clearly believed he had scored a victory over the spy master.[37]

Babington's damning letter was handed over to an 'unknown boy' who delivered it to Phelippes at his home in Leadenhall Market. It was quickly decoded and given to Walsingham, who, sensing that the defining moment was imminent, ordered Phelippes to take it himself to Chartley, where he was to watch for Mary's reply. Phelippes left London at nine o' clock on the evening of 7 July and would have arrived at his destination sooner 'but for the extreme carelessness of constables and contempt of some of them, wherein,' Phelippes crossly told Walsingham, 'your honour needs [to] take order upon special services [such] as this.'[38]

The decipherer eventually arrived at Chartley on 9 July, the day before the Burton brewer was due to make his weekly beer delivery to the household. Babington's letter was secreted and duly retrieved.

Mary's secretaries Gilbert Curle and Claude Nau deciphered Babington's letter and handed it to the Scottish queen. Nau, apprehensive and suspicious, strongly advised her to leave the missive unanswered.[39] Mary, the chance of freedom and accession to the English throne tantalisingly held up before her, was less wary. Her immediate concern was where to hide the letter in a household so closely monitored by her enemies; perhaps she hid it about her person. The next day, 11 July, she decided to accept the situation and talked further with her secretaries. After several drafts, a letter was eventually written in French and translated into English by Curle before being enciphered and sent off on 18 July.

Phelippes wrote to his master in London on 14 July, reporting that he and Paulet attended Mary's 'very heart. She begins to recover health and strength and did ride abroad in her coach yesterday.' In a chillingly sinister aside, he described how he had seen her as she left the manor house and 'had a smiling countenance. But I thought of the verse: *Cum tibi dicit Ave, sicut ab hoste cave*'[40] – 'when he greets you, beware him as if he were an enemy'.

Her reply to Babington was dated 17 July and takes up six and half pages.[41] Its dramatic contents were finally to seal her fate and as such became a matter of controversy then and for historians in the centuries to follow. Mary certainly encouraged the conspirators:

> I cannot but greatly praise and commend your desire to prevent in time the designs of our enemies for the extirpation of our religion from this realm, with the ruin of us all.
>
> I have long ago shown to the foreign Catholic princes, and experience proves it, that the longer we delay to put in hand the matter on this side, the greater leisure have our enemies to prevail over the said princes . . . In the meantime, the Catholics here, exposed to all sorts of persecution and cruelty, daily diminish in number, force, means and power, so if remedy is not hastily provided, I fear they will become altogether unable to rise again and to receive any aid at all, whenever it were offered . . .

Mary astonishingly then goes on to deny that she had 'any particular interest in this cause' – other than for 'the public good of this state'. Swiftly laying aside such diffidence, she then moves on to the mechanics of the plot to overthrow Elizabeth. The words demonstrate just what a seasoned campaigner she had become in the ways of intrigue and conspiracy:

> Now to ground the enterprise substantially and to bring it to good success, you must examine deeply:
>
> 1. What forces on foot and horse may be raised amongst you all and what captains you will appoint for them in every shire in case a general in chief cannot be had.
> 2. Of what towns, ports and havens you may assure ourselves in the

north, west and south, to receive succour from the Low Countries, Spain and France.

3. What place you think fittest and of great advantage to assemble the principal company of your forces and the same being assembled, whether or which way you are to march.

4. What foreign forces on horse and foot you require from the said foreign princes – which would be compassed according to the proportion of yours – for how long paid; what munitions and ports fittest for their landing in this realm from the three aforesaid foreign countries.

5. What provision of armour and money (in case you want [lack]), you would ask [for].

6. By what means do the six gentlemen deliberate [plan] to proceed.

7. Also, the manner of my getting from this [strong]hold.

She also gave Babington some advice:

> You should impart the same with all diligence to Bernardino de Mendoza, ambassador lieger [resident] for the King of Spain in France, who besides the experience he has of the estate of this side [England], I may assure you will employ him therein most willingly. I shall not fail to write to him of the matter with all the earnest recommendations I can. You must make choice for managing this affair with the said Mendoza and others out of the realm of some faithful and very secret personage unto whom only you must commit yourselves . . .

Mary then moved on to the date for putting the *coup d'état* into action:

> The affairs being thus prepared and forces in readiness without and within the realm, then shall it be time to set the six gentlemen to work . . . [and] I may be suddenly transported out of this place and that all your forces [at] the same time be on the field to meet me in tarrying for the arrival of the foreign aid, which must then be hastened with all diligence.

The raid on Chartley to release her was, of course, uppermost in her mind, and she urged that those charged with assassinating Elizabeth should have 'always about them, or at least at court, four stout men furnished with good and speedy horses', and as soon as the deed was done, these

> should come with all diligence to advertise those that shall be appointed for my transporting . . . immediately they may be at the place of my abode, before my keeper can have advice of the execution . . . or at the least before he can fortify himself within the house or carry me out of the same.

Perhaps with the terms of the Bond of Association still ringing in her ears, the Scottish queen was also concerned about her security after her rescue. She wanted to be guarded

> in the midst of a good army, or in some very good strength, where I may safely stay on the assembly of your forces and arrival of the said foreign succours, it were sufficient cause given to that queen in catching me again to enclose me for ever in some hole, [from] which I should never escape . . .

Mary, all too aware of Walsingham's network of informers and agents, emphasised the dangers of spies

> and false brethren that are amongst you, especially of some priests, already practiced [subverted] by our enemies, for your discovery . . . In any way, keep never any paper about you that in any sort may do harm; for from like errors have come the only condemnation of all such as have suffered heretofore, against whom there otherwise have been nothing proved.

The fates of Throgmorton and Norfolk must have haunted her as she dictated these words.

At the end of her letter she returned to the issue of her rescue and suggested three alternative plans:

The first that at one certain day appointed in my walking abroad on horseback on the moors betwixt this [house] and Stafford, where ordinarily, you know, very few people do pass, fifty or three score men well horsed and armed, come to take me there, as they may easily, my keeper having with him . . . but eighteen or twenty horsemen, [armed] only with daggs [pistols].

The second means is to come at midnight or soon after to set fire in the barn and stables, which you know are near to the house, and whilst my guardian [and] his servants shall run forth to the fire, your company (having every one a mark whereby they may know one another under night) might surprise the house, where I hope, with the few servants I have about me, I were able to give you some correspondence [signal].

And the third, some that bring carts hither . . . early in the morning, their carts might be so prepared and with such cart leaders that being just in the midst of the great gate, the carts might fall down or overthrow [their loads] and that thereupon, you might come suddenly with your followers to make yourself master of the house and carry me away. So you might do easily, before that ever any number of soldiers (who lodge in sundry places [outside] of this place, some half and some a whole mile off) might come to the relief.

Whatever issue the matter takes, I do and will think myself obliged, as long as I live, towards you for the offers you make to hazard yourself as you do for my delivery, and by any means that ever I may have, I shall do my endeavour to recognise by effects your desserts herein.

I have commanded a more ample alphabet [cipher] to be made for you, which herewith you will receive.

Mary ends her letter, the product of a mind constantly immured in conspiracy, with the solemn instruction: 'Fail not to burn this privately and quickly.'

The letter was retrieved from the beer keg and handed over to

Phelippes, still at Chartley, on the evening of 18 July. After deciphering its contents, Walsingham's man gloatingly drew a gallows on the cover before dispatching it to the spy master. With a detective's intuition, he knew the letter would become the instrument of Mary's death.

He did something else as well: Phelippes could not resist adding a forged postscript to the letter, seeking more information about those planning to murder Elizabeth:[42]

> PS I would be glad to know the names and qualities of the six
> gentlemen which are to accomplish the [design] for it may be, I
> shall be able upon knowledge of the parties to give you further advice
> necessary to be followed . . . and even so do I wish to be made
> acquainted with the names of all such principal persons [etc.]. [And]
> also from time to time particularly how you proceed . . .

In making his copy, he also inserted a number of phrases that drew the noose tighter around Mary's neck, specifically in her enquiry regarding the method of assassinating Elizabeth.

Phelippes wrote to Walsingham on 19 July:

> You have now this queen's answer to Babington. If he be in the
> country, the original will be conveyed into his hands and like enough
> an answer returned.
>
> I look for your honour's speedy resolution touching his appre-
> hension or otherwise, that I may dispose of myself accordingly. I
> think . . . you have enough [on] him, unless you would discover
> more particularities of the confederates, which may be [done] even
> in his imprisonment. If your honour means to take him, ample
> commission and charge would be given to choice persons for
> search of his house.

Phelippes fully understood the import of Mary's letter:

> I wish it for an evidence against her, if it please God to inspire her
> majesty with that heroic courage that were meet for avenge
> [vengeance] of God's cause and the security of herself and this state.

At least, I hope she will hang Nau and Curle, who justly make Sir Amyas Paulet take upon him the name she imputes to him of a gaoler of criminals.

He took an impudent side-swipe at Elizabeth's notoriously tight grip on government expenditure by reporting that Paulet now hoped the queen would have 'better consideration' of the costs of guarding Mary than when Burghley, on her behalf, had complained that his garrison was too large. This 'pinching at charges' was no small offence to Paulet, Phelippes told Walsingham. He added: 'I am sorry to hear from London that Ballard is not yet taken and that searches by forewarning have been frustrated.'[43]

Three days later, on 22 July, his master, then at Elizabeth's court, told Phelippes that his work was appreciated: 'At your return, you shall, from her majesty's self, understand how well she accepts your service.' He looked ahead to finally resolving the lingering problem of Mary Queen of Scots:

I hope there will be a good course held in this cause. Otherwise, we that have been instruments in the discovery shall receive little comfort for our travail [labour].

At your return, come as quietly as you may, for the practisers [plotters] are jealous of your going down and the gallows upon the packet sent has greatly increased their suspicion. Some of them are very inward with our post of London.

[I] hope Babington will be taken before your return. My friend [Gifford] remains still here. And so in haste I commit you to God.

Your loving friend
Francis Walsingham

[Postscript] Babington shall not be dealt with until your return. He remains here. The original letter [sent] to him you must bring with you.[44]

That hapless conspirator received Mary's letter on 29 July, as he was unexpectedly away from his base at Lichfield in Staffordshire. He wrote to the Scottish queen on 3 August from London with some bad news:

In the meantime, your majesty may understand that one Maude (that came out of France with Ballard, who came from Mendoza concerning this affair) is discovered to be for this state. Ballard acquainted him with the cause of his coming and has employed him of late into Scotland with letters.

By whose treachery unto [what] extreme danger myself have been and the whole plot is likely to be brought, and by what means we have in part prevented and purpose by God's assistance to redress the rest, your majesty shall be by my next letter informed.

The plot was therefore dangerously compromised, or 'blown' in espionage parlance. Nevertheless, Babington remained hopelessly optimistic:

My sovereign, for His sake that preserves your majesty for our common good, dismay not, neither doubt of happy issue. It is God's cause, the church's and your majesty's, and enterprise honourable before God and man, undertaken upon zeal and devotion, free of all ambition and temporal regard and therefore no doubt will succeed happily. We have vowed and we will perform or die.[45]

These are the noble, reckless words of an innocent moving inexorably to his slaughter.

At some stage during this tight little drama, Walsingham met Babington in an attempt to persuade him to switch sides. He posed the conspirator several questions about Mary Queen of Scots and, according to the Jesuit priest William Weston, 'charged [Babington] to cultivate affection for his own country and the fidelity of a subject towards his own sovereign'. After several days, he summoned the conspirator again, but this time took a gentler, more conciliatory tone:

Stretching out his hand, [Walsingham] said: 'Come now, act with confidence, and do not fear to speak out freely.' All these particulars Babington narrated to me with his own lips . . . I knew full well what a master of deception this Walsingham was and how powerful to accomplish what his mind was set upon.

Weston told Babington:

> I cannot tell you in what manner you can escape out of his snares. If you yield, you give up your religion; if you decline his offers, you inevitably incur the peril of death.[46]

Not much comfort there. Despite these less than subtle hints from Walsingham about cooperation – he clearly wanted everyone involved named and arrested – Babington recklessly, stupidly decided to take the path of religion and the road to martyrdom.

Ballard had returned to London on 9 July with depressing information about the likelihood of Elizabeth's Catholic subjects joining an open rebellion. They may have voiced wholehearted support for the destruction of the Protestant state, but were less than enthusiastic about taking up arms against it. However, with the terrible certainty of a religious zealot, or perhaps as a result of an unrealistic belief in miracles, he refused to read the writing on the wall for his grand conspiracy. He told one of the plotters, John Savage, that he had been promised that 60,000 were ready to assist him in the north, but most of them did not own armour, which would, of course, be provided 'out of France'.[47]

Knowing that Maude had been discovered, the spy master decided it was high time to haul in his far-flung net around the conspirators. Always the efficient planner and administrator, he first needed to create some room in London's crowded prisons for the large number of arrests he expected to make as the full extent of the conspiracy was exposed. At the end of July, therefore, Walsingham sent a list of names of those priests and recusants incarcerated, prison by prison, to Phelippes for decisions on their ultimate fate.

Of the thirty-four priests and suspected seminarists and fifty-six recusants then detained in London, many had been committed to the jails by the Secretary himself.[48] Some were clearly already destined for execution. The codebreaker sent on a copy of the list to Walsingham's spy Nicholas Berden, alias Thomas Rogers, for his comments and recommendations, based on his personal knowledge of the prisoners.

Walsingham's document,[49] bluntly entitled *Prisoners to be Disposed of*, makes grim reading. Their ultimate fate rested upon the mere whim of someone they would fully regard as an enemy and a traitor. Phelippes made his own annotations before Berden added his comments (shown here in italics).

The Marshalsea Prison [Southwark][50]

Priests – (*Meet* [fit for] *for Wisbech* [Castle, Cambridgeshire], *if not for the gallows*)

[Edward] Caverley, gentleman and priest.[51]

Palmer alias Stamford, gentleman and priest. Brother to Mr Stamford, justice of the peace in Staffordshire . . . proud, arrogant fellow.[52]

[James] Edwards, of great learning accounted;[53] [William] Clareregent.[54]

Meet to be banished: [John] Lyster,[55] [John] Habberley,[56] [Francis] Tilleson,[57] [Nicholas] Knight,[58] [Thomas] Bramston,[59] [John] Bolton, [Ralph] Crockett, [Robert] Wilcocks.

Thought meet for the gallows (*or the galleys*)[60]

[John] Smith, alias Owen, a banished man but not so [well] known as Owen; [George] Potter – a shrewd fellow and obstinate.

Laymen[61] – Gentlemen and of wealth (*meet for Wisbech*): Mr Beckett, Mr Moore the elder, Mr [John] Williamson, Mr Shaxton and Mr [Walter] Blunt.

Poor fools but very knaves (*neither wealthy or wise but all very arrant* [downright knaves]): [Richard] Webster, [William] Green, [Peter] Lawson, [Robert] Holland, [Lionel] Edes alias Jennings, [John] Tucker, [Henry] Webley, [William] Crabb and Thomas Shelley's man.

The Poultry[62]

Little Ralph [Emerson], sometimes servant to the Jesuits in England.[63]

King's Bench Prison, Southwark

Clifton, priest condemned in praemunire

Two brothers passing poor.

The Gatehouse at Westminster[64]

Priests: John Bawdwin,[65] meet for banishment; Ralph Bickley.[66]

Laymen – Gentlemen and of ability (*Meet for Wisbech*): Humfrey Cumberford, Walter Whitehall, Thomas Worthington,[67] John Hewes, a collector and maker over of money.

Mean persons (*meet for what place you please*): Owen Fletcher, Richard Johnson, Thomas Edwards, Roger Astell, John Aparry, Anthony Snape – William Shelley's man and of his secret counsel and acquainted with Paget's being in England.

The Counter in Wood Street[68]

Priests: Dr [John] Bavant, an old man, no seminary;[69] [John] Maddox, an old man meet enough for Wisbech; [Richard] Davis, alias Winckfield and the corrupter of William Flitton and all his family and a great guide to the Jesuits. A gentleman and no priest; Richard Sherwood, alias Carleton, well known.

Laymen:[70] Thomas Shelley, gentleman and of ability; [Roger] Lyne and [William] Higham, gentlemen under nineteen years; [John] Chaundler and Dutton, passing poor.

The White Lion, Newington, Southwark[71]

Priests: George Collinson to be banished; [Thomas] Higate alias Simpson, a banished man . . .

Laymen – Gentlemen of abilities (*Wisbech*): Mr [John] Becken-sale; Mr Smith, a great collector and maker over of money; Richard Sampson and Richard Waldren,[72] poor knaves (*gallies or gallows*).

The Clink, Southwark[73]

Priests – None of them of any account (*of small wit or honesty*): [John] Adams, a banished man; [John] Lowe, meet for Wisbech; [John] Robinson, an old priest; Edward James; Parry, alias Morgan; Paul Spence.

Laymen – Benjamin Stookwith of some ability (*meet for Wisbech*).

Poor fellows – John Lawnder; [John] Bradstock, [Stephen] Chester, Richard Dowse, Old [John] White.

Newgate

Priests – Alban Dolman, no seminary but known. (*A Justice of the Peace of Paget's description.*) [Here Berden inserts a small sketch of a gallows.][74] [William] Wiggs, [Isaac] Higgins, [Leonard] Hyde – bad fellows. [Robert] Rowley (*Roley*) and Nutter – banished men.

Laymen – Of Abilities (*Wisbech*) Mistress [Dorothy] Pawnsfoot; Moore the younger. Poor men: [Thomas] Penkeville; [Robert] Bellamy, [Brian] Lacy.

The time had come to swoop down on the conspirators, but for Wals-ingham, fully engaged in court business at Richmond Palace on the banks of the River Thames, there were lurking, nagging fears that he had waited too late to strike. Concerned that his trap would snap shut but miss the suspects, he fired off four letters in two days to Phelippes, who was now back in Seething Lane.

Writing on 2 August, Walsingham[75] ordered Phelippes to decode Babington's answer to Mary's letters, sent to him by Paulet.

So soon as you ... have deciphered the letter, so earnestly looked for by her majesty [Elizabeth], I pray you bring it with you, for I think it right you should deliver it yourself.

I directed Francis Milles to confer with you about the apprehension of Bal[lard] which I wish now executed out of hand, unless you shall see cause upon the decipher of the letter to the contrary.

It shall be right also to apprehend Bab[ington] and such as are noted to be his friends. I am sorry that G G[ifford] is absent. I marvel greatly how this humour of straying ... comes upon him.

I pray you think [?of a] man to apprehend Bab[ington] and consider also of the manner [of the arrest].

I mean both he and Bal[lard] shall be kept in my house until they be thoroughly examined.

I hope you have thought on the articles [questions] that are to be ministered unto them both, [and the evidence] as also caused [Nicholas] Berden to set down the names of the principal practisers [conspirators] as well as clergy men and temporal.

I would be glad to understand who accompanies Sir George Peckham[76] for I take him to be a great practiser and his companion Sir Thomas Gerard.[77]

The next day, 3 August, Walsingham, still occupied with royal business but clearly preoccupied by his all-consuming worry that his quarry would escape, hastily penned another letter to Phelippes from Richmond Palace:[78]

I am sorry the event [has resulted] so ill. I doubt greatly her majesty has not used the matter with that secrecy that [is necessary]. The circumstances show [Babington has] departed [after] some doubt [or] apprehension.

I fear he has come to some knowledge by Dunne.[79] I have dispatched a letter [to] Sir Amias [sic] Paulet and have acquainted him with Bab[ington's] departure and desired him to give some secret order for his apprehension. But I doubt he will repair [to] those parts.

Touching your going down, I think it not necessary. Our way

will be to discover here what is the cause of his departure wherein great secrecy would be used.

I look for Pooley [Walsingham's spy] from whom I hope to receive some light.

Ballard would be taken but with no other course of proceeding than with an ordinary Jesuit.[80] Accordingly as I have directed Francis Milles, with whom you may confer, who is most secret . . .

You will not believe how much I grieved with the event of this cause. I fear the addition of the postscript has bred the jealousy. And praying God to send us better success than I look for, I commit you to his protection.

I pray you learn of Mr H. Offley what is become of G[ilbert] G[ifford] whose straying manner of withdrawing himself I know not what to think of. Let the messenger repair this day to Bab[ington] to solicit [an] answer.

Within hours, Walsingham dashed off a third letter to Phelippes from Richmond:[81]

. . . Your Latin letter comforted me. I think [if your] messenger receives no answer this day at Bab[ington's] hands, then were it not good to defer the apprehension of him, lest he should escape. If you hope by giving of time that an answer will be drawn from him, then I wish the stay [of arrest].

It may be yet the deferring of the answer proceeds upon confer- ence, which if it be so, then were it a great hindrance of the service to proceed over hastily to the arrest.

These causes are subject to so many difficulties as it is a hard matter to resolve. Only this, I conclude it were better to lack the answer than lack the man.

I do not mean to speak with [Babington] for many causes. And therefore, if Pooley repair[s] hither, I will put off the meeting until Saturday, to the end he may in the meantime be apprehended.

I like well that Ball[ard] should be apprehended in such sort as is agreed on . . .

I mean to acquaint her majesty with the contents of your letters. In the meantime, I [want] the messenger you use [to] be directed to solicit answers, unless you shall see some cause to the contrary. And so in haste I commit you to God.

Walsingham adds a postscript: 'I send you two blanks signed to be converted into [arrest] warrants.'

That evening, Walsingham wrote for the final time that day to Phelippes:[82]

Pooley has been with [me and] has given me great [assur]rance of Bab[ington's] devotion both to myself and the public service.

To strengthen my opinion and good concept towards him, he has told me from Bab[ington] that there is one Ball[ard], a great practiser in this realm with the Catholics to stir up rebellion within the realm, being set on by the Amb[assador] of Spain and Charles Paget.

I [asked] him to give him great thanks for this advertisement [news] and to require him in my name to draw from Ballard what he could touching such parties as he had dealt with and to meet me at my house on Saturday next.

Though I do not find but that Pooley has dealt honestly with me, yet I am loath [to] lay myself any way open to him but have only delivered such speeches as might work . . .

I do not think good, not withstanding, to defer the apprehension of Bab[ington] longer than Friday. *Ne forte* [Not chance or luck].

I like well therefore that he hasten the Fr[ench] Amb[assador's] dispatch. And yet can I not think that he should use his help in the matter; but do rather judge it he doubted what to answer.

I long to hear of Ball[ard's] apprehension which I have caused to be done by a warrant signed by the Lord Admiral[83] for that I would not be seen in the matter.

Sorry I am that I hear not of G[ifford] who might at this present [time] have given good assistance.

The Lord Admiral's warrant is in Francis Mille's hands.

Within hours of the dispatch of this letter, Phelippes tracked down Babington in the garden of Pooley's house in London. The hole in Walsingham's net now seemed closed.

The following day, 4 August, at between eleven o' clock and noon, Pooley's home was surrounded and Ballard seized by agents of the London Magistrate Richard Young. Babington, in bed, was not apprehended, to his astonishment, and Pooley, still keeping up his pretence as his friend, went to court to plead for him with Walsingham. He was arrested there and thrown into the Tower. The break-up of the conspiracy was taking on all the hallmarks of a farce.

Babington, unaware of Pooley's detention, wrote him a letter, saying that

> proceedings at my lodgings have been very strange . . . Take heed to
> your own part, lest of these my misfortunes you bear the blame.
> Farewell sweet Robin, if as I take it, you are true to me. If not, adieu!
> *Omnium bipedim nequissimus* [of all two-footed things, the wickedest].[84]

By this point, Babington must have been confused and frightened. After hearing the seductive offers from Walsingham and escaping arrest by the skin of his teeth, he decided to flee.

But he met some of his fellow conspirators amongst the crowds in Paul's Walk, the two aisles within Old St Paul's Cathedral which then were the habitual daytime haunt of loiterers, adventurers and broken-down gallants.[85] He asked them: 'Ballard is taken, all will be betrayed! What remedy now?' John Savage replied: 'No remedy now, but to kill her presently.' Very well, said Babington, 'Then go you into the court tomorrow and there execute the fact.' But Savage said he was not dressed properly, limply adding: 'In this apparel I shall never come near to the queen.' Babington crossly gave him his ring and all the money in his purse to buy some new clothes and told him bluntly to 'dispatch it'.[86]

The spy master sent a letter to Babington via his man Scudamore,[87] explaining that Ballard's arrest had been nothing to do with him and to stay close to Scudamore to avoid being taken by Young's men. They went for a meal at a nearby tavern, and while they nervously ate, a messenger

brought a note for Walsingham's man. Babington immediately suspected
it was an order for his detention and, leaving his cloak and sword on the
back of his settle, said he was going to the bar to pay the bill. He fled the inn
and ran to Westminster where he met Charnock and another plotter,
Robert Gage. By now thoroughly panic-stricken, the trio retreated to rural
St John's Woods, north of London, and then north-west, on to Harrow in
Middlesex, having cut their hair and stained their faces with walnut juice
in an attempt at disguise. They and two more conspirators, Robert Barnwell
and Henry Dunne, were arrested on 14 August near Uxendon Hall, the
home of the Bellamys, a prominent recusant family,[88] where they had
sought food. All the rest were quickly rounded up and taken to the Tower.

A month later they were tried in two groups at Westminster with Walsingham sitting as one of the commissioners. There was little mention of
Mary Queen of Scots during the proceedings, other than Ballard's plea:

> That I practised [plotted] the delivery of the queen of Scots, I am
> guilty. And that I went about to alter the religion, I am guilty – but
> that I intended to slay her majesty, I am not guilty.[89]

There were also references to Mary's letters to Babington. All of the conspirators were inevitably condemned and sentenced to the usual death for
traitors – hanging, drawing and quartering. That was not enough for
Elizabeth, for once genuinely fearful of her life. She told Burghley that
extra agonising torment should be added to the plotters' last moments –
'for more terror', as she stressed.[90] This was an extraordinary crime, said
the queen, and it deserved 'further extraordinary pain'.[91] Following her
orders, the first group of seven to be executed on 20 September, including
Ballard and Babington, died more slowly than was usual on such occasions
on the scaffold at St Giles in the Fields.[92] This was not popular with the
watching crowd and the second batch, the following day, were allowed
to hang until they were dead.

Propaganda at such times is all important, and it was probably Walsingham who ensured that the printed accounts of the executions suggested
that Elizabeth, 'detesting such cruelty', had ordered clemency.

Pooley was soon after released from the Tower.

CHAPTER FIVE

The Trial of Mary Queen of Scots

'Look to your consciences. Remember that the theatre of the whole world is wider than the kingdom of England.'

MARY QUEEN OF SCOTS TO THE COMMISSIONERS BEFORE HER TRIAL,
13 OCTOBER 1586.[1]

Elizabeth entertained no doubts at all that Mary Queen of Scots was 'the worst woman in the world'. In May 1578, she had bluntly told a French envoy who had come to London to plead on Mary's behalf that her 'head should have been cut off years ago'. Elizabeth angrily declared to Jerome Gondi, Comte de Retz, that she 'could never be free as long as she lived, even though it cost her realm and her liberty'.[2] But when Walsingham's plans to finally destroy the Scottish queen came to fruition in the aftermath of the Babington plot, the sometimes ruthless Tudor monarch was tormented by doubts, fears and unaccustomed anxiety.

The antiquary William Camden generously described Mary Queen of Scots as a 'woman most constant in her religion; of singular piety towards God, invincible magnanimity of mind; wisdom above her sex and passing beauty'. She was, he wrote, 'A lady to be reckoned amongst those princesses that have exchanged felicity for calamity.'[3]

In 1586, Mary was aged forty-three. Beneath all her regal poise and charm lay the harsh medical and psychological impact of almost two decades of captivity at the hands of Elizabeth. Five years earlier,

Robert Beale had reported to Walsingham that the Scottish queen

> desires earnestly to have the benefit of taking the air sometimes, not
> that she would be out of Queen Elizabeth's hands, but in order to
> recover herself from that indisposition and weakness of her body
> [to] which want of air has reduced her.
>
> She said also that though she's not old in years, she found
> herself old in body and that her hair was turned grey. She would
> never have another husband.[4]

There is a sadness, a sense of dreary inevitability, in his description of
Mary's state of mind. She knew that her beauty had become blurred by the
years of boredom and sedentary life: she was now doubled-chinned and
stood painfully, with stooped shoulders, her legs swollen and crippled
with arthritis. During her imprisonment at various houses in the English
North and Midlands she had suffered from a veritable medical lexicon
of afflictions – a gastric ulcer, dropsy, headaches, constipation, neuralgia,
viral fevers and rheumatism. Some may have had psychosomatic causes;
others, such as vomiting, abdominal pain and weakness in the arms and
legs, may have been symptoms of the hereditary metabolic disorder
porphyria.[5]

Just as importantly, for almost twenty years, Mary had been completely separated from the real world beyond the walls of her prisons.
She had also been denied access to uncensored information from her
correspondents between December 1584 and January 1586.[6] In her
isolation and in her sequestered state of mind, hopes of rescue and her
succession to the English throne were undoubtedly unrealistic, sometimes
hopelessly optimistic. Perhaps that was the crutch upon which she leant
to enable her to endure the loneliness of the stateless, lost world she
unwillingly inhabited. Throughout her ordeal she remained a proud,
showy cockatoo, caged within the bars of a gilded jail, always conscious
of her status, always jealous of her position and the respect it merited
from those around her.

For all her ill-health and her own growing perception that she was
losing a battle against time for the throne, Mary truly personified the

mounting foreign and internal threats both to the survival of the Protestant state of England and Elizabeth's own crown – indeed, her very life. In Elizabeth's view, and that of her supremely loyal ministers, during the 1580s the Catholic forces of Counter-Reformation were marshalling their awesome strength against her realm.

They saw the Spanish sun now firmly in the ascendancy across Western Europe, growing in strength and power, and feared the consequences for England. Across the North Sea in the Netherlands, where a revolt against Spain had been continuing bloodily since the 1560s, the rebel cause now faced disaster after the assassination of William, Prince of Orange, in July 1584. In December 1585, Elizabeth had reluctantly sent 6,000 English troops under the lacklustre command of her favourite, Robert Dudley, Earl of Leicester,[7] to reinforce the Dutch rebels in their campaign for independence against the Imperial forces under Governor General Alexander Farnese, Duke of Parma. Further south, three years earlier, Philip II of Spain had won control of Portugal and her lucrative empire, together with her mighty naval forces to augment his already powerful fleet.

On the other side of the English Channel, the new French king Henry III had, to all intents, capitulated in June 1585 to the dominant Catholic party within his country, led by Mary's cousin Henry, Duke of Guise.

In Rome, Walsingham's spies had earlier reported that Pope Gregory XIII had been encouraging Philip II to invade troubled Ireland. After Gregory's death on 1 June 1585, the new Pope Sixtus V was a dedicated supporter of the Counter-Reformation; an over-enthusiastic member of the Inquisition in Venice earlier in his career,[8] he was a ruthless reformer of papal finances and governance. Under his hand, the papacy was to become both leaner and meaner and wholly dedicated to reclaiming the former Catholic states and provinces that had been lost to Protestantism.

Across the Irish Sea, the four-year-long Desmond Rebellion had finally ended in 1583 after a brutal counter-insurgency operation by English forces that had left around 30,000 Irish non-combatants dead from starvation. Savage subjugation had left that restive nation a bubbling cauldron of dissent and resentment.

All around, therefore, grave doubts and dangers beset Walsingham, Burghley and the other Privy Councillors – not least within Elizabeth's own realm, where many of her Catholic subjects viewed Mary Queen of Scots as their rightful monarch, if not the sole legitimate heir in the event of Elizabeth's death. Mary's pivotal role in any attempt at restoration of the Catholic faith in England was also fully appreciated overseas by the Catholic exiles, and by their paymasters in the Vatican and Madrid.

Some were prepared to back their beliefs with actions, however ill-judged and hopeless. In early June 1586, Henry Radcliffe, Fourth Earl of Sussex, was tipped off about an intended rebellion 'in the country near Portsmouth'. Within days, he reported that he had quelled it and had arrested some of its leaders, adding on 13 June that 'some recusants, privy to the insurrection, were going to sea' and that he would attempt to apprehend them.[9]

Away from all these alarums, Mary was ostensibly merely quietly biding her time for her succession to the throne, 'which I will wait for patiently, without getting myself into trouble', as she wrote to one supporter.[10] In truth, she was always deep in trouble; always well over her head in conspiracy.

Walsingham's efficient spy network had uncovered plot after plot aimed at assassinating Elizabeth, some planning to include foreign troops landing in England to support the *coup d'état*. The fumbling, bumbling Babington debacle of 1586 was the last straw as far as Burghley and Walsingham were concerned. On 2 October that year, Burghley wrote to Stafford, the English ambassador in France:

> Here has been of late upon the prosecution for discovery of the great horrible conspiracy very great diligence used, so as in our opinion we have seen the bottom of this later purpose . . .
>
> I was never more toiled than I have been of late and yet am with services that here do multiply and whosoever scapeth I am never spared. God give me his grace.[11]

It was time to act against Mary – 'that devilish woman', as Walsingham called her – and remove the dire threat she posed.

Cohorts of distinguished lawyers were assembled to consider the legality of trying her in England, sparking a legal debate that presaged similar discussions before the trials of the surviving leaders of the Third Reich at Nuremburg from November 1945, or indeed of Saddam Hussein in Iraq in 2005. Then, as now, page after page of legal argument were scribbled, well spattered with Latin phrases, as learned counsel cast back into antiquity in a quest for precedents.

Objection: If it be objected in respect of her person that she is an anointed queen and an absolute princess and therefore not subject to the jurisdiction of her majesty . . .

Answer: It may be doubted whether she is a queen because she stands deposed [in] . . . Scotland and she has willingly left all her right and interest in the same realm to her son [James VI]. A king deposed is not after to be taken for a king. Therefore Frederick, King of Naples, being deposed by the King of Spain was afterwards judged [as] no king by sentence.

Every prince without his own territory is no more than a private person.

Objection: If it be objected that the offence wherewith she is charged is not *delictum consummatum* [a complete crime] and therefore not punishable by death in her person . . . to which law she submits herself?

Answer: It may be said in respect to her allegiance to the Crown of England, her actions are to be measured according to the positive laws of the said realm than by the law of nations.

By these laws, her actions are treason.

Aliens and strangers are not exempt from the force and penalties of the laws which are enacted and published whereby they remain . . . A king in all other kings' territories may commit treason as another private person.[12]

After days spent sifting through their lawyers' opinions, Burghley and Walsingham decided that they could convince both Elizabeth and public opinion that Mary could be tried for treason quite lawfully. The all-important legal gloss had been deposited upon her destruction. She would be tried by a commission of no fewer than twenty-four Privy Councillors and other nobles, under the terms of the Act for the Surety of the Queen's Person passed the previous year. Elizabeth needed little persuasion of the Scottish queen's guilt. She urged Mary's jailor, Sir Amyas Paulet:

> Let your wicked murderess know how with hearty sorrow her vile desserts compel these orders and bid her from me [to] ask God forgiveness for her treacherous dealings towards the saver of her life many a year to the intolerable peril of her own.[13]

Elizabeth declared that Mary's money should be seized and her servants sacked, possibly in the hope that such pressure would make her seriously ill and even kill her, thus neatly sparing the queen the problem of ordering her execution. Walsingham doubted the wisdom of such a policy. On 5 September, he told Paulet:

> Her pleasure being such I do not see why you should now any longer forebear the putting of the same in execution. If afterwards the inconveniences happen . . . her majesty can blame none [but] herself for it.

He was away from the court because of an inflammation in his right leg, 'caused by a painful boil', and therefore 'I cannot debate the matter with her majesty as I would'.

Despite his affliction, Walsingham was wasting no time in making his arrangements to bring the Scottish queen legally to book, anxious as he was to execute her before Christmas 1586. That afternoon, he told Paulet, he was meeting with Burghley and Hatton to decide whether Mary should be moved to Fotheringay Castle in Northamptonshire, or to the Tower of London for the trial.[14] Their sensible recommendation was the Tower, for greater security, but for Elizabeth that would be too close to home and she flatly rejected the idea. Hertford Castle, north-east of London, was also considered but again turned down as a prison.

On the morning of 9 September, Paulet moved to confiscate Mary's cash. 'We found [her] in her bed, troubled after the old manner with a defluxion [open sore] which was fallen down into the side of her neck and had bereft her of the use of one of her hands,' he recounted to Walsingham afterwards.

> After many denials, many exclamations and many bitter words
> against you (I say nothing of her railing against myself) with flat
> affirmation that her majesty might have her body but her heart she
> should never have, refusing to deliver the key of her cabinet, I called
> my servants and sent for [crow]bars to break open the door,
> whereupon she yielded and caused the door to be opened.[15]

Inside Paulet found 5,000 French crowns, two bags containing £104 2s (or £14,500 in modern monetary values) and three pounds of silver, the latter left with her as she claimed she had no more money in the house and she owed her servants their wages. More money was found in the chamber of her secretary Claude Nau, amounting to £1,445 18s (£199,500). Further searches found a casket containing all Mary's seals, and further cash in gold and silver.[16]

On 25 September, Mary arrived under heavy armed escort at Fotheringay, seventy-five miles from London, after a four-day journey from the unhealthy manor house at Chartley where she had been imprisoned since the previous December.[17]

Preparations for the trial were already in full swing. Walsingham employed Patrick, Master of Gray,[18] one of James VI's Gentlemen of the Bedchamber and Master of his Wardrobe, to discover the Scottish king's attitude towards the trial of his mother. Robert Douglas, Provost of Lincluden and a Scottish Privy Councillor, wrote to Archibald Douglas, the Scottish ambassador in London, of James's

> misliking [of] the wicked intentions of her majesty's evil disposed
> subjects and thinks, if the same had taken effect, to have been no
> less in danger thereby as if it had been meant against his own
> person . . . In so far as his mother may be burdened . . . I find his
> majesty [in] no ways mind[s] that rigour shall be used against her.[19]

Gray also reported that James believed that Mary should be 'put in the Tower or sum [sic] other firm manse and kept from intelligence; her own servants taken from her and such as be culpable punished rigorously' and that in future, those about her should be in the pay of Elizabeth.[20]

Burghley, meanwhile, sketched a plan of the Great Chamber on the first floor of Fotheringay,[21] with special fittings for the trial. Against one wall was a canopied cloth of state, brightly blazoned with the arms of England, positioned above a throne set on a dais for Elizabeth – although the chances of her attending the hearing were less than slim. 'A [waist-high] rail, as in the Parliament Chamber' was stretched across the room, separating the well of the court from 'the nether part, for all persons not being in [the] commission, nor of the Queen's learned counsel'. Despite Burghley's original plans, a high-backed chair upholstered in crimson velvet was placed for Mary not directly facing the throne as he had ordered, but immediately to its right. Before her would be a table for the lawyers and their papers and behind and in front, along the walls, low benches to seat the commissioners. The room was draped with velvet, intended to add to the majesty, if not the appearance of legality, of the occasion.

On 6 October, Thomas Randolph, the English ambassador to Mary's court in Scotland during the 1560s, announced his intention (with permission) to attend the proceedings 'because of his knowledge of that woman's former dealings against her majesty'.[22]

The scene was now set for one of the most poignant and tragic dramas in British history.

Most of the commissioners gathered at Fotheringay on Tuesday 11 October; Walsingham, although keen to seal the Scottish queen's fate, was seemingly not amongst them.[23] Early the following morning, Burghley – who had just arrived – sent Chancellor of the Exchequer Sir Walter Mildmay, escorted by Paulet, together with Elizabeth's public notary Edward Barker[24] and another man called Stallenge, the Usher of Parliament, to Mary's privy chamber to deliver a letter from Elizabeth. It informed the Scottish queen, as she fully expected, that she now faced trial for treason – and for her life.

Whereas we are given to understand that you to our great and inestimable grief . . . pretend with great protestation not to be in any sort privy or assenting to any attempt either against our state or person, for as much as we find by most clear and evident proof that the contrary will be verified and maintained against you.

We have found it therefore expedient to send unto you diverse of our chief and most ancient noblemen of this our realm together with certain of our Privy Council, [and] also some of our principal judges to charge you . . . with the privety [secret] assent to that most horrible and unnatural attempt.

To the end you may have no just cause (lying as you do within our protection and thereby subject to the laws of our realm and to such a trial as by us shall be thought most agreeable to our laws) to take exception to the manner of our proceeding, we have made choice of the chief honourable personages to be used in this service, having for that purpose authorised them by our Commission under our Great Seal to proceed therein.

Therefore [we] do both advise and require you to give credit and make answer to that which the said honourable personages so authorised by us, shall from time to time during their abode there, object or deliver unto you in our name, as if it were to our self.

Given at our Castle of Windsor

6 October 1586[25]

Mary read it quietly and with little expression on her face as they stood anxiously waiting for her response. Eventually, she told them:

It grieves me that the queen, my royal sister, is misinformed of me . . . It seems strange to me that the queen should command me as a subject to appear personally in judgment.

I am an absolute queen and will do nothing which may prejudice either my own royal majesty or other princes of my place and rank . . .

My mind is not yet dejected; neither will I sink under my calamity . . .

The laws and statutes of England are to me most unknown. I am destitute of counsellors and [of] who shall be my peers I am utterly ignorant.

My papers and notes are taken from me and no man dares step forward to be my advocate.

I am clear [innocent] from all crime against the queen. I have excited no man against her . . . Yet can I not deny but I have commended myself and my cause to foreign princes.[26]

It was a brave, confident speech, delivered with royal dignity and composure and displaying all the signs of careful preparation and thought.

It would have come as no surprise to Burghley, waiting uneasily elsewhere in the castle, that her regal status was to be her prime weapon for attacking the legality of her trial. There must have been nervous discussions amongst Burghley and his advisers overnight as they considered their tactics to persuade the Scottish queen to attend the proceedings. It was vital to have the prisoner present at the bar to complete the picture of due legal process and to create a public impression of a fair trial.

The next day, Thursday, Burghley led a delegation of commissioners in another attempt to convince her to appear before the special court. She remained obdurate in her opposition.

I am a queen, not a subject.

If I appeared, I should betray the dignity and majesty of kings and it would be tantamount to a confession that I am bound to submit to the laws of England, even in matters touching religion.

I am willing to answer all questions, provided I am interrogated before a free Parliament and not before these commissioners who doubtless have been carefully chosen and who have probably already condemned me unheard.[27]

The Lord Treasurer angrily interrupted her telling words. He built a picture of Elizabeth's kindnesses to her – hardly an eloquent argument to one kept confined as a prisoner for so long – and then flatly stated that legally the commissioners could and would try her in her absence.

'Will you therefore answer us nor not?' he demanded. Mary repeated: 'I am a queen,' but Burghley snapped back: 'The queen, my mistress, knows no other queen in her realm but herself.' He told Mary that Elizabeth had

> punished those who contested your pretensions to the English crown. In her goodness, she saved you from being judged guilty of high treason at the time of your projected marriage with the duke of Norfolk and she has protected you from the fury of your own subjects.[28]

Mary merely smiled sadly, and the meeting, which had lasted two hours, broke up in mutual anger and frustration.

The government's game plan was to firmly deny Mary her royal status. They had no choice. If they had allowed Mary's claims of being a queen, the indictment would have failed, as it was universally acknowledged that a queen was not required to take cognisance of any plots against a neighbouring sovereign.[29]

That afternoon, Burghley returned to Mary's privy chamber with another committee of commissioners. She referred to one passage in the third paragraph of Elizabeth's letter to her and demanded to know the meaning of the word 'protection'. She told them: 'I came into England to seek assistance and I was immediately imprisoned. Is that protection?' Burghley neatly side-stepped the question. He had read the letter but declared that neither he nor his colleagues were so presumptuous as to dare to interpret the meaning of their royal mistress's words. Mary responded with cold, penetrating logic:

> You are too much in the confidence of your mistress not to be aware of her wishes and intentions.
>
> If you are armed with such authority by your commission as you describe, you surely have the power to interpret a letter from the queen.[30]

This letter, she added adroitly, 'was written by Walsingham. He confessed to me that he was my enemy and I well know what he has done against me and my son.' Her sharp rejoinder wrong-footed the commissioners.

It sent them into a huddle, to discuss whether the spy master really was in London when the letter was written. But why debate the matter? Such talk was completely irrelevant. They held the power to legally try her. Further discussion was therefore nugatory. But still they whispered amongst themselves.

By now, it was getting dark outside the walls of Fotheringay. Eventually, Elizabeth's Vice-Chamberlain Sir Christopher Hatton tried a conciliatory approach. He told Mary:

> You are accused (but not condemned) to have conspired [in the] destruction of our lady and queen anointed.
>
> You say you are a queen, so be it.
>
> But in such a crime, the royal dignity is not exempted from answering, neither by the civil nor canon law, nor by the law of nations, nor of nature. For if such offences might be committed without punishment, all justice would stagger, yes, fall to the ground.
>
> If you be innocent, you wrong your reputation in avoiding a trial.

After these fine lawyer's words, he slipped up in his anxiety to crush her arguments: 'You protest yourself to be innocent, but Queen Elizabeth thinks otherwise and that neither without grief and sorrow for the same.' These words gave the lie to the honesty and impartiality of the proceedings. It was an admission that she had been judged and convicted before the trial had even begun. The shadow of the executioner's axe had fallen across the room.

Hatton hurried on hastily, realising his error. His royal mistress had appointed 'most honourable, prudent and upright' commissioners to hear Mary's case, who would, he added disingenuously, 'rejoice with all their hearts if you clear yourself of this crime'. 'Believe me,' Hatton went on, even 'the queen herself will be much affected with joy. [She told] me at my [departing] from her, that never anything [made] her more grieved [than] that you were charged with such a crime'. Put aside any notion of the privileges of royalty, he urged Mary: 'Appear in judgment and show your innocence, lest by avoiding trial, you draw upon yourself suspicion and lay upon your reputation an eternal blot.'

Mary was not swayed by his rhetoric, nor did she entertain any naïve doubts regarding the certain outcome of the commissioners' trial. Moreover, even at this dangerous hour, she clung tenaciously to her perceived right of succession to the English crown. She insisted on appearing before Parliament 'lawfully assembled, so I may be declared the next [in] the succession [to the English crown]'. Better still, she would agree to her case being heard directly by Elizabeth and her Privy Council so that her 'protests may be admitted and [that] I may be acknowledged the next of kin to the queen'.

She looked directly into the grim faces of her judges and told them boldly: 'To the judgment of my adversaries, amongst whom I know all defence of my innocence will be barred, flatly I will not submit myself.'

Burghley, exasperated, stopped the discussions there with an imperious wave of his hand. Bluntly, he told Mary that the commissioners 'will proceed tomorrow in the cause, though you be absent and continue in your contumacy [stubborn and wilful obstinacy]'. She snapped back: 'Search your consciences! Look to your honour! May God reward you and yours for your judgement against me.'

With her words ringing around the presence chamber, the delegation retired, bowing and retreating backwards from the Scottish queen, displaying their respect and an incongruous attention to royal protocol in stark contrast to their constant attempts to demean her royal status.

Late that night, a courier arrived post-haste from London bearing another letter from Elizabeth to Mary that hinted of a possible reprieve. But the queen, clearly well briefed about the latest discussions at Fotheringay, began with a forthright accusation:

> You have planned in diverse ways and manners to take my life and to ruin my kingdom by the shedding of blood.
>
> I never proceeded so harshly against you; on the contrary, I have maintained you and preserved your life with the same care which I use for myself.
>
> Your treacherous doings will be proved to you and made manifest in the very place where you are. And it is my pleasure that

you shall reply to my nobles and to the peers of my kingdom as you would to myself were I there present.

I have heard of your arrogance and therefore, I demand, charge and command you to reply to them.

But answer fully and you may receive greater favour from us.

ELIZABETH

By the same messenger came another letter, this time to Burghley, instructing him that the commissioners should not pronounce sentence until they returned to London and that a full report of the proceedings should be dispatched to Elizabeth without delay. She was already becoming infected by doubts over the Scottish queen's fate.

Early on the morning of Friday 14 October, Mary asked to see a small group of the commissioners. Walsingham was now amongst them, presumably having arrived overnight at Fotheringay. It was the first time she had met her great adversary face to face. In the brief silence that followed the delegation's arrival, each must have studied the other's expression, trying to divine and comprehend their thoughts and intentions.

But compromise seemed to linger in the air: the Scottish queen had realised overnight that being tried *in absentia* would harm her cause, as her voice would effectively be silenced. Perhaps Elizabeth's less than subtle hints of possible clemency weakened Mary's earlier resolve to stand fast upon her royal rank and dignity. Now, Burghley asked her again if she would attend the imminent legal proceedings, if her protests of regal status were received in writing 'without allowance [concurrence]'. After some debate, Mary reluctantly agreed, as she was anxious, above all, to purge herself of the allegations made against her.

In order to prove my goodwill towards [Elizabeth] and to show that I do not refuse to answer to the charges of which I am accused, I am prepared to answer to that accusation only, which touches on the life of Queen Elizabeth, of which I swear and protest that I am innocent.

I will say nothing upon any other matter whatsoever as to any friendship or treaty with any other foreign princes.[31]

Later that morning, shortly after nine o'clock, thirty-six commissioners[32] assembled in the Great Chamber, taking their places on the low settles along each wall. In the well of the court sat the seven judges[33] and the lawyers Valentine Dale[34] and Ford, two doctors of the civil law; John Popham, the queen's Attorney General;[35] Thomas Egerton, her Solicitor-General;[36] Edward Barker, Elizabeth's notary or registrar; Thomas Gawdy, the serjeant at law; and finally two clerks to record what was said.[37]

Mary, after breaking her pious fast by drinking a small cup of wine 'as she felt weak and ill', made a stately entrance to the courtroom, dressed in a gown and mantle of black velvet with a long white gauze veil over her widow's cambric cap, her train carried by one of her maids of honour, Renée Beauregard.

Her carefully stage-managed procession, escorted by soldiers armed with halberds, had a distinctly medical flavour. Because of her rheumatism, she walked with great difficulty, supported on either side by her steward Andrew Melville and her physician Dominique Bourgoing. Her surgeon, Jacques Gervais, followed on behind with her apothecary Pierre Gorion and three gentlewomen, Gillis Mowbray, Jane Kennedy and Alice Curle. But if Mary believed all this would engender any shred of sympathy amongst her judges, she was sadly mistaken.

As she entered, the commissioners politely removed their hats, their action acknowledged by a regal gesture of her hand. Mary paused as she saw the throne beneath the canopied cloth of estate and, nodding towards it, said: 'I am a queen by right of birth and my place should be there, under the dais.' After a brief, poignant pause, she recovered her composure and took her seat, positioned to the right of the throne. As she sat, she turned to Melville, standing next to her, and commented: 'Alas, here are many counsellors, but not one for me.'[38] Some of her judges' faces were unfamiliar and she asked Paulet, standing behind, about the identities of the commissioners around her.

Sir Thomas Bromley, Lord Chancellor, rose and faced her as the muttering and whispers died away in the courtroom. He opened the trial:

The most high and mighty Queen Elizabeth, being not without
great grief of mind, advertised that you have conspired the destruction of her and of England and the subversion of religion [and] has,
out of her office and duty lest she might seem to have neglected
God, herself and her people, and out of no malice at all, appointed
these commissioners to hear the matters which shall be objected
unto you and how you can clear yourself of them and make known
your innocence . . .[39]

Madam, you have heard why we have come here; will you please
listen to the reading of our commission and I promise you that you
shall say all that you wish.[40]

But Mary, rising painfully to her feet, repeated her protest that she was an
independent sovereign and princess, and expressed her fervent desire
to show 'by my replies to all the world, that I am not guilty of this crime
against the person of the queen [with] which it seems I am charged'. Her
objection was duly recorded by the clerks, scribbling with their pens at
their table, and the royal commission in Latin, appointing her judges,
was read out.

Gawdy, the serjeant at law, resplendent in his blue robes, a red hood
on one shoulder and wearing a round cap upon his head, opened the
case for the crown against Mary. He laid out the details of the Babington
plot, including the correspondence between Babington and Mary, and
claimed that she knew of the conspiracy to kill Elizabeth and had 'approved
it, assented unto it, promised her assistance and showed the ways and
means' to achieve its successful conclusion. The Scottish queen interrupted him with a fierce, defiant rebuttal:

I knew not Babington. I never received any letters from him, nor
wrote any to him. I never plotted the destruction of the queen. If you
want to prove it, then produce my letters signed with my own hand.

There was a moment's silence. Gawdy, smilingly triumphant, quickly
responded: 'But we *have* evidence of letters between you and Babington.'
Mary, still feeling sure of her ground, answered:

If so, why do you not produce them? I have the right to demand to see the originals and the copies side by side. It is quite possible that my ciphers have been tampered with by my enemies. I cannot reply to this accusation without full knowledge. Till then, I must content myself with affirming solemnly that I am not guilty of the crimes imputed to me.

I do not deny that I have earnestly wished for liberty and done my utmost to procure it for myself.

In this I acted from a very natural wish – but I take God to witness that I never either conspired against the life of your queen nor approved a plot of that design against her . . .

Then, damningly, she began to lie and to embroider the fabric of her protest:

I declare formally that I never wrote the letters that are produced against me. Can I be responsible for the criminal projects of a few desperate men, which they planned without my knowledge or participation?[41]

Suddenly, with a timely sixth sense, she must have begun to experience a sudden, terrible foreboding of Walsingham's ambush that was closing, relentlessly, around her. Another lawyer stood up and read two letters, one from Mary to Babington and another from him to her. One of Walsingham's men carefully translated the passages in French for all to hear and understand. The Scottish queen tried to bluster herself out of harm's way:

It may be that Babington wrote them – but let it be proved that I received them. If Babington or any others affirm it, I say they lie openly. Other men's crimes are not to be cast upon me.

A packet of letters, which had been kept from me almost a whole year came to my hands about that time, but by whom it was sent I know not.[42]

Mary continued: 'If Babington really confessed such things, why was he put to death without being confronted with me? It is because such a meeting would have brought to light the truth, that he was executed so hastily.'

In the teeth of such evidence, the Scottish queen decided to play her powerful sympathy card – seeking pity from those in the court, she was sure, who could not publicly own up to their private thoughts. She pointed to the injustice of her long imprisonment:

> I have, as you see, lost my health and the use of my limbs. I cannot walk without assistance, nor use my arms and I spend most of my time confined to bed by sickness.
>
> Not only this, but through my trials, I have lost the small intellectual gifts bestowed on me by God, such as my memory, which would have aided me to recall those things which I have seen and read and which might be useful to me in the cruel position [in which] I find myself. Also the knowledge of matters of business which I formerly had acquired for the discharge of those duties in the state to which God called me, and of which I have been so treacherously despoiled.
>
> Not content with this, my enemies now endeavour to complete my ruin, using against me means which are unheard of towards persons of my rank and unknown in this kingdom before the reign of the present queen and even now not approved by rightful judges . . .[43]

Mary maintained that she did not fear

> the menaces of men. I will never deny Jesus Christ, knowing well that those who deny him in this world, He will deny before His Father. I demand another hearing, and that I be allowed an advocate to plead my cause, or that I be believed on the word of a queen. I came to England relying upon the friendship and promises of your Queen. Look here my lords, [drawing a ring from her finger] see this pledge of love and protection which I received from your mistress – regard it well.

But all her powerful pleas for sympathy, all the theatre of her emotional eloquence, were swept away by Walsingham's carefully constructed web of evidence, like a child's collapsing tower of playing cards. Her fatal letter, written to Babington on 17 July 1586, was read out – including its final condemning plea: 'Fail not to burn this privately and quickly.'

The Scottish queen burst into tears of frustration and despair. But her defiance was undimmed. Wiping her eyes, she pointed at Walsingham, seated down the room from her, beyond the end of the lawyers' table:

It is easy to imitate ciphers and handwriting, as has been lately done in France by a young man who boasts that he is my son's brother.

I fear that all of this is the work of Monsieur de Walsingham for my destruction. [He] I am certain, has tried to deprive me of my life and my son of his.

Her eyes flashing, still gesturing down the room at Elizabeth's spy master, she issued a challenge: 'But Mr Walsingham, I think you are an honest man and I pray you say in the words of an honest man whether you have done so or not.'[44] She then turned her attention to some of the allegations made against her:

As to Ballard, I have heard him spoken of.

Information has reached me from France that he was a very firm Catholic and that he wished to serve me but I was also told that he had great intelligence with Monsieur de Walsingham and that I must be on my guard . . .

I protest that I never even thought of the ruin of the Queen of England and that I would a hundred times rather have lost my life than see so many Catholics suffer for my sake and be condemned to a cruel death through hatred to my person.[45]

Lord Treasurer Burghley was sitting on the settle directly in front of Mary. He jumped to his feet and stated firmly: 'No faithful subject has ever been put to death on account of religion. Some have been for treason, because they maintained the Bull and the authority of the Pope against that of our Queen.' Mary retorted: 'Yet I have heard just the contrary and read so in printed books.' Burghley replied: 'The authors of such books also declare that the Queen has forfeited the royal prerogative.'

At the other end of the room, Walsingham stood up and interrupted these exchanges. Bowing his head respectfully in the direction of the royal prisoner, he was uncharacteristically anxious to answer her accusations against him.

> I protest that my soul is free from all malice. God is my witness
> that, as a private person, I have done nothing unworthy of an honest
> man and as Secretary of State, nothing unbefitting my duty.

He paused as if to lend emphasis to his words, and then addressed Mary directly. The two adversaries at last each confronted their own personal deadly enemy:

> You have been told that I wish you ill; that I have often said things to
> your disadvantage; that I have confessed myself to be your enemy –
> no, even that I planned that the death of yourself and your son
> should happen on the same day.
>
> But I assure you that I bear no ill-will to no one.
>
> I have attempted no one's death.
>
> I protest that I am a man of conscience and a faithful servant to
> my mistress.
>
> I confess that I am ever vigilant regarding all concerning the
> safety of my queen and country; I have closely watched all conspira-
> cies against either.
>
> As for Ballard, if he had offered me his assistance I could not
> have refused it, and should probably ha[ve] rewarded him. If I had
> any secret dealings with him, why did he not declare them in order
> to save his life?[46]

She had clearly twanged a raw nerve in Walsingham's psyche, forcing him to speak of his private thoughts and motives. This was an astonishingly frank explanation of his personal and professional creed from Elizabeth's spy master, although in parts – notably the references to the Scottish queen – suitably weasel-worded for a man of the shadowy world of espionage finding himself in the unaccustomed glare of a state trial.

Mary was impressed by his denials. Perhaps chastened by his eloquence and apparent sincerity and exhausted by the strain of the trial, she begged Walsingham not to be angered by her words; she had merely repeated freely what she had heard reported. The Secretary now should give no more credit to those who slandered her than she did to those who accused him. 'Spies,' she said, 'are men of doubtful credit, who dissemble one thing and speak another.' She burst into tears once more and added: 'I would never make shipwreck of my soul by conspiring the destruction of my dearest sister.'

Gawdy quickly interjected that this statement would be disproved by testimony that afternoon. So, at one o'clock, after the heady drama of the morning, the proceedings broke up for the midday meal. Mary told her followers that the trial reminded her of the Passion of Jesus Christ and that she was being treated just as Christ had been by the Jews when He was in the hands of Pontius Pilate. She was seemingly already willingly taking on the mantle of a holy martyr.

After the break for refreshments, the prosecution moved on to the confessions of Claude Nau, her secretary, and Gilbert Curle, her cipher clerk, obtained by Walsingham after the arrest of the Babington conspirators. Their evidence must have come like a thunderbolt to Mary, rocking her supreme confidence, but she stoutly maintained a brave face. She stood up and faced her accusers, and said it might be that these two may have inserted into her letters such things as she had not dictated to them – indeed, letters might have come into their hands that she had never seen.

The majesty and safety of all princes falls to the ground if they depend upon the writings and testimonies of secretaries. I delivered nothing to them but what nature delivered to me, that I might at length recover my liberty.

I am not to be convicted but by my own word or writing.

If they have written anything which may be hurtful to the queen, my sister, they have written it altogether without my knowledge.

Let them bear the punishment of their inconsiderate boldness. I am sure, if they were here present, they would clear me of all blame in this cause. And I, if my notes were at hand, could answer particularly to these things.[47]

More evidence was produced at the next and final day's hearing at Fotheringay, with one last telling exchange between Burghley and the Scottish queen. Mary had accused the minister of being her enemy. 'No,' said the Lord Treasurer: 'I am enemy to the queen's enemy.'[48]

The trial was adjourned to be reopened ten days later in the Star Chamber, within the security of the Palace of Westminster. There the commissioners reviewed the evidence against Mary and unanimously judged her guilty of having 'compassed and imagined within this realm of England, tending to the hurt, death and destruction of the royal person of our said lady the queen'.[49] Walsingham wrote to Leicester:

We had proceeded presently to sentence but we had a secret countermand and were forced under some colour to adjourn our meeting until the 25th of the month to Westminster. I see this wicked creature ordained of God to punish us for our sins and unthankfulness for her majesty has no power to proceed against her as her own safety requires.[50]

One can sense vividly Walsingham's intense frustration at the slowness of events.

Even after the commissioners pronounced sentence, Elizabeth havered over issuing a public proclamation announcing the verdict against Mary. She needed a nudge towards signing the death warrant. Parliament reassembled on 29 October and petitioned the queen to agree to the execution.[51] Burghley and Walsingham's fingerprints were all over the wording:

Having of long time to our intolerable grief seen by how manifold most dangerous and execrable practices, Mary . . . commonly called Queen of Scots has encompassed the destruction of your majesty's sacred and most royal person, in whose safety (next under God) our chief and only felicity does consist; and thereby not only to bereave us of the sincerer and true religion of Almighty God, bringing us and this noble crown back again into the thraldom of the Romish tyranny, but also to utterly ruin and overthrow the happy state and commonwealth of this most noble realm.

The judgement and sentence upon Mary were 'in all things most honourable, just and lawful'. Parliament could not discover 'any possible means to provide for your majesty's safety but by the just and speedy execution of the said queen, the neglecting whereof, may procure the heavy displeasure and punishment of Almighty God'. It is always comforting to have God agreeing with you in such matters, as Walsingham undoubtedly believed He did.

Elizabeth, with growing doubts over the planned regicide, eventually replied to the petition 'with an answer without an answer'. It was an impressive display of semantics:

> Your judgement I condemn not, neither do I mistake your reasons but pray you to accept my thankfulness, excuse my doubtfulness, and take in good part my answer answerless.
>
> If I should say I would not do what you request I might say perhaps more than I think.
>
> And if I should say I would do it, I might plunge myself into peril, whom you labour to preserve.

No doubt her loyal Commons and Lords read over her convoluted prose many times and discussed its true import. But for all its foggy phrases, the meaning was crystal clear: Elizabeth had very real doubts about being seen to order the execution of the Scottish queen.

Burghley tried to force her hand and she eventually agreed to proclaim Mary's sentence on 4 December – news greeted joyously by celebratory bonfires lit by the citizens of London.[52]

CHAPTER SIX

'Thirst After Her Blood'

*'You may see that this dreadful delay breeds
dread and danger on every side and that every
day brings forth new mischief . . . There will be no
end until . . . the wrath of God be appeased by the
sweet-smelling sacrifice of justice [be] executed
upon this lady, whose life threatens ruin both to
Prince and people.*

SIR AMYAS PAULET'S LETTER TO WILLIAM DAVISON,
JUNIOR SECRETARY OF STATE, 27 JANUARY 1586.[1]

Walsingham drafted a warrant for the execution of Mary Queen of Scots sometime during early December 1586.[2] With an eye towards its public consumption, he made sure that the document graphically recounted the plans of Babington and his fellow conspirators. He added:

> Mary, pretending title to the crown of this realm of England, had compassed and imagined . . . diverse things tending to the hurt, death and destruction of our royal person . . . By our proclamation under our great seal of England bearing date at Richmond the [blank] day of this month of December have published the said sentence and judgement . . .

By the ancient laws of this our realm, they do justly deserve death and that all the favours and tolerance by us heretofore used towards the said Mary have and do embolden her and her confederates to persevere in their mischievous attempts against us and this our realm, have therefore in like manner . . . moved us that execution of death, which she has so justly deserved, might be done on the same Mary.

The warrant directed 'any two or more' of the designated commissioners at 'our castle of Fotheringay in our county of Northampton you do immediately cause the head of the same Mary to be cut off, whereof fail you not'. The document was endorsed carefully by Walsingham: 'Note that this must bear date the day after the proclamation [be] made.'

On 19 November, at Fotheringay, Lord Buckhurst and Robert Beale, clerk to the Privy Council, told Mary of the sentence of death passed upon her. Two days later, her keeper Paulet and his new assistant Sir Dru Drury told her that as she was now legally regarded as a dead woman – moreover, one 'without honour or dignity' – they would remove the glittering cloth of estate that hung over a regal chair in her presence chamber. Her own attendants refused to remove it, but eight of Paulet's servants tore it down in a deliberately callous attack on her royal status. He also churlishly and needlessly ordered the removal of her billiard table.[3] The Scottish queen wrote to Mendoza in Paris on 23 November:

Praise God for me that, by His Grace, I had the courage to receive this very unjust sentence of the heretics with contentment, for the honour . . . to shed my blood at the demand of the enemies of His Church.

They honour me so much as to say, that theirs cannot exist if I live. The other point they affirm to be, that their queen cannot reign in security and for the same reason.

On both these conditions, I, without contradicting them, accepted the honour they were so anxious to confer upon me, as very zealous in the Catholic religion for which I had publicly offered my life.[4]

She was finding considerable comfort and moral strength in her new role of Catholic martyr.

On 1 December, a mere six days after the proclamation announcing the sentence on Mary was published, Burghley issued instructions to hand Mary over to Sir Thomas Andrews, the Sheriff of Northampton-shire, ready for her immediate execution after delivery to him of the as yet unsigned death warrant.[5] Burghley and Walsingham clearly believed the matter would be wrapped up speedily – preferably before Christmas.

But all was not as clear cut as they hoped.

There remained nagging fears amongst Elizabeth's advisers that Mary would throw herself on the queen's mercy – and that such an emotional appeal, woman to woman, queen to queen, could win her a reprieve. Their concerns were heightened when Mary wrote to Elizabeth on 19 December, piously thanking her for the 'happy tidings' of her impending execution, adding, 'While abandoning this world and preparing myself for a better and for all those whom you doom . . . I desire that my blood and my country may be remembered in that time.' Paulet took it upon himself to delay delivery of the letter, fearing its impact on his emo-tionally tortured queen, but Elizabeth eventually received it by 23 December.[6] It must have added to her torment of indecision, and could hardly have brightened her Twelve Days of Christmas.

Possible reaction to the execution overseas and the diplomatic con-sequences of the act were also troubling her.

Roger Aston, the confidential agent to Mary's estranged son James VI reported that the 'only thing' the Scottish king craved 'is her life; all other things to be just as her majesty [Elizabeth] pleases, her life only [be] saved'.[7] Despite this emotional response, reports suggested there would be no ultimatum, no threat of war from Edinburgh, if the Scottish queen was executed.

Pompone de Bellièvre, a special ambassador from the French king Henry III, travelled to London to hand over a letter of protest to Elizabeth. He warned that his master would 'look upon it as a personal affront' if Mary was killed. Such weak, half-hearted coercion did not worry the English queen, who replied defiantly that any such intimidation was the 'shortest way to make me dispatch the cause of so much mischief'. But behind her bluster and bravado, Elizabeth was still far from convinced of the wisdom of slaughtering Mary.

Walsingham wrote her a closely reasoned paper arguing for a speedy execution: *The Dangerous Alteration likely to ensue both in England and Scotland in case the Execution of the Scottish Queen be Stayed.* He warned that

> The number of Papists, atheists and malcontents will marvellously increase in respect of the hope they will conceive that the . . . Scottish Queen shall come to the crown as a thing fatal [to Elizabeth].
>
> The Jesuits and seminaries and their confederates that build only the hope of alteration of religion upon her person, doubting that in respect of the infirmity of her body that a more strait keeping of her will hasten her death, will use the greater expedition for the prevention thereof in putting in execution such practices as may shorten her majesty's days . . .
>
> Now touching the perils that are to ensue either by the King of Scots or the King of Spain by a particular consideration of them, it will appear that they are nothing equal to the peril that is likely to grow from her.[8]

All his eloquence, all his passionate belief, were to no avail. The queen remained unable to take a decision.

In late December, frustrated and vexed by Elizabeth's havering, Walsingham retired from the court in a huff to his home at Barn Elms.

Another perhaps more compelling factor behind his sudden departure was her refusal to grant him Babington's forfeited estates (which she awarded to Sir Walter Raleigh early in January 1587)[9] at a time when he was facing serious financial problems over the considerable debts left by his dead son-in-law Sir Philip Sidney and worried over the difficult delivery of a child by his newly widowed daughter, Frances.[10] He may also have become jealous over the queen's recent attention to Sir Christopher Hatton's advice and opinions. On 16 December Walsingham wrote to Burghley, explaining his swift disappearance from court, the anger scorching off the page, his bitterness shining out like a fiery beacon:

> I humbly beseech your lordship to pardon me in that I did not take my leave of you before my departure from the court.
>
> Her majesty's unkind dealing with me has so wounded me as I could take no comfort to stay there.
>
> And yet, if I saw any hope that my continuance there might either breed any good to the church or furtherance to the service of her majesty or of the realm, the regard of my particular should not cause me to withdraw myself.

In an angry jab at some of those at court opposed to Mary's execution, he added: 'But seeing the declining state we are coming into and that men of best descent are least esteemed, I hold them happiest in this government that may be rather lookers-on than actors.'

Walsingham begged Burghley not to press Elizabeth any further on the issue of Babington's lands 'which I am fully resolved to give over'. But, now faced with Sidney's mountainous debts, he remained disappointed and disgruntled that further honours or other marks of royal favour had not come his way:

> Whatsoever conceit her majesty makes either of me or of my [service], I would not spend so long a time as I have done in that place, subject to so infinite toil and discomfort, not to be made Duke of Lancaster.[11]

Here he was referring to his attempts to be appointed to the lucrative sinecure of Chancellor of the Duchy of Lancaster. Piously, he added: 'My hope is, however I am dealt with by an earthly prince, I shall never lack the comfort of the Prince of Princes.'

Eight days later, on Christmas Eve, Walsingham had recovered enough from his chagrin to write to Leicester, bemoaning Elizabeth's indecision over Mary's death: 'The delay of the intended and necessary execution doth more trouble me, considering the danger her majesty [faces] than any other grief.'[12] He repeated his forthright views in a letter to Burghley on 5 January:

There is but one way (next after God) and that is that her majesty will be persuaded to preserve her safety before her treasure.

The diseases of her estate will not be cured with slight remedies, nor can endure long delay.

I pray God therefore, direct her majesty's heart to do that which may be for her safety.[13]

Walsingham was now almost beside himself with frustration at Elizabeth's vacillation – so much so that he had fallen ill. He told Burghley that the grief of his mind 'has thrown me into a dangerous disease, as by [speaking to] Dr Baily [Walsingham's physician], your lordship may understand'.

A flavour of those angry conversations taking place in the privacy of Elizabeth's chambers may possibly be supplied from overseas. The Spanish perceived dissension amongst Elizabeth's chief ministers and advisers over Mary's death, but chose the wrong actors in the drama. Mendoza in Paris reported to Philip II in late January that Burghley

says that although he had constantly shown himself openly against the Queen of Scotland, the earl of Leicester and secretary Walsingham, his enemies, had tried to set [Elizabeth] against him by saying that he was more devoted to [Mary] than anyone.

But she had seen certain papers in his coffers which had told greatly against Leicester and the queen had told the latter and Walsingham that they were a pair of knaves and she saw plainly now that, owing to her not having taken the advice of certain good and loyal subjects of hers, she was in peril of losing her throne and her life by having burdened herself with a war which she was unable to sustain or carry on.

She said if she had done her duty as a queen, she should have had them both hanged.[14]

In addition to Burghley and Walsingham, others were maintaining the pressure on the queen to authorise the execution. A document entitled *Reasons Touching the Execution of the Scottish Queen*, probably drawn up by Hatton during this period and clearly intended only for Elizabeth's eyes, lists ten cogent arguments why Mary should die:

1. Her majesty, in not executing justice upon the S[cottish] queen, shall foster and nourish the only hope which the Catholics have to re-establish their religion within this realm.

2. The S[cottish] queen's life cannot stand [continue] with her majesty's safety and the quiet estate of this realm being (as she is) the only ground [source] of all practices and attempts [conspiracies] both at home and abroad.

3. Mercy and pity (where impunity does not assuage but increase malice) is nothing else but *misericordia crudelis* [cruel compassion] but [with] the S[cottish] queen, experience teaches [us] that the more favour she receives, the more mischief she attempts.

4. When public health and necessity enforces a speedy execution (as in this case it does) there ought [to be] no respect of kindred, affection, honour ... whatsoever, to enforce the contrary; as being all of no account in regard of a matter so important as public necessity.

5. What dishonour or rather impiety were it, sparing the life of so grievous an offender, to hazard the lives of so many thousands of true subjects, being left to the spoil and revenge of so malicious a woman.

6. By taking away the S[cottish] queen's life, her majesty shall quench the malice of foreign princes who, notwithstanding they will not be quiet during her life, will never trouble themselves to revenge her death.

7. Her majesty, being a public person, is to have especial regard of a matter that imports [impacts] so greatly [on] both her own safety and the public state of her whole country.

8. The saying which politic men have so much respected without regard to justice, *mortui non mordent* ['the dead don't bite'] may well be used by her majesty in a case of so great and apparent justice.

9. Albeit there were some hope[s] of good success by sparing her life, yet wise men in doubtful cases have always allowed of this rule – *prudentius est timere quam sperare* ['it is more prudent to fear than to hope'].

10. If her majesty shall omit this occasion to take away so dangerous a person, when law and justice condemn her, there may hereafter

more dangerous practices [conspiracies] be attempted, when law and justice cannot take hold of her.[15]

But mere philosophical argument was not enough to galvanise Elizabeth's mind. To convince the queen of the need for execution, a sensational new plot to murder her was conveniently discovered that January.

It was a baffling affair that bears all the hallmarks of Walsingham's genius for both disinformation and timing. Despite his petulance at his less than gracious treatment by Elizabeth, despite his continued ill-health, his determination to destroy his old arch enemy was as strong as ever.

On 8 January, the French ambassador Châteauneuf was suddenly placed under house arrest in London, suspected of involvement in a new conspiracy to assassinate Elizabeth. William Stafford, the 'lewd, mis-contented' younger brother of Sir Edward, the English ambassador in Paris, had allegedly contacted Châteauneuf's secretary Leonard Des Trappes, offering to carry out a plan to kill the queen. It involved the recusant debtor Michael Moody (then a prisoner in Newgate, by order of the Archbishop of Canterbury), notoriously a 'discontented man and one that would do anything for money'. Elizabeth's death would be caused 'either by gunpowder or by poisoning her stirrup or her shoe or some other Italian device'.[16] Des Trappes allegedly dismissed these methods as mere 'fancies' and wished 'that there was such a man to be found in England as he that did the execution upon the Prince of Orange'.[17]

Both Stafford and Des Trappes[18] were thrown into the Tower and questioned. On 10 January, Elizabeth sent urgently for Thomas Phelippes 'to attend without fail' and to bring with him Châteauneuf's intercepted letters. The next day Stafford confessed to Walsingham, and Moody was questioned by Vice-Chamberlain Sir Christopher Hatton and Elizabeth's senior law officers, Attorney General Popham and Solicitor-General Egerton.

Moody was well briefed, with a script that must have been specially written to goad the queen into action over Mary. He told his interrogators that all hope was not yet past.

His meaning by these words was that the Scottish queen was still living and there was still hope of her life . . . William Stafford had declared to him that she should not die and that, he understood from the French ambassador here.

Stafford would deal with the princes of the Scots' queen's blood [guises] in France to procure money and other necessary provision . . . for some attempt against the queen's majesty.

On New Year's Eve, Stafford told him that the French ambassador said it was necessary that there should be more in the action for destroying her majesty and not to lay it upon two or three only.

Thereupon, Stafford said that his servant, Godson, was a tall fellow and a gentleman and was fit to be used in the matter.[19]

In light of the 'plot', the number of bodyguards around the queen was doubled as an extra security measure, an act no doubt intended to emphasise the grave peril she faced every day that Mary remained alive.

Châteauneuf angrily denied any involvement or, as Stafford claimed, giving his approval to the plan. There seems little doubt that Stafford was one of Walsingham's agents provocateurs[20] and it is perhaps significant that two years earlier he had acknowledged some kind of deep obligation to the spy master. In June 1585 he told Walsingham

I am as ever at your command and there is no man living to whom I am so beholden. If I should live to see my blood shed in your cause I should think it but some recompense for the great good I have received at your hands.[21]

Moody was also known to Walsingham – the spy master had paid him to carry letters between London and Paris in 1580–4.[22]

Whatever the origins of the plot, Châteauneuf could not conceal the fact that he had not immediately exposed the conspiracy to Elizabeth's government, as any ambassador of a friendly country would do. In reality, he knew it was a trap, albeit a risky one diplomatically for Walsingham. However, not only was the plot a useful psychological weapon for putting pressure on Elizabeth, it also effectively neutralised the French ambassador for a month during a critical period for her government. It is noteworthy that Des Trappes was later quietly released from the Tower, and after two months, when the danger was past, Elizabeth's government acknowledged that it had all been a terrible misunderstanding and sought to smooth the ruffled French feathers. The whole episode was, the spy master later told the ambassador, merely an attempt by Stafford to extort money.[23]

In case the Stafford 'conspiracy' was not enough, both Walsingham and Burghley cunningly spread a host of rumours designed to stiffen Elizabeth's resolve to finally rid herself and England of the threat posed by Mary Queen of Scots.[24] The Secretary's agents were tasked with spreading a web of misinformation to both inflame public opinion and cause general consternation amongst the loyal subjects of the realm. Philip II of Spain, it was rumoured, was building up stocks of artillery and military equipment at Lisbon, ready to use against England. The Duke of Parma was to mount an operation from the Low Countries to rescue the Scottish Queen from Fotheringay, or, in another more lurid version, to abduct Elizabeth herself. Worse still, the Duke of Guise had actually landed strong forces in Sussex and was marching on London, to coincide with an invasion from Scotland. There were other rumours that Mary herself had escaped.

But the campaign of misinformation rebounded on the government and came back to haunt them. Amid the fevered, plot-laden atmosphere in the dark corridors of Elizabeth's court, it must have frustrated and angered Walsingham and Burghley to continually receive messages reporting back the disturbing output of their own rumour machine, although some of the communications may have been symptomatic of the general anxiety and tension felt throughout the country at this time.

The Earl of Pembroke wrote on 31 January that talk of a Spanish force landing at Milford Haven was happily unfounded.[25] The jittery Mayor and Aldermen of Exeter, Devon, anxiously sent to Burghley on 3 February, enquiring urgently for instructions in the hue and cry to retake the Scottish Queen. The following day, 'at the hour of one in the night', they dispatched a messenger to the Privy Council, seeking the truth of reports that she had really escaped and that London had been set ablaze by England's enemies.[26] As late as 6 February, Sir Owen Hopton, Lieutenant of the Tower of London, reported his interrogation of one William Bellinger who had heard Alexander Payne, 'a goldsmith's boy', recount how Mary had escaped and been recaptured, but had broken her arm in the attempt. He also discussed the 'general opinion that the Scottish queen should not be put to death'.[27]

Unaware of the true nature of the government-inspired rumours, Paulet himself had heard the stories and wrote to the newly appointed Junior Secretary of State William Davison[28] on 30 January:

> You may perceive by these letters enclosed . . . that the report of the Scottish queen's escape or of her taking away, as it is now termed, carries such credit in these parts . . .
>
> These seditious rumours are not to be neglected, in my simple opinion, and indeed there is not a more ready way to levy forces to the achieving of that which these lewd reporters pretend to fear.
>
> I cannot let them flatter themselves with vain hope, but by the grace of God I will not lose this lady, my charge, without the loss of my own life, neither shall it be possible for any force to take her out of my hands alive.[29]

The rumours had also spread overseas. On 1 February, Walsingham received information from one of his 'intelligencers' in France, reporting that

> Many Romanists laugh at the report of the Scottish queen's escape but the French ambassador never thought her dead till now, supposing the rumour to be spread by policy. If she yet lives, she lives too long and threatens loss.
>
> If she be dead, the thing must be handled with severity with a show of grievous offence towards those who had charge of her and a search [instituted] throughout the realm as never a milk maid, especially in Northamptonshire, must be left unexamined, lest otherwise the subtle enemy discovers the [truth].[30]

As if to substantiate the climate of treachery, another of Walsingham's agents reported rumours that Paulet himself had murdered Mary: 'God grant this is true for she has lived too long: good Protestants blame the queen for waiting so long for God commanded that rulers should govern with great severity.'[31]

He was closer to reality than he could have imagined.

Elizabeth, now desperate to avoid having Mary's royal blood on her hands, considered ordering her assassination to escape having to sign the death warrant herself. The still, small voice of conscience was never a factor in her thinking. To her, employing the law of the land to kill another queen struck at the very concept of the divine right of kings. She knew full well that such an action potentially had awesome political ramifications for her and her successors on the throne of England.[32] She sought solitude to wrestle with her uncertainty and was reportedly heard to mutter to herself: '*Aut fer, aut feri: ne feriare, feri*' – 'Either suffer to strike, not to be struck, strike'.

The queen somehow at long last steeled herself and signed the death warrant on 1 February at Greenwich, summoning Davison into the palace from the park, where he was taking the air, to fetch the document from his chamber.

After reading it 'she called for pen and ink, signed it and laying it from her, demanded [of Davison] whether I were not heartily sorry to see it done'. After some discussion, Elizabeth, 'with smiling countenance', asked him what other documents he had for her to sign, which 'it pleased her with the best disposition and willingness that might be to dispatch them all'. She instructed him to have the Lord Chancellor, Sir Thomas Bromley, set the Great Seal upon the death warrant and also to inform Walsingham of her action. The spy master was still away from court, now recovering from his illness at his London home in Seething Lane, and Elizabeth joked, with heavy irony, that the news would cause him 'grief . . . [to] go near to kill him outright'.[33] Then she stopped Davison dead in his tracks as he bowed out of her presence, suddenly complaining that Paulet and others 'might have eased her of this burden'.

He immediately guessed what she meant by this euphemism. She wanted Paulet to murder the Scottish queen.

Davison argued against such a plan, knowing full well the honesty and integrity of Paulet, 'whom I thought would not do so unlawful an act for any respect in the world, yet finding her desirous to have the matter attempted, I promised for her satisfaction to signify this, her pleasure, to Mr Secretary'.[34]

Walsingham wrote to Paulet later that day, mincing no words about Elizabeth's desire for him to assassinate Mary:[35]

> We find by speech lately uttered by her majesty that she notes in you a lack of that care and zeal of her service that she looks for at your hands, in that you have not in all this time . . . *found out some way to shorten the life of that queen, considering the great peril she is subject unto hourly so long as the said queen shall live* [author's italics].
>
> Wherein, besides a kind of lack of love towards her, she notes greatly that you have not that care of your own particular safeties or rather of the preservation of religion and the public good and prosperity of your country that reason and policy commands . . .
>
> She takes it more unkindly towards her that men professing that love towards her that you do, should in any kind of sort, for lack of the discharge of your duties, cast the burden upon her, knowing as you do, her indisposition to shed blood, especially of one of that sex and quality, and so near to her in blood as the said queen is.
>
> These respects we find do greatly trouble her majesty . . . We thought it very meet to acquaint [you] with these speeches lately passed from her majesty, referring the same to your good judgements.[36]

In a covering letter, Davison urged Paulet to destroy the communication: 'I pray let this and the enclosed be committed to the fire, which measure shall be likewise meet to your answer, after it has been communicated to her majesty for her satisfaction.'

Paulet received Walsingham's bombshell letter at five o'clock the following afternoon at Fotheringay. Within the hour, he wrote an indignant reply from both himself and his assistant Sir Dru Drury:

> I would not fail according to your directions to return my answer with all possible speed which shall deliver to you . . . great grief and

bitterness of mind, in that I am so unhappy to have lived to see this unhappy day, [when] I am required by direction from my most gracious sovereign to do an act which God and the law forbids.

My good living and life are at her majesty's disposition and [I] am ready . . . to lose them this next morrow if it shall please her . . .

But God forbid that I should make so foul a shipwreck of my conscience, or leave so great a blot to my poor posterity, [as] to shed blood without law or warrant.[37]

Although the letter was signed by both Paulet and Drury, it is clear from the tumbling, anguished words that the former was the author. Indeed, in a postscript, Paulet adds that his assistant 'subscribes in his heart to my opinion'. Fearing that his reaction would anger the queen, the last portion of the letter is an anxious appeal to her good nature:

Trusting that her Majesty, of her accustomed clemency, will take this, my dutiful answer in good part . . . as proceeding from one who will never be inferior to any Christian subject living in duty, honour, love and obedience towards his sovereign.

Later, when the Privy Council clerk Robert Beale was at Fotheringay, he heard talk of Elizabeth's desire to murder Mary, with one 'Wingfield'[38] chosen to do the deed. The queen pretended that the Scottish ambassador Archibald Douglas had suggested assassination as a suitable solution and that the Earl of Leicester had supported the idea.[39] But 'both the secretaries misliked [it]' and certainly, the belief in Elizabeth's government was that Mary should die openly, in contrast to earlier slain monarchs like Edward II and Richard II.[40] Paulet's letter would have come as no shock to Walsingham: he knew the Puritan and his godly ways well enough to believe that he would not stoop to administering poison, or wielding the assassin's knife, to rid Elizabeth of her unwelcome decision.

Despite his queen's arch and less than subtle hints regarding what for her would be the quick, easy and more palatable outcome, Walsingham was convinced that a judicial execution was the only route to take. On 2 February, probably even before Paulet received his electrifying letter,

he sat down quietly to draw up a memorandum about the official arrangements that had to be made for the execution of Mary at Fotheringay.[41]
We can only speculate on the thoughts that ran through his mind as he
scribbled across the parchment in his untidy, spindly writing. So much
of his official life had been concerned with thwarting the Scottish queen's
machinations and foiling the conspiracies inspired by her presence in
England. His own royal mistress had constantly ignored his warnings
of the dangers she posed to her. Now Mary was entrapped in a net he
had woven for her and the threat to the English crown would soon be
neutralised.

Walsingham was never anything but methodical. His two pages of
notes coldly and calculatingly lay down the critical path to the axeman's
block. Once completed, he sent the document off by special messenger
to Burghley to review and to add his own comments. Always conscious of
the importance of propaganda, the Secretary suggested that speeches
should be specially written for the Earls of Kent and Shrewsbury to make
at the execution. These are Burghley's comments on their content, which
he scribbled alongside Walsingham's proposals:

> To express her many attempts both for destruction of the queen's
> person and the invasion of this realm; that the hope and comforts
> she has given to the principal traitors of this realm, both abroad and
> here at home . . .
>
> All the attempts that have been against her majesty's person,
> and so confessed and yet do continue, so as sure by the laws of God
> and man, she is justly condemned to die.
>
> The whole realm has often times vehemently required that
> justice might be done, which her majesty can not longer delay.

Walsingham also urged that only Mary's 'chief officers and servants'
should attend her on the scaffold, 'excluding the women'; he wanted to
avoid emotional outbursts that might disrupt the gruesome proceedings. He also suggested giving the earls precise instructions regarding
what they should do in the event of Mary wanting 'private speech' with her
servants – Walsingham was clearly anxious that no secret instructions, no

damaging testament to Mary's memory should be smuggled out of the great hall at Fotheringay. Burghley added: 'Not to refuse it, [but be limited] to three or two at the least.' The fewer people involved, the easier the interrogation of them afterwards. Indeed, the Secretary goes on: 'Her servants, both Scottish and French to be stayed [held] for a time in this realm,' to which Burghley adds in the margin: 'To remain also in the castle until further order.' Moreover, Paulet should ensure that the stronghold's gates were firmly locked.

Walsingham then moved on to the grim practicalities. 'The body to be buried in the night in the parish church in such uppermost place as by the two earls shall be thought fit.' He queried whether it should be embalmed. Then:

> To send down the sheriff of Northampton, if he be here.
>
> The executioner to be sent down.
>
> To take order that her jewels and plate may not be embezzled by her servants.

Here Burghley added: '[Andrew] Melville [Mary's steward] and her principal women [must] be acquainted therewith and their seals to be put to the cases etc.' Finally, in an astonishingly cynical attempt to ensure that no unwelcome, last-minute reprieve came from Elizabeth, Walsingham added: 'The lords at the court to give out that there will be no execution.' Burghley underlined the three words 'at the court' to emphasise his agreement and his shared anxiety about the prospect of an eleventh-hour reprieve.

Later that day, the Lord Treasurer received the signed and sealed death warrant, personally delivered by Davison.[42] He decided to act quickly to avoid giving the fretful queen any further time, or opportunity, to change her mind again.

The next day, 3 February, despite a painful injury received in a riding accident two weeks earlier, Burghley convened a special Privy Council meeting, called solely on his own authority in his chamber at Greenwich. Burghley proposed, and the other Councillors unanimously agreed, to dispatch the warrant to Fotheringay without telling Elizabeth, together with the Council's special instructions to Henry, Earl of Kent, and the Earl Marshal, George, Earl of Shrewsbury, appointed by Elizabeth to super-intend the execution.[43] It was neither 'fit nor convenient to trouble her majesty any further', they decided, a telling indication of their rampant fears that Elizabeth would think of 'some new concept of interrupting and staying the course of justice'.[44] The documents were signed at two o'clock and Robert Beale, clerk to the Privy Council, was ordered to deliver the warrant to Paulet, as well as briefing the two earls on their grim duties, under the disguise of a special commission to investigate the still-troublesome hues and cries in Hertfordshire and Bedfordshire. The warrant probably reached Fotheringay on 5 February.

The two-and-a-half-page document is full of explanations – almost excuses – for the need to judicially kill Mary. Finally, it directs Shrews-bury, Kent and three other peers

> as soon as you have time convenient, to repair to our castle of
> Fotheringay where the said Queen of Scots is in custody of our right
> trusty servant and counsellor Sir Amyas Paulet, and then taking her
> into your charge to cause by your commandment, execution to be
> laid upon her person in the presence of yourselves and the said Sir
> Amyas Paulet . . .
>
> The same to be done in such manner and form and at such
> time and place there and by such persons as to you, five, four, three
> or two of you shall be thought by your discretions convenient
> notwithstanding any law, statute or ordinance to the contrary.[45]

The Privy Council's instructions to Kent also included an exhortation to keep the matter strictly covert:

> Your lordship shall understand by this bearer [Beale] how needful it
> is to have the proceeding herein to be kept very secret and upon
> what occasion no more of the lords in commission are at this time
> used herein.[46]

Davison meanwhile was still worrying about the fate of the incrim-inating 'assassination' letter written to Paulet. The same day, he sent a note to Mary's keeper repeating his earnest entreaties to destroy all the correspondence, adding:

> I pray you let me hear what you have done with my letters because they are not fit to be kept, that I may satisfy her majesty therein, who might take offence thereat and if you [deal] with this postscript in the same manner, you will not err a whit.[47]

In the event, the cautious Paulet carried the originals with him to London, leaving, perhaps as a wise precaution given the political climate and the tensions at court, copies with his family in case he was arrested. On 8 February, he replied to Davison:

> If I should say that I have burned the papers you [wrote] of, I cannot tell if everybody would believe me and therefore I reserve them to be delivered to your own hands at my coming to London. God Bless you and prosper all your actions to His glory.[48]

Walsingham now had other things to worry about. On 4 February, Elizabeth smilingly told Davison that she had been troubled the previous night by a dream that Mary had been executed. Her words must have sent a shiver of terror and trepidation down his back. Had she somehow learnt of that secret Privy Council meeting, convened behind closed doors? Did another of her infamous rages lurk behind that beguiling smile? He nervously asked whether she did not intend to 'go through' with the execution, according to the warrant. 'Her answer was "yes" confirmed with a solemn oath [with] some vehemence . . . She thought that it might have received a better form, because this threw the whole burden upon herself.'[49]

The next morning the queen heard of Paulet's refusal to assassinate the Scottish queen. She now threw a terrible tantrum, worthy of any testy Tudor monarch, complaining of the 'niceties of these precise fellows, who in words would do great things for her surety, but in deed perform nothing'.[50] As she angrily swept up and down the gallery at Greenwich, Elizabeth petulantly said she could 'have it well enough done without them', naming 'one Wingfield' who, she assured Davison, 'would with

some others undertake it'. He told the queen that if Paulet and Drury
had murdered Mary, they would have exposed themselves to 'great
extremity':

> If in a tender care of her surety, they should have been what she
> desire, she must either allow their act or disallow it.
>
> If she allowed it, she took the matter upon herself, with her
> infinite peril and dishonour.
>
> If she disallowed it, she should not only overthrow the
> gentlemen themselves, but also their estates and posterities.[51]

But in truth, Elizabeth knew her law. And the law of England was very
clear, whether for the highest or lowest in the realm. Mary Queen of
Scots could not legally be killed unless her death was sanctioned by a
death warrant issued under the Great Seal of England. Without that,
Paulet and Drury would be common murderers, their lives, estates and
possessions immediately forfeit to the crown. Even Elizabeth, in this,
her darkest moment of rage and frustration, could see the injustice of
that.

Walsingham pressed grimly on with the arrangements for Mary's
judicial murder. One of his servants, Anthony Hall, interviewed the
notorious Bull, the expert public executioner employed at the Tower of
London, at his dwelling outside Bishopsgate in the City of London. He
agreed a price of £10 (or £1,560 in today's prices) for beheading Mary.
The Secretary then sought to lodge Bull with his brother-in-law Sir Walter
Mildmay, the Chancellor of the Exchequer, at his home at Apthorpe just
three miles north-west of Fotheringay, and therefore convenient for the
execution. But Sir Walter 'misliked' the idea of putting up such a socially
unacceptable guest and the headsman and his assistant were eventually
accommodated 'in an inn at Fotheringay', their presence 'kept secret
until the day'.[52] Walsingham also warned Paulet of Bull's arrival:

> I send down the executioner [escorted] by [a] trusty servant of mine
> [George Digby] who will be at Fotheringay sometime upon Sunday
> night.

His instrument [the axe] is put into a trunk and he passes as a
serving man.

There is great care taken to have the matter pass in secrecy.

Sometime after dinner on Tuesday 7 February, Beale, having collected
and briefed Henry Grey and George Talbot, the Earls of Kent and Shrewsbury, arrived with them at the castle of Fotheringay. Escorted by Paulet
and Drury, they went upstairs to Mary's apartments to tell her of her
impending execution. The death warrant was read out. She was remarkably calm – but then a frown crossed her brow. Remembering her English
history, she enquired politely whether she would be murdered as Richard
II had been in Pontefract Castle in 1400.[53] Sir Dru Drury, who had only
days earlier received that outrageous letter containing Elizabeth's dark
suggestions as to Mary's fate, told her: 'Madam, you need not fear it, for
that you are in charge of a Christian Queen.' A heavy sense of irony must
have almost overwhelmed him as he uttered these reassuring words.

The Scottish queen then turned to the two earls:

I do not think the queen, my sister, would have consented to my
death, [as I] am not subject to your law and jurisdiction.

But, seeing her pleasure so, death shall be to me most welcome,
neither is that soul worthy of the high and everlasting joys above,
whose body cannot endure one stroke of the executioner.

I thank you for such welcome news. You will do me a great
good in withdrawing me from this world, out of which I am very
glad to go . . .

I am of no good and of no use to anyone.[54]

Mary devoutly crossed and blessed herself and added: 'I am quite ready
and very happy to die and to shed my blood for Almighty God, my Saviour
and my Creator and for the Catholic Church and to maintain its rights
in this country.' She asked if she could talk to her almoner, confessor
and Andrew Melville, her steward. The almoner, Camille de Préau, was
denied her, and the staunchly Protestant Kent told her: 'Your life will be
the death of our religion, as contrariwise, your death will be the life
thereof.'[55]

She ate a small supper, drank to her servants' health and prayed privately for more than an hour. Then she wrote out her will in French, naming her cousin Henry, Duke of Guise, James Beaton, Archbishop of Glasgow, and John Leslie, Bishop of Ross, amongst her executors, and asking that her body should be buried in France.[56] At around two o'clock in the morning she wrote her last letter – to her brother-in-law Henry III, king of France – in her best italic hand, three pages in the fashionable, neat Italian style:

Royal brother, having by God's will, for my sins, I think, thrown myself into the power of the queen my cousin, at whose hands I have suffered much for almost twenty years, I have finally been condemned to death by her and her estates . . .

Tonight, after dinner, I have been advised of my sentence. I am to be executed as a criminal at eight o'clock in the morning.

I have not had enough time to give you a full account of everything that has happened but if you will listen to my physician[57] and my other unfortunate servants, you will learn the truth and how, thanks be to God, I scorn death and vow that I face it innocent of any crime, even if I were their subject.

The Catholic faith and the defence of the rights, which God has given me to this [English] crown are the two reasons why I am condemned.

Yet, I fear they will not permit me to say that I die for my religion, for fear of interference with theirs. As a proof of it, they have taken from me my chaplain, who though he is in the house, I cannot obtain leave for him to come and confess me and give me the Communion at my death but they are very pressing that I should receive comfort and instruction from their minister, brought here for that purpose.

I beg you as a Most Christian Majesty, my brother-in-law and my oldest ally, who has always protested your love for me . . . to reward my unfortunate servants by leaving them their wages and . . . [to] offer prayers to God for a queen who has borne the name of

Most Christian and dies a Catholic, stripped of all her possessions.

I have taken the liberty of sending you two precious stones of rare virtue, talismans against illness, trusting that you may enjoy good health, and a long and happy life . . .

For the sake of Jesus Christ, to whom I shall pray for you tomorrow as I die, I be left enough to found a memorial Mass and give the customary alms.[58]

She signed it: 'Your most loving and most true sister, Mary R.'

Mary managed to get a few hours' sleep but was awakened by her ladies at six o' clock. She dressed carefully in a black satin dress over a bodice of crimson velvet, her sombre appearance only relieved by a flowing long white linen veil fastened to her head beneath a cap of white cambric. Her household was summoned to her presence, her will read out and committed to her physician Dominique Bourgoing for safekeeping. Prayers were said, amid the weeping of her women.

Shortly after eight, the two earls and Andrews, the sheriff, knocked loudly on the outer door of her privy chamber. The time had come for her to die.

There were more tears, more prayers, many more farewells. Then Mary's procession to the scaffold formed up and left her apartments.

In the ground-floor ante-room to the great hall of Fotheringay Castle, her steward Andrew Melville awaited her on his knees, his face also puckered by tears. Supported by two soldiers, Mary paused and told him:

Lament not but rather rejoice. By and by, you shall see Mary Stuart freed from all her cares. Good servant, all the world is but vanity and subject still to more sorrow than a whole ocean of tears can bewail.

Tell them that I die a true woman to my religion and like a true woman of Scotland and France.

But God forgive them that have long desired my end and thirsted for my blood as the hart the water brooks.[59]

Turning to the two earls, she asked for 'womanhood's sake' that her 'poor distressed servants' could attend the execution, 'that their eyes might behold and their hearts might be witnesses how patiently their queen and majesty should endure' death.

Kent immediately turned down her request, fearing trouble from her household or that her servants might 'put some superstitious trumpery [into] practice . . . In dipping their handkerchiefs in your grace's blood whereof it were very unmeet for us to give allowance'.

Mary burst into hopeless tears once again and for a terrible moment her escorts feared they would have to drag her, screaming, to her place of execution next door in the great hall. After a hurried whispered consultation, the earls agreed that she could choose 'half a dozen of her best loved men and women' to accompany her. Mary, drying her eyes, chose Melville, her surgeon Jacques Gervais, the apothecary Pierre Gorion 'and one other old man',[60] together with her two favourite gentlewomen, Elizabeth Curle and Jane Kennedy.[61] '*Allons* done. Now let us go,' said the Scottish queen, her composure swiftly recovered after her bout of histrionics.

The scene that confronted her was dominated by the scaffold – a black-draped, five-foot-high wooden stage, twelve feet wide, built alongside a large fireplace in which a huge log fire blazed against the raw, damp chill of the morning.[62] A high wooden chair had been placed in one corner of its straw-strewn floor, but all eyes were quickly drawn to the squat block positioned at the opposite corner of the platform. The axe, the instrument of Mary's destruction, was casually propped up against the eighteen-inch-high rail that ran around three sides of the scaffold. The executioner Bull and his assistant, both masked and dressed in black gowns with white aprons, awaited their victim to one side. Despite the arrangements to keep the execution secret, word of what was happening had quickly spread locally. The hall was crowded with spectators of quality – the local gentry and their neighbours from adjacent counties – come to see a page of history written that morning. The hoi polloi, probably more than a thousand strong, waited shoulder to shoulder outside in the cold courtyard of the castle's lower bailey.

Mary slowly climbed the low steps to the scaffold, a soldier on each arm to assist her, and sat down on the high-backed chair. Robert Beale read out the death warrant and the loyal onlookers dutifully cried out, 'God save the queen.' Mary listened silently as if the dread words had not concerned her at all – 'nay with so merry and cheerful a countenance as if it had been a pardon from her majesty for her life',[63] according to one onlooker.

Richard Fletcher, Dean of Peterborough,[64] then stepped forward to administer to the Scottish queen's soul. 'Madam,' he began politely,

The queen's most excellent majesty . . . standing this preparation for the execution of justice justly to be done upon you for your many trespasses against her sacred person, [and] state, a tender care upon your soul which presently departing out of your body must either be separated in the true faith of Christ, do offer you the comfortable promises of Almighty God to all penitent believing Christians . . .

As he continued with his long and rather pompous Protestant dissertation, Mary interrupted him two or three times.

Mr Dean! Trouble not yourself nor me, for know that I am settled in the ancient Catholic and Roman religion and in defence thereof, I mean, by God's help, to spend my blood.

What was intended as a pious sermon had suddenly lapsed into an unseemly religious debate. Fletcher was forced to abandon his discourse and, kneeling, began to pray aloud. But he was again interrupted by Mary, saying her own prayers in Latin, the tears pouring down her face, with her six servants on the scaffold joining in, louder and louder, intentionally trying to drown out the dean's words. She slipped weakly, painfully from her chair and slumped down onto her knees, and continued, now in English, praying for 'Christ's afflicted church; for an end to her troubles, for her son [James VI] that he might truly and uprightly be converted to the Roman Catholic church' and, rather cheekily, for Elizabeth, 'that she may long and peacefully prosper and serve God aright'.[65] It was a scene of pure tragedy, an act of high theatre – as she had intended it to be. Clasping her ivory crucifix to her bosom, she begged the saints to intercede for her soul and that God, in his mercy and goodness, might avert his plagues from England, 'this silly island'.[66]

This was all too much for the devout Kent, sitting behind her. 'Madam,' he said earnestly, 'I beseech you: settle Christ in your heart . . . and leave the addition of these Popish trumperies to themselves.' Mary flatly ignored him and continued her prayers, milking the inherently powerful drama of the occasion for all she was worth.

Bull the executioner and his assistant, menacing and sinister in their black masks, then stepped forward and knelt before her, making their traditional request for the victim's forgiveness for what they were about to inflict upon her. The Scottish queen told the axeman: 'I forgive you with all my heart, for I hope that this death shall give me an end to all my troubles.'[67]

Helped by her two weeping ladies, Elizabeth Curle and Jane Kennedy, the executioner then began to disrobe Mary. Bull lifted the *Agnus Dei* medallion from around her neck, as custom asserted that he could claim all valuables worn by the queen on the scaffold as his own property, as part of his professional fee. It was just one of the perks of the job. She swiftly stopped him, saying it would be given to one of her women as a gift. Now smiling, Mary remarked dryly that she 'never had such grooms before to make her ready, nor ever did put off her clothes before such a company'. She stripped down to her petticoat, and as this was revealed, there came an astonished and horrified gasp in the crowded hall.

Mary Queen of Scots was now dressed all in blood-red satin – the universally acknowledged colour of Catholic death or martyrdom.

She quickly knelt down on the cushion placed in front of the block, without 'the least token of the fear of death', and Jane Kennedy took out a white cloth embroidered in gold with the Corpus Christi. She kissed it, folded it three ways into a neat triangle and tied it over her mistress's eyes as a blindfold. Mary prayed, using the words of the *Te Deum* taken from Psalm 30: '*In te Domino confido me confundar in eternum*' – 'In thee, O Lord, I put my trust. Let me never be confounded' – and groped forward, reaching out for the foot-high wooden block, finally laying her head and neck in the hollowed recess. Bull's assistant removed her hands from the block and she stretched out her arms and legs, crying out 'three or four times': *'In manus tuas, Domine, commendo spiritum meum'* – 'Into thy hands, O Lord, I commend my spirit.'

It was now around eleven o'clock. A breathless silence fell in the hall. Shrewsbury signalled to the executioner.

The moment of Mary's death had finally come.

Bull lifted his axe high above his head for the fatal strike and brought down the weapon with the full force of his considerable weight behind it.

His blow was misaimed. The blade hit the knot of the blindfold and, glancing off, cut deeply into the back of Mary's skull. The Scottish queen made 'a very small noise' but did not move.

Bull's second strike severed her head from her neck, apart from 'a very little gristle'. Crouching over her, he hastily shortened his grip on the heavy axe to finally slash through the last remaining sinews, using it like a butcher's cleaver to finish his grisly task.[68] He then picked up the severed head by the pinned cap and, straightening up, cried out in a loud voice: 'God save the queen!'[69]

Suddenly, shockingly, the head fell from his grasp, leaving him dumbly holding only her white cap and her auburn curls in his gory hands. Mary had been wearing a wig, and her bloody head now rolled across the scaffold, very grey and nearly bald. Horribly, her lips continued to move soundlessly, as if she was trying to speak. The nerves in her dead face were twitching still.

Robert Wingfield, who earlier may have been earmarked to assassinate the Scottish queen, was watching in the packed hall. He reported:

> Her dressing [cap] of lawn fell from her head, which appeared grey as if she had been seventy years old, cut very short . . . Her lips stirred up and down [for] almost a quarter of an hour after her head was cut off.[70]

Mary had largely dictated the grim proceedings throughout and even after death she had destroyed her adversaries' moment of triumph with another telling piece of theatre. A stunned and speechless Shrewsbury helplessly burst into tears.

The dazed silence was at last broken by Fletcher, the Dean of Peterborough, stepping forward and shouting: 'So perish all the queen's enemies!' – bravely echoed by Kent: 'Such be the end of all the queen's and the Gospel's enemies!'

The hall was quickly cleared of spectators, some exultant, some cowed by what they had witnessed. Mary's weeping household were shepherded under guard to their quarters and locked in. Bull and his assistant began to strip her body but found her small pet Skye terrier Geddon, hiding amongst her blood-soaked clothes. It 'would not be gotten forth but without force and afterward would not depart from the corpse but came and lay between her head and shoulders ... The same dog, being imbued in her blood, was carried away and washed.'[71]

All her clothes and belongings that were covered in blood were burnt outside on a huge bonfire, together with the black cotton hangings from the scaffold – to avoid any scrap being used as a sacred relic of her death. Walsingham wanted no trappings of martyrdom to survive for use as a rallying point for future conspiracies.

The body, crudely wrapped in the baize stripped from her confiscated billiard table,[72] was taken upstairs on a stretcher for embalming by a physician from the nearby town of Stamford, assisted by two surgeons. Her heart and other organs were secretly buried within the castle by Andrews, the Sheriff of Northamptonshire.[73]

News of Mary's death was taken to the court by Henry Talbot, Shrewsbury's fourth son, with strict instructions to hand over the official reports of what had happened only to the Privy Councillors.

The businesslike Paulet, writing to Walsingham later that day, enclosed a lengthy inventory of Mary's possessions – plate, hangings and 'other household stuff'.

All the best stuff was removed from hence yesterday under the conduct of some of my servants, praying you to signify forthwith to my servant Robert Hacksaw remaining in London, in what place there the said plate and other stuff shall be discharged.

The jewels, plate and other goods belonging to the late Queen of Scots were already divided into many parts before the receipt of your letters . . . the whole company (saving Kennedy and Curle's sister) affirming that they have nothing to show for these things from their mistress in writing and that all the smaller things were delivered by her own hands.

I have, according to your direction, committed the custody of the said jewels, plate and other stuff to Mr Melville, the physician and Mrs Kennedy, one of the gentlewomen.[74]

The following morning, Burghley decided it was 'not fit to break suddenly to her majesty' the news of Mary's execution, and he kept it from Elizabeth all that day. However, she heard of Mary's death that evening 'by other means' and took it quietly enough, but having a whole night to work herself into a torrent of righteous indignation, she sent for Sir Christopher Hatton early the next morning. As Davison reported, she 'fell into some heat and passion' and denied having commanded or intended the execution, 'casting the burden generally upon them all, but chiefly upon my shoulders'. She told him angrily that 'I had, in suffering it [the death warrant] to go out of my hands, abused the trust she reposed in me.'[75]

Outside, in stark contrast, Protestant London rejoiced at the news of Mary's death. Bells were rung joyfully in all the towers of the city churches for twenty-four hours and bonfires were lit in the streets at every crossroads.[76]

Elizabeth's Councillors had fully anticipated her ritual tantrum and warned Davison to absent himself from court for a day or two, to allow time for the regal rage to blow itself out. He was compelled to be away regardless because of 'an unhappy accident [which had] befallen me the day before, together with some indisposition of my health at that time'. Truly a well-timed diplomatic illness! But Elizabeth needed a scapegoat and now had Davison firmly in her sights.

I returned home where the next news I heard was that her majesty resolved to commit me to the Tower; which at the first seemed a matter very strange to me and such as I could by no means believe until my lord Buckhurst came with orders from her majesty to execute this her pleasure, which by reason of my sickness was deferred for two or three days and afterwards on the fourteenth of this month accomplished.[77]

On 12 February, a chastened Privy Council tried, rather pathetically, to rationalise and explain their actions to a still incandescent Elizabeth. Two rough drafts of their obsequious and remorseful letters to her survive, bearing Burghley's holograph. It remains uncertain whether either was sent. If they were, the letters would have seemed, at the very least, over-anxious in their protestations of innocence to the queen.

The first described England's domestic situation as

every hour grow[ing] daily more and more dangerous . . . whilst the Queen of Scots was suffered to live.

This danger we found even at our daily meeting to increase upon the universal hourly hues and cries with rising of multitudes of people in arms in all corners of the realm and sundry of them concerning the Queen of Scots, whereof we had cause to fear that some great treasons were hid under these stirs and that the Queen of Scots might by force . . . be recovered out of the place where she was and her majesty be brought thereby into great danger.

We thought it our most bounden duty and that we were charged in our consciences after God not to delay the proceedings . . . and therefore perceiving that it pleased almighty God to incline her mind to sign a commission lawfully devised and being showed to us by Mr Davison under her hand and Great Seal of England, whereby, according to honour and justice, the said great dangers might be prevented and her majesty's life surely continued and preserved, we did with one mind conclude it was most necessary to use all secrecy herein and to delay no time for fear of greater danger.[78]

So why was Elizabeth kept in the dark about the instructions for the execution? The Councillors pleaded that

it was thought by us all unwell to acquaint her majesty with the
form and circumstances for the time and manner of the doing . . .
presuming it for diverse causes not convenient to trouble her
majesty therewith . . .

They did not elaborate on these 'diverse causes'. These were hardly convincing explanations and they were far from enough to quell the royal
rage.

The second draft is much more repentant, much more contrite, and
written after they had been told that Elizabeth's fury had made her ill. It
seems likely she had suffered some form of nervous collapse, refused
food and sleep was denied her.[79]

> We, your born, bound and sworn servants and counsellors . . . do
> most lowly, humbly and sorrowfully pray and beseech your majesty
> that you will suspend your heavy censure against us until we may
> declare the intention of our late counsels for the orderly removal of
> the danger of your life and the manner of our proceeding therein.
>
> And in the meantime, to the bottom of our hearts, we confess
> that we are most heartily sorry to hear that your majesty is so deeply
> grieved in your mind as thereby your health, the maintenance of
> your life, must needs be hindered and the present government of
> your state, being now environed with many difficulties or rather
> dangers for lack of your favourable audience to be given to us, must
> needs receive great detriment and hardly to be recovered.[80]

Robert Beale, the agent of the Privy Council, was less repentant. 'I thought
that I ought to fulfil the order,' he wrote.

> I was the queen's servant and bound to obey her. If, in those cir-
> cumstances, the queen had been exposed to some danger, it would
> have been my fault. I was convinced that her safety depended upon
> the death of the Queen of Scotland [and] I found sufficient warrant
> in an order signed by herself.[81]

Elizabeth, however, was not going to be placated and was looking for retribution amongst more senior members of her government. On 13 February, Walsingham pleaded with the Lord Treasurer to intervene with the queen on his friend Davison's behalf: 'I beseech you to use all means to remove her majesty's heavy displeasure from Mr Secretary Davison.'[82]

But he was too late. Davison was sent to the Tower.

Burghley was the next to feel the full weight of the queen's ire. She refused to see him, refused even to read his letters – although they were filled with a torrent of self-deprecating remorse. One pleaded that the Lord Treasurer might 'be laid upon the floor near your majesty's foot' to soak up 'some drops of your mercy to quench my sorrowful panting heart'.[83] After almost three decades of faithful service, her Chief Minister had fallen perilously from grace.

On February 14, Elizabeth wrote to Mary's son, James VI of Scotland, astonishingly denying any part in the execution of his mother. She began:

> My dear brother: I would you knew, though felt not, the extreme dolour that overwhelms my mind for that miserable accident which, far contrary to my meaning has befallen . . .
>
> I beseech you that as God and many more know how innocent I am in this case . . .
>
> For your part, think you have not in the world a more loving kinswoman nor a dearer friend than myself, nor any that will watch more carefully to preserve you and your estate.[84]

The queen also sent Sir Richard Wigmore to Scotland 'on secret employment'. His mission was to discover James's private feelings, 'divert him from all thoughts of revenging his mother's death', induce him to resolutely profess his Protestant faith and depend upon Elizabeth and England's friendship rather than any other potentate.[85]

Mendoza heard news of the execution in Paris on 28 February and dashed off a quick dispatch to his master, King Philip II. He claimed that a Privy Council cabal had forced Elizabeth to sign the death warrant by threatening that Parliament would otherwise refuse to approve funds for the war in Holland.

As Secretary Walsingham was ill, this warrant was taken to the queen for her signature by Davison and after she signed it she ordered him not to give it to anyone unless she gave him personally her authority to do so.

Davison, who is a terrible heretic and an enemy of the Queen of Scotland, like the rest . . . delivered the warrant to them.

They took a London executioner and sent him with the warrant to the justice of the county where the queen was. The moment the justice received it, he entered the Queen of Scotland's chamber with Paulet and Lord Grey who had charge of her, and there they had her head cut off with a hatchet in the presence of the four persons only . . .

They did not even give her time to commend her soul to God . . . [Elizabeth] the queen orders her ambassador to inform this king [Henry III] of it and assure him, as she will more fully by a special envoy, that the deed was done against her will. Although she had signed the death warrant, she had no intention of having it carried out.

She cannot avoid blaming herself for having trusted anyone but herself in such a matter.[86]

Mendoza's informant was Sir Edward Stafford, the English ambassador in Paris. Here, then, is Elizabeth's own version, her own 'spin', on these tragic events, for diplomatic consumption. At home, her rage against her government ministers and advisers had to be public to be believed. By now feeling somewhat better, she enquired of her learned judges whether her royal prerogative could be used to hang the wretched Davison without the tiresome formality of a trial. A cornered and panic-stricken Burghley sent a messenger with a desperate civil servant's appeal to them to consider their advice to the queen very carefully: 'I think it is a hard time if men, for doing well before God and man, shall be otherwise punished than law may warrant with an opinion gotten from the judges that her prerogative is above the law.'[87]

But Elizabeth was not to be moved in her righteous anger at what she saw as a betrayal of her trust. She eventually referred Davison's case to the Court of Star Chamber, where he appeared on 28 March, accused of dire disobedience in issuing the death warrant and of concealing the proceedings from her. He was inevitably found guilty of misprision,[88] fined the huge sum of 10,000 marks (or £1,080,000 in today's monetary values) – 'too much for Davison, yet little for his offence'[89] – and returned smartly to the Tower to be detained there at the queen's pleasure. In the event, Elizabeth having firmly and publicly made her point, the fine was never imposed and Davison was released nineteen months later after a letter from Burghley and Walsingham to Sir Owen Hopton, Lieutenant of the Tower, ordered that Davison be moved 'in a secret manner' to private custody.[90] He was never employed in royal service again, but continued to draw his salary as Secretary of State and, thanks to Walsingham's influence, continued to receive some of his official perks.

Burghley also remained out in the cold. The queen's fury against the Lord Treasurer was increased, like petrol being poured onto a fire, by the dispatches sent to London by Stafford in Paris regarding the anger felt there at Mary's death; so much so that Walsingham ordered him to stop sending them, for his reports 'increased the more her majesty's offence against her Council'. On 15 March, after she condescended to receive Burghley but had immediately fallen into another rage, the Lord Treasurer wrote to the queen:

> I am so wounded in the heart with the late sharp and piercing speeches of her majesty to myself in the hearing of my lord of Leicester and Mr Secretary Walsingham, expressing therewith her indignation, at such time as I was called to her presence for matters of the Low Countries; myself giving no occasion by any speech of the matter of the queen of Scots, until her majesty did charge me therewith as since regarding, in great anguish of heart, the weight of her majesty's displeasure so settled and increased . . .
>
> I have certainly felt of long time many sharp effects for doing my duty, yet now being so publicly, in town, in court, and field known, as I daily find it, her majesty is so grievously offended with me, whereby my enemies may presume that her ears are open to any sinister calumniations to be devised against me for anything I shall do in this time of disfavour.

I am therefore urgently moved to live wanly in token of the reverend fear I bear to her majesty to forbear all voluntary public actions of state, wherein I am not by her majesty expressly commanded, until I may be relieved to have her presence. [91]

His old rival at court, Leicester, wrote to him on 9 April, suggesting that the harshness he was experiencing at the queen's hands was because his 'place and credit heretofore with her makes it heavier to you and more noted to the world than to all the rest . . .' He also added these ponderous words of comfort:

So my good lord, being most heartily sorry for your absence as much for her majesty's and the realm's service as for your own particular, I will leave you to His protection that rules all and can give you more true comfort in an hour than all the world can do in the longest man's life.[92]

Eventually, Elizabeth realised she could ill afford to shun the political skills and acumen of so experienced a minister as Burghley, and after a few late outbursts – calling him traitor, and wicked wretch – he was received back into the bosom of her good esteem.

Walsingham, meanwhile, as befits a man of the shadows, kept his head down and quietly carried on with his official duties. Elizabeth knew she could not afford to lose the services of both of her Chief Ministers, and consequently he escaped much of her disfavour, having the dubious advantage of being at home sick until the middle of February 1587 and therefore absent from court during the critical period. However, any triumph, any satisfaction he may have felt at the destruction of his enemy Mary Queen of Scots was to be short-lived.

England now faced a more grievous clear and present danger.

CHAPTER SEVEN

Defeating the Armada

'This I am sure of: if her majesty would have spent but 1,000 crowns to have had some intelligence, it would have saved her twenty times as much.'

CHARLES HOWARD, LORD EFFINGHAM, ADMIRAL OF THE ENGLISH FLEET,
FROM HIS SHIP *THE BEAR*, TO WALSINGHAM, 24 JANUARY 1587.[1]

Many believe that the execution of Mary Queen of Scots triggered, or at least accelerated, King Philip II of Spain's ambitious and financially crippling plans to assault England. In truth, the genesis of the invasion was more the anger caused in 1585 by Francis Drake's plundering, burning voyage to the West Indies and Leicester's expedition to the Low Countries.[2] These were the English actions that finally goaded the Spanish into preparations for an amphibious offensive. The plans were made despite Philip's strong misgivings that an attack on Elizabeth's realm might provoke France – fearing total encirclement by his dominions – into an uncomfortable and unlikely alliance with England.

Walsingham, with his aggressive, almost fanatical desire to protect and promote his fledgling Protestant religion, had long feared Spanish military action against England. In October 1585, the spy master wrote to William Harborne,[3] sent at his suggestion three years before to become English ambassador at the Turkish court in Constantinople, instructing him to persuade the Turks to attack Spanish interests in the Mediterranean, or indeed the southern coast of Spain itself.

These pre-emptive strikes would serve as an archetypal diversionary tactic, focusing Spanish attention onto the Turks rather than the English. This ambitious diplomatic master stroke vividly demonstrates not only Walsingham's firm grasp and understanding of the complete European picture, but also the breathtaking depth of his strategic vision, as well as his full appreciation of the value of sea power. Harborne had actually first received these orders verbally the previous April via Walsingham's trusted Florentine agent Jacomo Manucci, but now, impatient for action, the Secretary confirmed his instructions in cipher. Recent Spanish successes in the Low Countries were likely to foment 'hot wars' between England and Spain, and therefore Harborne was to

use all your endeavour and industry on that behalf . . . for . . . it is most evident that if the said king [Philip II] might be kept thoroughly occupied, either by some incursion from the coast of Africa in itself, or by the galleys of the Grand Seigneur [the Sultan of Turkey] in his dominions in Italy or otherwise, as may be best considered of you in those parts.

With the order taken to annoy him from this side of Europe, his power should be so weakened and divided as it would be no small advantage to her majesty presently, but to all Christendom hereafter.

The limbs of the devil [Catholic Spain and Muslim Turkey] being thus set against one another by means thereof, the true church and doctrine of the Gospel may, during their contention, have leisure to grow to such strength as shall be requisite for suppression of them both . . .

Let them [the Turks] understand that there could never be . . . better occasion than at this time that he [Philip] is entered into a quarrel with her majesty who shall have the means to give him such annoyance on this side of Europe that if the Sultan will embrace the opportunity of assailing him on the other side, there is no question but that he shall sink under . . . so heavy a burden.[4]

At the very least, Walsingham suggested that Harborne should convince the Turks to make a show of mobilising their ships in the west to threaten the Spanish and thereby distract them from mounting any hostilities against England.

A war fought on two fronts against Spain – with the eventual prize being the ascendancy of the Protestant religion in Europe! It must have been the stuff of Walsingham's most compelling and pleasant daydreams; but, always realistic, he would also have known from the outset that success looked remarkably unlikely.[5] Harborne laboured hard for three years to fulfil these grand, sweeping plans, but was constantly defeated by the Turks' total preoccupation with the fighting on the eastern borders of their empire against Persia and by their lack of naval resources to attempt a fresh military adventure elsewhere.

During this period, Walsingham was desperately short of reliable informants in Spain. The English merchants based there supplied intelligence on a somewhat haphazard basis, and their activities were further limited when Spain imposed a trade embargo on English ships in May 1585 and denied its ports to them. His earliest report that an armada of warships and military transports was being assembled and troops being mustered in the Spanish possessions in Italy came to England via a merchant who landed at Dartmouth in Devon in December 1585.

Initially, Walsingham, after sifting through a pile of conflicting reports from Spain in early 1586, was not convinced of the immediacy of the threat of the Armada, dismissing stories of shipping movements and warlike preparations as mere 'Spanish brag'.[6] He wrote to Leicester on 24 March that the Spanish threat '(as the report that came from Lisbon the tenth of this month), will prove nothing this year and I hope less the next'. Then doubts began to gnaw insidiously at his self-confidence and certainty. That same month, the spy master sent Antony Poyntz (who was in the service of the Spanish ambassador in Paris) to Spain to gather more intelligence. But Poyntz was a double agent, serving both sides, as he admitted to Walsingham, who clearly planned to use him to supply disinformation to the Spaniards.

In fact, Walsingham's instincts were entirely correct. Detailed planning for the invasion had only been submitted to the Spanish king for approval two weeks earlier, on 12 March, envisaging the deployment of 556 ships of all types, including 150 'great ships of war', 85,332 sailors and soldiers and a further 8,890 gunners and cavalry. Philip firmly vetoed these plans as far too grandiose and expensive and instead initially relied for his land forces on the 30,000 battle-hardened veterans drawn from the Duke of Parma's army in the Low Countries, to be transported across to England in towed flat-bottomed barges.[7] The Armada was also to carry roughly the same number of soldiers as Parma's multinational contingent.

The true import of all that activity in the Spanish ports may have been revealed to Walsingham through one of his spies in Rome, one of many placed there to monitor and report on the exiled English Catholics and the seminarists still being sent into England.

One account, first written eighty years after Walsingham's death, tells how he learnt from a well-placed source in Spain of a letter from King Philip, written, for security, in his own hand, to Pope Sixtus V, briefing him on the invasion plans. The English agents in Rome were then alerted, and one of them bribed, threatened or in some way induced an august but possibly venal member of the pontiff's Gentlemen of the Bedchamber to steal (or more likely copy) the Spanish king's letter, safely locked up in the Pope's writing desk or cabinet in the Vatican. This was apparently achieved by stealing Sixtus's keys out of his pocket while he slept.[8]

It is a nice story and probably apocryphal, but certainly confirmation of the Spanish intentions against England later did come from Rome, when Philip informed the full college of cardinals of his invasion plans in order to secure their support in the event of the Pope's death. Their collective noun perhaps should be a 'chatter' of cardinals, as the intelligence quickly leaked out and very soon after was gratefully received in London.

By February 1587, information on the Spanish preparations for invasion was flowing more strongly to Walsingham. An assessment of the strength of the gathering Armada, with the displacement and location of seventy-six vessels in northern Spain and elsewhere, is listed in a document in Lord Admiral Howard's hand.[9]

The renowned naval commander John Hawkins wrote to Walsingham on 1 February, urging a naval reconnaissance expedition to Spain or imposing a small blockade. He understood very well which arguments would convince the reader of his letter:

> Having of long time seen the malicious practices of the papists combined generally throughout Christendom to alter the government of this realm and to bring it to papistry and consequently to servitude, poverty and slavery, I have a good will from time to time to do and set forward something as I could have credit to impeach their purpose . . .
>
> If we stand at this point in a mammering [hesitation] and at a stay, we consume [burn in a fire], and our commonwealth utterly decays . . .
>
> Therefore, in my mind, our profit and best assurance is to seek our peace by a determined and resolute war, which in doubt, would be both less charge, more assurance of safety and would best discern our friends from our foes . . . abroad and at home and satisfy the people generally throughout the whole realm.[10]

Hawkins urged that a permanent force of six English warships should be stationed off the Spanish coast, with enough food, water and munitions for four months, supported by six smaller scouting vessels. This naval force would 'be a sufficient company to distress anything that goeth through the seas'. He estimated the resources required should include a complement of 1,800 sailors, with a monthly pay and supplies bill of £2,700 (or £442,792 at today's prices). Finally, Hawkins added persuasively: 'By open wars, all the Jesuits and ill-affected persons would be discerned and cut off from the hope of their malicious practices.'

The following month, Walsingham received, by a circuitous route,[11] alarming intelligence of the progress of the Spanish build-up: 400 ships and fifty galleys were now in and around Lisbon, with 74,000 soldiers being mustered in Italy, Spain, Portugal and Flanders. This order of battle did not include the 1,200 gunners and 8,912 sailors already in Spain, together with accumulated provisions including 184,557 quintals of biscuit, 23,000 quintals of bacon, 23,000 butts of wine, 11,000 quintals of beef and 43,000 quintals of cheese.[12] The invasion clock was ticking faster.

Early reports received by Walsingham also concerned the Armada's armament, which was for 'the most part . . . cast iron pieces [cannon] and lying very high, not to do great damage'[13] – important intelligence about Spanish firepower that later helped determine the English tactics for the coming battle at sea.

In London, news of these preparations suggested that a pre-emptive naval strike on the growing Armada was now becoming imperative – to win more time for the painfully slow preparations for the defence of England, which were constantly hampered by Elizabeth's procrastination and penny-pinching.

The queen was urged to send Sir Francis Drake with a squadron of warships, ostensibly to support the pretender to the Portuguese crown, Don Antonio. In reality, an attack was planned on Spanish ports and the provisions necessary for invasion stored there and to destroy as much enemy shipping as possible. There was absolutely no hope of totally neutralising the mounting threat posed by the Armada, but the invasion plans could be disrupted and its sailing date delayed.

Elizabeth, as was her usual wont, hesitated over giving approval to the daring plan despite Walsingham, Leicester and Lord Admiral Howard arguing strongly for such decisive action. Raleigh, if later Spanish spy reports are believed, was an equally vociferous opponent.[14] On 15 March 1587, the queen eventually (and reluctantly) permitted Drake's bold mission, involving twenty-seven ships and 2,200 men, for what was to become a punitive expedition against Spain. With typical parsimony, she agreed to only four of her own warships[15] accompanying Drake, with the remainder fitted out and paid for by London merchants or other private investors.

He departed on 2 April, embarrassingly delayed by a large-scale desertion by his sailors on the eve of sailing, perhaps subverted by those in government opposed to the naval adventure, as the operation had been kept strictly secret from all but the highest ranks. On board his flagship, the 600-ton *Elizabeth Bonaventure*, on the River Thames, Drake penned a last flamboyant letter to Walsingham:

> Let me beseech your honour to hold a good opinion not only of myself, but of all these servitors in this action . . .
>
> The wind commands me away.
>
> Our ship is under sail. Haste![16]

Despite the clandestine preparations for the voyage, the Spanish soon learnt of Drake's departure. On 7 April, one of their agents across the English Channel in Rouen recounted his conversations with a French merchant who had arrived the previous day from England. He reported that

> Captain Drake had left the Thames with forty well-armed ships, five belonging to the queen, of 800 or 900 tons each and carrying 5,000 men. The merchant saw the fleet pass before Rye [Sussex] on the way to Falmouth, where they are to join forty or fifty more . . .
>
> The rumour was that this fleet was going to encounter the [West] Indian flotilla.
>
> We are astonished at the great diligence and secrecy with which this fleet has been equipped, for up to the moment, not a word of it has reached us here.[17]

The southern English ports had been closed by government order to prevent news of Drake's mission leaking out. Afterwards, the Spanish claimed that

> so much cunning was employed that even Secretary Walsingham refrained from sending hither [Paris] a dispatch from his mistress [Elizabeth] so that the courier might not say anything about it.[18]

It was almost inevitable that Elizabeth would begin to have second thoughts. Reports reached her – perhaps simply propaganda issued by the Spanish – that preparations for invasion had slowed and the phantom of peace materialised before her eyes, replacing the spectre of an expensive war that had haunted both her waking hours and her closely guarded purse. A week after Drake had sailed, she sent an urgent message to Plymouth instructing him to attack only Spanish shipping at sea, and to steer well clear of Spanish ports. Her new orders prohibited him from entering 'forcibly into the said king's [Philip's] ports or havens, or to offer violence or to do any act of hostility upon land'.[19] Walsingham feared, as suggested by the rumours he picked up at court, that the queen would now recall the force altogether. Elizabeth's new orders were sent on by a pinnace,[20] but it was delayed by storms in the Bay of Biscay. Drake was long gone. The queen's change of heart had come too late; quite literally, she had missed the boat.

By 20 May, Mendoza had discovered the true mission of Drake's squadron. After tapping a source obviously close to his English counterpart in the French capital, he wrote immediately to King Philip, reporting that Walsingham and Howard had described in letters just

how diligent they were in getting Drake away with the fleet, without anything being known about it a week before its departure.

[Drake's] orders were to prevent the junction of your majesty's fleet and enter what ports he could.

They have fresh letters from Spain reporting that . . . the [West] Indian flotillas were not coming this year, so they have sent a dispatch boat after Drake, ordering him on no account to enter any port in Spain, but to confine himself strictly to preventing the junction of the fleet, especially the galleasses[21] coming from Italy. He was to wait and capture two argosies[22] which were to bring munitions from Italy.[23]

But events overtook even this astonishingly accurate intelligence. On 19 April, Drake sailed audaciously into the harbour of Cadiz in Andalucia in south-west Spain, surprised the garrison and destroyed thirty-seven of the eighty ships anchored there, setting them ablaze or blowing them up in an enjoyable twelve-hour orgy of demolition.[24] Drake wrote to Walsingham on 27 April that he had burnt one ship of 1,500 tons and brought away four 'to sell to the Moors. God make us all thankful that her majesty sent out these few ships in time. There must be a beginning of any great actions, but continuing to the end yields the true glory'.[25]

But he made no mention of a disquieting incident that occurred during the action. Drake's second-in-command William Borough[26] was outraged at his foolhardiness in launching the attack and sulkily took his flotilla out of the harbour during the action. Despite this less than shining example of English naval dash and derring-do, after wreaking destruction at Cadiz, Drake cast around for other convenient targets of opportunity. Lisbon was too strongly fortified, and after taunting the Spanish admiral there in the vain hope of luring his ships into the open sea and battle, the English squadron sailed on to Cape St Vincent.

An assault on Lagos was beaten off, but Drake personally led the force that attacked, up a steep slope, the fort perched high on Cape Sagres. Timber, pitch and bundles of firewood were piled high up against the fort's wooden gates under covering small-arms fire and set alight, but before the blaze could provide entry into the stronghold, its defenders cravenly sought terms for surrender.

Drake daringly held the fort for three weeks as a base from which he could harry Spanish shipping, and around 100 ships were captured and their cargoes destroyed. Thomas Fenner, one of Drake's captains, told Walsingham in a dispatch on 17 May:

> The marquis of Santa Cruz [the Spanish naval commander] was near with seven galleys . . . but would not attack. Twelve of her majesty's ships were a match for all the galleys in the King of Spain's dominions.[27]

One important coup was the destruction of a year's supply of iron hoops and oak staves for making barrels. This alone was later to prove a tactical disaster for the Armada: food and water had to be stored in unseasoned, leaky casks that depleted water supplies or quickly rotted the food stored within.

The small English force then headed west for the Azores in the hope of intercepting a treasure ship from the Americas and winning some more booty for their merchant backers. Drake's luck still held good. He captured the Portuguese carrack[28] *San Felipe* on 18 June, together with her cargo of precious spices, ivory and silks from the East Indies, valued then at £114,000, or £17,900,000 at today's prices.

Elizabeth, her earlier doubts now swiftly and conveniently forgotten, told the French ambassador Châteauneuf that she had heard on 13 May that Drake 'had burnt the ships at Cadiz and had sacked the country'. The envoy found her dramatic news difficult to believe and she told him acidly: 'Then you do not believe what is possible.'

The squadron arrived back in Plymouth on 26 June 1587 to national hero-worship and unbridled adulation. Drake had destroyed or crippled about 10,000 tons of Spanish shipping, ruined much of the Armada's stock of provisions and, as an added benefit, captured a cargo that paid for the adventure many times over, no doubt thrilling the queen and his number-crunching financial backers in London. Furthermore, his awesome, reckless exploits had created a lasting moral ascendancy for English seamanship and naval tactics, and the much-vaunted Spanish naval and military power now seemed impotent against him. Most importantly, he had achieved the strategic objective of his mission: to delay the sailing of the Spanish invasion force for at least twelve months. No wonder the fearful Spanish called him *El Dracque* – the Dragon.

Walsingham was cock-a-hoop at the success of the expedition. He urged that Drake should immediately be sent back to the Azores to prey on the ponderous treasure ships that regularly brought silver bullion from the Americas, as a means of waging bruising economic warfare on King Philip. The best way 'to bridle their malice is the interrupting of the Indian fleets', he advised Burghley on 16 July.[29] Elizabeth, however, unsurprisingly turned down the idea.

Attacking the Armada in and around its home ports was one thing, but Walsingham clearly had other methods for crippling or delaying the projected invasion. There are indications that he regularly monitored Spain's annual revenues as a means of evaluating its financial ability to wage war against England.[30] One of his schemes for countering the invasion fleet was to turn off the cash tap that financed it. To achieve this, he recruited the assistance of the powerful foreign banks.

The spy master suggested, via the London financiers, that the great banking houses of north Italy, like the Corsinis, and the gold exchanges of Genoa and Florence should refuse to provide any lengthy credit to the king of Spain – thereby starving the Armada of necessary funds. Thomas Sutton, the merchant, financier and founder of the Charterhouse almshouses in the City of London, may have been one of his prime agents in negotiating such useful cooperation from the hard-nosed Italian bankers,[31] and they turned down or delayed the Spanish king's request for loans.

Shortage of cash, therefore, forced Philip to turn to the Vatican in 1587. His ambassador there, Henry de Guzman, Count de Olivarez, was not sanguine about the prospect of obtaining financial support from Sixtus V: 'When it comes to getting money out of him, it is like squeezing his life blood,' he reported despondently to his royal master.[32] The Pope, one of history's great reformers of Vatican finances, no doubt wanted to preserve its riches. Moreover, although an implacable opponent of everything Elizabeth stood for, politically and religiously, there are indications in some of his letters and pronouncements that he held a sneaking regard for her courage and single-mindedness. Perhaps he also had serious doubts about the chances of success for the Spanish plans. Eventually, however, on 29 July Sixtus signed a treaty with Spain, promising Philip one million gold ducats, or £40,000,000 in today's money, to help fund the 'Enterprise of England'.

Despite the ambassador's efforts to obtain a munificent advance, the final canny agreement was that one half was to be paid when Spanish forces actually landed on English soil and the remainder in equal instalments every two months thereafter. Lawyers today would recognise the deal as a 'no win, no fee' arrangement. In return, Philip could bestow the crown of England on anyone he wished, providing that the new monarch pledged that the defeated realm would be restored to the Catholic faith.[33] One would not expect the Pope to reject outright appeals for help to reclaim a recalcitrant nation back into the Catholic fold, but the terms and conditions he imposed were less than generous – and hardly immediately helpful to Spain.

A correspondent in Rome told Burghley that the Spanish plan was to capture Elizabeth and send her triumphantly as a prisoner to the Vatican:

> He heard the cardinal say that the King of Spain gave great charge . . . to all the captains that in no way they should harm the person of the queen; but upon taking her, use the same with reverence, looking well to the custody of her. And further . . . take order for the conveyance of her person to Rome, to the purpose that his Holiness the Pope should dispose thereof in sort, as it should please him.[34]

Pleasant dreams of success aside, Philip of Spain was still left with an immediate cash-flow problem in paying for the Armada preparations. This was partially solved in August when the Spanish Plate Fleet arrived safely from the West Indies with sixteen million gold ducats on board, of which twenty-five per cent, or £160,000,000 at current prices, went straight into the king's depleted coffers in his exchequer.

Elizabeth still clung obstinately to her fond hopes of peace, and an irritated Walsingham wrote to Leicester on 21 September complaining of her failure to appreciate the dangerous reality England and her throne were now confronting:

> To think that the king of Spain, having his treasure now come home in greater quantity than ever he had, his forces doubled in those countries [Holland] when the levies made in Italy and Germany shall be arrived and the Pope ready to back him with three million crowns[35] and all against England, will make a peace but with such conditions as will work then [to the] overthrow both of her majesty and of those countries [the Low Countries] is but a mere vanity, for always the strongest gives law to the weaker.[36]

Soon after Drake's return from 'singeing the King of Spain's beard', as his exploits were now popularly labelled, Walsingham sat down and drew up plans to gather more timely and accurate intelligence out of Spain. He could no longer rely on the serendipity of a report being sent casually by a merchant in that country as this extracurricular activity was becoming more and more risky for such amateur informants in the face of heightened Spanish security.

In April 1587, Mendoza wrote to King Philip that he had heard

> from a good quarter that a Scots merchant, who says he is the King of Scotland's banker, is in Spain with twelve well fitted English boats freighted with merchandise from [England] – the mariners also being English. It would be well for your majesty to send orders to the ports to have this merchant arrested. His name is Hunter.[37]

Hunter was based in Lisbon and was quickly arrested, put on trial as an English spy and supporter of heretics, and imprisoned in the city. A later letter from him, still in the British Library, confirms Mendoza's suspicions as fully justified. In the correspondence, Hunter describes his incarceration, but boldly adds details of the armaments and munitions stored in the city. He appends a crude sketch of a horn as his signature in cipher, but the true provenance is confirmed by Walsingham's marginal note, written safely back in London: 'From Mr Hunter of Lisbon.'[38] His motivation for undertaking this dangerous work can only be guessed at – perhaps he was a fervent Scottish Protestant?

Another brave man was the Englishman Nicholas Ousley, who resided in Malaga and who smuggled his intelligence out of Spain hidden in wine casks. Again, it was Mendoza who identified his clandestine work in a note to the Spanish king on 12 July 1587:

> Ousley . . . sends advertisements [news] to the queen [Elizabeth] and on Walsingham receiving certain letters from him, he said he was one of the cleverest men he knew and the queen was much indebted to him for his regular and trustworthy information.[39]

Ousley was captured, then bribed himself out of jail, and was still sending reports to London as late as April 1588. He later served as a volunteer soldier aboard the *Revenge* in the skirmishes against the Armada up the English Channel. Lord Admiral Howard wrote of him to Burghley:

It has pleased her majesty, in respect of his good service heretofore in Spain, in sending very good intelligence thence, and now since in our late fight against the Spanish fleet, to grant him a lease of St Helen's in London.[40]

Back in 1587, Walsingham needed a more reliable intelligence network to counter the threat of the Armada and his scheme to achieve that end demonstrates his customary methodical planning. He wrote a document to plan his way out of the problem of a dearth of information on military capabilities and intentions, entitled *A Plot for Intelligence out of Spain*:

1. Sir Edward Stafford [Elizabeth's ambassador in Paris] to draw what he can from the Venetian ambassador.
2. To procure some correspondence with the French king's ambassador to Spain.
3. To take order with some at Rouen to have frequent advertisements [news] from such as arrive out of Spain at Nantes, Newhaven [present-day Le Havre] and Dieppe.
4. To make choice of two especial persons, French, Flemings or Italians to go along the coast [of Spain] to see what preparations are a making there. To furnish them with letters of credit.
5. To have intelligence at the Court of Spain, one of Finale,[41] one of Genoa.
6. To have intelligence at Brussels, Leiden[42] [and in Denmark].
7. To employ the Lord Dunsany.[43]

The plan capitalised on the spy master's experience and knowledge won in his younger days in Europe, and no doubt exploited his surviving contacts in the Low Countries and Italy. How much of this plan Walsingham managed to put in place remains unknown. Elizabeth grudgingly made grants of £3,300 (£574,800 at current prices)[44] in March and June 1587 towards the cost of the spy master's secret services, which probably proved insufficient for his intelligence-gathering needs, and a further £2,000 the following year. There seems little doubt that he was forced to supplement this budget out of his own pocket, in fulfilment of his own maxim that the acquisition 'of knowledge is never too dear'.

His pressing need to improve intelligence on Spain came at a time when he was still running a secret police operation against what he saw as the subversive seminaries in England. Leicester's military campaign against the Spanish in the Low Countries – and more importantly, its expense – was also preoccupying the queen's attention.[45] Despite the mountain of tasks facing a Secretary of State, Walsingham recognised the bigger issue and drew up his plans accordingly.

Total reliance on informants in Spain seemed far too risky, although Walsingham continued to receive titbits from a range of sources, and in June 1587 he made arrangements for two 'intelligencers' to be inserted into the Spanish court and two more to spy on the Spanish preparations on the coast. He looked more to cosmopolitan Venice, Florence and Rome as the most fruitful areas to exploit. Walsingham already had a substantial network of agents in Italy, watching the English Catholics there, and it would have been an easy and cost-effective matter to redirect their energies rather than set up a new, purpose-built ring of spies. However, he did dispatch one Stephen Paule to Venice in early 1587 who sent weekly reports for more than a year of the gossip and rumour he picked up in that thriving, cosmopolitan city. In November, Paule reported that Michael Giraldi, a 'Bergomase',[46]

has set sail for England, pretending to be a merchant. It is thought that for several reasons, [he is] to poison her majesty at the instigation of the Pope. The Pope, under pretence of supporting the war against the heretics and for performing some great enterprise, has enriched himself exceedingly.[47]

Walsingham's best overseas agent was the reckless Catholic Anthony Standen, alias Pompeo Pellegrini, alias 'B. C.',[48] who in 1565 was a member of the household of Henry Stuart, Lord Darnley, Mary Queen of Scots' second husband, and later lived and worked in Tuscany. He was a great friend of Giovanni Figliazzi, the Duke of Tuscany's ambassador in Madrid, and his dispatches, many routed through Walsingham's agent Manucci, began to tap this useful friendship. Standen was also proactive in his intelligence-gathering. In May 1587, he reported that four galleys from the Genoese fleet had sailed for Spain and the Armada and he had heard that four more were to leave Naples. He added in cipher:

> Since your last [letter], in which you desire intelligence on Spanish matters, I have borrowed 100 crowns and dispatched to Lisbon a Fleming who has there a brother in service with the [Spanish Grand Admiral] marquis of Santa Cruz and of his chamber.
>
> I have given him [the] address for his letters to me at the [Tuscan] ambassador's house in Madrid who straight will send them to me.
>
> He is a proper fellow and writes well and I sent him away with these four galleys.[49]

What a triumph of espionage! Walsingham now had an agent within the household of the Spanish naval commander-in-chief, although the route necessary to retrieve the vital information was lengthy and time-consuming and Santa Cruz himself died on 9 February 1588, his demise said to have been caused by Philip II's constant reproaches over delays in readying the Armada. One of the first fruits of this new agent was a copy of the grand admiral's most recent order of battle, dated 22 March 1587, complete with the fleet's wages bill, signed by Santa Cruz himself and Navy Secretary Barnaby de Pedrosa.

Three months later, Standen informed Walsingham of his firm belief that the Spanish could not be ready in time that year to take advantage of good weather to dispatch the Armada. He also reported Spanish reactions to Drake's punitive expedition:

> The attempts of Sir Francis Drake upon the Spanish coasts make these people tremble. If upon him entering the port of Cadiz he had immediately landed, he might certainly have plundered that rich town, though [as] it was the mischief he did them came to 1,000,000 crowns.

The spy master passed on his letter to Burghley with the comment: 'I humbly pray your lordship that Pompey's letter may be reserved to yourself. I would be loathe [sic] the gentleman should have any harm through my default.'[50] Security over the identity of sources was as vital then as it is now, to protect their cover.

On 28 August 1587, Standen sent in more intelligence, partly in cipher. He reported that the city of Ragusa had promised to provide Philip of Spain with eighty ships and 4,000 sailors.

> The king's . . . enterprise upon England proceeds not so much out
> of his inclination, as for the necessity he has . . . of preserving the
> Indian navigation, being the fairest flower in his garland. The Pope
> bends his whole thoughts upon the invasion of England.[51]

The Spanish already had substantial land forces on England's doorstep – across the southern North Sea in the Low Countries. Reports in 1587 from spies watching the Duke of Parma's headquarters confirmed their plans to use these troops in the invasion forces after the Armada had neutralised Elizabeth's navy in the English Channel.

An example of Walsingham's espionage methodology is provided in a report by two Spanish prisoners of war in England, Francisco de Valverde and Pedro de Santa Cruz.[52] In late February 1588, they informed Mendoza about the espionage ring operated by relatives of Dr Hector Núñez,[53] a distinguished Portuguese physician in London who was one of Walsingham's correspondents, or in modern spy jargon a dead letter box – receiving letters from abroad on his behalf. The two prisoners told the Spanish ambassador:

> We understand that your lordship has friends in the city [London]
> from whom [you] can learn more about the forces and armaments
> here than we can tell you. All we can say is that they are simply a
> mob of riffraff, with but few leaders, and they are more cunning at
> banquets than at war.
>
> We are sure they are not as diligent [as] the Portuguese Geronimo
> Pardo in Lisbon and Bernaldo Luis in Madrid,[54] who are relatives of
> Dr Núñez, who lives here. They carefully report hither everything
> that passes at Madrid and Lisbon and transmit their news by ships
> which they send from Spain . . .
>
> [Pardo] brought . . . two packets of letters in cipher, giving a

full account of the warlike preparations which were being made by Spain. After translating them, he carried them to Secretary Walsingham . . .

[Another vessel brought] full accounts of the ships, men and stores for the Armada in Lisbon. The dispatches were delivered to Dr Núnez whilst he was at a dinner . . . He rose in great haste and went direct to Secretary Walsingham's house.[55]

The prisoners questioned Núnez's servant and relative Francisco de Tapia regarding whether there were any more letters from Pardo, and he told them that the Portuguese had been arrested in Lisbon on suspicion of being a spy and being traitorously in the service of England. Despite this, he had apparently persuaded the master of a German ship to take back letters to London, telling him:

It is a matter of life or death to him that you should carry this letter to Dr Hector Núnez . . .

The shipmaster hid the packet in a feather bed and on coming up the Channel in a storm, he ran ashore and lost everything but the lives of his crew.

This Tapia may be captured in Lisbon as he is going thither in a ship bound for Brazil. She must call at Lisbon and will be taken from there by Tapia, Pardo or by one Pero Freire of Lisbon.

She will also land in a port of Galicia or Portugal a man well disguised in the garb of a pilgrim. The ship and cargo are entirely English property, nothing belongs to the Portuguese who ostensibly own her . . . Another English ship, called the *Black Crow*, is also going to Spain carrying a false deed of sale and transfer in favour of certain Flemings. We have all the information set down here from good Catholics and we swear upon this cross [†] that we are writing it in all zeal for the service of God and our king.

It seems inconceivable to us now that two prisoners of war should either enjoy enough freedom in their place of captivity to gather such useful intelligence, or have the means to send it out of the country. Finally, how could they be allowed free access to 'good' Catholics, given the paranoia about the dangers posed by recusants in London? They were apparently not even held under lock and key: Valverde and Santa Cruz were lodged with two London merchants, Simon Borman and James Naunton, and they had been told by the English authorities that 'unless certain Englishmen in Seville were released, we should not be set at liberty'.[56]

Walsingham also sought professional advice about the size and type of forces that the Spanish would require for a successful invasion, to enable him to quantify the intelligence he was receiving. Sir William Winter, the English naval commander in the Low Countries, had been asked about the technical problems of amphibious operations and establishing a bridgehead on an enemy shore:

> It seems from your honour's letters that the Prince of Parma's intention is towards [the Isle of] Sheppey, Harwich or Yarmouth, two of which I know perfectly as Sheppey and Harwich, the other not so well . . .
>
> Whereas it is said the Prince's strength is 30,000 soldiers, then I assure your honour, it is no mean quantity of shipping that must serve for the transporting of that number [of men] and that which doth appertain to them, without the which I do not think they will put forth: 300 sail must be the least . . .[57]

The English were anticipating a Spanish landing somewhere along the south coast: Portsmouth or Southampton, perhaps, or even on the Isle of Wight – 'the place for which the enemies of this realm have principally desired'.[58] Some experienced army commanders, knowing the dire problems of resupplying an invading force on a hostile beach, suggested that the Spanish might seize a large harbour, and Plymouth, as the nearest major port to Spain, was suggested as the Armada's probable first military objective.

In Madrid and Lisbon, the Spanish were also building up an intelligence picture of their adversaries. It was not always accurate, influenced at times by wishful thinking. Philip II advised the new

Armada commander, the Duke of Medina Sidonia, reassuringly that

> the ships of the enemy are all old or small – different from those
> we make here in quality and soundness, leaving aside the advan-
> tages our men have in their numbers and in the experience many of
> them have.[59]

They also considered the kind of welcome they would receive. In 1587, they drew up a lengthy list of Englishmen, county by county, who were known practising Catholics and who might be relied upon to support, or even join, the invasion. It was not information collected or assessed alto-gether objectively. For example, under the list of Catholics living in Norfolk, we have:

> *Sir Henry Benefield*, who was formerly the guardian of Queen
> Elizabeth the pretended queen of England, during the whole time
> that his majesty was in England. Sir Henry kept her by order of
> King Philip and Queen Mary.
> I wish to God they had burnt her then, as she deserved, with the
> rest of the heretics, who were justly executed.
> If this had been done, we should be living now in peace and
> quietness.

In the County of York:

> *Sir Richard Stapleton*
> *Sir Brian Stapleton*, who would risk his life for his majesty [Philip II]
> *Edward Clerker* of Risby
> *Henry Constable* of Holderness
> *William Babthorp* of Babthorpe
> *Robert Clerker* of Clerker, and many other gentlemen.

Others listed were likely opponents – a ready-made schedule of those to be arrested in the event of the Armada's victory and Elizabeth being toppled from power.[60] The document is naturally headed by the Privy Council, led by Leicester with Walsingham last, all of them named as 'the principal devils that rule the court'.

The document urged a landing not on the south coast but in the restive North of England, in Northumberland or Westmorland where Catholicism was still endemic:

> If his majesty [Philip II] intends to send a fleet . . . it will have to encounter strong resistance if it does not come to one of these counties. The way by Ireland is dangerous.
>
> It would therefore be safer to enter and disembark at Kirkcudbright in the territory of the earl of Morton, who is now in Lisbon and would be glad to accompany them.
>
> If the force be landed there, they might enter the rest of England with less risk than elsewhere.[61]

This was not sound tactical advice and it would have been unwelcome reading for Philip and his naval and land commanders. Not only would a voyage to the North of England increase considerably the logistical problems of the invasion fleet, but it would provide better opportunity for the English ships to split up the Armada and pick them off, one by one, en route. Moreover, they would face enough problems invading one country, let alone a second – Scotland.

As well as controlling England's foreign and domestic espionage and counter-insurgency, Walsingham was also heavily involved in spreading disinformation, or black propaganda, amongst the enemies of England and his queen. Mendoza describes one such operation in a dispatch to King Philip in July 1587:

> Some newsletters, in English, have been sent to me from Rome, which letters have been received, addressed to an English gentleman who had died here. The count de Olivares had seen them and thought they should be sent to our majesty.
>
> I know of these letters . . . they were written by one of Walsingham's officers who is the son of a Spanish friar who fled many years ago from St Isidro in Seville with a nun of Utrera, to whom he is married.
>
> The son is a much worse heretic than the father and when he

wrote the letters he had them dated March to deceive the
Englishman . . .

He wished to pledge the English gentleman here by this civility,
in order that he might send him some news.

I mention this matter to your majesty that you may understand
that although these reports have some appearance of probability,
they are really hatched by Walsingham's knavery.[62]

Richard Gibbes, one of Walsingham's agents in Lisbon who posed
as a Scotsman, was questioned by the Spanish about the suitability of
various English harbours and rivers for use by the Armada ships. He
told them misleadingly that the Thames was 'very ill, full of sands within
and without sight of land and not possible to bring in a navy'.[63] As events
turned out, they did not believe him because their final plan was to aim
for the Thames, in order to land troops on either bank of the river.

Walsingham also employed the black art of psychological warfare.
Those with the precious skills to divine the future foretold disasters and
great storms for the summer of 1588, and these predictions received
wide circulation in pamphlets and almanacs printed both in Paris and
Amsterdam. In Spain, recruitment for the Armada began to suffer in
the teeth of these prophecies and in Lisbon an astrologer was arrested
for making 'false and discouraging predictions'.[64] It is entirely plausible
that Walsingham encouraged these demoralising forecasts.

But his greatest opportunity to hoodwink the Spanish government
lay in Paris. The English envoy there, Sir Edward Stafford, appointed in
1583, had become a double agent for the Spaniards. He had accumulated
substantial gambling debts by playing cards with the French king's
brother Francis, Duke of Alençon,[65] and his companions during his first
year as ambassador, but maintained that he now avoided such expensive
(and dangerous) pastimes.

But he remained always short of money. Stafford had been recruited
by Mendoza who had offered him financial inducements to supply information – the classic espionage scenario for 'turning' an individual into a
useful agent. He perhaps became the 'illegal' in Paris (in modern parlance)

Sir Francis Walsingham, attributed to John de Critz the Elder, *c.*1585. The grim-faced spy master would have found today's counter-terrorism legislation too limp-wristed for his battle against the frequent conspiracies against both England and Queen Elizabeth's life. (National Portrait Gallery, London)

Sir Francis Walsingham, possibly after John de
Critz the elder, and painted *c*.1587, just before
Walsingham's ultimate test: the Spanish Armada.
(National Portrait Gallery, London)

Unknown woman, possibly Ursula Walsingham.
Unknown artist, painted in 1583. Walsingham's second
wife must have been a formidable lady: there is something about her expression and that thin, disapproving
mouth that strongly suggests this was not a woman to
be trifled with. (National Portrait Gallery, London)

Queen Elizabeth I, *c*.1585–90, by unknown artist.
The queen, who called Walsingham her 'Dark Moor',
subjected him to tantrums and jibes and her parsimony
and indecision frequently frustrated him. (National
Portrait Gallery, London)

Mary Queen of Scots – 'That devilish woman', as
Walsingham called her – painted c.1559–60, by Francois
Clouet. She recognised the spy master as her greatest
enemy and he was to become the devious means of her
eventual downfall and destruction. (The Royal Collection
© 2006, Her Majesty Queen Elizabeth II)

ABOVE LEFT William Cecil, first Baron Burghley, painted after 1572. Lord Treasurer Burghley oversaw the plans for the trial and execution of Mary Queen of Scots and took the full brunt of Elizabeth's anger when the deed was done. (National Portrait Gallery, London)

ABOVE RIGHT Queen Elizabeth I, Sir Francis Walsingham and William Cecil, first Baron Burghley, by William Faithorne, line engraving, 1655. They saw the wars in the Netherlands as a grim harbinger of what could happen in England if the Catholic threat was not destroyed. (National Portrait Gallery, London)

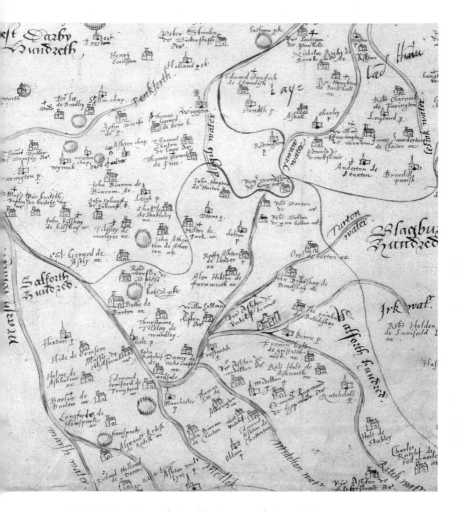

ABOVE A section of Burghley's map of Lancashire showing homes of named Catholic recusants, from information supplied by Walsingham's spies. From the Burghley-Saxton Atlas of c.1579. (By permission of the British Library)

OPPOSITE CENTRE Sir Amyas Paulet, Copy by George Perfect Harding, after unknown artist. This strait-laced Protestant refused to assassinate Mary Queen of Scots to save Elizabeth's conscience. (National Portrait Gallery, London)

ABOVE The Trial of Mary Queen of Scots at Fotheringay
Castle from a contemporary sketch. The figures in the drawing
are identified by numbers inserted by the Privy Council clerk
Robert Beale to correspond to a key written on the verso. The
Scottish queen sits in a chair to the right of the unoccupied
royal dais, faced directly by Burghley, shown as number 2 on
the sketch. Walsingham is seated, with his back to the reader,
at number 28. Add. MS 48027 f.569*. (By permission of the
British Library)

OPPOSITE The execution of Mary Queen of Scots at
Fotheringay Castle on Wednesday 8 February 1587. A contemporary ink and pencil drawing that corresponds closely to
eye-witness accounts. Add MS 48027 f.650* (By permission
of the British Library)

RIGHT Sir Philip Sidney, poet and soldier, who was Walsingham's impoverished son-in-law. He was wounded in action at Zutphen in the Low Countries, through recklessly not wearing leg armour. He died from gangrene at Arnhem on 17 October 1586, aged thirty-one. (By kind permission of Parham House, West Sussex)

OPPOSITE Frances Walsingham, the spy master's daughter and wife of Sir Philip Sidney. This and the portrait of her husband, now at Parham Park, were probably painted as marriage portraits after their wedding on 21 September 1583. (By kind permission of Parham House, West Sussex)

The English
fleet fighting
the Spanish
Armada off
Gravelines in
1588 from
*The Holy Bull
and Crusado of
Rome* by Pope
Gregory XIII,
London 1588.
(By permission
of the British
Library)

codenamed 'Julio'.[66] The Spanish ambassador had reported to Philip II in 1585 that 'now was the time for your majesty to make use of him [Stafford] if you wished any service done. You should see by his acts how willing he was to do so. This ambassador is much pressed for money'. The Spanish king suggested paying him 2,000 crowns 'or the jewel you suggest'.[67] Stafford also accepted 3,000 crowns from the Duke of Guise for showing him English diplomatic correspondence and was in regular contact with Charles Arundel, a Catholic exile in Paris and a congenital conspirator. There is no doubt that Walsingham deeply mistrusted the envoy, even sending one of his agents, Thomas Rogers, alias Nicholas Berden, in 1586 to monitor Stafford's relationships with exiled English Catholics in Paris.

Stafford may well have suspected Walsingham's doubts about his loyalty and honesty. He wrote to him on 10 July 1588 complaining of his shortage of funds:

> If you did know what unseasonable times and unreasonable, I have had to pass . . . ordinary bounds of expense and especially the Queen of Scots' time, above all other, and this last both for mine own con-servation and preservation of things in good state for her majesty's service here, I think you would not wonder at the expense.[68]

But his treachery also provided Walsingham with an opportunity to use him as an innocent conduit for feeding false information regarding English intentions and military strength to the Spanish, and no doubt the spy master spotted this and seized his chance. But why the ambassador was not eventually impeached remains a mystery.[69] Certainly, the flow of intelligence to the Spanish in Paris ceased after the defeat of the Armada.

In Rome, the Pope was also carefully monitoring the progress of the Armada and the constant diplomatic posturing in the courts of Europe. The Count de Olivares, King Philip's ambassador to the Vatican, reported in October and November[70] that Sixtus had been told that the French king Henry III had refused to take any role in the Spanish invasion 'until he pacified his own affairs'. The pontiff heard that Châteauneuf in London had written that the English were 'in the utmost confusion and discouragement'. In Scotland, King James VI was reportedly deeply suspicious of the motivation behind the Armada invasion plan and, perceptively, believed that Philip of Spain wanted to deprive him of his rights to the English crown. A Scottish diplomatic source also said that Elizabeth had ordered Burghley and Walsingham 'by all means to make peace with' Spain and when the Secretary asked her 'what about religion, she replied angrily that she would agree about religion and everything else'.

Again, there is a very strong element of wishful thinking in these reports, coupled with the age-old problem in any intelligence-gathering operation of military or political leaders being told what subordinates believe they want to hear.

But in London, there *were* real problems in creating a credible defensive strategy and with its implementation, mainly due to the queen's unwillingness to fully comprehend the danger her realm and crown now faced – and, more pertinently, to part with the necessary funds to defend them. Elizabeth also still believed in giving peace a chance, and Burghley, seeking to comfort a frustrated Walsingham, told him:

> As God would be best pleased with peace, so in nothing can her
> majesty content her realm better than in procuring of peace, which,
> if it cannot be had, yet is she excused before God and the world . . .
> In short, seek peace, but prepare for war.[71]

On 9 October 1587, the Privy Council heard a list of defensive measures drawn up by Burghley, including mobilisation of the standing navy, commandeering of merchant ships as warships and supply ships,[72] purchase of further vessels from the Low Countries and the arrest or surveillance of dangerous Catholic recusants within the population.[73] Most were put in train, with the addition, inserted more in hope than of any chance then of realisation, that the Lord Lieutenants of the English counties were ordered to put their local forces on one hour's notice for military service. An important omission from the orders issued was the royal warships being placed on a war footing. Elizabeth point-blank refused to implement this sensible precaution and the most her discouraged Councillors could wring out of her exchequer was an additional two ships to join the small fleet stationed in the English Channel – but this for only six weeks' service.

Walsingham, who suffered more bouts of ill-health for much of 1587, could not believe that the queen would risk everything at such a time of great danger. He despairingly told Leicester on 12 November:

> The manner of our cold and careless proceeding here in this time of peril . . . makes me take no comfort of my recovery of health, unless it please God in mercy and miraculously to preserve us, we cannot long stand.[74]

A war council met in London on 27 November to debate where the Spanish might land and establish a bridgehead in England. A scare later that month that the Armada had sailed for England and was off the Irish coast – a report subsequently proved incorrect – at least provided the opportunity for a dry run for the defensive plans. The navy ships mobilised with surprising rapidity and merchant ships were speedily requisitioned and fitted out with ordnance from stocks in the Tower of London. Iron braziers were erected on poles on hilltops along the southern coast to act as beacons, to warn of the approach of the Spanish invaders, and local magistrates ordered to ensure 'the beacons' guarding and good usage'.[75] Walsingham also ordered experienced officers to inspect the militias based in the southern maritime counties,[76] and issued an instruction to the Lord Lieutenants for the physical restraint of Catholic recusants. But as the naval forces stood down after this false alarm, the queen halved the complement of the main fleet – again to save money.

Walsingham's health remained uncertain, but his brief appearances at court must have stiffened the resolve of those, such as Howard, Hatton and Leicester, who were determined to take the war to the Spanish in another pre-emptive strike. The spy master was determined to fight, if needs be, personally on the front line, and he had already ordered new armour from the Low Countries.[77]

On 15 December 1587, Howard received his orders to take the Navy's warships to sea as a forward protective screen in the Western Approaches of the English Channel, and Drake (now a vice admiral), with around twenty ships, was instructed to attack the Armada in its ports. But bad weather and an epidemic of some disease amongst Drake's crews fatally delayed the sailings.

False alarms continued, as must be expected during periods of high tension. On 10 March 1588, Howard wrote to Walsingham from his anchorage in Margate Roads, off the Kent coast, with news of a Spanish departure:

> Last night there came to me of purpose from Dunkirk, one who assures me that on Wednesday last, there came a Scottish gentleman out of Spain to the duke of Parma and brought a packet from the king and declared that the Spanish forces by sea are for certain to depart from Lisbon the 20th of this month with the light moon and that the number of the fleet when they all meet will be 210 sails and the number of soldiers, besides the mariners, are 36,000 ...
>
> I fear me ere it would be long her majesty will be sorry that she has believed some as much as she has done, but it will be very late.[78]

As well as gathering intelligence, Walsingham was also in charge of the organisation and deployment of Elizabeth's land forces. Like so many of the nobility and gentry, he also personally paid for a small contingent of troops – in his case fifty mounted lancers, twenty horsemen armed with petronels[79] and 200 foot soldiers.[80] A document drawn up in April 1588, in his handwriting, provides a fascinating glimpse of the administrative nightmare of organising England's defences. It is a checklist of what now must be done urgently:

> The defence to be made by land and sea.
> The defence by sea committed to the Lord Admiral [Howard].
> Defence by land – to be considered:
> What number of men are put in readiness throughout the realm, horse and foot?
> How they are directed to assist upon any invasion?

Who be the lieutenants of the shires and captains of the men both
trained and untrained?
What pioneers [military labour] appointed for every band and what
carriages [for supply]?
What [gun] powder appointed for every band?
What field pieces [artillery] and munitions are placed in certain of
the maritime counties?

Then Walsingham considers the best tactics for repelling the invasion:
should the defence forces fight the Spanish on the beaches or lure them
inland, burning and laying waste to the countryside in a 'scorched-earth
policy' to deny them food and fodder for their cavalry and horse-drawn
transport?

Where is it likely that the enemy will attempt anything against this
realm?
How may he best be withstood? – whether by offering a fight
when he has landed or in avoiding a fight (which it is likely the
enemy will affect) and to make head[way] against him with the use
of pioneers and withdrawing of victuals.
What men of sufficiency meet to be sent to those places where
the descent [upon the shore] is likely to be made?
What engineers are there in this realm meet to be used for the
direction of the pioneers?
What forces were [best] to be about her majesty's person, both
horsemen and footmen [her bodyguard]?
If anything should be attempted against the city of London,
which way would it be attempted and how may it best be withstood?

By this time, the strategic picture had changed dramatically and the
threat was imminent. On 22 April, on the eve of the glorious pomp
and circumstance of the Order of the Garter ceremonies at Windsor,
Walsingham wrote sarcastically, if not confidently, to his cousin Sir
Edward Norris, then at sea:

This bearer can tell you that here we do nothing but honour St George, of whom the Spanish army seems to be afraid for that, as we hear, they will not be ready to set forward before the middle of May, but I trust it will be May come twelve month.

The King of Spain is too old and too sickly to fall [attempt] to conquer kingdoms.[81]

The spy master's information was amazingly accurate: the Armada departed, under the command of Medina Sidonia, from Lisbon for England and glory between 18 and 20 May. That month, he also received an updated order of battle for the Armada from one of his agents in Spain, plus a breakdown of shipping available to Spanish forces based in the Netherlands.[82]

In late June, Cornish sailors came across some Spanish ships waiting at an agreed rendezvous off the Scilly Islands:

A barque of Mousehole in Cornwall, being bound for France to load salt, encountered nine sail of great ships between Scilly and Ushant bearing north east with the coast of England. Coming near to them, he, doubting [suspecting] they were Spaniards, kept the wind of them. They perceiving it, began to give him chase. In the end, three of them followed him so near that the Englishman doubted hardly to escape them.

At his first sight . . . there were two flags spread which were suddenly taken in again. They were all great ships, the least of them from 200 to five [500] and 800 tons.[83]

But this was just the vanguard of the Armada. Bad weather forced the vast bulk of the fleet, some vessels badly damaged by storms, to take shelter in northern Spanish ports like Corunna, and this respite allowed the English to hone their defensive plans.

On 18 June, the queen called the English gentry and their followers to the colours and a few days later, the Lord Lieutenants of the counties were ordered to place their militias on maximum readiness.[84] Some forces were mobilised: 1,000 cavalry and 5,000 infantry were speedily stationed in the eastern county of Essex, where Parma's forces were now expected to land, and measures put in place for the defence of the Thames Estuary, including building barriers of 120 ships' masts (priced at £6 each) chained together in the river.[85]

Walsingham wrote to Norris on 9 July:

For the navy of Spain, we have lately received [news] that by reason of their great wants, as well of mariners as of necessary provisions, but especially through the infection fallen among their men, they are forced to return and have dispersed themselves.[86]

Walsingham's information was out of date. Three days later, on 12 July, the reprovisioned and repaired Armada, under the command of the Duke of Medina Sidonia, the Captain-General of Andalusia, finally left for England, his flagship hoisting a sacred flag bearing the design of a crucifix between the figures of the Blessed Virgin Mary and St Mary Magdalene. The weather was rough, making progress slow. Medina Sidonia reported later:

The sea was so heavy that all the sailors agreed they had never seen its equal in July. Not only did the waves mount to the skies, but some seas broke clean over the ships . . . it was the most cruel sight ever seen.[87]

Seven days later, the Armada arrived off the south-west coast of England. On 21 July, Howard wrote hurriedly to Walsingham from his flagship, the *Ark Royal*:

Sir – I will not trouble you with any long letter – we are at present otherwise occupied than with writing.

Upon Friday at Plymouth, I received intelligence that there were a great number of ships descried off the Lizard. Whereupon, although the wind was very scant, we first warped[88] out of harbour that night and upon Saturday turned out very hardly, the wind being [in the] south west.

About three in the afternoon, [we saw] the Spanish fleet and did what we could to work for the wind which [by this] morning we had recovered, [observing] their f[leet] to consist of 120 sail, whereof there are four g[alleasses] and many ships of great burden.

At nine of the [clock] we gave them fight, which continued until one.

[In this] fight we made some of them to bear room to stop their leaks; notwithstanding, we dare not adventure to put in among them, their fleet being so strong. But there shall be nothing either neglected or unhazarded, that may work their overthrow.

Howard adds an urgent appeal for cannon shot in a hasty postscript:

Sir, for the love of God and our country, let us have, with some speed, some great shot sent us of all bigness, for this service will continue long, and some powder with it.[89]

Walsingham's old spy Nicholas Ousley reported the sea battles from Drake's ship *Revenge*, off Portland Bill, on 23 July:

We passed the Spanish fleet the 21st and this day, was the taking of the galleon wherein was Don Pedro de Valdes, who is third person in this army [after] the duke [of Medina Sidonia], and Juan Martinez de Recalde, vice-admiral. They have reported to me they are now left 150 sail, divided as I do see, twelve in squadron, and do keep such excellent good order in their fight that if God do not miraculously work, we shall have wherein to employ oursel[ves] for some days.

It was going to be a close-run battle, fighting all the way up the English Channel. Then Ousley, with a strangely awkward sense of timing given Walsingham's obvious preoccupation with the defence of the realm and the almost permanent sessions of the Privy Council at Richmond, turns to more personal issues, seeking that

there may be some consideration of the long time I was prisoner for a spy, for writing the letters to London that came to your honour's

hands; which being proved I could not have release but with great
expenses and bribes.

Also, the three months I spent in riding to most ports where
this army was made, whereof I have given true relation to your
honour; anything that your honour shall think convenient for me,
either in England or Ireland.[90]

As we have seen, he was rewarded for his services in Spain.

By the date of Ousley's letter, around 20,000 men had been mobilised
for the defence of England on land. All were expected to provide their
own equipment and probably the majority were thus ill-armed and only
partially trained. Attempts had been made to purchase small arms and
more armour in Germany but Elizabeth's exchequer was remarkably
bare and stocks of old and rusty equipment stored in the Tower of London
and Windsor Castle were less than satisfactory both in quality or quantity.
Leicester told Walsingham on 1 August:

A number of burgonets[91] have arrived from the Tower but not a
man will buy one, being ashamed to wear it. The armoury must be
better looked to. [There is] a great want of powder and munitions,
which is known abroad.[92]

But Walsingham and his fellow Privy Councillors knew that if Spanish
forces were allowed to land on English soil, their hastily mustered and
inexperienced militias would be no match for Parma's seasoned cam-
paigners. The Spanish had to be held and defeated at sea, and they strove
to maintain supplies of gunpowder and shot to the English fleet, sending
forty-seven 'lasts' of powder off to Portsmouth and the Kent coast between
23 and 26 July.[93] Unfortunately, because of the nature of the running sea
battle, little reached the guns of the English ships. Captured Spanish
vessels had to be plundered of powder and shot to maintain war stocks.
These vital shortages prevented Howard's gallant captains from administering any kind of killer blow.

In spite of suffering considerable battle damage in the Channel skirmishes, the Armada emerged largely unscathed as an effective fighting

force. The fleet anchored off Calais on 27 July, ready to escort Parma's troops across the southern North Sea to the invasion beaches in and around the Thames Estuary. But Medina Sidonia had no means to inform Parma of their imminent arrival, and the land-forces commander needed at least six days to fully embark his troops, already seriously depleted in numbers by disease and desertion, from Nieuport and Dunkirk.[94] There was a fateful pause in Spanish fortunes.

The nimble English ships were easily able to outmanoeuvre their enemy's ponderous attempts to come alongside and board them with their superior forces. But the effects of the English broadsides, fired at long range, were disappointing. Now the Armada, resting peacefully at anchor, was a sitting duck for a fresh weapon deployed by Howard: fireships. Eight small vessels were packed with combustible materials – barrels of pitch, tar, wood and oil – turning them into floating incendiary bombs. Just after midnight on 28 July, these were set alight and steered in amongst the Armada. Panic-stricken, the Spanish cut their anchor cables, hoisted sail and headed out into the open sea in great confusion.

As dawn broke, the English, now reinforced with more ships, attacked and battered the Armada with ferocious gunfire off Gravelines, forcing them eastwards until some ships were in danger of running aground on the treacherous sandbanks off the coast of Zeeland.

The wind suddenly veered and drove the Spanish ships northwards, eagerly pursued by the English, like hunting dogs now scenting a famous victory. They were forced to break off the chase as the Armada entered Scottish waters because of their desperate want of fresh water, food and, most importantly, powder and shot. The Spaniards were left to limp around the north coast of Scotland and out into the tempestuous Atlantic, in the hope of steering a course south and to safety in their home ports.

Where English gunnery had failed to destroy, fierce storms devastated the Armada. More than twenty-five ships were wrecked on the west coast of Ireland, drowning around 6,000 of their soldiers and sailors. Well over 1,500 survivors were hunted down and killed by English forces in Ireland.

One survivor of the shipwrecks, Francisco de Chéllar, wrote afterwards of the horrors experienced by the stranded Spaniards, recounting how Sir William Fitzwilliam, Lord Deputy of Ireland and English military commander

> set out at once with 1,700 soldiers in search of the wrecks and the people who had escaped. There could not have been very many, fewer than 1,000 men, roaming naked, unarmed, in the places where each ship foundered. Most of these, the governor caught and hanged at once. He inflicted other penalties too and imprisoned the people he found sheltering us, doing them all the injury he could.[95]

By the autumn, when the last ships straggled back into Spanish waters, of the mighty Armada totalling 130 ships only sixty got home. More than 20,000 Spanish sailors and soldiers had perished on the voyage. Medina Sidonia told Philip in limp explanation: 'The troubles and miseries we have suffered cannot be described to your majesty. They have been greater than have any been seen in any voyage before.'[96]

The astrologers' prophecies of disaster had come all too true for the Spanish. But England had been saved. Despite Walsingham's pleas, the queen immediately began to stand down the English forces to save money. On 18 August, Drake wrote to him:

> I will not flatter you, but you have fought more with your pen than many have in our English navy fought with their enemies, and but that your place and most necessary attendance about her majesty cannot be spared, your valour and desserts in such place opposite to the enemy had showed itself.[97]

Even Elizabeth showed some gratitude to her spy master. After the exertions of the summer of conflict, he had fallen sick again. On 14 September, the Clerk of the Signet, Thomas Windebank, wrote to Walsingham:

> After her majesty had read these letters, the first thing she said was to know how you did . . . I answered that you had begun your physic [medicine] yesterday because you would lose no time.

Her majesty . . . willed me to write to you, that such as having power to seek and take remedy in time for any [of] their griefs were like to find remedy and she hoped you should do so.

Whereupon I said that . . . [God] had given you health and strength in these late occasions of troubles to attend to the service and spared you from sickness hitherto.

Her majesty confirmed my saying with many gracious and comfortable words towards you.[98]

Here was a rare moment when the queen at last showed some compassion for her loyal spy master. The defeat of the Armada had been a triumph for his intelligence-gathering and the crowning moment of his long and arduous career in her service.

CHAPTER EIGHT

Death in Penury

'I will that my body, in hope of a joyful resurrection, be buried without any extraordinary ceremonies as usually appertain to a man serving in my place, in respect of the greatness of my debts and the mean state I shall leave my wife and heirs in.'

WILL OF SIR FRANCIS WALSINGHAM, SIGNED 12 DECEMBER 1589.[1]

Francis Walsingham suffered a fraught, stormy relationship with Elizabeth. As her Principal Secretary of State, earning an annual salary of £100[2] plus the provision of two hot meals a day, he was responsible for implementing her wishes and decisions and the instructions of her Privy Council. He also supplied guidance and advice on the thousand and one issues – legal, political and diplomatic – that demanded her urgent attention on a day-to-day basis. His duties as head of overseas espionage and chief of security at home meant that he was frequently the unwelcome bearer of grave and tumultuous news.

No such relationship ever runs smoothly, but in the fevered atmosphere of rumour and intrigue that surrounded Elizabeth's court, he often had to endure the sharp edge of her tongue and the devious attempts of his opponents to discredit him in her eyes.

Walsingham, in turn, was often frustrated, sometimes in total despair,

at her constant pig-headed procrastination on those military and diplomatic issues (as well as her cheese-paring in spending) that he saw as
vital to the interests of both throne and state. She sometimes became
locked almost in a state of denial about the imminent dangers confronting
her crown – indeed, her life – and it took a brave, perhaps reckless, official
to shine the cold light of reality upon her false sense of security. All too frequently, Walsingham was destined to be that unlucky official.

Furthermore, there is evidence that at times she disliked intensely
her spy master and secret policeman. Alone amongst her ministers and
advisers, his counsel was always frank, sometimes even censorious, and
frequently shorn of some of the polite niceties of court etiquette. His
letters of reproach and remonstrance must have been difficult for *Gloriana*,
God's chosen sovereign of the realm of England, to read, let alone tolerate,
amid the splendour and panoply of her monarchy.

Then there were his recurrent absences from court, mostly due to
illness, but occasionally departures in high dudgeon at the way his advice
had been ignored, or because he felt slighted, insulted even, by Elizabeth's
jibes or tantrums, and her failure to acknowledge his loyal services. On
22 December 1582, he wrote from his country home at Barn Elms to Sir
Christopher Hatton:

> In men's absence from court, envy often work[s] most malicious
> effects and therefore I . . . pray you, as my friend, to procure [ensure]
> that I may enjoy the orderly course of justice, not to be condemned
> unheard. I trust there will be no fault found with my absence for . . .
> I see no use, for the present, of my service.
>
> And if there were, I hope as it has not been hitherto, so shall it
> never be found that I shall prefer my particular before the public.[3]

When Elizabeth havered over sending Drake to interdict the Armada
preparations, Walsingham was singled out to suffer her sharp tongue.
He told Hatton:

> I hear that I stand in so hard terms with her majesty as I fear any
> persuasion I can use further . . . of Sir Francis Drake's voyage will

hurt more than help. I am blamed as a principal counsellor thereof . . . although I did concur with the rest in a matter of advice.[4]

On other occasions, he defended colleagues before the throne – but paid dearly for such temerity with the testy monarch. In June 1584, for example, Elizabeth became affronted by George Carey, Lord Hunsdon, and Walsingham sought to intercede with her on his behalf. But this only increased her anger and 'seeking to qualify her displeasure' he 'received hard speeches himself'.[5]

Once she *had* made a decision, she could be wholly obdurate. The queen selected Walsingham to embark on an almost hopeless diplomatic mission to Scotland in July and August 1583, despite his earnest pleas not to go. Mendoza, the Spanish ambassador in Paris, whilst hardly an impartial observer, reported triumphantly that Walsingham, then still sick, threw himself at Elizabeth's feet and swore by 'the soul, body and blood of God' that he would not travel to Scotland, even if she ordered him to be hanged for it.[6] Walsingham knew he would be blamed for any failure in the mission and told a colleague:

I shall be ready to set forward about the 13th or 15th [of August], though it be with as ill a will as ever I undertook any service in my life, finding . . . that things are now grown into so bad terms as I fear . . . I shall be [un]able to do any good there and therefore I would most willingly abide [avoid] the journey if by any means I might do it without her majesty's extreme displeasure.[7]

The queen could also be spiteful. She vehemently opposed the marriage of Sir Philip Sidney to Walsingham's sixteen-year-old daughter Frances. Her motivation remains unclear, other than mere unkind caprice, or perhaps her ire was sparked by fears that Leicester, Sidney's uncle, would become closer to Walsingham through the marriage, and a new power bloc would emerge at court.[8] Her principal Secretary of State was away sick in March 1583 when she objected to the love match and he wrote a bitter and disappointed letter from Barn Elms, again to Hatton:

I think myself bound to you for your honourable and friendly
defence of the intended match between my daughter and Mr Sidney.
I do find it strange that her majesty should be offended withal . . .

I hope that her majesty shall weigh the due circumstances of
place, person and quality [so] there can grow no just cause of offence.

[It] may be thought a presumption for me to trouble her majesty
with a private marriage between a free gentleman of equal standing
with my daughter. I had well hoped that my painful [painstaking,
conscientious] and faithful service done unto her majesty had merited
that grace and favour at her hands [and] that she would have counte-
nanced this match with her gracious and princely good likes.[9]

He added that if the queen raised the issue again, she should understand
that the match was near 'concluded and [you should] let her know [what
a] just cause I shall have, to find myself aggrieved if her majesty shall
show her mislike thereof'.[10] The queen's disapproval continued into May,
when Roger Manners wrote to his father Edward, Third Earl of Rutland,
that 'Mr Secretary . . . is somewhat troubled that her majesty conceives no
better of the marriage . . . but I hope shortly all will be well.'[11] And so it
proved. Despite Elizabeth's transparent displeasure, the couple were
married on 21 September 1583 and the following July, Walsingham settled
on them some of his substantial properties and lands in Wiltshire and
Surrey.[12]

The spy master was reported 'well contented' with the match.
However, the marriage settlement included a clause whereby he undertook
to pay or discharge all Sidney's debts 'so far as shall amount to £1,500' (or
more than £250,000 in today's monetary values) and allowed the young
couple and their household to live at his home at Barn Elms.[13] Just over two
years later, in November 1585, a daughter was born. She was christened
Elizabeth at the Walsinghams' parish church of St Olave, Hart Street,
around the corner from their London home in Seething Lane, with the
queen, her sulks forgotten, and Leicester acting as godparents.[14] No doubt
the Christian name was chosen very deliberately to placate and please
her royal susceptibilities.

In June 1586, the young wife, now pregnant again but 'well and merry', joined her husband in Flushing in the Low Countries, where he had been appointed military governor.[15] A Spanish convoy under the Marquis de Vasto and protected by 3,000 infantry and 1,500 cavalry moved to resupply the besieged town of Zutphen on the banks of the River Ijssel. Sidney joined the English forces in the trenches around the town and, following the fad amongst cavalry officers of the time, did not wear his full armour – leaving off his cuisses, or thigh defences.[16] His horse was shot from under him during a second charge against the Spanish troops and he remounted on a fresh charger. As he wheeled to withdraw after penetrating the Spanish lines in a third assault, he was struck by a musket ball in the right leg, just above the knee, shattering his femur. Sidney was taken in Leicester's barge to Arnhem, twenty miles (32 km) away and given medical treatment at the home of Madame Gruithuissens, the widow of a judge.

On 27 September, Leicester wrote a hopelessly optimistic note to Walsingham, reporting a 'most comfortable letter' from the surgeons about his son-in-law's condition. They were in 'very good hope' of his recovery, 'albeit yesterday evening, he grew heavy and [fell] into a fever. About two o'clock, he fell into exceeding good rest and after his sleep, found himself very well and free from any ague at all.'[17] Sidney died from gangrene in the early afternoon of Monday 17 October 1586, aged just thirty-one.[18]

Leicester, aghast at the death of his nephew, brought his young widow to Utrecht

> till she may recover some strength, for she is wonderfully overthrown
> through her long care since the beginnings of her husband's hurt
> and I am the more careful that she should be in some strength ere
> she take her journey into England, for that she is with child.[19]

Burghley wrote to Walsingham on 5 November, offering his condolences. Ever practical, the Chief Minister was more smugly concerned with the debts that his colleague was now taking on:

> If your authority shall die with him for lack of foresight in making
> the conveyance for your safety and that you, as the lawyers' term is,
> assumed upon yourself, you are in very hard case . . . I shall be sorry
> if this is your hazard, which came of love, shall be a teaching to
> others to adventure with more surety.
>
> You do very well to provide as much comfort as you can for the
> young lady, your daughter, considering that, as I hear, she is with
> child, which I wish may prove to be a son for some diminution of all
> your common grief.[20]

Unhappily, Frances' child, another daughter, died.

Sidney's estate was insufficient to pay off even a third of his debts,
which were estimated at a stupendous £6,000, or £1 million in today's
spending terms. Walsingham told Leicester:

> This hard estate of this noble gentleman makes me to stay [delay] to
> take order for his burial until your lordship's return [from the Low
> Countries]. I do not see how the same can be performed with that
> solemnity that appertains without the utter undoing of his
> creditors, which is to be weighed in conscience.[21]

In the event, Sidney's funeral, held over until 16 February 1587, was
a grand and awesome spectacle, with 700 mourners winding their way
through the thronged streets of London behind the cortege to his grave
in the north aisle of Old St Paul's Cathedral. As it slowly passed to the
beat of black-draped and muffled drums, the crowd called out: 'Farewell,
the worthiest knight that lived.' As befits a Protestant military hero,
soldiers from the city's trained bands fired a two-volley salute as Sidney's
coffin was lowered into the grave.

The funeral came eight days after the execution of Mary Queen of
Scots at Fotheringay, and some cynics at court suggested that it was
planned deliberately by Walsingham to counter any public mourning
over her death. The splendour of the occasion was commemorated by a
specially commissioned and expensive book, illustrated with thirty-two
plates depicting the procession engraved by the herald and draughts-
man Thomas Lant.[22]

In spite of Walsingham's dedicated service to queen and country, Elizabeth did not shower honours on her faithful spy master, and he had to wait until 1 December 1577 for his knighthood, conferred upon him at Windsor. The queen was strangely loath to ennoble even those close to her, with Burghley being a rare recipient of a barony. With no son to pass a title on to, Walsingham may not have sought such an honour, and the patronage system may also have offended his Puritan ideals. Indeed, shortly before he died, he wrote scornfully:

> As for titles, which at first were the marks of power and other rewards
> of virtue, they are now according to their name . . . like the titles of
> books, which for the most part, the more glorious things they
> promise, let a man narrowly peruse them over, the less substance
> he shall find in them.
>
> I say, let a man by doing worthy acts deserve honour and
> although he do not attain it, yet he is much happier than he that
> gets it without dessert.[23]

Elizabeth did, however, grant him a number of offices. He was appointed to the long awaited Chancellorship of the Duchy of Lancaster in June 1587. This post administered and protected the royal interests within the duchy and brought with it a regular fee of £142 16s, together with a £4 allowance for ink and paper. Burdened by all his other duties, Walsingham's administrative skills may not have shone in dealing with the duchy's tenantry and other issues connected with the estates. A letter written in 1595 by an individual who had been tasked to come up with reforms in its governance suggests that his management style was none too successful:

> Seeing those matters far past and so far out of all course that I saw
> no manner of reformation was likely to take place, I did therefore
> cast all my notes into the dungeon of silence for that I would be
> deemed to be a busybody . . .
>
> In my conscience that honourable gentleman [Walsingham]
> was abused by such in whom he put his trust who are right

worthy . . . to be called to answer for such . . . disorders as have been by them committed.[24]

Walsingham was also appointed Chancellor of the Order of the Garter on 22 April 1578, which came with a pension of £100 a year together with lodgings within the walls of Windsor Castle and a daily allowance for food. He held this post of dignity and honour for nine years before being succeeded by his old friend Sir Amyas Paulet in 1587. Elizabeth also granted him lands and revenues: the manor of Barnes in 1579; Odiham in Hampshire in August 1585; Little Otford in Kent in 1587; and manors in Durham and York in March 1588. He also enjoyed a number of local appointments: Chief Steward of Salisbury, with an annuity of £62 8s 4d; High Steward of Ipswich, Winchester and Kingston upon Thames; and Recorder of Ipswich in Suffolk. He was also *Custos Rotulorum*, or the queen's representative or guardian of her interests, in Hampshire.

Elizabeth also presented Walsingham with a large allegorical painting depicting the Tudor family group. In the centre was the seated Henry VIII, shown presenting the Sword of Justice to his son, Edward VI, kneeling beside him on his right. On the left was Mary, his daughter by Catherine of Aragon, and her husband, Philip II of Spain, behind whom, significantly in propaganda terms, stood a figure of Mars, the bringer of war. Opposite was Elizabeth herself, portrayed with figures of Peace and Plenty, treading underfoot the weapons of discord. Inscribed in gold letters at the foot of the painting was this doggerel verse:

The Queen [to] Walsingham this Tablet sent
Mark of her people's and her own content.[25]

This gift represented a rare public display of her appreciation of the services of the man she called 'Her Dark Moor' because of his swarthy appearance. The painting has been attributed to the Flemish artist Sir Antonio Moro, alias Mor van Dashorst. As he died in Antwerp around 1575, the picture might have been given to Walsingham soon after his appointment as Secretary of State in 1573, and its theme of peace may link it to the Treaty of Bois, signed the year before, in which he took a leading role.[26] Just as likely, it was already hanging in one of Elizabeth's royal apartments and she merely had the inscription added before handing it over as a gift later on in her reign.

More profitable was Walsingham's success in securing from the queen her lease of the customs of all the important western and northern ports for six years from 17 August 1585, at an annual rent of £11,263 0s 7d.[27] This was basically a privatisation of the state's collection of customs dues on goods imported and exported from Plymouth,[28] Fowey, Exeter, Poole, Bridgwater, Bristol, Gloucester, Milford, Cardiff, Chester, Berwick, Newcastle, Hull, Boston, King's Lynn and Great Yarmouth. His hopes for profit, however, were seemingly quickly dashed. In the first three years, he paid the royal exchequer £21,050 instead of the £33,789 1s 9d agreed under the lease, and Walsingham claimed in 1589 that the shortfall was caused by the 'fear of war' with Spain and other constraints on trade, which caused a decline in revenues.[29] On 28 May 1586, he wrote to his brother-in-law Sir Walter Mildmay, Chancellor of the Exchequer, asking that the £829 owed in customs dues by Sir Walter Raleigh and others be accepted as part of his payments required by the customs agreement.[30] Elizabeth, surprisingly for one so careful of the contents of her purse, forgave the debt and accepted a much-reduced annual payment of £7,000 for the remainder of his lease.

In reality, as Conyers Read has demonstrated,[31] Walsingham *was* making a generous margin out of the administration of the customs: £2,053 in 1585–6; £3,852 in 1586–7; £6,695 in 1587–8 and £1,765 in 1588–9, revenue in the latter years reduced by the impact of the Armada on maritime trade. Overall, he was taking a handsome fifty-eight-per-cent profit annually out of the business, but much of it was probably being used to augment secret service funds.

There is little doubt that Walsingham had a ready eye for commercial opportunity. On 30 January 1584, William Paget wrote to him proposing a project to supply 'marble out of Ireland' to the North African coast for building purposes. 'Mr Alderman Starkey has communicated this [plan] to the earl of Leicester,' he announced, and strongly advised the Secretary to be a partner in the venture.[32] Walsingham was also involved in the export of unfinished cloth, receiving licences in September 1574 to trade in 8,000 broad cloths or kerseys over four years, and permission for a further 200,000 over the next eight years.[33] Here, he almost certainly sold his rights on to trading companies such as the Merchant Adventurers.

Walsingham paid out £25 as one of the financial backers for Martin Frobisher's first unsuccessful expedition in 1576 to discover the elusive Northwest Passage around North America and on to the Far East, and probably £200 for a second voyage in search of precious metals. But Frobisher returned in September 1577 with only 200 tons of iron pyrites – fool's gold – in the hold of his ship. Despite this disaster, Walsingham was inveigled into putting up more than £800 for a third voyage in 1578 that proved just as disappointing. More profitable was his probable investment in Sir Francis Drake's plundering cruise along Spanish settlements on the west coast of North America in the late 1570s.

Walsingham also secured from the queen a charter on 11 June 1578 enabling the explorer Sir Humfrey Gilbert[34] to find and colonise 'remote heathen and barbarous lands, countries and territories not actually possessed of any Christian prince or people' for the 'inhabiting and planting of our people in America'. Some of the financial backing for this enterprise may have come from Catholics in England, and there is no doubt that Walsingham actively encouraged these voyages of discovery, seeing a Catholic colony in North America as an elegant method of ridding himself of some troublesome citizens. He successfully urged Bristol merchants to support the project and his stepson Christopher Carleill, or Carlyle, was active in convincing the Muscovy Merchants in London to make a substantial investment. Gilbert set sail with five ships on 11 June 1583 and landed in Newfoundland, but was lost at sea when his tiny vessel *Squirrel* foundered off the Azores on the return journey.

Aside from these forays into mercantile endeavour and exploration, Walsingham's burden of paperwork must have been almost unbearable. Despite his frailty and his illnesses, he still managed to handle the voluminous daily correspondence that came with the job. It is none too difficult to picture him, gaunt-faced, lying in bed and wracked with pain, surrounded by sheaves of paper and parchment: the letters from the great and good at home and overseas; the accusations of recusancy against their neighbours by malicious citizens; and perhaps some vital intelligence from his network of spies.

One of his faithful secretaries must always have been in attendance, sitting in a corner of the room and taking dictation as his master digested the contents of each letter and decided on the appropriate action: prison for some poor Catholic; a painful meeting in the Tower with the torturer Richard Topcliffe for an arrested Jesuit priest; or, more mundanely, whether to grant petitions seeking favour from some anxious suitor greedy for advancement and enrichment.

There were other, more tiresome problems that took up Walsingham's valuable time and energy. For example, the Earl of Shrewsbury wrote to him on 9 January 1584 seeking 'favour for the town of Doncaster' which had been impoverished by the plague. He warned that the queen's recent grants of forest rights to Nicholas Pudsey in Hextroppe, Hunter Woods and Rossington Park would now force her mills in Doncaster into decay for lack of timber.[35] A pretty administrative pickle! In September the same year, his faithful old agent Manucci had 'information against Filippo Corsini for illegal export of wool' in London and proposed a conference with the English traders regarding the problems caused by alien, or foreign, merchants in the wool trade.[36]

Around 1584, Walsingham became involved in a dispute between the inhabitants of Farnham, Surrey, and their vicar Daniel Craft, who, it was reported, could not 'read plainly and distinctly and is a drunkard'.[37] His curates were little better – Thomas Moore and William Owen were also drunkards or, worse still, 'gamesters' and Thomas Hogge was 'unlearned'. The bishop refused to act on the parishoners' complaints, even though Walsingham supported their case. Then there were the usual little domestic difficulties, such as bailing out his servant Stephen Ellis who had been seized by the night watch at Whitechapel in East London on 10 May 1580.

Finally, his reputation as a sober man of integrity often led to him being called on to arbitrate in delicate family matters, such as the clandestine marriage in 1582 of Lord Beauchamp to Honora, daughter of Sir Richard Rogers of Bryanston in Dorset. The young bridegroom wrote to Walsingham seeking his assistance to reconcile him both to his father, the Earl of Hertford, and the queen – who frequently took a dim, old maid's view of such wilful activity amongst her nobility. Walsingham took a hard-headed stance. He wrote to Hertford from Windsor on 3 October, advising him to consult church divines regarding whether his son 'may free himself of the match' and if this were not possible, to put up with it. He told Beauchamp the same day to behave 'in a humble and dutiful sort' towards his father, 'considering how deeply you have offended [him] by matching yourself against his will'.[38]

Walsingham's reputation also made him an attractive employer: in 1582, a man called Johnson told the Secretary that he desired 'to have his honour's cloth for a livery this year, for it is a great comfort to be known to be one of your servants'.[39]

Walsingham's onerous duties were made even less bearable by his frequent bouts of ill-health. Although the symptoms vary, his illnesses were long-standing and sometimes removed him from court for lengthy periods. His maladies began early on in his royal service. In 1571, during his first embassy to France, Walsingham wrote to Burghley that his disease 'grows so dangerously upon me' that Elizabeth should send a substitute for him. 'I hope my life shall stand her majesty in more stead than my death and upon these extreme points stand the deferring of my cure.'[40]

His departure from Paris to attend an important diplomatic meeting at Blois with the Huguenot leader Admiral Gaspard de Coligny and the king of France early that September was delayed by 'the necessity of taking physic [medicine]'.[41] But there were no obvious signs of cure, and Walsingham's medical condition grew steadily worse, forcing him to repeat his pleas to London to be temporarily relieved of his duties. The queen eventually sent the diplomat Henry Killigrew to France in October to replace him and belatedly but sternly ordered Walsingham to consult his doctors. He was off sick until the end of the following February, writing to Burghley on 2 December: 'I am diseased by three sundry carnosities which will require the longer time to cure.'⁴² A 'carnosity' is a morbid fleshy excrescence, sometimes a fungous growth, and may be a symptom suggestive of some form of cancer afflicting Walsingham. After returning to his post, he suffered a slight relapse early in April 1572. In the tumultuous aftermath of the St Bartholomew's Day massacre of Huguenots in Paris in August that year, Walsingham again fell ill, which prevented him from delivering diplomatic correspondence in person to the French king.

After he returned to England and had been in post as Secretary of State for about two years, Fénelon, the then French ambassador in London, reported in January 1575 that Walsingham was absent from Elizabeth's court for about a month for treatment for 'son accoustumé difficulté d'urine' (problems in passing water).⁴³ In fact, he was off sick much longer. In April that year, he wrote from his home in London to James Douglas, Fourth Earl of Morton and Regent of Scotland: 'As yet, I remain at my own house under the hands of the physicians of whom I hope shortly to be rid, being in very good way of thorough cure.'⁴⁴

Walsingham was ill again in February 1576 and was in bed, suffering 'a pain in his head and stomach' in January 1578.⁴⁵ Three years later, he wrote a letter to Anthony Bacon,⁴⁶ the son of Lord Keeper Sir Nicholas Bacon, that reveals his frequent and excessive use of medicine for his illnesses in his younger days:

> . . . a thing which I have, by experience, found hurtful in myself when I was of your years, so you will find in time, many incommodities if you do not in time break it off.
>
> Your years will better wear out any little indisposition by good order of exercise and abstinence with some other little moderation in diet, than abide to be corrected with physic [medicine], the use whereof alters nature much – yes, makes a new nature, if it be without great cause used in younger years.⁴⁷

By now Walsingham was approaching fifty, a good age for a period that regularly saw far more limited life expectancies,⁴⁸ even though he had suffered debilitating illnesses for at least the last two decades. Whether his medical condition, be it a cancer or some disease of the kidneys, had been worsened by what today would be regarded as quack remedies must remain debatable, although it seems likely they were frequently of little assistance. Given the kinds of drugs prescribed by doctors to their hapless patients during the Tudor age – some of them remarkably toxic – perhaps the spy master was lucky still to be alive.[49] If he was seeking relief from pain, he may have sought solace from draughts of opium-based potions, which could explain why his 'taking of physic' so inconveniently rendered him *hors de combat*. The drugs may also have affected his immune system, making him vulnerable to other infections and illnesses such as fevers. Certainly, his dogged determination and total self-belief kept him functioning when lesser mortals would have gratefully and gracefully retired from a taxing, tiring and turbulent public office.

He was taken ill once more in the hot summer of 1583, and on 2 July wrote to Burghley after he had visited him in his sickbed:

> The same night your lordship departed from hence, I was taken
> with an extreme fit of the colic which held me until next day at
> noon. Since that time till now I have been so greatly troubled with
> pain in my back and head as I am not able to write, whereof your
> lordship is to pardon me that I use not my own hand[writing].[50]

Two days later, a letter to one of Walsingham's friends, Sir Thomas Heneage, now Vice-Chamberlain, reported that 'Mr Secretary has not been well at ease since your departure [and] has kept [to] his chamber. I delivered your letters to him and he desired a note whether to send to you in York'.[51] Walsingham was still suffering from the pain in August, as he told Hatton:

> This last night I was troubled with an extreme pain in my right side
> which bereaves me of my sleep. It continues with me still and
> therefore I mean to use both Gifford's and Hector's advice.[52] I find
> the pain accompanied with an unaccustomed faintness and a
> disposition altogether subject to melancholy.
>
> I hope I shall enjoy more ease in another world than I do in this.[53]

As we have seen, his fury and bitterness over being denied Babington's forfeited properties by Elizabeth and his despair over her continued indecision regarding the execution of Mary Queen of Scots in January 1587 made him 'dangerously ill', and at that time he may have been attended by a Dr Baily.[54] Later that year, Walsingham suffered a seizure while on official duties in London and frankly told Leicester that for one moment he feared he would die. He was also afflicted again with his old problem of being unable to pass water and a number of remedies failed to provide any relief from this distressing and painful condition, perhaps caused by a urine infection, which could also trigger high fevers.[55]

Although he recovered, by September he was again in the hands of his doctors. On 9 September, Burghley wrote from court to Walsingham, who was then staying at the Chief Minister's opulent home at Theobalds in Hertfordshire, expressing his gladness about 'the comfort that your physicians and surgeons give you'[56] – presumably another liberal dose of opiates. However, a relapse must have occurred, for more than two weeks later, the Lord Treasurer wrote again with fears that his fever 'comes of some extraordinary pains'.[57] Whatever Walsingham was suffering from, it was a debilitating disease, for it ensured that the spy master was frequently away from his desk at the crucial time of the Armada preparations until the early spring of 1588,[58] and on 19 June he was again in bed, 'waiting for a recurrence of his fit'.[59]

The following year he was laid low once more and ordered by his doctors to stay in bed. His letter of 27 August to Burghley enclosed some of his papers which had been

> read to me, being advised by my physicians to keep my bed, waiting whether I shall be visited with another fit of my fever, whereof I am in no doubt for that I have this night taken no good rest.[60]

By 1590, it was clear to many that Walsingham's health was irretrievably in decline, and perhaps fearing that he was losing his mental as well as physical faculties, he once again sought Elizabeth's permission to appoint a replacement. In March, he delivered a batch of state papers held in his custody to Burghley for safekeeping because of his incapacity.[61] On 2 April, Thomas Windebank wrote to Walsingham reporting his conversation with the queen about a fit that the spy master had just suffered, probably while at court:

> I told her majesty of your last night's fit, which I heard [of] by Mr Lake[62] and thereupon took occasion to move her for speedy easing of your honour; whereunto, she answered that shortly she would call another to the place, so that I hope when a full presence of councillors shall be here, the effect of her resolving will take place.[63]

Even in this last service for her loyal minister, Elizabeth was delaying her decision on who would be his successor. Windebank also informed Walsingham that Burghley should 'speak with the Italian who had lately arrived' if he was too unfit to do so.

Walsingham was now fully aware that his death could not be far off and had prudently made a number of preparations, both financial and spiritual. In July 1584, he had conveyed a large parcel of lands to create a small income for his wife and daughter Frances. Ever the devout Protestant, he also wanted to leave his mark firmly on the religious life of London. In April 1589, he drew up a plan for 'catechising' within the city, with the appointment of 'two eminent persons from the universities . . . to be supported by a fixed stipend and by public subscription' to preach in the (new) Greyfriars in the city's Farringdon Ward. 'Some stage may be erected [in the church] theatre-wise, for the receiving of great numbers; a special place to be appointed for all women, apart by themselves'.[64] He also wrote three essays on philosophical and moral themes during the last months of his life, the last entitled *Sir Francis Walsingham's Anatomising of Honesty, Ambition and Fortitude*.[65]

The spy master had drawn up his will on 12 December 1589, while of 'good and perfect memory (praise be to God)'. Much of the very simple and direct document, as befits a committed and devout believer, has a religious content. He bequeathed his soul

> when it should please . . . almighty god, my creator and maker, to separate the same from this my most sinful earthly and mortal body,

to the Holy Trinity, God the Father, my creator, God the Son, my
only redeemer, and God the Holy Ghost, the true comforter . . .

He felt assured that Christ would continue to defend him while still
living, 'especially in this time wherein sin and iniquity so much abound'.
He hoped that he would make a 'good and Christian end' – a good death
– 'in perfect sense and memory' – this, perhaps, a telling reference to
his very real fears about his diminishing mental capacity, perhaps adversely
affected by his drugs. Walsingham asked that his body, 'in hope of a
joyful resurrection', should be

> buried without any such extraordinary ceremonies as usually appertain
> to a man serving in my place, in respect of the greatness of my debts
> and the mean state [I] shall leave my wife and heir in.[66]

The will mentions a £200 annuity (nearly £28,000 at current prices) to
his daughter Lady Sidney, already executed by a deed he had previously
signed, and a further £100 to be paid to her every year while Walsingham's wife Ursula lived. This latter sum was in lieu of the lands in Lincolnshire owned by Frances' husband that Walsingham had earlier
ordered to be sold.

His 'well-beloved wife' was to be his sole executor and after payment
of his debts, the residue of 'all my goods, chattels, plate and jewels, I do
give to Dame Ursula'. In addition, bequests of plate worth £10 each were
to be given to 'my most loving brethren' – his brother-in-law Robert
Beale, Edward Carle and William Dodington – 'in token of my good
affection towards them' who were appointed overseers of the will.

There was clearly anxiety in his mind to make suitable arrangements
before he met his Maker. On 3 April 1590, Walsingham sold his manors of
Axford and Chilton in Wiltshire, with annual rental incomes of £44 and
£13 6s 8d respectively, to William Gerrard, Francis Milles (his old secretary)
and John Willard, presumably to help pay off his immediate debts.[67]

Three days later, in the early hours of 6 April, Walsingham died at
his house in Seething Lane.[68] His will was discovered there, hidden in
a secret cabinet.

The contemporary historian William Camden, who probably knew Walsingham well, noted that he died of 'a carnosity growing, *intra testium suntcas* [testicular cancer] . . . or rather through violence of medicines'.[69] Pertinently, Camden also claimed that the spy master's efforts to 'diligently [search] out the hidden practices against religion, his prince and country' had left him with 'so great charges, that he weakened his private estate and [was] surcharged with debt'.

As a result of this indebtedness and in fulfilment of his last wishes, Walsingham was buried privately the following night at ten o'clock. His final resting place was in the north aisle of the choir of Old St Paul's Cathedral, hard by the grave of his son-in-law Sir Philip Sidney.

It must have been a short, sombre ceremony, the torches lighting the sad faces of the mourners amid the gloom of the huge gothic cathedral. The funeral was totally bereft of the trappings of honour and power that would be expected to have accompanied him to the grave, as a personage of such great importance and magnitude in Elizabethan England. There were no serried columns of professional black-clad mourners, no pomp and circumstance for Walsingham. Neither was a certificate of his funeral entered at the College of Heralds, as was normal practice for someone of his status.[70] It cannot now be determined how big a factor his shortage of ready cash was in the decision to have a simple funeral – certainly, holding it at night absolved his estate from having to pick up the bill for draping Old St Paul's in black mourning, the usual custom for marking the obsequies of such an important figure. His own bleak, self-denying brand of Protestantism may also have figured in the choice of ceremony.

Certainly, afterwards there was no grand, imposing tomb of alabaster columns and gilded heraldry, sculpted by one of the fashionable Dutch refugee sculptors in Southwark, erected over his mortal remains, as commemorated many of his fellow Privy Councillors. Wags maintained that the lack of appropriate monuments for Walsingham and Sidney was because the stupendous tomb of Sir Christopher Hatton, the Lord Chancellor,[71] towering as high as a two-storied house, left little room for them.[72] A rhyming couplet of the time by a 'merry poet' maintained dryly:

Philip and Francis have here no tomb
Since great Sir Christopher has all the room.[73]

There was some official debate over the content of his epitaph. One of several surviving documents suggested some suitable words and phrases focusing on his life and works 'to be considered'. One or two passages were plainly extravagant:

> His birth . . . parents, the father . . . descended of the house of gentry of the Walsinghams being of greater antiquity than the [Norman] conquest. [In another hand:] His mother of the Dennys . . .
>
> [He] did foster and help to prevent many dangers, practices [plots] as well as abroad as at home against his Prince and his country in discovery of which he was so largely liberal that he neglected much of his private estate as well as for health and wealth.[74]

In the event, a Latin inscription, probably merely painted upon a modest wooden board, was later fixed on the wall or a pillar above Walsingham's unmarked grave. It was destroyed when the Great Fire of London consumed the old cathedral in 1666. Translated, it read:

Sacred to Virtue and Honoured
Sir *FRANCIS WALSINGHAM*
Descending from a Family every way splendidly conspicuous
Excell'd and out-shined the splendour of his Family
By the Shining Lustre of his quaint wit,
And the beautiful embellishments of a Noble Mind.
In his Childhood, he was ingeniously educated at home.
In his Youth, he travel'd into many foreign Countries
Whose manners, Laws, Languages and Policies
He accurately studied and critically understood
As he practically improved the knowledge of them
Both to his private advantage,
And indeed public Emolument of the whole Realm.
In his Virile Age, he voluntarily (during the Reign of *Queen Mary*)
Forsook his Country for the preservation of his Religion.

In his riper years

He was sent Ambassador by Queen *Elizabeth* into *France*, even in the most turbulent times: In which Employment, he continued there many years.

After some interval he was again sent Twice Ambassador to that Kingdom.

Moreover, once into *Scotland* and once into the *Netherlands*.

He was also of the Privy Council to that Queen

And her Principal Secretary of Estate for seventeen years together.

Besides all this he was Three Years Chancellor of the Duchy of *Lancaster*.

In all which Offices, he demeaned[75] himself

With so much Prudence, Temperance, Generosity,

Moderation, Piety, Industry and Circumspection

That he hereby freed his Country from many apparent Perils,

Preserved the Republic and ratified the peace of the Realm,

And consequently still studied to be beneficial and helpful to all

Especially those who were eminent in the possession of Arts or Arms

And thus evermore regardless of himself,

he was ever ready to help and assist others

Though to the consumption and much impairing of his own purse and person.

He had a choice and virtuous wife named *Ursula*

By whom he had only one daughter named *Frances*

First married to Sir *Philip Sidney* Knight,

Secondly to the right honourable then Earl of *Essex*

And lastly to the right honourable *Richard*, Earl of *Clanrickarde*.

He died the 6th of April in the year of our Lord 1590

And was buried in a manner Privately.[76]

Some acrostic verses – in which the initial letter of each line vertically spells out his name – were also later attached to the pillar. They were signed 'E. W.' – probably Elizabeth Walsingham, his grand-daughter, who is known to have been a poet.

As we have seen, his espionage activities involved 'much consumption and much impairing of his own purse' – how big a factor was the running of Elizabeth's secret service in the near bankruptcy of Walsingham? Shortly after his death, Burghley calculated a balance sheet for his debts, which included £12,016 owed to the queen and a further £15,308 to other individuals, totalling £27,324, or nearly £4 million in today's money. Of the private creditors, the vast bulk – more than £12,000 – was owed to Sir Thomas Shirley. This is probably the Shirley who was treasurer-at-war to the English army in the Netherlands but got himself into dire straits over his own debts to the crown,[77] or his soldier son, who was knighted in 1589 and ended up in the Tower two years later for marrying secretly, to Elizabeth's obvious displeasure.

In 1611, nine years after the demise of Dame Ursula, Walsingham's brother-in-law Robert Beale conducted an inquiry into Walsingham's estate and drew up another, far more favourable estimate of his finances at the time of his death. It also provides some insight into the very large sums of money that passed through the Secretary's hands on government business. Beale's figures suggested that the Secretary had paid out the colossal sum of £38,089 6s 11d 'for the Queen's service', which, added to another £10,438 3s 6d refunded to his 'servants' for their spending for the same reason, totalled £48,527 10s 5d, or nearly £7 million at today's values. Debts to the crown were then calculated, rather precisely, at £43,181 7s 10d. This left a healthy credit in Walsingham's favour of £5,346 2s 6d, in today's terms worth £729,000. Of course, his widow and daughter would have seen nothing of this cash, so the claims of near-insolvency may well be justified. The learned judge Sir Julius Cæsar decided in 1611 on a just quid pro quo – wiping out the debts owed by both sides,[78] thereby at least lifting this burden from the family.

This decision was formalised on 5 August that year, when a release was granted to Frances, as executor to Sir Philip Sidney, and Elizabeth, daughter and heir to Walsingham, of 'all sums and debts owing to the crown'.[79]

On 30 June 1590, Burghley wrote to Count Giovanni Figliazzi in Florence – the Tuscan diplomat whose information about the Armada proved so useful to Walsingham – thanking him for his offer to mediate between Elizabeth and the king of Spain. He also informed him of the spy master's death:

> I cannot otherwise think but you have before this time heard or else I am sure you will hear . . . of the death of Mr Secretary Walsingham who left this world the 6th of April . . .
>
> Though he has gained a better state, as I am fully persuaded, for his soul in heaven, yet the queen's majesty and her realm and I and others, his particular friends, have had a great loss, both for the public use of his good and painful long services and for the private comfort I had by his mutual friendship.[80]

A change in command is always a disruptive period in any intelligence operation. For Elizabeth's government, it was imperative to establish from where and from whom the secretive Walsingham received his valuable information. Burghley's staff must have made a frantic search amongst his papers to discover the identities and locations of his agents. Within a month, they had built up a partial list:

> The names of foreign places from whence Mr Secretary Walsingham was accustomed to receive his advertisements of the state of public affairs. [The names of] agents on the Borders and in Scotland, about the Queen of Scots [and] among the foreign ambassadors and Papists.[81]

Burghley's agents probably also combed through Walsingham's papers and sequestered a huge number of documents, to protect the powerful and safeguard the reputation of Elizabeth's government.

Some of his informants were still anxious to ply their sordid trade under a new master. Burghley had received, on 28 June, a note from one of Walsingham's informants – the London grocer Thomas Millington – who wrote of his obligations to the spy master, 'who had befriended him in his grievous distress and protected him from the malice of his enemies'. He had supplied secret intelligence from abroad to Walsingham and was clearly interested in continuing these services for Elizabeth's government. As an indication of his talents, and an appetiser for future services, he told of the 'dangerous practices of Catholics, as shown by the example of one Robert Morris who carried away a young kinsman of his to be christened in Spain'.[82] Walsingham's intelligence network was alive and breathing, albeit with its members' usual vested interests intact to the last.

His arch-enemy Spain was also quick to learn of his decease. On 18 April, a Spanish spy in London provided details of an English fleet then being fitted out 'with much activity' and possibly destined for the Azores, sailing under the Portuguese flag. He added finally: 'Secretary Walsingham has just expired – at which there is much sorrow.'

More than a thousand miles away in the Escorial Palace in Madrid, King Philip II of Spain later read the spy's report. After musing for a few moments, he picked up his pen and scribbled in the margin alongside his personal reaction to the spy master's death: 'There . . . yes. But it is good news here.'[83]

Walsingham would have smiled wryly at this unexpected tribute to his life's work.

CHAPTER NINE

Epilogue

'Madam, I beseech you, be content not to fear.
The Spaniard has a great appetite and
an excellent digestion but I have fitted him with
a bone for this twenty years . . . Your majesty
have no cause to doubt him, provided
that if the fire chanced to slack which I have
kindled, you will be ruled by me, and
now and then cast in some English fuel which
will revive the flame.'

SIR FRANCIS WALSINGHAM TO QUEEN ELIZABETH REGARDING
SPANISH PLANS AGAINST FRANCE.[1]

Walsingham was clearly a famous Protestant hero in his time. William Camden, writing only a little while after his death, said that in subtlety and official services

> he surpassed the queen's expectation and the Papists accused him
> as a cunning workman in complotting his business and alluring
> men into dangers, whilst he diligently searched out their hidden
> practices against religion, his prince and country.[2]

Sir Robert Naunton had read many of Walsingham's 'letters . . . and secrets, yet if I might have been beholding to his ciphers (whereof they are full) they would have told pretty tales of the times'.[3]

Men of letters also paid their tributes. The poet Edmund Spenser acknowledged his virtues and accomplishments in a sonnet prefixed to his *Faerie Queene*, published in 1596:

This lowly Muse that learns like steps to trace,
Flies for like aid unto your patronage;
That as the great Mecænas of this age,
As well to all that civil arts profess
As those that are inspired with martial rage
And craves protection of her feebleness
Which if ye yield, perhaps ye may her raise
In bigger times to sound your living praise.

Another poet, Thomas Watson,[4] who befriended the spy master in Paris in 1581, wrote a Latin and English *Eglogue upon the death of the Right Honourable Sir Francis Walsingham* in 1590, in which he appears under the pastoral name of Melibœus and his daughter as Hyane. The English version was dedicated to Frances and talks of Walsingham as 'a sound pillar of our commonwealth and chief patron of virtue, learning and chivalry'.

For all these fine, elegant words, however, Walsingham in truth was a ruthless instrument of the state.

With the benefit of our twenty-first-century liberal values, we could easily share the oppressed English Catholics' view of his character and actions. It would be all too simple for us to glibly equate Elizabeth's ubiquitous Minister with the most notorious and cruellest enforcers of any modern-day totalitarian nation, such as Lavrenty Beria of the Soviet NKVD, or Reichsführer Heinrich Himmler, who controlled Nazi Germany's *Schutzstaffel* (SS) and Gestapo. But such a hasty judgement would be wholly wrong, as it conveniently discounts the callous reality of the times in which Walsingham lived and the challenges he confronted almost daily.

Religious belief is a powerful, unforgiving emotion and, down the

ages, countless barbarities have been piously committed in its sancti-
monious name against many good and innocent men, women and
children. Sadly, such outrages continue today under the same justification
and there remains a widespread failure to fully comprehend the compelling imperative of religious motivation behind so many of the horrific
acts that stun us when we turn on our televisions or read our news-
papers. The only change, over the years, is our increased capacity to be
shocked by them. But more than four centuries ago, the conflict arising
from differences in religious belief was more starkly defined and fiercely
fought over upon a less sophisticated and more violent stage. In sixteenth-
century England, lacking much of the painfully acquired veneer of the
civilised behaviour norms we enjoy today, life was not only far cheaper but
contained fewer complexities, certainly no niceties. Pain and death were
never far away in everyday life.

In this harsh environment, we find Walsingham to be a deeply
spiritual man, driven always by the overarching need to protect and
preserve his precious Protestant state, beset, like a small ship in a fierce,
threatening storm, by enemies all around – indeed, even within.

Never far from the forefront of his mind was the brutal suppression
of Protestantism by Mary, Elizabeth's Catholic half-sister, in the mid-
1550s, a persecution he had wisely fled from as a youth. He would have
returned from exile certain that those burnings and that bloodshed would
inevitably be repeated in England if Catholicism were ever restored as
the state religion.

Subsequent events just across the English Channel bore out his worst
fears and hardened his resolve to prevent that happening, at whatever
cost. Like the rest of the English government, he had heard with horror
the graphic accounts of the mass atrocities inflicted on 'infidel' Dutch
Protestants by the crusading Spanish army of occupation in the Low
Countries. He must also have been traumatised and scarred by witnessing
the bloody and genocidal St Bartholomew's Day massacre in Paris in
August 1572. Later, as Secretary of State, reports endlessly crossed his
desk from his spies and informers regarding plot after plot to assassinate his queen and the planned invasions, by battle-hardened Catholic

forces, of his ill-defended nation. Couple the impact of these events with his own religious fervency, and we might begin to understand his personal determination that Spanish troops would never forcibly return the Mass to English parish churches on the needle-sharp points of their pikes.

Such fears could rarely have deserted him in either his waking or sleeping hours. They can have left no room for any doubts or scruples to prevent him from deploying all the dark instruments of the Tudor state to destroy any threat he perceived as emanating from the repressed Catholic majority or from England's enemies overseas. To him, bribery, treachery, blackmail, coercion, internment, torture and state-sponsored murder were merely handy tools to be employed unhesitatingly to stamp out the contagion of Popish treason and conspiracy. In addition, let us also remember that these tools were the customary penal methods of the period, used similarly by oppressive Catholic governments and administrations in the Low Countries, in Spain, France and Italy.

Walsingham's writings demonstrate the extent to which his simple but dour version of Protestantism shaped his thoughts and actions. Walsingham perhaps held a brutally logical, Old Testament view of the world. 'Right' – represented by decency, humility, obedience and even patriotism – was clearly God's work, and 'wrong' was often equated with the wicked actions and sinful will of a Popish Anti-Christ. The continuance of his religion in England, as an island haven from or bastion against what he saw as the florid evils of Catholicism in Europe, was to him the complete and absolute personal mission in life. Its importance to him perhaps exceeded his concern for and loyalty to his queen, as she sometimes testily but shrewdly pointed out. Indeed, sixty years on, he might have felt comfortable in the humourless Puritan Republican Commonwealth of Protector Cromwell. He was therefore something of a fanatic, a religious fundamentalist in modern terms, who saw issues purely in black and white, always measured against what he and his God stood for. You were either on Walsingham's side or judged to be against his aims and objectives, and therefore treated accordingly. There was no room for grey areas of indecision: right had to be defended by might and, in his terms, might was right.

So much for his motivations. To secure the state religion and the sacred person of Elizabeth, we have seen how he employed a substantial network of overseas spies and domestic informers – the direct forerunners of today's secret intelligence and security services in Britain. In the face of always inadequate funding from the state, his belief that the 'acquisition of knowledge is never too dear' often had to be supported by contributions from his own private finances. His methodology, his total obsession with secrecy, would be familiar tools of the trade to any desk officer in a modern spy agency, as would the systematic way in which he collected evidence against individuals, although some of his tactics – such as forging incriminating material – would be shunned in Western societies.

If he had one fault, it may have been an unwillingness to pounce on a suspect until he had collected every available piece of information. Perhaps such caution or occasional hesitancy is understandable in any secret policeman who operates amongst the shifting sands of rapidly changing political allegiances at court, or has to rely on a corps of unreliable informers, motivated only by cash handouts.

But despite all the obstacles, he succeeded in staunchly and successfully protecting both England and Elizabeth.

His intelligence-gathering played a major role in defeating the Spanish Armada – a role acknowledged by that ultimate man of action, the swashbuckling corsair Francis Drake – as well as foiling conspiracy after conspiracy, including the continual machinations of Mary Queen of Scots. His attempts to counter her constant plotting against queen and state must count as one of the greatest and most dramatic personal confrontations of English history. Elsewhere in this undeclared and covert religious war, Walsingham's mind encompassed a remarkable grand strategic vision focused on containing the Spanish and papal threats and recognising that his front-line defences lay not along the English coast, but on the continent of Europe. He fully understood the necessity of using naval power to exert political and diplomatic pressure; he utilised economic warfare to hinder the Armada preparations; he employed black propaganda to lower morale amongst the forces of England's enemies.

Unfortunately, Elizabeth did not always embrace the wisdom of his strategies, and the audacity of some of his proposals, together with their potential cost, was often too much for her to swallow, or for her exchequer to bear. And who can blame her? After all, she had far more to lose from an unlucky throw of the dice in Walsingham's 'great game' against the Spanish.

For Walsingham, his onerous duties as spy master came on top of the workload of the routine bureaucratic grind of government and a series of difficult diplomatic missions. His career as a Minister is a breathtaking intellectual achievement, made more impressive by his frequent and debilitating bouts of ill-health. His capacity for paperwork must have been awesome, even aided by a bevy of secretaries. Walsingham was not a man cursed with tunnel vision: he had an unquenchable thirst for detail, as befits any spy master. While Burghley's papers often consist of only a tautly disciplined half-page of handwriting, Walsingham's correspondence goes on for page after page – confirming details, seeking information, giving instructions, offering advice. Despite his pressure of work, no issue went unresolved. He must rank as one of England's greatest administrators.

His sure, safe hands manipulated many of the levers of power in the Elizabethan state. No wonder he burnt himself out.

Today, Walsingham still remains a man of the shadows, like a play's leading actor speaking his lines off-stage, unseen by the audience. We know something of him by reputation, but few of us have seen his performances to admire his consummate skills. Those quizzical eyes are rarely caught by the bright glare of the footlights of history, but the drama of the past is incomplete without his physical presence. It is now time for him to come out of the darkened wings to receive the audience's applause for his unique role in creating the England, the Britain, we know today.

Walsingham's wife Ursula lived on for twelve years after the death of her husband. She continued to play a role in the life of Elizabeth's court, exchanging New Year gifts with the queen, although their relationship was sometimes stormy. At one point, Elizabeth refused to ask a favour of her, saying imperiously that she would see Ursula hanged first. She died suddenly at Barn Elms on 18 June 1602, probably in her late sixties, and was buried quietly near Francis in Old St Paul's the following night.[5] In her will, dated 30 January 1599, she left bequests of £20 each to eight servants, if they remained in her service at her death; £3 each to her cooks Henry Calthorpe and John Cordell, and £50 to her 'waiting woman' Alice Poole, who must have given faithful service. Amongst those of higher station, her brother-in-law Robert Beale and Thomas Fleming, the queen's Solicitor-General, each received a piece of plate worth twenty marks. Aside from bequests to the poor in Barnes and to the ministers of the parish churches she attended, her 'plate and jewels' and her property at Boston and Skirbeck in Lincolnshire went to her surviving daughter Frances, who was appointed sole executor.[6]

Barn Elms – 'my poor cottage', as Walsingham referred to it[7] – was granted by James I on his accession to the throne to Peter Vanlore, afterwards made a baronet.[8] The house was rebuilt by Thomas Cartwright in 1694 and remodelled in 1771 by the banker Richard Hoare. The site later became famous as the Ranelagh Polo Club, but the buildings were demolished in 1954. Nothing remains except an ornamental pond, an icehouse from the later house and an artificial mound.[9]

Elizabeth, the surviving daughter of Sir Philip and Lady Frances Sidney, married Roger Manners, Earl of Rutland, in March 1599, but died without issue at the age of twenty-nine in 1614. She was something of a poet, with the dramatist Ben Jonson describing her as 'nothing inferior to her father in poetry'.[10]

The widowed Frances took as her second husband the dashing Robert Devereux, Second Earl of Essex, in a secret marriage probably in March 1590, only days before Walsingham's death, to the chagrin of Queen Elizabeth. She bore him one son, Robert, in January 1591, and two daughters, Frances and Dorothy, before he was executed on Tower Hill for attempting rebellion on 25 February 1601, in the dying years of Elizabeth's reign.[11] Robert became a leading Parliamentary general in the Civil War.

Twice-widowed Frances then married for a third time in 1603 – this time to Richard de Burgh, Fourth Earl of Clanrickarde. She bore him one son in 1604 – Ulrick, later Marquis of Clanrickarde – and a daughter, Honora, who married John Paulet, Fifth Marquis of Winchester. Frances herself died on 17 February 1633.

Burghley expired on 4 August 1598 after four decades of faithful service to Elizabeth. His last years were afflicted by poor health, especially the painful gout in his legs. His son Robert had deputised for him for some years before his official appointment as Principal Secretary of State on 5 July 1596. For once, the churlish queen unbent sufficiently to show gratitude for Burghley's loyalty, saying that she gave 'hourly thanks' for all his services, and urged him 'to use all the rest possible you may, that you may be able to serve her at the time that cometh'. She came to his bedside and spoon-fed him during his last days.[12]

The code-breaker and forger Thomas Phelippes worked for Essex after Walsingham's death and his dismissal by Sir Robert Cecil. By 1596, he was so inundated with intelligence reports from Europe that four secretaries were employed to handle the deciphering.[13] A grateful government appointed him Collector of Petty Customs for the Port of London, deputising for that old recusant-hunter, the magistrate Richard Young. But in this lucrative sinecure Phelippes managed to come a cropper. He may have been good at the arithmetic of code-breaking but he was hopeless at the management of money and cash accounts. In just two years, he built up a debt to the crown totalling £11,682 6s 6d, lost his office and was thrown in jail.[14] In 1598, he asked to repay the cash by instalments and to use the exchequer to recover his own debts.[15]

After the accession of James I, Phelippes was quick to write an apology to the new king for his 'meddling in the cause' of his mother, Mary Queen of Scots. He pleaded that he had merely deciphered the letters relating to Babington intercepted by the government.[16] Sir Robert Cecil re-employed him to decode the correspondence of new suspects; one letter has an annotation written in Cecil's hand: 'Letters written by Phelippes and suggested by him to be counterfeited.'[17] An old dog continues with his favourite tricks. In 1605, he was arrested and questioned about his correspondence with undesirables living overseas[18] and four years later, his old debt problems caught up with him again, with a warrant issued to pay Sir Robert Carey £800 for the redemption of the lease of Phelippes, 'late collector of subsidies for the port of London'.[19]

His last appearance in the State Papers is in 1622, by which time he must have been an old man. He was then imprisoned in the Marshalsea, 'arrested upon an old warrant between me and one Tytten'. Sir Robert Cotton reported that Phelippes had been advised to leave England

> and to expect entertainment abroad to sell his skill. He was told . . . by others to have recourse to the king's bounty here, being also of himself loth to wander at these years, especially without leave of the state.
>
> He thereupon presented a petition to his majesty, importing that he had been forced . . . to part with a pension [he] had for deciphering, towards satisfaction of a debt owing to the late queen, which she was in mind to have pardoned . . .
>
> His majesty therefore may be moved – if not for his feat of deciphering, by the which . . . England was sometime preserved to him and sometime his majesty to England, when he knew not of it – for these other abilities to bestow upon him for the present, for to pay his debts till something may occur to repair his estate and to entertain such a servant, perhaps to some ecclesiastical dignity of the inferior sort . . .[20]

History does not record whether Phelippes received his lowly church job, a post remarkably ill-suited to his lurid past as a forger and deceiver.

The spy Anthony Standen heard of Walsingham's death while in prison in Bordeaux after, ironically, he had been arrested on suspicion of being a Spanish agent. He languished in jail for nine months before he could smuggle a letter out to his friend Anthony Bacon, signed with the fictitious name 'Andrew Sandal'. In June 1591, Standen wrote to Burghley complaining about lack of payment for his espionage on behalf of the English crown and seeking his help in obtaining his freedom. Walsingham had told him of a pension of £100 a year that had been granted to him by a grateful sovereign.

At my coming back from Spain to Florence in 1588, I found the effect by the receipt of a year's pay and now this year another towards my voyage which has not sufficed for my expenses in travelling to and especially now this last time being forced to remain for passage at Genoa for five month[s].

The year 1588 was the time that huge armada went and perished: I was, by his [Walsingham's] order, at the court of Lisbon, where I had the view of all and by the way of Italy, gave advice of the whole manner of their designs, which, by his letters I found in Florence, seemed most grateful to her majesty.[21]

Standen was freed on 12 October and went on to Spain, sending a new cipher to Burghley and using the new alias of 'La Faye'. He was later knighted by Elizabeth but fell foul of James I and was imprisoned in the Tower from 1603 until the November of the following year after the discovery of some letters he wrote to various cardinals in Rome about the possible conversion of James's wife, Anne of Denmark, to Catholicism.[22]

Gilbert Gifford, Walsingham's agent provocateur in the Babington case, also came to an ignominious end. Back in France, he astonishingly got himself ordained as a priest but was discovered in flagrante delicto in a brothel in Paris in December 1587. He was immediately imprisoned and an attempt to prosecute him for his treachery against the Catholic cause was launched unsuccessfully by the Papal Nuncio in France. He died in prison in November 1590.

Thomas Morgan, Mary Queen of Scots' agent in Paris, was freed from the Bastille after appeals from Rome for his release, much to Elizabeth's fury. Mendoza arranged a small pension for the Welshman and sent him to Flanders in 1588 to help with the preparations for the invasion of England by Spanish forces. He returned to England after James's accession but was speedily deported back to France, where, bizarrely, he became involved in an intrigue over the custody of the bastard children of Henry IV. He was imprisoned again in the Bastille from June 1604 to April the following year for his inveterate plotting. He made the last of his shuttlecock journeys across the English Channel in 1608 and died in England shortly afterwards.[23]

Bernardino de Mendoza, that most canny of all conspirators, had become blind by 1590 and retired from public life, his scheming and duplicity stilled at last. He died in the convent of San Bernardo in Madrid in 1604.

Richard Topcliffe, the odious rackmaster, prospered. He became the Member of Parliament for Old Sarum, Wiltshire, and developed commercial interests in all manner of enterprises from peat extraction to fuel-iron smelting[24] and in droving cattle. His use of torture to extract information eventually became notorious even in those hard times: a letter from Standen in 1592 refers to an individual having 'such mildness and affability, contrary to our *Topcliffian* [author's italics] customs as he has won with words more than others could ever do with racks'.[25] Despite this sly dig, Topcliffe was effective in arresting suspected priests and breaking down their resistance: the State Papers contain a number of confessions from his victims.[26]

But the tide was slowly turning against Topcliffe and his savage, sadistic methods. Questions over the legality of and official authorisation for his torture emerged after his torment of the priest Robert Southwell in 1592, whom he had arrested in June that year. At his trial three years later, Southwell said he had been tortured on ten separate occasions, but the newly appointed Attorney General Sir Edward Coke asserted that Topcliffe 'had no need to go about to excuse his proceedings in the manner of his torturing'.[27] The rackmaster was able to prove that he had official sanction to torture the priest 'short of death or maiming'.

Always cocksure, always arrogant, Topcliffe was briefly jailed in the Marshalsea in 1595 for insulting the Privy Council, and from there he wrote to the queen, complaining that 'by this disgrace . . . the fresh dead bones of Father Southwell at Tyburn[28] and Father Walpole[29] at York, executed both since Shrovetide, will dance for joy'.[30]

Released, he returned to his winning ways with prisoners, being employed by the Privy Council for a further four years in the interrogation of prisoners in the Bridewell Jail in London, where he widened his net to include thieves, murderers, 'Egipcians [gypsies] and wanderers'.[31] He also interrogated the author and actor Thomas Nash and other players in the lost satirical comedy *The Isle of Dogs* in the Fleet Prison in 1597.

Topcliffe also enjoyed a little light homework at his house hard by St Margaret's Churchyard in Westminster, where he constructed a 'strong chamber' fitted with various sets of manacles'[32] to torment priests 'in his own house in such sort as he shall think good'. Here, he boasted, he had 'a machine, of his own invention, compared with which, the ordinary rack was mere child's play'. One shudders to consider its workings and the effects on the bodies of his victims, or Topcliffe's leer as he inflicted this home-made device on some hapless prisoner.

Topcliffe was now aged sixty-six and afflicted by lameness – no doubt caused by arthritis brought on by all the time he spent in all those damp prisons. His nephew Edmund renounced the family name as an acknowledgement of his uncle's notoriety and his eldest son Charles was convicted of a felony. Topcliffe left London and spent the remainder of his life at his family estate at Somerby in Lincolnshire and, from 1603, at a new property at Badley Hall, Derbyshire, previously owned by the Catholic Thomas Fitzherbert, which he acquired as part of an agreement involving the persecution of the Fitzherbert family.[33] He died peacefully in his bed in November or December 1604.

There is clearly little natural justice in his end.

For six months after her execution, the body of Mary Queen of Scots lay seemingly forgotten at Fotheringay, encased in an anthropoid coffin of lead. At last, in mid-July 1587, orders were issued to give the executed queen a royal burial. This may have been the result of a rare attack of conscience on Elizabeth's part, or more prosaically because the smell of the rapidly decaying corpse was beginning to unpleasantly pervade her castle.

On Sunday 30 July, Sir William Dethicke, Garter King at Arms and the principal herald, plus five of his colleagues and escorted by forty horsemen, arrived at Fotheringay with a 'royal coach' covered in black velvet and decorated with shields bearing the arms of Scotland. Mary's body – the lead shell now encased in a wooden coffin – was reverently placed in the coach and the sad little procession headed off for the city of Peterborough at ten o'clock at night. Some of the Scottish queen's household – her steward Andrew Melville, Dominique Bourgoing, Pierre Gorion and Jacques Gervais[34] amongst them – followed the heralds on foot in the flickering torchlight for the duration of the eleven-mile journey.

At the door of the cathedral, the cortege was met by Richard Fletcher, Dean of Peterborough – ironically, the same clergyman who had fared so badly at Mary's hands at her execution. Sometime around two o' clock in the morning, her coffin was quickly lowered into a vault in the south aisle at the entrance to the choir, 'without bells or chanting'.[35] A small opening was left in the top of the brick vaulting. It had been decided to bury Mary in advance of the funeral because her coffin

> was so extremely heavy by reason of the lead, that the gentlemen could not endure to have carried it with leisure in the solemn proceeding[s] and besides, [it] was feared that the [lead] might rip and being very hot weather, [there] might be found some annoyance.[36]

The funeral service was held on Tuesday 1 August. Although a cloth of estate of purple velvet had been hung over a regal chair in the black-draped presence chamber of the bishop's palace, Elizabeth, as at Mary's trial, had no desire to suffer the embarrassment of attendance. The role of chief mourner therefore fell to Bridget, Countess of Bedford, who wore the insignia of the sovereign she represented. She was attended by a number of court functionaries and thirty-one lords and ladies, together with eight Scottish gentlemen. Despite the ceremonial trappings of royalty, it was deemed indiscreet to invite foreign ambassadors. Outside the palace, one hundred poor men waited patiently to fulfil their symbolic role as mourners in the Scottish queen's obsequies, wearing specially made black gowns.

In lieu of the body or a coffin, a life-size wax effigy of Mary had been carved,[37] which now lay in the great hall of the episcopal palace. Promptly at ten in the morning it was carried in great state into the cathedral and placed in the choir within a hearse measuring twenty feet square, twenty-seven feet in height and richly covered with black velvet.[38] A 'close crown of gold with precious stones' was set on the effigy's head, which rested upon a purple velvet cushion.

An anthem was sung, and the Scottish contingent then all hurriedly departed, save Andrew Melville, Mary's steward, and one of her attendants, Barbara Mowbray, the Scots saying they would 'not tarry [for the Protestant] sermon or ceremonies'.[39] William Wickham, the Bishop of Lincoln, then preached from Psalm 39: 'Lord, let me know my end and the number of my days, that I may be certified how long I have to live.' Today, we would perhaps feel this was a singularly inappropriate choice of text for such a sermon. After being told of her impending execution, Mary at least knew when and in what violent manner her life would be ended. He concluded his discourse with these comforting words for all those who had come *not* to mourn the Scottish queen:

> Let us give God thanks for the happy dissolution of the high and mighty Princess Mary, late Queen of Scotland and Dowager of France, of whose life and death at this time I have not much to say because I was not acquainted with the one, neither was I present at the other.
>
> I will not enter into judgement further but because it has been signified to me that she trusted to be saved by the Blood of Christ, we must hope well of her salvation.
>
> For, as father Luther was wont to say, many a one that lived a Papist died a Protestant.[40]

There is sometimes something insufferably smug about Protestant divines in the late sixteenth century, but his sentiments reflected the perceived threat that Mary Stuart had represented to the continued existence of the English Protestant nation.

Her heraldic accoutrements – the tabard bearing her arms, the sword, shield and helmet – were solemnly laid before the altar[41] and the funeral service was read over the vault containing her body by the Bishops of Lincoln and Peterborough. The officers of Elizabeth's household then ceremoniously and symbolically broke their white wands of office over their heads and hurled the pieces into the void below.

Everyone then departed to consume 'a most royal feast' at the bishop's palace, while alms were distributed to the patient poor gathered outside.[42] The remnants of Mary's household were invited to attend this banquet, their hosts 'praying them to eat well and to ask for anything they wished, so that nothing should be wanting to them, such being the orders of their mistress, [Elizabeth]'.[43] But they sat apart from the official mourners, in a separate room, 'mingling many tears with their food and drink'.[44]

Mary's body remained in the vault at Peterborough for twenty-seven years. After her son, James VI of Scotland, succeeded Elizabeth as King James I of England in 1603, he built a new vault in the south aisle of Henry VII's chapel in Westminster Abbey to receive his mother's body.[45] A magnificent tomb was commissioned from the carver Cornelius Cure of Southwark and was completed by his son William in 1613.[46] Its iconography significantly includes the figure of Victory.

Across on the north side of Henry VII's chapel lies Elizabeth's sumptuous tomb, also commissioned by King James I in 1606 from the Protestant refugee sculptor Maximilian Colt. Elizabeth had died in her sleep at Richmond Palace, on the banks of the River Thames in Surrey, in the early hours of Thursday 24 March 1603, probably from septicaemia caused by the poisonous infection of her rotten teeth and bronchopneumonia.[47] She was aged sixty-nine.

The two queens may have been divided by politics and religion in life, but they are now united in the same church in death. Walsingham had been the prime mover in the cruel slaughter of one, and the protection and survival of the other, one of the greatest of England's monarchs, despite her parsimony and procrastination. He was truly the guardian of the gates of this fledgling Protestant nation, soon to spread its creed and values like a creeping tide across the globe.

Walsingham's Spy Network

This is the first attempt to produce a consolidated list of the many spies and informants employed by Walsingham. Names, locations and details are inevitably sparse because of the spy master's famed obsession with secrecy.

Aldred, Solomon. Double agent. Set up a tailor's shop in the French city of Lyons. Later moved to Rome with his wife, became tailor to the English College there and was granted a pension by Pope Gregory XIII. Recorded as a visitor to the English Hospice in Rome 10–20 March 1581 and 11–19 March 1583.[1]

Dr Owen Lewis, a leading Catholic in Rome, told the Pope's secretary in March 1582 that Aldred was able to supply copies of letters intercepted from English ambassadors in Europe.

In 1583, the Inquisition in Milan imprisoned Edward, brother of Henry Unton (or Umpton). At Walsingham's suggestion, Henry Unton negotiated for his release. A cash payment was demanded, the money destined to support English Jesuit priests in Rome.[2] Lewis sent Aldred to Lyons to represent the Catholics' interests in the negotiations. Henry Unton told Walsingham on 2 June 1583:

I have won over Aldred, the player of my brother's tragedy, to come into England upon your . . . assurance of his safety. He is one [who seems] simple, but better acquainted with Romish practices against England than any. He has delivered much to me and promised me upon my writing to him out of England and performance of certain conditions, he will become a right Englishman. Whereas now he is unnatural and of little honesty, yet he is one very worth the winning.[3]

William Parry, one of Burghley's spies in Lyons, told the Chief Minister on 18 August that 'Aldred departed for Milan the 10th of this month in hopes of bringing Mr Umpton away' and later reported that on 'the 20th of this month Mr Edward Unton was in good health but not yet delivered. Aldred was within two or three days after to depart from Milan to Rome, in very good hope to procure his dispatch.'[4]

The following year, Aldred went to England and met Walsingham. On 15 November 1584, Aldred wrote to him from Lyons, pledging his services as a spy: 'I assure you of my faithful and true service both to her majesty and to your honour. If you ever have cause to doubt me, cause one of your servants to write to me and I shall show myself an honest man.'[5]

News of his unexpected visit to London reached Rome via Paris and the belief that he had turned traitor was prevalent in the Holy City by February 1585. The Pope stopped his pension and some Catholic exiles warned Aldred that if he set foot in Rome 'he would be evil entreated even to the death'. William Lewknor, Walsingham's agent in Lyons, told his master that

poor snack, not having other means to live than his pension was constrained to hazard himself and to strain his conscience, God knows how, for the obtaining of his stipend, the which he has obtained and has brought himself into more credit than ever he was, insomuch as he is one of the Inquisitors.[6]

At this time, Walsingham planned to create dissension between the Jesuits and the exiled Catholic seculars abroad, and to that end employed

Aldred to sow the seeds of discord in Paris. Aldred brought Batson, a friar (and later a member of the Jesuit order) to London in 1585 for discussions with Hatton, Burghley and Walsingham 'about moderation in religions' but 'all fell out to be subtle dealing from the first', according to the leading Jesuit priest, Father Robert Persons.

Intelligence received by Walsingham from the French capital in September 1585 warned that 'here is a great looking into Aldred [and] his doings and they are very diligent upon him. They intend to do him mischief, except he looks warily to his business'.[7] Stafford, the English ambassador there, warned Walsingham that Aldred was 'somewhat long-tongued' and that the spy should be 'more circumspect, if only for his own safety for there are here eyes enough that neither sleep nor wink'.[8] The spy was still on Walsingham's payroll in Paris in July 1589, sums having been paid to him for travelling expenses for the previous three years.

Persons commented in 1592 that Aldred was

a Catholic layman . . . [who] seemed to be honest [but] falling into the factious was first employed into England diverse times and often he returned to Paris to have conference with Thomas Morgan, Gilbert Gifford and others of the crew, by which he so profited in spirit, as he soon after became Walsingham's man openly, and professed heresy and atheism, and died most miserably in Rome, showing no faith at all, in the year 1592.[9]

Almond or Amon, Roger, alias **William Vavasour**. A renegade Catholic and betrayer of the Jesuit priest William Holt at Leith, near Edinburgh, in March 1583. Almond was later constantly in and out of prison. He was tortured in jail in Arras in France in September 1583 and Walsingham eventually won his release. He returned to England and was almost immediately imprisoned at Winchester. In October 1584, Roger Manners, Fourth Earl of Rutland, detained Almond at Newark, Nottinghamshire.[10] The agent 'called himself Walsingham's servant, showed a warrant surreptitiously obtained and pretended to have been robbed of his horse'. The warrant, dated 26 September 1584, was addressed to High Sheriff

Sir John Spencer, directing him to assist William Vavasour in arresting the Jesuit Robert Persons and any other Papists. He was imprisoned yet again for having an unauthorised warrant.

He last appears in 1612, incarcerated in Newgate Prison, London, after being convicted of praemunire, and offering a composition of £100 to James I for his freedom.[11]

Barnard, Robert, alias **Robert Woodward**. Also signed himself 'P. H.' Tracked down priests and recusants in England. When he first worked for Walsingham in January 1581, he was living in London. He seems to have been frequently impecunious, at one stage begging Walsingham: 'I must humbly beseech you to consider of me I owe my host above £4 who threatens to have me in prison for the same. I have not received anything from you in three months past.'

He became a kind of roving spy, rooting out recusants and hidden priests during a tour of Middlesex and Nottinghamshire and later Cheshire, Lancashire, Westmorland, Northumberland and Yorkshire in December 1584.

Barnes, Thomas, later used the alias '**Robinson**'. Cousin of the agent provocateur Gilbert Gifford and stayed with him in London. Implicated in the Babington conspiracy as a messenger for Mary Queen of Scots, carrying letters to and from the French ambassador. Secured his pardon from the government by agreeing to spy on Catholic exiles in Paris.[12] Barnes travelled there in March 1588 and became a confidant of Thomas Morgan, Charles Paget and their Catholic exile circle. Barnes returned to London in April 1589 and maintained his contacts with English Catholics in France after Walsingham's lifetime.[13]

Baynebridge, Patrick, alias **Tompson**. Worked as a spy for Sir Robert Bowes, English ambassador in Edinburgh, but sent intelligence to Walsingham on Scottish Catholics in France via the English ambassador in Paris.[14] He disguised himself to accompany the French envoy in Scotland, François de Roncherolles, Seigneur de Mainville, when he was forced out of Scotland in May 1583.[15]

'B. C.' Alias of **Anthony Standen**.

Beckner, Thomas. An English cloth merchant in Rouen, France, who provided regular information about Catholics and general intelligence about events in France from 1584 in return for Walsingham's help in settling a local lawsuit against him.

Berden, Nicholas, alias **Thomas Rogers**. Able to disguise his handwriting and used a variety of names. He was the servant of a prominent Catholic layman, George Gilbert, and accompanied him to Rome.

His first contact as a spy was a note to Walsingham concerning 'the proceedings there, touching the Queen of Scotland' in 1583. Berden was quickly suspected of treachery by the Catholic exiles and imprisoned in the papal castle of Sant Angelo in Rome. On swearing an oath of loyalty to Catholicism, he was freed and returned to England. He was soon spying again for Walsingham and in March 1585 was operating in London, tasked with observing the activities of Philip Howard, Earl of Arundel, who was under suspicion of conspiracy.

From August 1585 to January 1586 he was sent to France to spy on the English Catholic communities in Paris and Rouen, using invisible ink for his reports. He was, in effect, a double agent, as he was being used to receive and deliver letters for them and also to circulate intelligence gathered in England amongst them. He proposed 'to keep an entire correspondence with all the parties for the avowed purpose of communicating it to Walsingham'.

On his return to England, Berden vetted a list of names of priests and recusants imprisoned in London in advance of the Babington conspirators' arrests in the midsummer of 1586. He told Phelippes:

> I return his honour's [Walsingham's] note, which I have well perused, according to my knowledge and intelligence. Such persons as I have noted to be hanged are of most traitorous minds and dispositions. Such as I have marked for banishment are most meet for the said purpose, for that they are exceedingly poor and contentious. Such as I have marked for Wisbech [Castle] are well able to defray their

expenses, of the graver sort and best accounted for learning. And it might stand with the pleasure of his honour, it were meet they should all be hanged.

In 1588, the Catholic exile Charles Paget (signing himself 'Nauris') wrote to Berden bitterly complaining about 'the knavery' that caused the death of Mary Queen of Scots and that 'Secretary Walsingham has been a great instrument therein'.[16]

That same year, Berden decided to quit the exciting world of spying and adopt a 'more public course of life' after five years of service. He wrote to Walsingham seeking the post of Royal Purveyor of Poultry that he had performed for three years in 'my father's lifetime'. It was granted to him within a month, upon the Secretary's recommendation.

'Best'. Agent disguised as a disaffected Englishman to discover the extent of the papal plans to overthrow Elizabeth. Best's source was the secretary of the Spanish ambassador in Paris. Brutally killed in July 1580 in a suspicious street brawl in the French capital.

Bodenham, Roger. English merchant based in San Lucar in Spain. In 1580, he reported that elaborate naval preparations were underway.

Boucher, Friar. Provided information about English Catholics in Paris.

Bridges, Edward. Alias of **Edmund Grateley**.

Bruce, Robert. Scottish gentleman, younger brother of the Laird of Binnie. Supplied information about Thomas Morgan and the other Catholic exiles in Paris through Stafford, the English ambassador in Scotland. The envoy told Walsingham in January 1585:

> He promises and offers great things, but plainly he says that a 'working man is worthy of his hire' and will not put himself in danger without certainty of a reward.
>
> He is in debt almost 200 crowns here. Because it is an extraor-

dinary reward I thought it good to advertise [tell] you that her majesty's pleasure may be known as also what he shall trust to have while he does service to deserve it.

This man is a great Papist . . . in my judgement, 200 crowns were well ventured to get such a service, for I think he will be able and willing to discover matter of importance.'[7]

Bruno, Giordano, alias **Henry Fagot**. Signed messages with the astrological sign for the planet Jupiter. Italian house guest in the French ambassador Castelnau's home in Salisbury Court, off Fleet Street. Supplied information to Walsingham that led to the uncovering of the Throgmorton plot in late 1583.

Burnham, Edward. Servant to Walsingham. In 1577, he was sent to Picardy and elsewhere in northern France to 'see and learn what French forces were levied there to enter the Low Countries'. Later a watcher on the Duke of Parma's military encampment in the Low Countries in the run-up to the Armada.

Casey, Thomas. Phelippes' servant. Messenger and escort of captured priests and suspects.

Catlyn, Maliverny. Signed himself 'II'. A Puritan and former soldier with a burning religious hatred for actors and stage-plays. Worked for Walsingham in the Low Countries and, writing from Rouen on 22 April 1586, offered his services to spy on Catholic exiles in France. In July of that year, imprisoned in Portsmouth and deliberately transferred to the Marshalsea to spy on imprisoned priests. From August 1586, acted as an informer in the disaffected North of England and that autumn returned to London to spy on members of the nobility suspected of harbouring Catholic sympathies.

Cobrett, David. Based in Dieppe.

Dunne, John. English merchant in Coruna in north-west Spain. Reported on elaborate naval preparations for Philip II's campaign against Portugal in 1580. Later, disguised as a Catholic, he was told by a Spanish monk that an Irish bishop was organising an expeditionary force of twenty ships for an invasion of Ireland.[18]

Fagot, Henry. Alias of the Italian **Giordano Bruno**.

Fowler, William. Scottish poet and theologian. Arrived in England after being expelled from his studies in France in 1583 and was immediately imprisoned. In return for his freedom, Fowler agreed to spy for Walsingham. He persuaded the French ambassador Castelnau that he could supply intelligence on Scottish affairs, and in turn told the English government about Castelnau's dealings with the Scots.

Foxley, John. Alias of **Edmund Grateley**.

Franchiotto, Captain Tomaso, alias **Captain François**. Of Lucca in Tuscany. Tipped Walsingham off regarding a plot to kill Elizabeth by secreting poison in her bedding in August 1568. Had been in the pay of the French crown for forty years before.

François, Captain. Alias of **Captain Tomaso Franchiotto**.

Germin, Thomas. His opinion was sought by Walsingham on 24 May 1584 regarding which people could be trusted for a secret channel of communication.[19]

Gibbes, Richard. Englishman based in Spain; while in Lisbon, posed as a Scotsman. He reported to Walsingham in 1587 that he had seen about 150 warships in various ports and was questioned by the Spanish about the suitability of various English harbours and rivers for use by the Armada ships.

Gifford, Gilbert. Described as 'young and without any beard'. Member of a Catholic family with a chequered career as a trainee priest. He had been expelled from the English College in Rome but had been allowed to join the Rheims establishment in 1582. After three years there, he became a deacon and a reader in philosophy. He left France for England in early December 1585 with letters for Mary Queen of Scots from the Archbishop of Glasgow, Thomas Morgan and the fugitive Catholic Charles Paget and was arrested at Rye. He had an interview with Walsingham and became his agent provocateur in the Babington plot to entrap Mary Queen of Scots.

Back in France, he continued to spy for Walsingham. He was ordained a priest but was discovered in flagrante delicto in a brothel in Paris in December 1587. He was immediately imprisoned and an attempt to prosecute him for his treachery against the Catholic cause was launched unsuccessfully by the Papal Nuncio in France. He died in the bishop's prison in Paris in November 1590.

Gilpin, Henry. English merchant in Naples who reported Sir Thomas Stucley's dealings with the Pope in 1575–6 regarding a possible invasion of England.

Grateley, Edmund, alias **John Foxley**, alias **Edward Bridges**. Private chaplain to Philip, Earl of Arundel, who fled to France in the summer of 1584. Informant who led to the earl's arrest and later involved on Walsingham's behalf in intrigues against the Jesuit clergy. He told the spy master on 4 August 1586: 'I remain a true born subject to her majesty and most affectionate to you and will not alter though you should change to me.'[20] With Gifford, he completed a book in June 1586 defending Elizabeth's policy towards the Catholics and the English military presence in the Low Countries. It was an unwise piece of writing – even Phelippes, Walsingham's chief decipherer, called it a 'mad book' – and Grately spent five years in an Inquisition prison in Rome for penning it.

Gregory, Arthur. Walsingham's expert in opening and resealing letters. After Walsingham's death, employed for similar work by Sir Robert Cecil, Burghley's son.

Hart, John. Jesuit priest. A prisoner in the Tower of London in 1581, he sought a pardon in return for spying on the Catholic community. He claimed that he enjoyed 'intimacy with Dr Allen [the de facto leader of

English Catholic exiles] . . . [which would enable him] to discover all his designs and to know the very secrets of his whole heart'.[21] His confession was used as evidence against Philip Howard, Earl of Arundel, at his trial in Westminster Hall on 14 April 1589.

Holder, Botolphe. English merchant in Lisbon who reported in 1578 that the Irish rebel James Fitzgerald, or Fitzmaurice, had loaded an eighty-ton vessel, recruited '100 tinkers and other rascals' as soldiers and had bought 200 culverine or cannon.[22] In 1580, he reported elaborate Spanish naval preparations.

Hunter, Mr. Scottish merchant based in Lisbon. Arrested in 1587, tried as an English spy and supporter of heretics, and imprisoned.

Jernegan, John. English agent at Calais in 1584 who spoke to the expelled Spanish ambassador to London, Bernardino de Mendoza, and confirmed Spain's 'malicious designs' against England.

Jones, David. Sought information for Walsingham on priests in London prisons in July 1574. Stony-broke and rapacious, he informed on a Mrs Cawkins, a 'notorious Papist' who had saved him from starvation.

Leclerc, Nicholas. Seigneur de Courcelles, Secretary to Castelnau, the French ambassador in London. Suborned by Henry Fagot into spying for Walsingham and supplied copies of letters to the spy master.

Lewknor, William. English merchant at Lyons who provided intelligence about Catholics in that French city.

Manucci, Jacomo. Florentine. Worked for Walsingham in Lyons and elsewhere in France in 1573–4 but imprisoned by Catherine de Médici.[23] He eventually returned to London, living in the parish of St Andrew Undershaft, to control part of the English network of agents in Europe and to act for Walsingham on sensitive missions, often passing on the Secretary's instructions verbally rather than in writing.

Marlowe, Christopher (1564–1593). Worked for Walsingham while a student in Paris and Rheims in 1586. Due to his espionage work, the award of his Master of Arts degree was placed in jeopardy, but the Privy Council told the Cambridge authorities in June 1587 that 'he had done her majesty good service and deserved to be rewarded for his faithful dealing'. He almost certainly continued as an agent working against Catholic intrigues in London, in return for escaping state prosecution over his blasphemous drama *Tamburlaine*, first produced in 1587. Murdered in a brawl in an eating house in Deptford on 30 May 1593. His death was witnessed by Walsingham's spy Robert Pooley.

Maude, Bernard or Barnard. Of Trinity College, Oxford. Formerly a member of the household of Edwin Sandys, the Archbishop of York; falsely accused the prelate of religious unorthodoxy and blackmailed him over allegations that he had had sex with the wife of William Sissons, landlord of the Bull Inn, Doncaster, in May 1582.[24] Sandys had handed over £600 in cash to Maude and his friends to keep them quiet. After an inquiry, he was forced to repay the archbishop, as well as a £300 'fine' to the queen, and served three years in the Fleet Prison, London, for blackmail. If he had not confessed, 'his ears would have been slit as a common offender'. He was another miscreant who was freed early by Walsingham in return for agreeing to undertake clandestine work for Elizabeth's government. Spied on the priest John Ballard in France and England.

Maude, Stephen. Recognised the seminary priest John Ballard on a boat crossing the English Channel.

Milles, Francis. One of Walsingham's private secretaries, involved in controlling the spy network and interrogation of prisoners in London.

Moffett, Thomas. An agent based in Rouen.[25]

Moody, Michael. Former Catholic servant of Sir Edward Stafford, the English ambassador in Paris, probable agent provocateur in the 'Stafford' plot of early 1587 and a double agent. Later a prisoner in Newgate (by order of the Archbishop of Canterbury) and notoriously a 'discontented man and one that would do anything for money'. Moody was well known to Walsingham – he paid him to carry letters between London and Paris in 1580–4. Jailed in London in January 1587 for three years. After 1591, worked for the Earl of Essex in the Low Countries.

Mulberry. Informer or spy against recusants and fugitive priests in England.

Munday, Anthony (1553–1633). A disaffected student at the English College in Rome, brought back to London to identify priests. Son of a London bookseller; apprenticed to John Alide, stationer, in 1576 and went to the English College in Rome two years later to study to become a priest. Returned to London and wrote *The English Roman Life*. Joined staff of Richard Topcliffe, the priest-hunter and torturer, who described him as a man 'who wants [lacks] no sort of wit'. In 1581 he wrote an anti-Catholic narration of the circumstances of Edmund Campion's capture. By 1584, appointed a messenger of the queen's Privy Chamber. Became a minor playwright and poet, producing eighteen plays of which four are extant, and some popular romances.

Needham, Francis. One of the spy master's most trusted servants. Appointed the Earl of Leicester's secretary in the Low Countries and used by Walsingham to spy on his behaviour and actions. Leicester wrote to Walsingham: 'I thank you Mr Secretary again and again for this honest, able young man.'[26]

Nowell, Thomas. Former student at the English College in Rome who returned to London to identify missionary priests.

Núñez, Dr Hector. Portuguese physician in London. One of Walsingham's correspondents, or in modern spy jargon a dead letter box, receiving letters from abroad on his behalf.

Ousley, Nicholas. Agent in Malaga who smuggled his intelligence out of Spain hidden in wine casks. Mendoza exposed his clandestine work in a note to the Spanish king on 12 July 1587. The ambassador added: 'On Walsingham receiving certain letters from him, he said he was one of the cleverest men he knew and the queen was much indebted to him for his regular and trustworthy information.'[27]

Ousley was captured, then bribed himself out of jail, and was still sending reports to London as late as April 1588. He later served as a volunteer soldier aboard the *Revenge* in the skirmishes against the Armada up the English Channel. Granted the lease of St Helen's Bishopsgate as a reward for his services.

Palavicino, Horatio. Genoese merchant who distributed Walsingham's funds to spies in northern France and spied on Sir Edward Stafford, the English ambassador in Paris.[28] In 1586, travelled to Germany to raise a Protestant army to invade France. Later knighted.

Parry, Dr William. Spy and double agent. Described as a 'passing proud, neat and spruce' man, he was probably insane. Spied on the English Catholics resident in Rome, Paris and Siena during the 1570s for Burghley.

In 1580, he escaped a death sentence for assaulting and badly wounding one of his creditors, Hugh Hare, after breaking into his room in the Temple in London. Parry spent more than a year inside the Poultry Prison before being bound over to keep the peace on a £1,000 bond. In return for his freedom, he was instructed to spy once again on English Catholics abroad for Burghley and Walsingham, firstly in Paris, then in Venice, and finally in Milan and Lyons.

In January 1584, Parry returned to London and told Elizabeth that he had been involved in dealings with Pope Gregory XIII and Thomas Morgan, Mary Queen of Scots' agent in Paris, in planning an attempt on her life.[29] His involvement, he maintained, had merely been to unmask the plans of 'malicious persons' at home. Given the Queenborough Seat in the Commons in the Parliament of 1584.

Parry returned to spying to augment his income, and sought the role of freelance agent provocateur in concocting a new plot against the queen. He suggested to Edmund Neville, cousin of the exiled rebel Westmorland, that Elizabeth should be murdered. Neville promptly betrayed Parry and he was arrested and executed in Great Palace Yard, Westminster, on 2 March 1585.

Paule, Stephen. Sent by Walsingham to Venice in early 1587 to discover information about the Armada. Sent weekly reports for more than a year. In November of that year, Paule reported that Michael Giraldi, a 'Bergomase'[30]

> has set sail for England, pretending to be a merchant. It is thought that for several reasons, [he is] to poison her majesty at the instigation of the Pope. The Pope, under pretence of supporting the war against the heretics and for performing some great enterprise, has enriched himself exceedingly.[31]

Pellegrini, Pompeo. Alias of **Anthony Standen.**

'P. H.' Alias of **Robert Barnard.**

Phelippes, Thomas. Codebreaker and forger. Also controlled a number of Walsingham's agents, notably Gilbert Gifford after his return to France. Son of William, a London customs officer. Cambridge Master of Arts, fluent in French, Italian and Latin but less skilled in Spanish. Described by Mary Queen of Scots herself as 'of low stature, slender every way, dark yellow hair on the head, [eaten] in the face with small pocks, of short sight, thirty years of age by appearance'.[32]

In 1578, Walsingham sent him to Paris to decode correspondence intercepted there. He was then used to control spies in France and to carry the cash that Elizabeth secretly supplied to the French Huguenots during the religious civil wars. At various times, he used the pseudonyms 'John Morice' and 'Peter Halins, merchant'.[33] His servant Casey was often used for delicate missions.

Appointed Collector of Petty Customs for the Port of London, deputising for Richard Young. In just two years he built up a debt totalling £11,682 6s 6d to the crown, lost his office and was thrown into jail.[34] In 1598, he asked to repay the cash by instalments and to use the exchequer to recover his own debts.

Pooley, Robert. A member of Walsingham's daughter's household. The Jesuit Father William Weston described him as 'quick-witted by nature and ingenious in deceiving'. He entertained many of the chief Catholics in London with meals at his own home 'at a table handsomely supplied'.[35] Francis Milles, one of Walsingham's confidential secretaries, thought him 'a notable knave with no trust in him'. Agent in the Babington plot. Worked for Sir Thomas Heneage in Flushing and Brussels in 1592 and was a witness to the murder of Christopher Marlowe in Deptford on 30 May 1593.

Poyntz, Antony. Acknowledged double agent. Brother-in-law of Sir Thomas Heneage, Treasurer of the queen's Privy Chamber, and student in the Inner Temple, but frequently in trouble with the law. Sent to Paris in December 1586 to spy on the Spanish ambassador Mendoza, but immediately revealed his true role. Sent by Walsingham to Madrid to discover information about the Armada.

Robinson. Alias of **Thomas Barnes**.

Rogers, Thomas. Alias of **Nicholas Berden**.

Sandal, Andrew. Alias of **Anthony Standen**.

Sassetti, Captain Tomaso di Vicenzo. Florentine decipherer who spied for Walsingham in France, later moving to London where he became a bodyguard to the Earl of Leicester for a fee of £50 a year.

Short. Informer or spy against recusants and fugitive priests in England.

Sledd, Charles. Masqueraded as a Catholic to infiltrate the English College in Rome in 1579, staying at the home of the tailor Solomon Aldred, who later became another of Walsingham's agents. On Sledd's return to England in May 1580, he wrote out long lists of Catholic exiles and priests, some with physical descriptions, all of whom he had met on his travels in France and Italy. These he supplied to Walsingham, together with a curious diary of his time in Rome. He remained in London, becoming a successful priest-hunter.

Somers, John. One of Walsingham's secretaries, expert in deciphering codes.

Stafford, William. Agent provocateur in the so-called 'Stafford' plot of 1587. Described as 'lewd, [and] miscontented', he was the younger brother of Sir Edward Stafford, the English ambassador in Paris. He allegedly contacted Leonard Des Trappes, secretary of Châteauneuf, the French envoy in London, offering to carry out a plan to kill the queen. Two years earlier he had acknowledged some kind of deep obligation to Walsingham, telling him in June 1585: 'I am as ever at your command.'

Stallynge, Richard. English merchant in Rouen who sent Walsingham news and gossip from his wide circle of correspondents.

Standen, Anthony, alias **Pompeo Pellegrini**, alias '**B. C.**'[36] Member of the household of Henry Stuart, Lord Darnley, Mary Queen of Scots' second husband, in 1565. Later lived and worked in Tuscany. Great friend of Giovanni Figliazzi, the Duke of Tuscany's ambassador in Madrid, and his dispatches, many routed through Walsingham's agent Manucci, began to tap this useful friendship. He also ran an agent within the household of the Marquis of Santa Cruz, the Spanish naval commander-in-chief.

Heard of Walsingham's death while in prison in Bordeaux after his arrest on suspicion of being a Spanish agent. In jail for nine months before he could smuggle a letter out to his friend Anthony Bacon, signed with the alias 'Andrew Sandal'. In June 1591 wrote to Burghley complaining about lack of payment of a pension of £100 a year for spying.

Later knighted by Elizabeth but fell foul of James I and was imprisoned in the Tower from 1603 until November of the following year after the discovery of some letters he wrote to various cardinals in Rome about the possible conversion of James's wife, Anne of Denmark, to Catholicism.

Thomas, Captain. Irish spy who had served with the royalist armies in the French civil wars. Escaped England and pretended to be a Catholic, thereby infiltrating the exiled Catholic community. Shadowed the activities of Maurice Fitzgibbon, Archbishop of Cashel, in Ireland in 1570. Five years later, he exposed plans for a rebellion in Ireland, but was arrested by the French government. The English ambassador Dr Valentine Dale eventually secured his release.

Tompson. Alias of **Patrick Baynebridge**.

Tomson, Lawrence. Walsingham's secretary. Sent to the northern Italian city of Bologna in 1580 to meet a papal agent with information to sell. He was told that Pope Gregory XIII intended to raise an army under Jacomo Bonacampanini. This general, with the assistance of Henry, Duke of Guise, was to invade England and dethrone Elizabeth.

Vavasour, William. Alias of **Roger Almond or Amon**.

Walton, Roger. Former ward and page to Lady Northumberland. Dispatched to Paris by Walsingham sometime in midsummer 1588 to spy on the Catholic exiles there. Stafford, unaware that Walton was an English agent, wrote of him:

> He [sleeps] here not far from me . . . To some he shows himself a great Papist, to others a Protestant . . . He has neither God nor religion, a very evil condition, a swearer without measure and tearer [blasphemer] of God, a notable whoremaster . . .
>
> This Walton is young, without any hair on his face, little above twenty, lean faced and slender, somewhat tall, complexion a little sallow, [mostly goes about] apparelled in a doublet of black carke [cloth], cut upon a dark reddish velvet.[37]

On his return to England, Walton boasted to Walsingham that he had wormed himself into the confidence of the Duke of Guise and of Father Darbyshire, leader of the English Jesuits in Paris, and had learnt important secrets.

Williams, Walter. Letter-carrier who sometimes dabbled in espionage. Former servant to Sir Thomas Copley, Catholic exile in France who tried to bribe Walsingham in 1582.[38] Inserted into Rye Prison in August 1582 to investigate Catholic sedition. One of those used by Walsingham to watch Sir Edward Stafford, but the envoy made Williams very drunk and when he was 'merry' succeeded in learning from him some details of the intrigue against him.

Woodshaw, Edward. Agent in Antwerp who replaced John Lee there in 1573 after his capture. A 'cunning but unprincipled man'[39] said to have considerable skill in a spy's tradecraft, specifically tasked to watch the English fugitives exiled in Flanders following the 1569 Northern Rebellion.

Woodward, Robert. Alias of **Robert Barnard**.

Notes

Prologue

1 'State Trials', Vol. I, p.145.

2 De Critz (c.1552–1642) was later one of the serjeant painters to James I. He is probably responsible for the two portraits of Walsingham, painted 1585–7, now in the National Portrait Gallery, London. Other works by him (or attributed to him) include portraits of Thomas Sackville, First Earl of Dorset (1601); Robert Cecil, First Earl of Salisbury (1602); and the famous painting of Henry Wriothesley, Third Earl of Southampton, with his pet cat in the Tower of London (1601), now at Boughton House, Northamptonshire.

3 See Ridley, p.264.

4 CRS, Vol. XXXIX, *Letters and Memorials of Father Robert Persons*, p.86.

5 From the Latin *recusare*, to refuse (the authority of the Church of England).

6 BL Add. MS 48,029 (Yelverton MS 33), fols.131-141B. This text is printed in CRS, Vol. LIII, *Yelverton MS Miscellanea*, pp.193-245. Another version, differing slightly in the text but containing a preface probably addressed to Walsingham, is contained in BL Add. MS 48,023, article nine. Worthington was captured and is recorded as being imprisoned in the gatehouse at Westminster in July 1586. See CRS, Vol. II, *Miscellanea*, p.254.

7 35 Henry VIII cap. 1.

8 NA PRO E 23/4/1 – Henry VIII's will, dated 30 December 1546. See Hutchinson, pp.210–16, for details regarding how the contents of the will enabled a Protestant *coup d'état* to form the government of Edward VI.

9 'Sadler Papers', Vol. II, p.325.

10 Wine sediment or dregs.

11 John Lothrop Motley, *Rise of the Dutch Republic*, 3 vols., New York, 1904; Vol. I, p.297.

12 Around £542,000 at today's prices. Was he claiming compensation?

13 Sharp, p.387.

14 Ibid.

15 Ibid., p.143.

16 Ibid., p.173.

17 Ibid., p.143.

18 Percy, born in 1528, had his estates restored by Mary I in 1557, his father having being attainted. He was beatified by Pope Leo XIII in May 1895. His wife Anne, Countess of Northumberland, took a very active part in the rebellion. Sir George Bowes reported: 'His wife, being the stouter of the two, hastened him and encouraged him to persevere, and rode up and down with their army from place to place' (Sharp, p.77). She fled to Flanders after the collapse of the rebellion, whilst Elizabeth fumed at her escape: the Countess 'behoved to be burnt and merited it well', according to the queen. See Somerset, p.301. She died of smallpox in 1591.

19 Neville was attainted for treason in 1571, thereby losing his estates. He died in Nieuport in Flanders in 1601.

20 Busse, p.14.

21 The austere and moral Pius, a former inquisitor in Milan and Lombardy, was Pope from 1566–72. He was beatified in 1672 and canonised by Clement XI in 1712.

22 Fuller, pp.93–4. Pius, 'constrained of the necessity to betake ourselves of the weapons of justice against her, not being able to mitigate our sorrow that we are drawn to take punishment upon one whose ancestors the whole state of Christendom have been so much bounden ... do out of the fullness of our Apostolic power, declare the aforesaid Elizabeth, being an heretic and a favourer of heresies, and her adherents ... to have incurred sentence of Anathema and to be cut off from the unity of the body of Christ. And moreover, we do declare her to be deprived of her pretended title to the kingdom and of all dominions, dignity and privilege whatsoever and also the nobility, subjects and people of the said kingdom and all other which have of any sort sworn unto her, to be for ever absolved from any such oath and all manner of duty ...' All were commanded and interdicted 'not to obey her, or her ... mandates and laws and those that shall do the contrary, we do likewise inundate with the like sentence of Anathema'.

23 It was nailed onto the gate between two and three in the morning on

25 May, the feast of Corpus Christi. The perpetrator, a wealthy Catholic gentleman called John Felton, of Bermondsey Abbey, Southwark, had received copies of the bull in Calais and was arrested within twenty-four hours. Felton, 'a man of little stature and of black complexion', was tortured on the rack three times and executed in St Paul's churchyard on 8 August 1570. He reportedly uttered the name of Jesus while the public hangman held his still-beating heart in his hand. Felton, whose wife had been a maid of honour to Elizabeth's half-sister Mary I and the widow of her auditor, was beatified by Pope Leo XIII in 1886.

24 Queen Mary I, Elizabeth's half-sister and predecessor on the throne of England.

25 This refers to Wyatt's Rebellion of 1554, which sought to prevent Mary's marriage to Philip II of Spain. It was crushed in the western suburbs of London in early February. Elizabeth had been implicated in the conspiracy because of her close contacts with two of the ringleaders, Sir William Pickering and Sir James Crofts. Elizabeth was dispatched to the Tower, but the treason case against her was eventually dropped through the influence of her great-uncle William Howard, the Lord Admiral. See Somerset, pp.47–55.

26 CSP Rome, Vol. II, p.551.

27 Margaret, who died in 1541, was the grandmother of Mary Queen of Scots.

28 CSPF, 1572–4, p.93. Letter from Walsingham to the Earl of Leicester, 31 January 1572.

Chapter One

1 Payments or bribes.

2 Written much later in his life, when he was Elizabeth's Principal Secretary of State. The advice was contained in a manuscript book owned by George Finch MP of Burley on the Hill, Rutland, but it was destroyed in a nineteenth-century fire. Walsingham told his nephew to read the classical histories 'to mark how matters have passed in governance in those days, so have you to apply them to these our times and states and see how they may be made serviceable to our age . . .' Cited by Read, *Mr Secretary Walsingham*, Vol. I, pp.11–12.

3 Some writers give the year of his birth as 1536, but as he is named in his father's will, dated 1 March 1534, this is clearly wrong. He was probably born at his father's house in Chislehurst in Kent.

4 For an account of Anthony Denny and his true role in the Henrician government, see Hutchinson, pp.151–8.

5 'DNB1', Vol. 59, p.228. He died in 1550 and was buried in the Scadbury Chapel of Chislehurst Church, Kent.

6 Webb, Miller and Beckwith, p.126.

7 BL Harleian MS 807, fol.4. Other pedigrees of the Walsingham family are in Harleian MS 1,174, fol.53 and Add. MS 5,520, fol.173, the latter being probably an eighteenth-century copy based on Glover's earlier work.

8 LPFD Henry VIII, Vol. IV, pt. ii, p.1,170. Henry's letter to the Common Council of the City is dated 17 November from Greenwich Palace and Catherine's 19 November. Some opposition was encountered: a second ballot was required for him to be appointed. The Common Serjeant was the legal adviser to the Lord Mayor.

9 Webb, Miller and Beckwith, p.377.

10 He was appointed bailiff of the royal manor of Hunsdon, Hertfordshire, in 1540, and was knighted in 1547, very soon after Edward VI became king. John Carey was the brother of William Carey, who married Anne Boleyn's sister, Mary.

11 The college possesses a portrait of Walsingham, painted in 1587 by an unknown artist.

12 According to his Latin epitaph, now lost, in Old St Paul's Cathedral in London.

13 Stählin, pp.89–90.

14 His stepfather died in 1552. Her funeral, on 6 April, was described by the London merchant tailor Henry Machyn, who today would be called an undertaker. Unfortunately, he names the wrong church as the venue, gives the wrong year and misspells the surname of Joyce's second husband. It was, however, a grand affair, with 'four great [wax] tapers and four torches and two dozen and a half of scutcheons of arms [heraldic shields]'. See: John Gough Nichols, *The Diary of Henry Machyn* . . ., Camden Society, London, 1848, p.193.

15 The eldest, Elizabeth, first married Geoffrey Gates, whose thuggish brother John was Sir Anthony Denny's 'fixer' in Henry VIII's Privy Chamber and who died for his role in the abortive accession of Lady Jane Grey. Following Geoffrey's death, she married Peter Wentworth of Lillingstone Lovell, Oxfordshire. The marriage of their daughter Mary is recorded in the Kent visitations of 1574 and 1592 by Robert Cooke, *Clarenceux Herald*. See 'Visitations', p.124. The second-eldest sister Barbara married Thomas Sidney, ironically the lord of the manor of Walsingham in Norfolk. Eleanor married Sir William Sherington and Christiana married firstly John Tamworth, a member of the royal household, and secondly William Dodington, an officer of the Mint.

16 The Walsingham arms appear, quartered with Mildmay, in a window in the hall at Emmanuel College.

17 Naunton, p.20.

18 Griffin provides the blazon for Walsingham's arms, recorded in the herald's visitation of Kent in 1592, 'Visitations', p.39. The motto is given by Philpot in BL Harleian MS 3,917, fol.2.

19 It met for the first time on 12 January 1562.

20 NA PRO PROB 11/47 PCC 32 STEVENSON. Also cited by Webb, Miller and Beckwith, p.380. The reference to 'exhibition' is provision for the child's education.

21 She was the daughter of the Somerset gentleman Henry St Barbe and held lands in her own right in Boston, Lincolnshire, and elsewhere in that county.

22 Worsley was Captain of the Isle of Wight. Appuldurcombe, 'the valley of the apple trees', was formerly a cell of the Benedictine monastery at St Mary Montsburg in Normandy, in the diocese of Coutances, founded by Richard de Redvers c.1090. See: Sir William Dugdale, *Monasticon Anglicanum*, Vol. I, London, 1718, p.73. An engraving of the house in 1690 is in Worsley, facing p.181. It was pulled down in 1710 by Sir Richard Worsley, Governor and Vice Admiral of the Isle of Wight, and a new house constructed. See: Percy Stone, *Architectural Antiquities of the Isle of Wight*, 2 vols., privately printed, London, 1891, Vol. I, p.57. A description of the later house is given in Nikolaus Pevsner and David Lloyd, *Buildings of England: Hampshire and the Isle of Wight*, Harmondsworth, 1967, pp.29, 729 and 800.

23 Worsley, pp.216–17 fn. This account was by Sir John Oglander, who heard a first-hand account of the accident from James Worsley, one of the survivors.

24 NA PROB 11/48 PCC 35 CRYMES and MORRISON, dated 9 March 1566, in Latin.

25 Read, *Mr Secretary Walsingham*, Vol. I, p.29 and Worsley, p.217.

26 Stählin, p.199. The name is London slang for priests and came from its use since 1430 by a fraternity or brotherhood of St Charity and St John the Evangelist, to house 'poor impotent priests'. The residents 'becoming lame or otherwise into great poverty, were here relieved, as to have chambers, with certain allowance of bread, drink and coal, and one old man and his wife to see them served and to keep the house clean'. The fraternity was suppressed in 1548 by Edward VI's government. See Stow, Vol. I, p.146.

27 Its full dedication was the parish church of 'St Mary the Virgin, St Ursula and the 11,000 Virgins', after the expedition throughout Europe staged by the latter saint and her cohorts of virgins. She suffered martyrdom by beheading. A sign showing an axe hung over the church's east end: hence the nickname.

The building disappeared early in Elizabeth's reign and its lower part was rebuilt as a free grammar school. See: Wilberforce Jenkinson, *London Churches Before the Great Fire*, London, 1917, p.105.

28 Stählin, p.194.

29 Painting NPG 1705. Not on public display in 2005. Oil on panel, measuring 15 1/2 x 13 1/4 in. (394 x 340 mm).

30 HMC, 'Finch', p.18.

31 Stählin, p.194, fn.4.

32 NA PRO PROB 11/75 PCC 33 DRURY.

33 NA PRO SP 46/17, fol.18.

34 A letter from Sir Thomas Smith, Walsingham's fellow Secretary of State, to Burghley on 7 January 1573 talks of his attempts to persuade the queen to recall Walsingham from France as he was 'undone, having been at great charge, all things waxing so dear, and his wife being here and great with child'. See BL Harleian MS 6,991, no.9.

35 Sir Amyas Paulet, who had just ended his tenure as English ambassador in Paris, wrote to Walsingham on 16 July 1580 offering his sympathies on Mary's death. See BL Cotton MS Titus B ii, fol.345.

36 SPD, *Edward VI, Mary & Elizabeth, 1547–80*, p.278.

37 Throgmorton (1515–71) was appointed ambassador in Paris in 1560 and was captured by Catholic forces at the battle of Dreux in 1562. He was sent to Scotland in an attempt to prevent the marriage of Mary Queen of Scots to Lord Darnley in 1565 and was imprisoned in 1569 on suspicion of being sympathetic to the rebels in northern England. Throgmorton Street in the City of London is named after him.

38 SPD, *Edward VI, Mary & Elizabeth 1547–80*, p.314, 18 August 1568. Cited by Read, *Mr Secretary Walsingham*, Vol. I, p.55.

39 Richings, p.117.

40 Ibid., p.123. In January 1569, Mary promised de Spes that with the aid of Philip II, she would be queen of England in three months and the realm returned to Catholicism. See Labanoff-Rostovsky, Vol. II, p.237 and 'Cal. Spanish', Vol. II, pp.97ff. De Spes was not so sanguine. He believed that the 'English hate the very name of foreigner and they wish the change to be made in a way that shall not hand them over to any other nation', Richings, p.157. How well he knew the English!

41 Richings, p.123. The Spanish ambassador's London home was at Winchester House, Southwark.

42 Naunton, p.60.

43 Richings, p.134.

44 Stählin, p.203.

45 SPD, *Edward VI, Mary & Elizabeth, 1547–80*, p.315.

46 Ibid., p.317.

47 Ibid., p.320. Dated 21 October 1568.

48 Ibid., p.324.

49 Letter dated 20 December 1568. Cited by Read, *Mr Secretary Walsingham*, Vol. I, p.58.

50 She was the daughter of Sir John Leyland of Cunswick, Westmorland, and had married Thomas Lord Dacre, who died in July 1566, leaving her with four young children. Norfolk married her on 29 January 1567 in London 'without any rejoicing or demonstration'. See Williams, p.127.

51 Robinson, p.52.

52 The others were Thomas Radcliffe, Third Earl of Sussex (the Lord President of the Council of the North), and Sir Ralph Sadler. Other delegates were to be appointed by Mary Queen of Scots and the Regent of Scotland, James Stewart, Earl of Moray.

53 He was strangled after escaping from a house at Kirk o' Field on the edge of Edinburgh, which was destroyed by an explosion got off in an attempt to assassinate him. See Guy, pp.299–303.

54 Mary's representatives withdrew from the conference on 6 December and the Scottish queen refused to offer a defence. On 10 January 1569 proceedings ended without any judgement being made.

55 Her mother Anne Boleyn, Henry VIII's second wife, was the granddaughter of Thomas, Second Duke of Norfolk. The French ambassador in London had already reported rumours of the marriage to the French king. See Fénelon, Vol. I, pp.17–18.

56 Robinson, p.60 and Williams, p.141. The reference to the pillow recalled the murder of Darnley.

57 She was also concurrently seeking annulment of her marriage, by Protestant rites, to James Hepburn, Fourth Earl of Bothwell, to ensure her freedom to marry Norfolk.

58 Brenan and Statham, Vol. II, p.453. Cited by Williams, p.159. The ducal palace at Norwich had been extended by Norfolk and now boasted a 180-foot-long bowling alley and a covered tennis court. It also had its own theatre.

59 Anderson, Vol. I, p.21ff., suggests that the text was sent to Thomas Randolph, then English ambassador in Edinburgh, for his comments before publication. This is entirely plausible. As well as Randolph checking the diplomatic implications, he and Walsingham had a friendly relationship, as he was married to Anna, one of the children of Sir Thomas Walsingham, first cousin of Francis.

60 It is ascribed to Walsingham in various contemporary hands on the manuscript copies in the British Library – Harleian MS 290, fol.117 and Harleian MS 4,314, fol.120. A printed version is in BL Cotton MS Caligula, C ii, fols.284–291. The manuscript version in Harleian MS 290 is printed in Read, *Mr Secretary Walsingham*, Vol. I, pp.68–79.

61 Her involvement in the murder of Darnley.

62 Mary's mother was Mary of Guise, the powerful French Catholic noble house.

63 A pamphlet, published as 'An answer to a slanderous book' – Walsingham's *Discourse* – and dated 15 March 1570, is in BL Cotton MS Julius F xi, fols.391ff.

64 Edwards, *The Marvellous Chance*, p.29.

65 Stählin, pp.246ff. The French ambassador Fénelon told the French queen mother in March 1569 that Ridolphi had 'received a commission from the Pope personally to negotiate with the Catholic lords . . . for the restitution of the Catholic religion in England. He has mainly dealt with the Earl of Arundel and Lord Lumley, with whom he has had business dealings concerning loans he had made to them . . . He found them . . . not brave enough to dare to undertake anything if the Duke of Norfolk does not take part. He has been very difficult to win over but at last he has allowed himself to be persuaded . . .' See Fénelon, Vol. I, pp.233–7.

66 SPD, *Edward VI, Mary & Elizabeth, 1547–80*, p.345. Ridolphi was to remain in Walsingham's house 'without conference [contact with the outside world] until he may be examined of certain matters which touch her majesty very nearly'.

67 Ibid.

68 Ibid., p.346. Cited by Read, *Mr Secretary Walsingham*, Vol. I, p.67.

69 Cecil wrote to Walsingham and Alderman Bowes on 26 January 1570, formally discharging Ridolphi's bond 'for keeping his house and restraint of liberty during the queen's pleasure'. See SPD, *Edward VI, Mary & Elizabeth 1547–80*, p.362.

70 Camden, p.394.

71 She was moved, as a security precaution, to Coventry on 25 November and was returned to Tutbury on 2 January 1571.

72 Stählin, p.299.

73 Ibid., pp.270–1

74 Cited by Read, *Mr Secretary Walsingham*, Vol. I, p.105.

75 Walsingham travelled by horse, using eight to reach Dover and a further sixteen from Boulogne to Paris, paying 2s 6d per horse. Shipping his belongings and geldings from Dover in two barques, or small sailing ships, cost a total of £12 13s 4d, including tips to porters and customs duties to 'searchers' at the ports. The bill also included £6 for two guides for himself and his cart from Boulogne. A letter of safe conduct was also issued for his servant John de Russe. See SPD *Edward VI, Mary & Elizabeth 1547–80*, p.432.

76 'Cal. Spanish', Vol. II, p.288.

77 See 'Journal', *passim*.

78 Ibid., p.5 – 'A bull set up against the queen my mistress *au pont de* [blank in manuscript] was brought up by Mr Dansett.'

79 Digges, p.45–6.

80 Walsingham's wife went to the French court on 21 April and was 'entertained by the Queen Mother [Catherine de Médici], the young queen, the Duchess of Lorraine, the lady Margaret [Marguerite de Valois] . . . and divers others'. One wonders what Ursula made of her entertainment.

81 Digges, p.29. Walsingham to Leicester, 28 January 1571.

82 Ibid., pp.29–30.

83 Killigrew was one of those Protestants who went into exile during Mary's reign. He was employed on various diplomatic missions by Elizabeth in Scotland in 1558–66 and 1572–91. He was knighted in 1591 and died in 1603.

84 Smith (1513–77) was ambassador to France 1562–6. He became a member of the Privy Council in 1571 and a Principal Secretary of State a year later. His work on the Tudor constitution, *De Republica Anglorum*, was published in English six years after his death.

85 CSPF, *1572–4*, p.9.

86 SPD, *Edward VI, Mary & Elizabeth, 1547–80*, pp.62–3.

87 Digges, p.343 and BL Cotton MS Vespasian F vi, fol.107, 13 July 1572.

88 Digges, p.212.

89 Gilbert (?1539–83), step-brother to Sir Walter Raleigh, used terror tactics to suppress the rebellion in Munster, killing men, women and children in disaffected areas and burning both homes and crops. He also decapitated the

corpses of those slain by his soldiers and stuck the heads on poles in his camps as an awful warning to the population.

90 An arquebus or 'hackbut' was a smoothbore matchlock and forerunner of the musket. It was fired by an 'S'-shaped lever pressing a lighted match into a small pan holding priming powder, which in turn ignited the gun's main charge.

91 Stählin, p.527, fn.1.

92 Fénelon, Vol. VI, p.330.

93 CSP Rome, Vol. II, p.45. Antonio Salviati, late Bishop of St Papoul, told the Cardinal of Como of Walsingham's 'dissatisfaction . . . at the execution done upon the Huguenots and the seizure of Briquemault in his house, as to which he has told his intimate friends that he has written to his queen that it is a point of honour for her to save him, whereof for the best of reasons I have not failed to apprise the Queen Mother [Catherine de Médici]'. The letter, in Italian, was dated Paris, 15 September 1572.

94 So many Lyonese corpses were floating in the River Rhône that the water was not drunk by the Arlesian population for three months.

95 According to a newsletter in Rome, dated 29 October, news of the massacre was brought to Charles IX 'while he was at church. He devoutly gave thanks to God that it has so befallen and announced that he was firmly resolved to tolerate no religion in his realm save the Catholic'. CSP Rome, Vol. II, p.64.

96 Stählin, pp.530–1.

97 Digges, p.238. He sent a list of women and children killed in Paris in a dispatch to London dated 14 September 1573. See BL Add. MS 48,126, fol.103B.

98 Bossy, *Under the Molehill*, p.55.

99 CSP Rome, Vol. II, p.42.

Chapter Two

1 APC, Vol. XV, p.330.

2 He was succeeded as ambassador by Dr Valentine Dale.

3 See Nuttall, pp.191–7.

4 BL Harleian MS 290, fol.88.

5 Edwards, *The Marvellous Chance*, p.35.

6 One reads: 'Wise men ought [circums]pectly to se[e] w[hat they] do, to examine [before th]ey speak, to pro[ve before] they take in hand, [to be]ware

whose compa[ny the]y use and above all [things to] whom they trust.' This is dated 10 April 1571. See: RCHM, Vol. V, p.84. Another carving is of an ornate panel containing the sacred monogram 'IHS' and with this additional inscription: 'Anno D[omini] 1571 10 September. The most unhappy man in the world is he that is not patient in adversities, for men are not killed with the adversities they have but with the impatience which they suffer. *Tout vient a poient quy peult attendre* ['Everything comes to him who waits']. *Gli sospirine son testimoni veri dell angoscia mia* ['My sighs are true witnesses to my sorrows']. Aged 29, Charles Bailly.' See RCHM, Vol. V, p.85 and Edwards, *The Marvellous Chance*, p.29. The panel is illustrated in RCHM, Vol. V, plate 31 and in Edwards, facing p.192. A third, in Latin, is on the ground floor.

7 Evidence for how the rack worked can be derived from an eighteenth-century edition of William Shakespeare's *Measure for Measure*. Its editor, Isaac Reed, wanted to illustrate the line: 'Some flee from brakes of vice' – 'the brake' being an alternative name for the rack – and after some searching in the Tower of London, he found the remains of 'this horrid instrument'. It still had its iron frame and three wooden rollers but was minus its levers and ropes. The rackmaster clearly turned the central roller using a lever, attached by ropes to the other rollers at the head and foot, so pulling and stretching the victim. A replica was created for a special exhibition at the Tower which opened in 2003.

8 Williams, pp.199-200.

9 Digges, p.95 and CSPF, 1569-71, p.445.

10 Robinson, p.63 and Williams, pp.200-2.

11 Information supplied by Herle is in BL Cotton MS Caligula C iii, fols.57–60 and 166–169. Herle begins by complaining of a 'great want of necessities'.

12 BL Add. MS 48,023, fol.150.

13 BL Cotton MS Julius F vi, fol.11 lists the questions put to Norfolk during the interrogations.

14 BL Cotton MS Caligula C iii, fol.96.

15 CSP Rome, Vol. II, p.3

16 Ibid., pp.2–3.

17 For accounts of his imprisonment and trial, see BL Cotton MS Julius F vi, fol.200B; BL Add. MS 48,027, fols.83–125B. The words recorded in Brown (*passim*) and in the report of the trial printed in the *Harleian Miscellany*, Vol V, pp.414–21 differ widely. His last moving letter to his children, dated 26 January 1572, is in Add. MS 48,023, fols.153–156.

18 Camden, p.140.

19 Brown, preface; Edwards, *The Marvellous Chance*, p.398.

20 Hatfield House, CP 90/150.

21 BL Cotton MS Vespasian F vi, fol.261, 18 January 1573.

22 SPD, *Edward VI, Mary & Elizabeth, 1547–80*, p.466.

23 Wotton (1548–1626) was briefly considered a candidate to succeed Walsingham as Secretary of State, together with Sir Edward Stafford. In the end, Burghley had to do the job.

24 CSPF, *1577–8*, p.457. Sir Amyas Paulet, then ambassador in Paris, had bought the satin and sent it over to London. Walsingham told him that the queen liked the gift 'so well that I have never had greater thanks of her for any present that I made her'.

25 Bertrand de Salignac de la Mothe Fénelon, French ambassador to London 1568–75, and Michel de Castelnau, Seigneur de la Mauvissière, French ambassador to London 1575–85.

26 Almost certainly a reference to Queen Elizabeth.

27 BL Add. MSS 48,149, fols.3B–9B.

28 BL Harleian MS 290, fol.84.

29 Cited by Read, *Mr Secretary Walsingham*, Vol. II, p.267.

30 'Cal. Spanish', Vol. II, pp.595–6.

31 Nicholas, *Memoirs of . . . Hatton*, p.361–2.

32 The original pamphlet was in Latin. An English translation was published under the name of J. Creswell.

33 See Meyer, p.177.

34 BL Lansdowne MS 97, fol.154.

35 SPD, *Elizabeth, 1581–90*, p.126.

36 Ibid., p.161. Mendoza also said that Edward Arden, Mary his wife and the priest Hugh Hall were to be executed; however, the woman's body would not be quartered as this was illegal in England. The sentence on her was deferred as she was pregnant. CSPF, *July 1583-July 1584*, pp.651–2. See also Read, *Mr Secretary Walsingham*, Vol. II, p.381 fn.

37 CSPF, *July 1583–July 1584*, p.651. Letter from Mendoza to ?the Prince of Parma, December 1583.

38 Ibid., pp.652–3.

39 Stucley (?1530–78) had been a privateer for Elizabeth in 1563 but escaped to Spain seven years later where he received a pension from Philip II. He later

joined an expedition against Morocco and died after a cannon shot took off both his legs during the battle of Alcazar.

40 CSP Rome, Vol. II, p.19.

41 Ibid., p.54.

42 Ibid., pp.140–1.

43 Ibid., p.208. The grants were signed on 13 June 1571.

44 For more information on Tregian (1548–1608), written in the seventeenth century by the Cistercian monk Francis Plunkett, see the text contributed by Mrs P. A. Boyan in CRS, Vol.XXXII, *Miscellanies*, London, 1932.

45 CRS, Vol. II, *Miscellanea*, p.191. The arrest party found a papal bull of indulgence amongst Mayne's papers. During his interrogation, he defiantly maintained that if any Catholic prince 'took in hand to invade any realm to reform the same to the authority of the See of Rome . . . then the Catholics in that realm invaded by foreigners should be ready to assist and help them'. See A. L. Rowse, *Tudor Cornwall*, London, 1941, pp.346–51. Tregian was imprisoned.

46 SPD, *Edward VI, Mary & Elizabeth, 1547–80*, p.32.

47 BL Harleian MS 360, fol.65. Undated document with amendments by Burghley.

48 The castle was built by William the Conqueror. It later became the palace of the Bishops of Ely and was sometimes used as a prison. In 1315, Richard Lambert of [King's] Lynn was illegally confined here and was 'so inhumanely gnawed by toads and other vermin, that his life was despaired of' – see VCH, Vol. 4, p.252. The castle was largely rebuilt in brick in 1478–83 and was surrounded by a moat. It was later pulled down and a house built on or near the site in 1816.

49 Watson was born in 1513 and died at Wisbech in September 1584. His see was left vacant for twenty years, with the temporalities remaining in the possession of the crown.

50 He was the last abbot. He was born c.1510 and also died at Wisbech in 1584.

51 VCH, Vol. 4, p.252.

52 Cited by Covington, p.70. For more on Wisbech, see Pritchard, pp.78–101.

53 VCH, op. cit. Quarrels broke out afterwards between the Jesuit and seminary priests held at Wisbech. William Weston, the leader of the Jesuit faction, arrived at the castle in 1587 and fell out with Christopher Bagshaw, a priest who had only been converted to Catholicism in 1582, over the living conditions at Wisbech. Weston and his supporters favoured a stricter

discipline as more fitting to their sanctity and accused the others of loose living and immorality. Relations were not helped by the Jesuits receiving the lion's share of the alms sent by the faithful outside the walls of their jail. Matters came to a head with the appearance of a hobby horse amongst the priests during the Christmas celebrations of 1594 (a hobby horse was a figure of fun used in popular entertainments – the forerunner, perhaps, of today's pantomime horses or cows). See Watson, *Historical Account of the Town of Wisbech*, p.127 and Collier, Vol. I, book vii, p.643.

54 NA PRO SP 12/141/29.

55 'Cal. Spanish', Vol. III, p.38.

56 Horsey was a Privy Councillor and a confidant of Leicester, and had commanded the royalist cavalry against the northern rebels in 1569. He died of the plague in the Isle of Wight in 1583.

57 SPD, *Edward VI, Mary & Elizabeth, 1547–80*, p.690.

58 23 Elizabeth I cap. 1.

59 27 Elizabeth I cap. 2.

60 Cottam, or Cotham, was recorded as a prisoner in the Tower in 1581 – see CRS, Vol.II, *Miscellanea*, p.221. He was ordained priest at Soissons in May 1580 and arrested at Dover but escaped. He surrendered himself to the authorities in London and was tortured in the Tower. Executed on 30 May 1582, his body parts being consigned to vats of boiling water, to prevent them from being used as sacred relics. Cottam was beatified in 1886 by Pope Leo XIII.

61 Kirby was subsequently executed in 1582 with Cottam and another priest, William Filby. His name appears in CRS, Vol. XXXVII, *Liber Ruber*, p.9, with the word 'martyr' written alongside in the margin.

62 In northern France. William Allen founded an English college there in 1568 to train priests.

63 Pound, 'a very obstinate recusant and a maintainer of that sect', is recorded by Walsingham as being in the White Lion Jail in Southwark in November 1586 and was listed as being 'fit' for transfer to Wisbech Castle in a document probably dating from the end of 1587. See CRS, Vol. II, *Miscellanea*, pp.262, 265, 278.

64 CRS, Vol. II, *Miscellanea*, p.200.

65 In 1587, Yates's home was again raided, this time by Edward Unton, who reported to Walsingham that 'many popish relics' were found within. Two of his servants, one suspiciously named John Doe and the other called Richard Buckley, were arrested. Both subsequently confessed to hearing Mass and

having been reconciled to Rome when Campion was sheltering in the house. See SPD, *Elizabeth, 1581–90*, pp.384–5.

66 Parading a prisoner was a deliberate policy to emphasise the power of the state. However, some priests saw the humiliating spectacle as more akin to Christ's sufferings before His crucifixion. See Covington, p.62.

67 R. Simpson, *Life of Edmund Campion*, London, 1866, p.338. Walsingham's departure that day is recorded in his 'Journal', p.43.

68 BL Harleian MS 6,991, no.57.

69 Both Cottam and Kirby were tortured with this instrument, the latter enduring it for more than an hour on 9 December 1580.

70 She was laid on her back with her arms tied to wooden posts, and a heavy weight lowered down upon her. See Morris, Vol. I, pp.397 and 432.

71 BL Lansdowne MS 97, Items 9 and 10.

72 See BL Add. MS 48,023, fols.26–58B; 26B–27; 33B; 42–43B; 48B. In 1572, Norton tried to organise a petition to the queen urging the execution of the Duke of Norfolk – ibid., fols.163–164B.

73 SPD, *Elizabeth, 1581–90*, p.48. On 3 May the previous year, the Privy Council had ordered Norton to examine 'a Jesuit naming himself Briant and if he refuses to confess the truth, then to put him to torture and by the pain and terror of the same, to wring from him the knowledge of such things as shall appertain'.

74 Ibid., p.22. Briant, from Somerset, was executed at Tyburn in 1581 and was one of those martyrs canonised in 1970.

75 Ibid., p.130.

76 Ibid., p.130. Walsingham to Thomas Wilkes, 18 November 1583.

77 BL Add. MS 48,029, fols.58–72B. This was not the first time Norton engaged in public polemics: in 1571 he wrote a tract against Mary Queen of Scots, a copy of which forms the vellum-bound BL Add. MS 48,098, with corrections and some of the text in his own handwriting. It has seventy-one pages in contemporary pagination.

78 BL Lansdowne MS 155, fols.84–106B.

79 SPD, *Elizabeth, 1581–90*, p.260. The fight was over a misunderstanding: the soldiers believed Bassano to be a Spaniard. Norton and Valentine Wood, said the musician, uttered 'opprobrious words' against the soldiers, and in the ensuing affray he was 'in danger of being slain'. He was one of three of the queen's musicians who came from Venice and acquired the Bell Inn in Mark Lane in 1572. Bassano's wife Margaret, who died in 1623, has a monumental brass inscription in All Hallows' Church, next to the Tower of London.

80 APC, Vol. XVII, p.205. Tankard was taken to Oxford Assizes the following month to stand trial. Ibid., p.329.

81 'DNB2', Vol. 55, p.28. Article by William Richardson.

82 Nichols, Vol. 2, p.217.

83 Caraman, p.69. Gerard escaped from the Tower in 1597 by clambering along a rope thrown across the fortress's moat from the wharf.

84 APC, Vol. XVI, p.235. Another sailor was George Ellis, who had been captured in later naval operations. He wrote to Burghley in 1595 complaining about Topcliffe and noting down the 'discoveries he could make on behalf of the realm'. See BL Lansdowne MS 79, Item 93. For other interrogations of Englishmen captured during the Armada campaign, see BL Add. MS 48,029, fols.85–91.

85 Alias Portmon, alias Whitgift. He was ordained at the English College in Rome in August 1587 and was executed on 20 February 1592. See CRS, Vol. XXXVII, *Liber Ruber*, p.27.

86 CRS, Vol. V, *Unpublished Documents*, pp.210–11. Pormont's notes were handed over to William Waad, clerk to the Privy Council, and shown to that august body in November 1592. Their reaction is not recorded but an apparently charmed Topcliffe continued a direct correspondence with the queen.

87 BL Lansdown MS 72, Item 39. Other documents include a report written by Topcliffe in 1592 to the Privy Council about 'discovering the haunts of several dangerous seminary priests' and a discourse on the 'best methods' of dealing with priests.

88 Southwell, born in Norfolk c.1561, was executed at Tyburn in 1595. He was canonised in 1970.

89 Covington, p.88.

90 Foley, Vol. I, p.350. She also disclosed the secret hiding places for priests built in the family home at Uxenden Hall, near Harrow on the Hill, Middlesex.

91 SPD, *Elizabeth, 1581–90*, p.207.

92 William Cobbett et al., *State Trials*, 33 vols., London, 1809–28, Vol. II, p.184. Cited by Covington, pp.160–1.

93 He was canonised by Pope Paul VI on 25 October 1970.

94 The Lord's Prayer.

95 CRS, Vol. V., *Unpublished Documents*, p.204.

96 Middleton was ordained priest on 30 May 1586 at Rheims and entered England later the same year. He was captured in Clerkenwell.

97 Jones was ordained priest in 1588 at the English College, Rome.

98 BL Add. MS 48,029, fols.121–141B. The text is reprinted in CRS, Vol. LIII, *Yelverton MS Miscellanea*, pp.193–245.

99 CRS, Vol. LIII, *Yelverton MS Miscellanea*, p. 227.

Chapter Three

1 SPD, *Elizabeth, 1581–90*, p.615.

2 Lloyd, Vol. II, p.514.

3 SPD, *Edward VI, Mary & Elizabeth, 1547–80*, p.477.

4 BL Cotton MS Caligula C iii, fol.217. Walsingham had also written two days before about the interview between a man he had sent 'under colour of a Catholic' and Thomas Darbyshire about Mary Queen of Scots. See HMC, 'Finch', p.19. Darbyshire is described as 'a very popular old Jesuit father generally living in Paris'. See CRS, Vol. XXI, *Ven. Philip Howard*, p.272 fn.

5 The Florentine Tomaso di Vicenzo Sassetti. He later moved to London and became a bodyguard to the Earl of Leicester at £50 a year. See Richings, p.137.

6 BL Harleian MS 6,991, no.39, 20 August 1573.

7 SPD, *Elizabeth, 1581–90*, p.373.

8 Ibid., p.140.

9 Ibid., p.633, 11 December 1589.

10 Kersey is a coarse ribbed cloth, woven from long strands of wool.

11 CSPF, *August 1584–August 1585*, p.40.

12 Ibid., p.358.

13 CSPF, *January–June 1583 and Addenda*, p.335.

14 Ibid., p.52.

15 SPD, *Elizabeth, 1581–90*, p.32.

16 BL Harleian MS 6,991, no.58.

17 Cockyn wrote to Burghley on 20 February with fresh intelligence about Mary Queen of Scots' friends in England and begging him to secure a pardon for him from Elizabeth. See BL Cotton MS Caligula C iv, fol.249. His debriefing took some time: on 18 March, he told Walsingham about a Spanish plot to kidnap the young James VI of Scotland. The examination of those he named and the draft charges against them are in BL Cotton MS Caligula C v, fols. 6–20. Alexander Hamilton's confession, dated 21 May, is on fol.15.

18 Cited by Read, *Mr Secretary Walsingham*, Vol. II, p.354, Walsingham to Leicester, 9 March 1575.

19 Tomson, a former lecturer in Hebrew at Geneva, edited a revision of the New Testament that was published in London in 1576. It was derived from the 1560 Geneva Bible, translated from the Greek by Theodore Beza. Tomson was elected Member of Parliament for Melcombe Regis in Dorset in 1584.

20 SPD, *Edward VI, Mary & Elizabeth, 1547–80*, p.486. Jones was referring to the fines imposed on obstinate recusants.

21 SPD, *Elizabeth, 1581–90*, p.36.

22 Ibid., p.51.

23 Henry Henshawe, former Rector of Lincoln College, Oxford. He was one of the 'old' Marian priests, recorded as being in the Fleet Prison in 1560. He died around 1598. See CRS, Vol. II, *Miscellanea*, p.3 fn.

24 William Holt, an Oxford man, was betrayed by another of Walsingham's agents, Roger Almond, in March 1583. See SPD, *Elizabeth, 1581–90*, p.207.

25 Jaspar Haywood, who was arrested at sea and committed by Walsingham on 9 December 1582. His name appears on a list of priests held in the Clink Jail in Southwark the following March, and he was indicted at the Court of King's Bench on 9 February 1584 and banished. He died in Naples in 1595. See CRS, Vol. II, *Miscellanea*, pp.177, 190 and 232.

26 SPD, *Elizabeth, 1581–90*, p.17.

27 Possibly the William Carter, bookbinder and citizen of London, recorded as a recusant prisoner in the Tower on 23 March 1583. See CRS, Vol. II, *Miscellanea*, p.228.

28 CRS, Vol. V, *Unpublished Documents*, pp.30–1.

29 According to a letter by John Hart, dated 15 November 1582 – see CRS, Vol. IV, *Miscellanea*, p.74.

30 Nonsuch was built by Henry VIII at a cost of £24,000 over nine years from 1538, but the house was later sold by Mary I to the Earl of Arundel, father-in-law of Lumley. In 1592, Elizabeth took it back into royal ownership in exchange for Lumley's debts to the crown. In 1670, Charles II gave it to his mistress Barbara Castlemaine, who began to demolish the huge structure in 1682. The site was excavated by the distinguished archaeologist Martin Biddle in 1959–60.

31 Robinson, p.77. Byrd (?1538–1623), a pupil of Thomas Tallis, was joint organist of the Chapel Royal in 1569 and recorded as a Catholic in Harlington, Middlesex, in 1578–88. He composed *Liber primus sacrarum cantionum* in 1589 and *Liber secundus* in 1591.

32 She was suspicious of him.

33 NA PRO SP 12/175/110, December 1584. His account of his sweep of Essex, Suffolk, Norfolk, Derbyshire, Nottinghamshire and Middlesex, exposing Papists, is in BL Add. MS 48,023, fols.110–111.

34 He was a friend of Persons and was later condemned with Campion. He was not executed but remained in the Tower until 1585, at which point he was banished from England.

35 Campion, Persons and George Gilbert were at the synod. Gilbert was a 'young man of good birth, ample fortune and in great favour at [the English] court, [who] dedicated himself and all his possessions to the defence of the Catholic religion', according to a letter from Persons to Pope Gregory XIII from London, 14 June 1581. Persons added: 'I know of nothing the queen craves so much as the capture of these brave men.' CRS, Vol. II, *Miscellanea*, p.67. Gilbert died in Rome in October 1583 and was admitted to the Society of Jesus on his deathbed.

36 Johnson was trained at Douai and only crossed to England on 2 May 1580. He was imprisoned in the Poultry Counter, tried and executed with Campion on 28 May 1582.

37 See Allen, pp.28–75 and 83.

38 CRS, Vol. II, *Miscellanea*, p.94, London, 24 August 1581. Persons left the capital and travelled to Sussex, to the recusant stronghold of the Shelley family at Michelgrove, before leaving England.

39 Strype, Vol. III, book ii, p.611.

40 Catlyn wrote to Walsingham complaining that 'the daily abuse of stage plays is such an offence to the godly and so great a hindrance to the gospel as the Papists do exceedingly rejoice at the blemish thereof. And not without cause. For every day of the week, the players' bills are set up in sundry places of the city: some in the names of [the actors' groups of] her majesty's men, some the Earl of Leicester's, some the Earl of Oxford's, some the Lord Admiral's . . . so that when the bells toll to the lectors, the trumpets sound to the stages, whereat the wicked faction of Rome laughs for joy while the godly weep for sorrow. Woe is me, the play houses are pestered when the churches are naked. At the one it is not possible to get a place, at the other void seats are plenty'. BL Harleian MS 286, fol.102.

41 SPD, *Elizabeth, 1581–90*, p.35.

42 BL Harleian MS 286, fol.266.

43 Ibid., fol.97 and Covington, p.68.

44 CRS, Vol. II, *Miscellanea*, p.179.

45 William Somerset, Third Earl (1526–89). Walsingham's suspicions may have been groundless: Worcester later raised land forces to repel the Armada in 1588.

46 Lewis, Third Lord Mordaunt (1538–1601), Sheriff of Bedfordshire. His father had taken an active role in the suppression of Protestantism during the reign of Mary I.

47 A small sailing boat.

48 SPD, *Elizabeth, 1581–90*, p.370.

49 BL Harleian MS 286, fol.95.

50 Also called Sything or Sydon Lane. Stow, Vol. I, pp.131–2, describes 'diverse fair and large houses built' in the thoroughfare. A near neighbour was the Earl of Essex.

51 Potassium aluminium sulphate. Used today in baking powder, for water purification and in the tanning of cattle hides.

52 Reports from one of Walsingham's spies, Nicholas Berden, alias Thomas Rogers, from Paris, were written in secret ink. The writing has turned dark brown over the passage of time and is difficult to read.

53 Hatfield House, CP Petitions 2,424.

54 Pollen, p.liv and 'Paulet', p.119.

55 A mark was worth 13s 4d.

56 'Paulet', p.115.

57 'Cal. Scot.', Vol. IX, p.109. Earlier, Phelippes was vexed by accusations levelled at him by one Lawrence Smith. In 1580, he wrote to Burghley complaining of the 'base and false informations' made against him. See BL Lansdowne MS 31, Article 23.

58 SPD, *Elizabeth, 1581–90*, p.614.

59 Birch, Vol. I, pp.14–15.

60 See Haynes, p.48.

61 Ibid., p.48 and Read, *Mr Secretary Walsingham*, Vol. II, p.371 fn.

62 CSPF, *January–June 1583 and Addenda*, pp.119–20.

63 SPD, *Elizabeth, 1581–90*, p. 207. See also BL Cotton MS Caligula C vii, fol.106, for Bowes' warning of 4 March about Englishmen coming to Scotland from Rome and French attempts to influence the Scottish king and nobility; see also ibid., fol.115 – Walsingham's letter of 14 March giving directions on what to do with Holt.

64 Almond was constantly in and out of prison. He was arrested in France in

July 1583, accused of betraying English Catholics in Paris. He had in his possession a letter from Walsingham 'mentioning some money' and had gone to
Artois with four Jesuits in order to accompany them to England. A note on a
French document adds: 'This young man has shown himself sufficiently
imprudent in many ways to put himself into danger to arrive at a good end. To
reconcile himself, he chose a bad means, worthy [more] of pity than of rigour
of justice' (CSPF, *July 1583–July 1584*, pp.47–8). Almond was tortured in jail in
Arras in France and in September Walsingham had to seek help to gain his
release (ibid., p.79). In October the following year, Roger Manners, Fourth Earl
of Rutland, detained Almond at Newark, Nottinghamshire. The agent 'called
himself Walsingham's servant, showed a warrant surreptitiously obtained and
pretended to have been robbed of his horse'. The warrant, dated 26 September
1584, was addressed to Sir John Spencer, High Sheriff, directing him to assist
William Vavasour in arresting the Jesuit William Persons and any other papists
– see SPD, *Elizabeth, 1581–90*, p.207. He last appears in 1612 in Newgate
Prison, London, after being convicted of praemunire, and offering a composition
[a payment in lieu of a larger sum] of £100 to James I as a 'get out of jail card',
but one that was hardly free.

65 Bowes wrote to Walsingham on 18 March warning him of the conspiracy
'between the Pope and the kings of France and Spain to invade this island' –
see BL Cotton MS Caligula C vii, fol.119B.

66 Bossy, *Giordano Bruno*, pp.75–7.

67 Ibid., p.191.

68 BL Cotton MS Caligula C vii, fol.155.

69 CSPF, *January–June 1583 and Addenda*, p.292.

70 BL Cotton MS Caligula C vii, fol.153. On the reverse is a notation
'April/Fagot', which is clearly a wrong date.

71 Howard (1540–1614) was the younger brother of the executed Duke of
Norfolk. Sir Anthony Weldon thought little of his 'venomous and cankered
disposition' and described him as a 'great clerk, yet not a wise man, but the
grossest flatterer of the world'. See Williams, pp.84–5.

72 His confession is in BL Add. MS 48,029, fols.64–65B.

73 Paget (d.1612) was the son of William, First Baron Paget. He went to Paris
in 1572 and became secretary to James Beaton, Mary's ambassador to the
Valois court.

74 'Heads of the causes of the dismissal of the ambassador of Spain', CSPF,
January–June 1583 and Addenda, pp.333–4. A letter from Walsingham to
Stafford, the English ambassador in Paris, also claimed that Mendoza allowed

English Catholics 'to repair to the Mass at his house contrary to the privileges of an ambassador'– ibid., p.301.

75 'Cal. Spanish', Vol. III, pp.516–17.

76 At Calais, one of the agents, John Jernegan, spoke to Mendoza and was told of 'the malicious designs' of Spain against England. See SPD, *Elizabeth, 1581–90*, p.158.

77 CSPF, *July 1583–July 1584*, p.594. Gilpin, the English agent in the Low Countries, informed Walsingham the same day that the assassin had been quickly executed. 'His right hand [was] pressed and burnt off with a hot iron engine made to that end. Afterwards the flesh pulled from his legs, arms and other parts with fired pincers and then his body cut open and quartered alive; during which torments he continued resolute and so little moved as was wonderful and incredible' – ibid., p.596.

78 Howard later received an annual salary of 1,000 crowns for supplying Mendoza in Paris with 'confidential and minute accounts twice a week' of events at court. See Robinson, p.85.

79 The list of his possessions in the Tower is given in BL Egerton MS 2,074, fol.108. Sir Owen Hopton, Lieutenant of the Tower, testified later that the door to Percy's room was barred from the inside and had to be broken down by his guards using their halberds. His body was on the bed, wounded in the chest, with the dagg, or pistol, lying on the floor about three feet away. See Howells, Vol. I, p.1,123.

80 SPD, *Elizabeth, 1581–90*, p.148. Endorsed by Phelippes: 'From "B"'.

81 CRS, Vol. XXI, *Ven. Philip Howard*, p.70.

82 Pierrepoint was described as 'a very obstinate recusant and a maintainer of all seminary priests and papists'. He was in the Marshalsea before being transferred to the Tower, and in June 1586 was sent on to Wisbech Castle.

83 Roscarrock, from St Endellion, Cornwall, was in prison 'for religion only . . . and for intelligence with Jesuits and priests'. He was reported in May 1585 to be 'a dangerous man and apt for any practice' and as such, was 'fit to be banished'. See CRS, Vol. II, *Miscellanea*, p.238.

84 Orton himself was a prisoner in the Tower.

85 CRS, Vol. XXI, *Ven. Philip Howard*, pp.70–1, 6 April 1585.

86 On the River Thames in Essex.

87 Probably the mouth of the River Arun at Littlehampton in Sussex.

88 CRS, Vol. XXI, *Ven. Philip Howard*, p.88.

89 Ibid., p.89.

90 Haynes, p.86.

91 Marlowe was murdered in a brawl over payment of a bill in an eating house in Deptford, east of London, on 30 May 1593. His death was witnessed by that habitual spy Robert Pooley.

92 'Cal. Scot.', Vol. IX, pp.306–7.

93 His grandfather was Peter Conway, Archdeacon of St Asaph. His father, Harry ap David, had thirty children by two wives. He apparently lived to the remarkable age of 108.

94 Firstly [?], daughter of Sir William Thomas of Carmarthan, widow of [?] Powell and secondly, Catherine, widow of Richard Heywood of London, an official of the Court of King's Bench.

95 On 17 December 1580, writing from the jail, Parry complained that he deserved better of his queen and country than having been 'tormented by a cunning and shameful usurer'. See SPD, *Elizabeth, 1581–90*, p.33.

96 Hasler, p.181.

97 Howells, Vol. I, p.1,103.

98 Strype, Vol. III, book i, p.336.

99 CRS, Vol. XXI, *Ven. Philip Howard*, pp.114–15.

Chapter Four

1 BL Harleian MS 290, fol.117.

2 BL Cotton MS Caligula B v, fol.159. A brief on the issues contained in the Bond, for debate in Parliament and drawn up by Walsingham's clerk, is in fols.222–223B.

3 BL Add. MS 48,027, fols.249–251B.

4 'State Trials', Vol. I, p.143.

5 BL Cotton MS Titus C vii, fol.80.

6 Translated from the Welsh, the song began: 'Thou Orange, fat and tedious. Everyone is glad when you are enclosed in your grave . . .' Hardly a catchy lyric. See CRS, Vol. V, *Unpublished Documents*, pp.98–9.

7 'Sadler Papers', Vol. II, p.36.

8 Hatfield House, CP 13/77 and BL Add. MS 48,027, fol.251B.

9 27 Elizabeth I cap. 1. Notes for Sir Christopher Hatton's speech promoting the legislation are in BL Egerton MS 2,124, fol.10. These stress the queen's subjects' 'duty to seek to preserve her with the service of our bodies, lives and

goods' and to resist 'all perils and dangers towards her person so far as the wit of men and force can reach'.

10 Tanner, p.419.

11 NA PRO SP 12/176/22. See Graves, p.94. Burghley had drawn up a similar plan in October 1562 when Elizabeth was laid low by an attack of smallpox and had lost the power of speech.

12 Lord St John of Bletso had been offered the job but, concerned at the costs involved in guarding Mary and Elizabeth's notorious tardiness in repaying them, he wisely declined the honour.

13 At Sheffield, Mary had already complained to Walsingham about the delays in receiving her letters. See BL Cotton MS Caligula C v, fol.129, 5 September 1579.

14 'Paulet', p.6.

15 Ibid., p.51.

16 Pollen, p.xxxi.

17 He was released in August 1587 by the efforts of the Papal Nuncio.

18 Pollen, p.xxxi.

19 Ibid., p.92.

20 Cited by Guy, p.480.

21 Labanoff-Rostovsky, Vol. VI, p.254.

22 'Paulet', p.153.

23 SPD, *Elizabeth, 1581–90*, p.307.

24 NA PRO SP 53/22 and SP 53/23.

25 NA PRO SP 53/22/6.

26 NA PRO SP 53/22/1.

27 Deacon, pp.27–8. See also Fell Smith, p.674.

28 'Paulet', p.191.

29 Ibid.

30 He married his guardian's daughter, Margaret Draycot. Their daughter Mary died aged eight.

31 Pollen, p.cvi.

32 Ibid., p.lxxxv.

33 Ibid., p.xcv.

34 Ibid., p.xciv.

35 A reference to Pope Pius V's papal bull of 25 February 1570, excommunicating Elizabeth.

36 Pollen, pp.19–22. Nau told him on 13 July that Pooley had written to Mary only once and she had not yet replied, not knowing his address. 'Her majesty's experience of him is not so great as I dare embolden you to trust him much.' Ibid, p.24.

37 That year Pooley had arrived at the Bastille, bringing letters to Morgan from Christopher Blount, a gentleman member of the Earl of Leicester's retinue who seemed to be a Catholic sympathiser. In fact, he was another double agent working for the English government.

38 'Paulet', p.218.

39 Labanoff-Rostovsky, Vol. VII, p.205.

40 'Paulet', p.224.

41 BL Cotton MS Caligula C ix, fol.326. A copy of the postscript is in NA PRO SP 12/193/54. Copies of the ciphers used by Mary and Babington are in BL Add. MS 48,027, fol.313B and their correspondence in fols.258–262B. See also 'Cal. Scot', Vol. VIII, pp.525–38.

42 Camden, p.438.

43 'Paulet', pp.234–5.

44 Ibid., p.245.

45 Ibid., pp.46–7.

46 Morris, p.184.

47 Ibid., p.381.

48 The Fleet Prison is omitted from the list as the June returns of Catholic prisoners contain only two as being held there by the warden, John Calton. In his report to Walsingham: 'Stephen Vallenger, committed from the Star Chamber [Court] by her majesty's Privy Council for publishing certain libels of [the executed priest] Edmund Campion and has here continued these four years. Likewise one Mr Francis Trudgeon committed by [the] Privy Council upon a praemunire.' Another priest or recusant, a Mr Travis, died in the Fleet the previous April. See CRS, Vol. II, *Miscellanea*, p.250.

49 SPD, *Elizabeth, 1581–90*, pp.373 and 342. See also CRS, Vol. II, *Miscellanea*, p.253.

50 The debtors' prison, long notorious for its poor conditions and nicknamed 'Hell in Epitome' or, as John Wesley wrote nearly two centuries later, 'a nursery of all manners of wickedness'. Rendle, p.13.

51 Arrested at Lydd, Kent. Committed to prison November 1585.

52 Detained at Battle, Sussex, with John Smith in March 1586.

53 Taken at Chichester in June 1585.

54 Arrested in Chichester. Jailed in November 1585.

55 Detained at Prescot, Lancashire, and imprisoned since June 1585. He had been examined by the Bishop of Chester and then interrogated twice by Walsingham.

56 In prison since June 1585.

57 Taken at Lowestoft, Suffolk, in June 1585.

58 Knight was detained with Bolton and Clareregent at Chichester and sent to prison in November 1585.

59 Bramston and Crockett were arrested with George Potter at Arundel in Sussex probably in April 1586.

60 Small ships propelled by prisoners working oars.

61 Williamson, Blunt, Webster, Green, Lawson, Holland, Edes and Tucker were listed as recusants in the June prison certificates – Green having been in jail since 1572. Webley and Crabb, listed amongst the 'poor fools' in the Marshalsea, were in a group of five detained in Chichester Harbour as they tried to flee to France that April.

62 This prison, called a 'Counter' or more probably 'Comptor', was in the City of London's Cheap Ward and belonged to one of the sheriffs of the city. See Stow, Vol. I, p.263.

63 Arrested for importing 'slanderous' Catholic books in 1584.

64 One of the entrances to the Palace of Westminster or Whitehall, near College Court. See Stow, Vol. II, p.122.

65 Bawdwin is described as a 'seminary priest', arrested in a boat on 'Yarmouth roads, coming over from beyond the seas'.

66 Inserted later. Berden was expecting £50 in bribes for their liberation. Their omission suggests Berden had fixed their release. See CRS, Vol. II, *Miscellanea*, p.252 fn.254.

67 Described as a boy who had been apprehended by Richard Topcliffe 'in the company of a priest, his uncle'.

68 Another of the sheriffs' prisons for the City of London, specially built and completed in 1555, on the east side of Wood Street near Lad or Ladle Lane. See Stow, Vol. I, pp.296 and 350.

69 Bavant and Sherwood are listed as 'released' in a later hand on the document. Bavant was made a doctor in Rome.

70 These are listed as recusants in the June prison lists.

71 The White Lion was an inn near St George's Church, Southwark, which was turned into a criminal prison for the county of Surrey in the 1560s. 'Newington' is a corruption of 'New Town', part of the Borough of Southwark. See Stow, Vol. II, pp.52 and 60. It was later converted into a Bridewell house of correction and was demolished in the late eighteenth century. See Rendle, p.92.

72 The June prison lists describe him as a 'poor simple man'.

73 The Clink was on the banks of the Thames in Southwark, west of London Bridge. Its name gave rise to a slang expression for prison.

74 Berden's little joke. An intercepted letter to Mary Queen of Scots written by Charles Paget in January 1584 says of Dolman: 'When attired like a gentleman of good calling, as commonly he goes, one would esteem him a justice of the peace'. See CRS, Vol. II, *Miscellanea*, p.256 fn. Dolman was ordained priest during the reign of Mary I, in 1557 (ibid., p.249).

75 Pollen, p.131.

76 Of Denham, Hall, Buckinghamshire. George Peckham had already been in trouble with the Privy Council in 1580 for harbouring the Jesuit Campion. His son was Edmund, patron of the 'exorcist movement' amongst the Catholic missionaries, led by Father Weston SJ, which reached its peak at Lent 1586. See Revd. R. H. Lathbury, *History of Denham*, privately printed, Uxbridge, 1904, pp.265–6.

77 Neither Peckham nor Gerard was involved in the Babington conspiracy. Peckham died almost immediately after this but Gerard remained a prisoner in the Tower until he was persuaded to give evidence against Philip Howard, Earl of Arundel.

78 Pollen, pp.132–3.

79 Henry Dunne, gentleman, late of London, one of the Babington conspirators.

80 The warrant for his detention should only describe Ballard as a priest.

81 Pollen, p.134.

82 Ibid., pp.135–6.

83 Charles, Second Baron Howard of Effingham.

84 BL Lansdowne MS 49, no.25.

85 Stow, Vol. II, p.349.

86 Howells, Vol. I, p.1,132.

87 Probably John Scudamore, clerk to the Privy Council.

88 The moated house at Uxendon. For the travails of the Bellamy family at the hands of the torturer Richard Topcliffe, see Chapter Two of this book.

89 Howells, p.1,136.

90 'Bardon Papers', pp.45, 47. Burghley wrote to Sir Christopher Hatton: 'I told her majesty that if the fashion of the execution shall be duly and orderly executed, by the protracting of the same both to the extremity of the pains in the action and to the sight of the people to behold it, the manner of the death would be as terrible as any new device could be, but therewith, her majesty was not satisfied.'

91 Ibid., p.47.

92 Their last speeches on the scaffold are in BL Add. MS 48,027, fols.263–271B.

Chapter Five

1 Scot, p.28.

2 'Cal Spanish', Vol. II, p.581.

3 Camden, p.323.

4 BL Harleian MS 290, fol.131.

5 Guy, pp.66 and 445–6. See also Antonia Fraser, *Mary Queen of Scots*, London, 1969, pp.443–6. In 1573, she had been allowed to take the spa waters at Buxton, Derbyshire.

6 Smith, p.18.

7 He was the son of John Dudley, Duke of Northumberland, executed for treason early in Mary I's reign.

8 His severity and enthusiasm nettled the Venetian Government, who obtained his recall to Rome in 1560.

9 BL Lansdowne MS 50, Items 19–21.

10 Labanoff-Rostovsky, Vol. IV, pp.236 and 314, and Lodge, Vol. II, pp.2 and 42.

11 Hatfield House, CP 164/114.

12 'Cal. Scot.', Vol. IX, pp.112–16. 'Reasons out of the Civil Law to prove that it Stands with Justice to proceed criminally against the Queen of Scots', October 1586. Another legal opinion written by Dr John Hammond at the request of Sir Philip Sidney – 'A Defence of the Roman Civil Law and the General Law of the World, untruly surmised to favour the Impunity of Mary late Queen of Scots notwithstanding her notorious and horrible treason against the Queen's Most Excellent Majesty' – is in BL Add. MS 48,027, fols.390–397B.

13 BL Cotton MS Caligula C ix, fol.606.

14 'Paulet', pp.286–7. The royal castle at Fotheringay is now gone, with just the high mound or motte marking the site of its eleventh-century keep over-

looking the River Nene and an earth bank, the remnant of the original inner bailey. A memorial on the site, commemorating both Mary and Richard II, was erected in 1913.

15 BL Cotton MS Caligula C ix, fol.378.

16 Mary had a notional income of around £7,500 a year from her French estates, paid via the French ambassador in London, but by the 1580s, this sum may have been reduced by more than a third. Out of this, she paid the wages of her household, but the running costs had to be found by her keepers. Food alone cost £3,000 a year under Paulet, and repayments from Elizabeth's parsimonious exchequer were often grossly inadequate. See Smith, p.12, 'Paulet', pp.172–3 and 183–4, and Leader, pp.442–3 and 609ff.

17 Reports from Spanish spies in London suggested that Mary was to be imprisoned in the Tower of London 'and no person was allowed to speak to her, except through two gratings like a nun and at so great a distance from her that it was necessary to speak very loudly, so that every word should be heard by others. She is treated with severity in all things. She was allowed to choose two women to cook her food to ensure her against being poisoned'. 'Cal. Spanish', Vol. IV, p.6.

18 Scottish ambassador to London 1584–5.

19 Hatfield House, CP 164/109.

20 Hatfield House, CP 164/105.

21 The room measured sixty-nine feet in length and twenty-one in width. An ink and pencil drawing of the courtroom at Fotheringay with the figures identified on the verso by a numbered key in the hand of Robert Beale, clerk to the Privy Council, is in BL Add. MS 48,027, fol.569. Burghley's sketch of his plan for the courtroom is in BL Cotton MS Caligula C ix, fol.635.

22 SPD, Elizabeth, 1581–90, p.360.

23 Poulet had written to Walsingham on 5 October about the arrangements for his accommodation. 'I was very willing to have provided a chamber for you and had taken order for it, but Sir Walter Mildmay hearing [of it] has given me to understand that the chamber appointed for him near adjoining the council chamber shall serve for you and him and that he knows [that] you would have it so. He has also made provision for your diet [meals] in that chamber . . . You will not be here so soon as I wish for you and indeed I think every day three until you come.' See 'Paulet', pp.294.

24 He was also registrar of the Court of Delegates and had been present at Babington's interrogation. He wrote a summary of the government's case against the conspirators that, no doubt, was to come in handy during Mary's trial. See BL Add. MS 48,027, fols.353–355B.

25 'Cal. Scot.', Vol. IX, p.82.

26 Steuart, p.38.

27 Guy, p.488.

28 Scot, p.30.

29 Pollen, p.cxciv.

30 Scot, p.32.

31 Ibid., p.42.

32 Forty-two had been named in the commission.

33 The judges included: Sir Christopher Wray, Lord Chief Justice of the King's Bench; Sir Edward Anderson, Lord Chief Justice of the Common Pleas; and Sir Roger Manwood, Chief Baron of the exchequer.

34 Valentine Dale (d.1589). Ambassador to Flanders in 1563 and to France, 1573–6 (succeeding Walsingham in that diplomatic post); MP for Chichester four times between 1572 and 1589. Dean of Wells Cathedral, 1575, and ambassador to the Prince of Parma, 1588–9.

35 Sir John Popham (?1531–1607), former Speaker of the House of Commons and later Chief Justice of the Court of King's Bench. Knighted 1592 and nominated as Lord Chief Justice the same year.

36 Sir Thomas Egerton (?1540–1617), Baron Ellesmere and Viscount Brackley. Appointed Attorney General in 1593 and Master of the Rolls, 1594–1603. Knighted 1593. Later Lord Chancellor.

37 Barker's notes of the proceedings at Fotheringay and later, when the trial reconvened in the Star Chamber at Westminster, are in BL Add. MS 48,027 fols.540–554. The marginal notes on this document are in Burghley's hand. A version in Latin, drawn up by Robert Beale, clerk to the Privy Council, is in fols.492–510.

38 Scot, p.46.

39 Steuart, p.43.

40 Scot, p.48.

41 Ibid., pp.50–1.

42 Steuart, p.47.

43 Scot pp.53–4.

44 'Cal. Scot.', Vol. IX, p.311.

45 Scot, p.60.

46 Ibid., p.61.

47 Steaurt, p.54.

48 'Cal. Scot.', Vol. IX, p.313.

49 A note in the hand of Thomas Egerton, Solicitor-General, of the documents produced in the Star Chamber hearing is in BL Add. MS 48,027, fols. 557B–568.

50 BL Cotton MS Caligula C ix, fol.2.

51 Notes of the Parliamentary proceedings 'in the cause of the Queen of Scots', BL Add. MS 48,027, fols.477–484.

52 The copy of the proclamation is in BL Add. MS 48,027, fols.448–50, with notes in the hand of Robert Beale, clerk to the Privy Council: 'Look ye [and] note how solemnly this was proclaimed in the presence of the Lord Mayor and his brethren.'

Chapter Six

1 'Paulet', p.353.

2 Hatfield House, CP 15/56 and Neale, *Elizabeth I*, pp.133–4.

3 Paulet was censured by Elizabeth for tearing down the cloth of estate. He told William Davison, the Junior Secretary of State, that he understood 'from some friend at court of her majesty's mislike that this lady did enjoy her cloth of estate'. On 27 November, he and Drury saw Mary in her dining chamber. She had hung 'eight or ten pictures in paper of the Passion of Christ and of other like stuff fastened upon the hangings over the chimney'. She told him: 'Although I had taken down her cloth of estate, she trusted that I would not take those things from her that she had set up in [its] place.' 'Paulet', pp.317–18.

4 Labanoff-Rostovsky, Vol. VI, p.461 and Pollen, p.cxcviii. Mendoza did not receive the letter until 15 October 1587.

5 Hatfield House, CP 165/10.

6 Labanoff-Rostovsky, Vol VI, pp.475–8 and 'Paulet', p.338. In January, Paulet was concerned that the 'still long delay of justice has stirred her [Mary] to hope of further mercy'. After hearing there had been no reply to her letter, she was willing to 'write again, and when her letter was ready would send it to me to see the enclosing and sealing of it. I answered that I would say nothing to that motion, forbearing flatly to deny her to promise to convey her letters. To be plain . . . being so well acquainted with her cunning, I would not wish that she might be permitted to write again to her majesty.' 'Paulet', p.346–7.

7 Hatfield House, CP 164/140.

8 Read, *Mr Secretary Walsingham*, Vol. III, pp.58–9.

9 Elizabeth claimed only a clock from the attainted estates. See BL Add. MS 6,997, fol.444.

10 Walsingham wrote to Leicester on Christmas Day, 1586: 'I thank my God for ... I am now in good hope of the recovery of both my daughter and her child.' Sadly, the baby died shortly afterwards. See BL Cotton MS Titus B vii, fol.24.

11 'Paulet', pp.341–2.

12 BL Cotton MS Titus B vii, fol.14.

13 'Paulet', pp.342–3.

14 'Cal. Spanish', Vol. IV, p.7.

15 BL Egerton MS 2,124, fol.55 and 'Bardon Papers', pp.93–4.

16 SPD, *Elizabeth, 1581–90*, p.380. A trail of gunpowder was to be laid to explosives in a bag hidden under or near her bed. Moody was described as 'a mischievous resolute person' by Burghley. See Hatfield House, CP 16/17.

17 Murdin, Vol. II, p.581.

18 He was arrested en route to the Channel port of Dover.

19 Murdin, Vol. II, p.579. Moody was formerly a servant to Sir Edward Stafford in Paris.

20 Stafford wrote to Elizabeth on 7 January urging that for her own safety Moody 'should be kept [a] close prisoner and no man suffered to speak with him but myself'. See HMC, 'Salisbury', Vol. III, p.216. What was he trying to hide?

21 Read, *Mr Secretary Walsingham*, Vol. III, p.60.

22 Haynes, p.82.

23 An abstract of Stafford's confessions is in BL Add. MS 48,027, fols.352–352B. A French account of the transactions between Stafford and the French diplomats is in BL King's MS 119, fol.50. The misunderstanding is acknowledged in the account of a conference between Walsingham and Châteauneuf on 13 April – see BL King's MS 119, fol.80. Stafford was recorded as still being in the Tower in August 1588.

24 Camden, p.485.

25 SPD, *Elizabeth, 1581–90*, p.383. Pembroke had been instructed to raise 2,000 men in Pembrokeshire 'to serve against [a] foreign attempt' and Lord Chandos commissioned to command 3,000 in Gloucestershire. See Murdin, p.785.

26 BL Lansdowne MS 51, Item 42. One enclosed a hue and cry signed by Justice of the Peace William Bowerman at Sampfield, Devon, ordering the local gentry to 'make your armour and artillery in readiness and that with all speed, upon pain of death'. Another commanded men to don their armour

'with all speed . . . for London is on fire. Let this go to Exeter upon horseback. Haste! Haste! Haste!'

27 SPD, *Elizabeth, 1581–90*, p.385.

28 Davison (?1541–1608) was a protégé of Walsingham and from 1574 one of his confidential men of business. He was fluent in French and Latin and had served on embassies to Scotland and the Netherlands. He was appointed Secretary of State and a Privy Councillor on 30 September 1586, having served as commander of Flushing in the Low Countries the previous year, although the Letters Patent confirming his appointment did not pass the Great Seal until 12 December.

29 'Paulet', p.356.

30 'Cal. Scot.', Vol. IX, p.263 and BL Harleian MS 290, fol.213.

31 BL Harleian MS 290, fol.104.

32 As another Stuart monarch, King Charles I, discovered to his cost when he was tried and beheaded by Parliament sixty-two years later in January 1649.

33 'Cal. Scot.', Vol. IX, pp.288, 297.

34 Ibid., p.289.

35 Walsingham must have written the letter by himself at his house. Davison recounts how he told his fellow Secretary of State of the queen's desires, departed and later returned to Seething Lane, when he found the letter 'ready to be sent away'.

36 'Paulet', pp.359–60.

37 Ibid., pp.361–2.

38 Possibly the Robert Wingfield who wrote an account of the execution of Mary for Burghley, who was a member of Paulet's team.

39 Leicester had written to the queen from the Low Countries, urging that Mary should be secretly removed by poison. See Camden, p.444.

40 Read, 'The Proposal to Assassinate Mary', p.235, quoting Calthorpe MS XXXI, fol.149. Several years later, there were reports in France that it 'had been better done to have poisoned her or to have choked her with a pillow, but not to have put her to so open a death'.

41 Hatfield House, CP 164/9.

42 Nicholas, *Life of William Davison*, p.264.

43 As well as Burghley, the Earls of Derby and Leicester, the Lords Howard, Hunsdon and Cobham, Sir Francis Knollys, Sir Christopher Hatton and Davison were present. Nicholas, *Memoirs of . . . Hatton*, p.460.

44 'Cal. Scot.', Vol. IX, pp.291 and 294.

45 Ibid., pp.262–3.

46 Ibid., p.264.

47 'Paulet', p.361.

48 Ibid., p.363.

49 'Cal Scot.', Vol. IX, p.291.

50 Ibid., pp.291–2.

51 Nicholas, *Life of William Davison*, pp.245–6.

52 Cited by Scot, p.177. The fifteenth-century building, formerly the inn, is now a farmhouse. Alongside is a public footpath to the site of the castle.

53 He was probably starved to death on Henry IV's orders while a prisoner in the castle's Gascoigne Tower.

54 Steuart, p.78 and Guy, p.499.

55 Hatfield House, CP 165/20-21 does not mention her chaplain being denied her, presumably so as not to offend Elizabeth's sensibilities.

56 Her original will, in the hand of her secretary Claude Nau with corrections in her own hand, was written while she was at Sheffield in February 1577, and is in BL Cotton MS Vespasian C xvi, fol.145. An extract, with notes by Robert Beale, clerk to the Privy Council, is in BL Add. MS 48,027, fol.530. It is reproduced, rather inaccurately, in Labanoff-Rostovsky, Vol. V, pp.352–62.

57 Dominique Bourgoing.

58 Prescott-Jones, pp. xii–xiii and Guy, p.501. It was addressed to: 'The most Christian king, my brother and old ally'. The original letter is in the National Library of Scotland, Adv. MS 54.1.1. It was purchased in 1918 by a group of subscribers and presented to the Scottish nation.

59 Dack, p.3, from the contemporary account of the execution by Robert Wingfield. See Steuart, p.80. She also told Melville: 'As you have been an honest servant to me, so I pray you to continue to my son and commend me to him. I have not impugned his religion nor the religion of others but wish him well and as I forgive all that have offended me in Scotland, so I would that he should also do and beseech God that he would send him his holy spirit and illuminate him.' See Hatfield House, CP 165/20–21.

60 Probably the Frenchman Baltazar, one of Mary's tailors, described by Paulet as 'old and impotent', or one Dedier, an old man who worked in her pantry. See 'Paulet', p.298.

61 Dack, p.5.

62 A contemporary pen and ink sketch of the execution is in BL Add. MS 48,027, fol.650; mounted separately. Eye-witness accounts are in fols.636–650B.

63 Dack, p.6.

64 He was one of Elizabeth's chaplains and the father of John Fletcher, the dramatist who worked with Shakespeare on the play *Henry VIII*. His account of the execution is in BL Add. MS 48,027, fols.654–658B.

65 Dack, p.13.

66 'Cal. Scot.', Vol. IX, p.317.

67 Dack, p.14.

68 Ibid., p.16.

69 Another report claimed he cried out: 'There is the head of Mary Stuart!' See 'Cal. Scot.', Vol IX, p.441.

70 Dack, p.16.

71 Ibid.

72 'Paulet', p.314.

73 One of her rings was found on the castle site and put on display at Peterborough in 1887.

74 'Paulet', pp.366–7.

75 'Cal. Scot.', Vol. IX, p 293.

76 Ibid., p.441.

77 Ibid., p.293.

78 Hatfield House, CP 164/10.

79 Smith, p.27.

80 Hatfield House, CP 164/15.

81 BL Add. MS 48, 027, fols.636–650B.

82 SPD, *Elizabeth, 1581–90*, p.387.

83 Strype, Vol. III, book ii, p.407.

84 BL Cotton MS Caligula C ix, fol.212.

85 BL Harleian MS 290, fol.238.

86 'Cal. Spanish', Vol. IV, pp.26–7.

87 Neale, *Elizabeth I and Her Parliaments*, pp.141–2.

88 A wrong action or omission, from the French '*mesprison*', an error.

89 BL Harleian MS 290, fol.224. A summary of Davison's communications with Elizabeth about the case of Mary Queen of Scots, written while he was a

prisoner in the Tower and dated 20 February 1587, is in BL Cotton MS Titus C vii, fol.48. See also BL Add. MS 48,027, fols.666–690B for an account of the Star Chamber proceedings against Davison.

90 Documents on the downfall and trial of William Davison, Secretary of State, including the letter dated 23 October 1588 ordering that Davison be moved, are in BL Add MS 48,027, fols.398–403.

91 Strype, Vol. III, book ii, p.410.

92 Hatfield House, CP 165/57.

Chapter Seven

1 Langton, Vol. I, p.46.

2 Drake's daring punitive mission to the West Indies in September 1585 to July 1586 sacked a number of Spanish towns and cities, amongst them Santo Domingo on the island of Hispaniola (today's Dominican Republic) and Cartagena, on Columbia's Caribbean shoreline, ransoming both under threat of further destruction. Audaciously, he also captured the fort of San Augustin on the Florida coast. The fleet returned to Portsmouth carrying loot valued at an estimated £8,300,000 at today's prices. Leicester was sent to the Netherlands to free its Protestant citizens from the Spanish army of occupation and to 'restore their ancient liberties and government by some Christian peace', but this mission was less than successful, and he failed to prevent the capture of several Dutch towns. The cost of the English expeditionary force also infuriated Elizabeth. See Somers, Vol. I, p.417.

3 He was dispatched primarily to promote English trading interests in Turkey, having negotiated a treaty to establish the London-based Turkey Company in 1579. Harborne served as ambassador to Constantinople until 1588. He died in 1617.

4 Read, *Mr Secretary Walsingham*, pp.226–8.

5 Walsingham repeated his instructions in cipher to Harborne in June 1587, when the danger from Spain loomed yet larger. He urged the ambassador to persuade the Sultan 'how necessary it is for him to attempt somewhat presently for the impeachment of the said Spaniard's greatness, much more in truth to be doubted than of Persia, against whom his forces seem to be altogether bent and may be performed by setting such princes as are in Barbary [the North African coast] at his devotion upon the King of Spain, furnishing them for the purpose with some number of galleys, which with small cost shall give him great annoyance'. See Bodleian Library, Tanner MS 79, fols.127ff.

6 BL Harleian MS 6,993, fol.125.

7 Langton, Vol. I, pp.xxv–vi. The original plans called for 150 warships, totalling 77,250 tons; forty store ships displacing 8,000 tons; 320 smaller vessels, amounting to 25,000 tons; six galleasses; and forty galleys.

8 Welwood, pp.8–9 and Read, *Mr Secretary Walsingham*, Vol. III, p.285. It has been suggested that this intelligence was gathered by the double agent Francesco Pucci, in Krakow. See Deacon, p.30.

9 'These in Guipuscoa: In Santander – sixteen new ships between 100 and 140 [tons]. In the Passage: fourteen of the like burden. In Laredo – eight *pataches* [fleet tenders or small communications vessels]. In San Sebastian – six ships of 300 [tons] and four of 200. In Bilbao – six *pataches*. In Figuera – four ships of 100 [tons]. Some built in the river of Fuenterrabia. In the river of Seville – eight ships of 300 and 200 apiece and four *pataches*. In Saint Mary Port – two galleys made short and broad and four *pataches*.' See Langton, Vol. I, p.56.

10 Ibid., pp.58–61.

11 Ibid., p.90. Much of the information came from a Portuguese living in Nantes in France who had sent his son to Lisbon, where he had a kinsman working on the provisioning for the Armada. There had also been reports from Brittany.

12 A quintal was 102 lbs (46.28 kg). The capacity of a butt – a large cask – varied, but may be estimated at 108 gallons (477 litres).

13 Fernandez-Armesto, p.163. The reports were broadly correct about the location of the ordnance in the Armada ships. With the exception of small-calibre ordnance, the Spanish shunned iron guns, made of welded rods bound together by hoops of steel, because of their habit of bursting open at inconvenient moments and killing their crews. Instead, their guns were mainly of cast bronze.

14 'Cal. Spanish', Vol. IV, p.24. Mendoza, the Spanish ambassador in Paris, described Raleigh as being 'very cold about these naval preparations and is secretly trying to dissuade the queen from them'.

15 The standing strength of the Royal Navy at this time was around twenty-five ships. In war, this would be augmented by chartering merchant ships, and various towns and cities also paid to fit out further vessels.

16 Corbett, Vol. I, pp.103–4.

17 'Cal. Spanish', Vol. IV, p.63. The estimates of the size and make-up of the squadron were inflated.

18 Ibid., p.97.

19 Corbett, Vol. I, pp.106–7.

20 A small two-masted, square-rigged vessel, displacing about twenty tons, designed to be used to carry dispatches from ship to shore and vice versa.

21 This type of sixteenth-century warship was a larger version of the galley, lateen-rigged on three masts and carrying 300 slaves to man the oars. It was able to fire broadsides from guns mounted above the banks of oars. Six galleasses were to sail with the Armada in 1588 but, being more suited to calmer Mediterranean waters, suffered in the storms of the North Sea and English Channel.

22 A large merchant ship, the name originating from a corruption of the Sicilian region and town of Ragusa.

23 'Cal. Spanish', Vol. IV, p.87.

24 They were unarmed and not manned.

25 SPD, *Elizabeth, 1581–90*, pp.411–12.

26 Borough (1536–1599), a famous navigator, was vice admiral for the Cadiz operation. He was placed under arrest by Drake in his own ship, the *Golden Hind*, for questioning his orders during the expedition, but the following year he commanded a ship in the battles against the Armada up the English Channel.

27 SPD, *Elizabeth, 1581–90*, p.412.

28 A three-masted ship with tall fore- and sterncastles, or superstructures, carrying up to 1,500 tons of cargo, which had great difficulty sailing against the wind.

29 BL Harleian MS 6,994, fol.76. Walsingham's plan was supported by Lord Admiral Howard and the Lords Cobham and Hunsdon on the Privy Council.

30 See, for example, the estimates of Spain's annual revenues *c.*1584–9 in BL Add. MS 63,742, fols.99–105.

31 Welwood, pp.8–9, Read, *Mr Secretary Walsingham*, pp.285–6 fn. and the 'Life of Sutton' in *Biographia Britannica, or the Lives of the Most Eminent Persons who have Flourished in Great Britain. . . .*, six vols., London, 1747–66, Vol. VI, p.3,852. There is no mention of Sutton's involvement in this economic warfare in the twenty-seven folios of his *Life*, written in the seventeenth century and now in BL Lansdowne MS 1,198.

32 Cited by Somerset, p.568 and 'Cal. Spanish', Vol. IV, p.127.

33 The full text of the treaty can be found in Meyer, p.454.

34 Strype, Vol. III, book ii, pp.551–2.

35 Walsingham was misinformed as to the amount of the loan.

36 BL Cotton MS Galba D ii, fol.86.

37 'Cal. Spanish', Vol. IV, p.62.

38 BL Cotton Vespasian C viii, fol.207.

39 'Cal. Spanish', Vol. IV, p.123.

40 Ibid., p.123 fn. The rectory of the Church of St Helen's Bishopsgate in the City of London formed the royal grant.

41 The city and port in north-west Italy, near Savona, occupied by the Spanish in the early 1570s.

42 In Holland. The city survived a siege by Spanish forces in 1573–4. Every year, on the anniversary of the relief of Leiden – 3 October – the inhabitants eat *hutspot*, a kind of stew made of carrots, onions and potatoes, the only food remaining following the siege.

43 Cited in Read, *Mr Secretary Walsingham*, Vol. III, p.287. This potential informant was Patrick Plunkett, Seventh Lord Dunsany, who was based in Ireland. He died in 1601.

44 This is mere peanuts compared to the £1.355 billion allocated in the 2004/5 budget for the British domestic Security Service MI5 alone – although these funds have been inflated considerably by current strategic concerns: the demands of the war against terrorism (67% of resources) and the prevention of the proliferation of weapons of mass destruction.

45 Leicester had been dispatched back to the Low Countries in June 1587 with £15,000 for the States General to pay for 5,000 extra troops.

46 Coming from Bergamo in Lombardy.

47 BL Harleian MS 296, fol.48.

48 A letter in BL Harleian MS 286, fol.46, addressed to Jacomo Manucci, Walsingham's trusted Florentine agent, signed 'B. C.' but in the same hand-writing as others by 'Pompeo Pellegrini', is endorsed: 'from Mr Standen'.

49 Cited by Read, *Mr Secretary Walsingham*, Vol. III, p.290.

50 BL Harleian MS 6,994, fol.76.

51 BL Harleian MS 296, fol.46.

52 Santa Cruz was captured by four English privateer ships when they attacked his vessel, en route from the Canary Islands to Lisbon in April 1587. Valverde was taken prisoner when his ship, separated from the rest of a Spanish flotilla by a storm, was boarded in 1586.

53 Núñez had been used effectively by Walsingham in 1582 as a go-between in negotiations over a peace treaty with Spain. See Read, *Mr Secretary Walsingham*, Vol. III, pp.125–6.

54 In the original document, Philip II underlined the names.

55 'Cal. Spanish', Vol. IV, p.221.

56 Two men who were to be exchanged for Valverde had already been set free and of the five Englishmen who were to be swapped for Santa Cruz, four had been freed and the fifth, James Lomas, was suffering 'from a malignant fever' whilst living in the home of the Archbishop of Seville's cook.

57 Langton, Vol. I, p.213.

58 Fernandez-Armesto, p.109. A French force had landed on the island in July 1545 as their fleet attacked Portsmouth. See Hutchinson, pp.117–18.

59 Fernandez-Armesto, p.114.

60 The German Gestapo compiled a similar arrest list for Operation Sea Lion, the plan to invade Britain in 1940–1.

61 'Cal. Spanish', Vol. IV, pp.184–6.

62 Ibid., p.123. Letter dated 12 July 1587.

63 Deacon, p.20.

64 Ibid., p.35.

65 Neale, *Essays*, p.174.

66 Mendoza was said to have three informants within the English embassy; all may have been one and the same person.

67 Deacon, p.18. Some modern historians, such as Neale (*Essays*, pp.147–69), defend Stafford and maintain his innocence of treachery, suggesting that he supplied deliberately misleading reports on his own authority. Others, notably James McDermott ('DNB2', Vol. 52, p.44), believe the evidence for his treason is both substantial and circumstantial.

68 Neale, *Essays*, p.153 and BL Harleian MS 288, fol.218.

69 Stafford remained as ambassador in Paris until November 1590 and died in February 1605. McDermott ('DNB2', Vol. 52, p.44) believes that the reason he was not impeached was because Walsingham felt less secure at court. Burghley remained a staunch friend to Stafford. Some of the ambassador's debts were cancelled by Elizabeth after the deaths of Leicester and Walsingham in 1588–9, but he had failed to repay several more at the time of his death.

70 'Cal. Spanish', Vol. IV, pp.164–5.

71 Read, *Lord Burghley*, p.405.

72 The practice remains in today's war-planning in Whitehall, known by the acronym STUFT – Ships Taken Up From Trade. Such vessels were used extensively by the British during the Falklands War in 1982.

73 APC, Vol. XV, pp.252–4.

74 BL Cotton MS Galba D ii, fol.178.

75 NA PRO SP 12/198/64.

76 A plan for an inspection two months before had been stopped by Elizabeth on grounds of cost. Burghley told Walsingham on 27 October: 'When her majesty was informed by me . . . of the names of such as should have been sent to the Lieutenants . . . she changed her mind, resting upon answer from the Lieutenants, as I think misliking the charge which would not have been above 200 marks [£60].' See Murdin, Vol. II, p.590.

77 Walsingham received a letter from the Low Countries, dated 15 July 1588, informing him that 'Adrian the armourer is gone to Utrecht and Amsterdam to get your armour done, in which there shall be no want of diligence used that your honour may be served speedily.'

78 Langton, Vol. I, p.107.

79 A large-calibre pistol, fired with the butt placed against the chest.

80 HMC, 'Cal. Foljambe', p.40. This force, probably raised in Wiltshire, was under the command of William Darell. Walsingham's contribution was larger than any other member of the English nobility or of the Privy Council save two – Hatton and the Earl of Essex.

81 Cited by Read, *Mr Secretary Walsingham*, Vol. III, p.302.

82 BL Cotton MS Vespasian C viii, fol.97, list of crew and equipment under command of Medina Sidonia, 1 May 1588; fol.205B, Spanish shipping in the Netherlands; fol.75, account of ships' ordnance and stores at Dunkirk, 13 June 1588.

83 Langton, Vol. I, p.221.

84 APC, Vol. XVI, p.138.

85 Ibid., p.168 and SPD, *Elizabeth, 1581–90*, p.507. Burghley admitted he had sleepless nights worrying about the defences of the River Thames. The cost of the barrier was £1,470, but the structure collapsed shortly after completion. See Fernandez-Armesto, p.111.

86 Motley, Vol. II, p.435 fn 1.

87 Fernandez-Armesto, p.237.

88 A laborious and repetitive method of moving sailing ships in the absence of wind. The anchor, attached to a cable, is rowed out ahead of the ship and dropped to the sea bed. The crew then wind in the cable using a windlass, and the ship is pulled in the direction of where the anchor has been dropped. The operation is then repeated as often as necessary.

89 Langton, Vol. I, pp.288–9 and SPD, *Elizabeth, 1581–90,* p.507.

90 Langton, Vol. I, pp.301–2.

91 A type of helmet with a peak and cheek pieces.

92 SPD, *Elizabeth, 1581–90,* p.520.

93 APC, Vol. XVI, pp.171, 176–81 and 187. A last was twenty-four barrels, each containing 100 lbs (45.06 kg) of powder.

94 Parma's original plan was to try to fool the English into believing he was attacking Ostend. His final invasion force numbered 4,000 Spanish, 9,000 Germans, 8,000 Walloons, 3,000 Italians and 1,000 Burgundians, plus 1,000 cavalry – a total of 26,000 troops. They would be transported to England in 173 vessels in three squadrons made up of *pleitas* – river boats, sixty to seventy feet long and fifteen to twenty feet wide – capable of carrying 200 troops apiece – and the smaller *huyas.* Each craft would be manned by three or four sailors. See Gallagher and Cruickshank, p.96.

95 Ibid., p.239. His estimate of the number of Spanish survivors who came ashore in Ireland is probably too low: Don Alonso de Leyra had 1,520 under his command after they were wrecked. Fitzwilliam left Dublin on 4 November and swung through Athlone to Sligo, on to Strabane and returned to Dublin on 23 December.

96 'Cal. Spanish', Vol. IV, p.432.

97 Laughton, Vol. II, p.126.

98 BL Harleian MS 286, fol.149.

Chapter Eight

1 NA PRO PROB 11/75 PCC 33 Drury.

2 His salary on appointment in December 1573 is worth £14,782 in modern monetary values, but had declined to £13,630 in 1590 as a result of the ravages of Elizabethan inflation.

3 BL Add. MS 15,891, fol.37.

4 Nicholas, *Memoirs of . . . Hatton,* p.189.

5 SPD, *Elizabeth, 1581–90,* p.181.

6 'Cal. Spanish', Vol. IV, p.499.

7 Stählin, p.57 fn.1. Letter to Sir Robert Bowes, Treasurer of Berwick. Walsingham, in fact, departed on 17 August with an eighty-strong escort. When he finally met the seventeen-year-old King James VI on 9 September, Walsing-

ham sternly remonstrated with him over his choice of councillors and bluntly pointed out his errors in government, including his tacit acceptance of outrages on the border between Scotland and England. The Scots retaliated by hiring a witch called Kate to sit at the palace entrance in Perth to taunt and revile Walsingham and his colleagues as they arrived and departed. She was paid partly in kind – a new plaid – and with £6 in cash for her efforts. See ibid., p.100 fn.1 and BL Harleian MS 291, fol.146.

8 Stewart, p.250.

9 BL Add. MS 15,891, fol.101. At the time of writing the letter, Walsingham was suffering from 'an indisposition' of his body and was expected to be absent from court 'until the end of the week'.

10 Stewart, p.349.

11 HMC, 'Rutland', p.149.

12 He conveyed lands including the manor of Bradford, buildings and lands in the villages of Atworth, Troile, Stoke, Leigh, Wraxall, Holt and Windesley in Wiltshire and property in Barnes, Putney and Mortlake to William Brunkhard and Thomas Fleming for their use, and after their decease to Sir Philip Sidney and Frances his wife. See Webb, Miller and Beckwith, pp.361–2.

13 Stewart, p.251.

14 Leicester paid £6 for the services of a midwife and nurse.

15 NA PRO SP 84/8/131.

16 It was said at the time that Sir William Pelham lacked his thigh armour and Sidney discarded his own armour as a gesture of solidarity, if not bravado.

17 Bruce, pp.414–15.

18 John Aubrey, in the next century, pruriently claimed that his death followed the overexertion of making love to his young wife on his sickbed.

19 Leicester to Walsingham, see Bruce, p.446.

20 SPD, *Elizabeth*, 1581–90, p.366.

21 Bruce, pp.456–7.

22 Lant (1555–1601) was successively *Portcullis Pursuivant* and *Windsor Herald* at the College of Arms. A copy of the book is in the Aldrich Collection in the library of Christ Church College, Oxford.

23 James Howell (ed.), *Cottoni Posthuma*, London, 1675, p.338.

24 Bodleian Library, Ashmolean MS 1,157, no.87.

25 See Webb, Miller and Beckwith, p.129. The painting, measuring 51 x 71 in. (1295 x 1803 mm), was bought from the Walsingham family seat of Scadbury

in Kent by James West. Later owners included Sir Joshua Reynolds and Horace Walpole. It was displayed in an exhibition in London in 1890 and is now at Sudeley Castle in Gloucestershire.

26 Strong, pp.79–80 and illustrated in plate 82. It was previously attributed to Hans Eworth (*fl.*1540–73) and there is also evidence it may be by Lucas de Heere (1534–84).

27 BL Harleian MS 306, fol.142.

28 Conditions for a grant of customs of Plymouth and Fowey, Cornwall, to Walsingham for six years from Michaelmas, 17 August 1585. NA PRO SP 46/17, fol.228.

29 BL Harleian MS 167, fol.39. Walsingham to Burghley, 23 April 1589.

30 NA PRO SP 46/34, fols.65–66B.

31 Read, *Mr Secretary Walsingham*, Vol. III, pp.388–9.

32 SPD, *Elizabeth*, 1581–90, p.156.

33 See, for example, the licences granted to Walsingham and others for 1575-80 in NA PRO SP 46/16, fols.223–224.

34 Gilbert (?1537–1583) was half-brother to Sir Walter Raleigh.

35 NA PRO SP 46/17, fol.166.

36 NA PRO SP 46/125, fols.143–143B. In June that year, Manucci, 'too ill to come to court', reported that Corsini was willing to lend Walsingham £400 – see fol.137.

37 Surrey History Centre, Loseley MS LM/1,042/14. The inhabitants' petition was addressed to Sir William More, amongst others. More was one of the overseers of the will of Sir Richard Worsley, first husband of Walsingham's wife Ursula.

38 Longleat House, Seymour Papers SE/Vol. V, fols.152–155. On 16 November, Beauchamp wrote to Hertford, his father, acknowledging his obedience to him but 'joining [it] with the duty of a husband as to his wife' (fol.156).

39 Liza Picard, *Elizabeth's London*, London, 2003, p.244 and SPD, *Elizabeth*, 1581–90, p.59.

40 Digges, p.136.

41 Cited by Read, *Mr Secretary Walsingham*, Vol. I, p.156.

42 Digges, p.145. Burghley wrote his instructions on 8 October 1571 and Killigrew departed for Paris on 20 October, carrying a letter from Elizabeth for Walsingham pointing out, rather obviously perhaps, that he should seek an immediate cure 'for . . . by your good service hitherto, we do plainly perceive that our election of you [as ambassador] has been well answered, and the continu-

ance of you in that service is to be much desired by the recovery of your health'. It was one of the rare occasions when Elizabeth showed some appreciation of Walsingham's efforts. Adverse winds in the English Channel and other difficulties delayed Killigrew's arrival in Paris to replace Walsingham until 31 October.

43 Fénelon, Vol. VI, p.358.

44 BL Add. MS 33,531, fol.151.

45 Elizabeth sent to Burghley, desiring his attendance at court, because of Walsingham's absence. See SPD, *Elizabeth, 1581–90*, p.578.

46 Bacon (1558–1610) was to become the Earl of Essex's private 'under-secretary for foreign affairs' in 1593. He would have been aged twenty-three when he received Walsingham's letter.

47 Birch, Vol. I, p.14 and cited by Read, *Mr Secretary Walsingham*, Vol. III, p.447.

48 The average male life expectancy in this period was around forty-five.

49 For a description of some of the more horrific Tudor medical techniques, see Hutchinson, pp.130–3.

50 BL Harleian MS 6,993, fol.50.

51 HMC, 'Finch', pp.24–5.

52 Presumably his doctors.

53 BL Add. MS 15,891, fol.110 and Nicholas, *Memoirs of . . . Hatton*, p.340.

54 Was this the same Dr Baily who lived next door to the French ambassador's house in Salisbury Court, off Fleet Street on the western edge of the City of London? See Bossy, *Giordino Bruno*, p.49. If so, one is tempted to speculate whether the physician was one of Walsingham's informants, providing details of the comings and goings at the residence.

55 BL Cotton MS Galba D i, fol.248, 14 August 1587. Walsingham talks of suffering a 'stoppage of water'.

56 SPD, *Elizabeth, 1581–90*, p.424.

57 Ibid., p.427.

58 The Earl of Derby wrote to Walsingham on 27 December 1587 with fervent hopes that he would 'recover his former health'. SPD, *Elizabeth, 1581–90*, p.446.

59 Ibid., p.491.

60 BL Harleian MS 6,994, fol.189.

61 SPD, *Elizabeth, 1581–90*, p.657.

62 Thomas Lake, just appointed Clerk of the Signet and regarded as Walsingham's man. He was afterwards knighted and became Secretary of State. See Birch, Vol. I, p.57.

63 SPD, *Elizabeth, 1581–90*, p.657. The letter also covers other matters of government business, such as the queen's decision to send one of her military commanders, Sir John Norreys, to Ireland.

64 Ibid., p.594.

65 All three were included in James Howell's *Divers[e] choice Pieces of that Renowned Antiquary Sir Robert Cotton*, first published in 1651. See Read, *Mr Secretary Walsingham*, p.441 fn. and p.442.

66 NA PRO PROB 11/75 PCC 33 DRURY – will of Sir Francis Walsingham, 12 December 1589. Also printed in Webb, Miller and Beckwith, p.384.

67 Inquisition Post-Mortem (hereafter 'IPM') on the death of Sir Francis Walsingham, conducted at Salisbury, Wiltshire, 27 September 1592, before John Hall esquire and others. Printed in Webb, Miller and Beckwith, p.361.

68 The note in the parish registers at Bexley, Kent, that he died 'about March 25' is clearly wrong. The date of death was reported officially at his IPM.

69 Camden, p.394.

70 Nichols, p.28.

71 He died in 1591.

72 Illustrated in Dugdale, p.82. The inscription on this megalomaniacal tomb even enjoined the passer-by to 'Stay [stop] and behold the mirror of a dead man's house'. It remained visible in the 'dismal ruins' of the cathedral after the ravages of the Great Fire of London, which destroyed Old St Paul's in 1666.

73 Fisher, p.8.

74 BL Cotton Vespasian C xiv, fol.215. Another suggestion in Latin on fol.185 more closely resembles his known epitaph.

75 Conducted.

76 Fisher, pp.8–11. The inscription, in Latin, is also transcribed by Dugdale, p.101 and Nichols, pp.28–9.

77 In 1588, the Sheriff of Sussex seized goods from Wiston (his home in that county) in payment of debts, including seventy-two feather beds and thirty-six Turkish carpets. As treasurer-at-war from 1586, he shamelessly embezzled large sums of cash raised to pay the English soldiers fighting in the Netherlands war – spending £8,000 before he even left the shores of England. One of the army's captains revealed how he loaned out much of the funds at interest, with £1.5 million passing through his hands in a decade. It was alleged that he made £20,000 a year through various scams. In the 1590s he unsuccessfully tried to bribe Burghley to procure for him the appointment of Comptroller of the Household and was declared bankrupt in disgrace in 1597,

when he owed the queen £35,175 in misappropriated funds. Perhaps Walsingham was trying to bail out his debts? See 'DNB2', Vol. 50, p.316 (article on Shirley by Janet Pennington).

78 BL Lansdowne MS 167, fol.294.

79 SPD, *James I, 1611–1618*, p.66.

80 BL Lansdowne MS 103, fol.68.

81 SPD, *Elizabeth, 1581–90*, p.664.

82 Ibid., p.674.

83 'Cal. Spanish', Vol. IV, p.578. Another Spanish report was written (in Italian) on June 9, adding that Walsingham was 'buried the next day in St Paul's church near the body of Philip Sidney, his son-in-law. He died greatly in debt.' See SPD, *Elizabeth, 1581–90*, p.670.

Chapter Nine

1 Naunton, p.21.

2 Camden, p.394.

3 Naunton, p.21.

4 Watson (?1557–159?) produced some sonnets that were closely studied by Shakespeare, and he was the 'Amyntas' of Spenser's *Colin Clout's Come Home Again* in 1595.

5 Webb, Miller and Beckwith, pp.130–1.

6 NA PROB 11/100 PCC 55 MONTAGUE.

7 Letter to Sir Christopher Hatton, 7 November 1582. See Nicholas, *Memoirs of . . . Hatton*, p.279.

8 Revd Daniel Lysons, *Environs of London*, Vol. I – 'Surrey', London, 1810, p.9.

9 Nairn, Pevsner and Cherry, p.105.

10 Webb, Miller and Beckwith, p.132.

11 A portrait of a lady 'in Persian dress', clearly pregnant, at Hampton Court, painted by Gheeraerts the Younger, has been identified by Sir Roy Strong as being of Frances Devereaux, painted in 1600 when she was carrying her second daughter Dorothy.

12 Graves, p.100.

13 Somerset, p.639.

14 See his humble request to the queen about his debts in NA PRO SP

46/39, fol.293 and the stay of legal process against him on 5 October 1596 in SP 46/40, fol.110.

15 NA PRO SP 4/19/38.

16 SPD, *James, 1603–1610*, p.13.

17 Ibid., p.72.

18 Ibid., pp.25, 29 and 314. Phelippes' brother Stephen was also questioned about Thomas' foreign correspondence.

19 Ibid., p.504.

20 BL Cotton MS Julius C iii, fol.297 and 'Paulet', p.375.

21 Birch, Vol. I, pp.66–8.

22 Ibid., pp.502–5.

23 Pollen, pp.ccvii–ccviii.

24 Edward Gage wrote to Burghley sometime in the 1590s asking that Topcliffe's 'manner of making iron with peat be investigated'. See BL Lansdowne MS 59, Item 74.

25 Birch, Vol. I, p.160.

26 See, for example, the confession of Richard Floyd, alias Lloyd, 'an imprisoned seminary priest taken [arrested] by Mr Topcliffe and [Justice of the Peace] Mr Young', 31 August 1590, in BL Lansdowne MS 64, Item 6.

27 James Heath, *Torture and the English Law: An Administrative and Legal History from the Plantagenets to the Stuarts*, Westport, Connecticut, and London, 1982, p.143.

28 Southwell was executed on 21 February 1595. Canonised in 1970.

29 Henry Walpole, born at Docking, Norfolk, in 1558; executed at York, 7 April 1595. Canonised in 1970.

30 BL Harleian MS 9,889.

31 'DNB2', p.29, article on Topcliffe by William Richardson.

32 BL Lansdowne MS 72, Item 49.

33 John Fitzherbert and his wife were reported as recusants at Badley Hall, 'with Mr Tanner, priest' by Walsingham's agent Barnard in the early 1580s.

34 Mary's physician, apothecary and surgeon, respectively.

35 The vault was opposite the tomb of Catherine of Aragon, Henry VIII's first and much wronged wife. The burial registers record: 'Anno domini 1587 et Regni Regine Elizabeth Anno XXIX. Item: The Queen of Scots was most sumptuously buried in the Cathedral church of Peterborough the first day of August who was for her deserts, beheaded at Fotheringay about Saint Paul's day before.'

Immediately after this entry comes another connected with Mary: 'Anthony More, one of the children of the queen's majesty's kitchen which followed at the funeral aforesaid of the Queen of Scots, was buried the third day [of August].'

36 'A Remembrance of the Order and Manner of the Burial of Mary Queen of Scots', *Archaeologia*, I, 3rd edn. (1804), p.383. The 'annoyance' is a euphemistic reference to the smell of the cadaver. The coffin was said to have weighed 9 cwt. (457 kg).

37 It was normal practice to lay such effigies on top of the coffin in royal or high-ranking noble funerals up to the end of the seventeenth century.

38 A hearse at this time was a temporary wooden structure used in the funeral service, covered with candles, rather than its modern meaning of a vehicle to convey the coffin. Dethicke described it as 'covered on the tips with black bays, garnished with escutcheons [shields] . . . of metal and beset with pinnacles from the top, on each quarter, most beautiful to behold. Whereupon was painted, on some, the Scottish arms alone and on others, the arms of France and Darnley impaled, and St Andrew's cross.'

39 Dack, p.23. Melville was a Protestant. See 'Paulet', p.371.

40 Dack, p.24.

41 Afterwards they were hung over her grave and remained there, even though her body was later moved to Westminster, until 1643.

42 Dethicke charged £406 (£63,150 at 2005 monetary values) for making the hearse and the heraldic decorations and accoutrements used in Mary's funeral. See NA PRO AO 1/2,119/2. His final accounts for the funeral, now sadly torn and water-stained, totalled a further £700 (£109,000 at today's prices), including £8 12s 8d for a 'strong chariot' to convey Mary's body to Peterborough; £3 6s 8d for the purple pillow, fringed with gold, on which the wax image's head rested; and £557 2s for the black velvet hangings in the cathedral. See NA PRO E 101/676/48. These charges were 'not accounted in the determination of the [final] account made by Anthony Paulet esquire, for his late father Sir Amyas Paulet, deceased, who had the custody and charge . . . for the said funeral charges of the late Scottish Queen so that the said Garter stands charged for the said account'.

43 Scot, p.241.

44 Adam Blackwood, *Martyre de Marie Stuart*, Paris, 1644, p.703.

45 James wrote to the Dean and Chapter of Peterborough in 1612 about the exhumation of Mary's body: 'We think it appertains to the duty we owe to our dearest mother, that like honour should be done to her body and like monument be extant of her, as others, hers and our progenitors, have been used to be done,

and ourselves have already performed, to our dear sister Queen Elizabeth. We have commanded a memorial to be made in our church at Westminster, the place where kings and queens of this realm are usually interred and ... we have ordered that her said body ... shall be removed to Westminster to her said monument and have committed the charge of the said translation of her body from Peterborough to Westminster to ... [Richard Neale] Bishop of Coventry and Lichfield, [the] bearer hereof.' Mary's body was removed from Peterborough on 12 October 1612. See Prescott-Jones, pp.xvii–xviii.

46 Payments for the tomb are contained in NA PRO E 403/2,726 and 2,727, and for its painting and gilding by James Mauncy in E 403/2,735.

47 Clifford Brewer, *The Death of Kings*, London, 2000, p.151.

Appendix

1 CRS, Vol. II, *Miscellanea*, p.34 fn.

2 CSPF, *January–June 1583 and Addenda*, p.280.

3 Ibid., p.383.

4 CRS, Vol. II, *Miscellanea*, p.34 fn., and CSPF *July 1583–July 1584*, pp.66 and 75.

5 BL Harleian MS 286, fol.56.

6 CSPF, *August 1584–August 1585*, p.193.

7 CRS, Vol. XXI, *Ven. Philip Howard*, p.81.

8 CSPF, *July 1583–July 1584*, p.257. Letter dated 25 January 1584.

9 CRS, Vol. II, *Miscellanea*, p.204.

10 SPD, *Elizabeth*, *1581–90*, p.207.

11 BL Lansdowne MS 153, fol.86.

12 Letter from Barnes to Walsingham, 17 March 1586. See 'Cal. Scot', Vol. IX, p.335.

13 SPD, *Elizabeth & James, Addenda, 1580–1625*, pp.267ff.

14 'Cal. Scot', Vol. VI, p.123. The letter is wrongly calendered as 1582.

15 Ibid., p.446.

16 SPD, *Elizabeth, 1581–90*, p.460.

17 Pollen, pp.xxxv–xxxvi.

18 CSPF, *1579–1580*, p.289.

19 SPD, *Elizabeth, 1581–90*, p.177.

20 SPD, *Elizabeth & James, Addenda 1580–1625*, p.184.

21 SPD, *Elizabeth, 1581–90*, p.32.

22 CSPF, *1577–8*, pp.493 and 675. He later made a landing in Ireland at Dingle Bay.

23 BL Cotton MS Galba E vi, fol.296.

24 Haynes, *Invisible Power*, p.47.

25 BL Harleian MS 287, fol.47.

26 Cited by Read, '*Secretary Walsingham*', Vol. III, p247 fn.

27 'Cal. Spanish', Vol. IV, p.123.

28 Haynes, p.44.

29 His confession to the queen is in BL Lansdowne MS 43, Item 47.

30 Coming from Bergamo in Lombardy.

31 BL Harleian MS 296, fol.48.

32 Pollen, p.liv and 'Paulet', p.119.

33 Haynes, p.13.

34 See his humble request to the queen about his debts in NA PRO SP 46/39, fol.293 and the stay of legal process against him on 5 October 1596 in NA PRO SP 46/40, fol.110.

35 Morris, Vol. III, p.169.

36 A letter in BL Harleian MS 286, fol.46, addressed to Jacomo Manucci, Walsingham's trusted Florentine agent, signed 'B. C.' but in the same handwriting as others by 'Pompeo Pellegrini' is endorsed: 'from Mr Standen'.

37 BL Harleian MS 288, fol.218.

38 He offered Walsingham's wife Ursula £100 a year from his lands. See SPD, *Elizabeth & James, Addenda, 1580–1625*, p.66. The offer was rejected.

39 Richings, p.139.

Chronology

1532	Probable year of birth of Francis Walsingham.
1542: December 8	Birth of Mary Queen of Scots at Linlithgow, daughter of King James V of Scotland and his second wife, Mary of Guise. She succeeds her father to the throne of Scotland on his sudden death on 14 December 1542. Her mother becomes Regent of Scotland on 12 April 1554 and holds this office until her death on 11 June 1560 in Edinburgh.
1548: November 12	Walsingham matriculates as a fellow commoner of King's College, Cambridge. He takes no degree.
1551	William Cecil appointed a Privy Councillor, Secretary of State to Edward VI and surveyor of Princess Elizabeth's estates.
1552	Walsingham admitted as a student at Gray's Inn to read law.
1555: December 29	Walsingham elected *Consularius* of the English Nation in the Faculty of Civil Law at the University of Padua in Italy.
1558: April 24	Mary Queen of Scots marries Francis, Dauphin of France, son of King Henry II, in the Cathedral of Notre Dame, Paris.
1558: November 17	Elizabeth succeeds her Catholic half-sister Mary as Queen of England. Cecil appointed Privy Councillor and Secretary of State.

1559: January 15	Coronation of Elizabeth I in Westminster Abbey.
1559: January 16	Mary Queen of Scots and her husband assume the style and title 'Francis and Mary, by the Grace of God, of Scotland, England and Ireland, King and Queen' and include the arms of England in her heraldry.
1559: July 10	Mary Queen of Scots' husband becomes Francis II, King of France.
1560: December 5	Mary is widowed.
1561: August 19	The Scottish queen returns to Scotland, landing at Leith, near Edinburgh.
1562	Walsingham marries Anne Carleill or Carlyle, widow of a London wine merchant and daughter of a former Lord Mayor of London. She dies in 1564, leaving a son, Christopher, by her first marriage.
1562: January 12	Walsingham returned as a Member of Parliament for both Banbury, Oxfordshire, and Lyme Regis, Dorset.
1562: October 10–25	Elizabeth falls ill with smallpox, temporarily loses power of speech.
1565: July 29	Mary Queen of Scots marries her second husband Henry Stuart, Lord Darnley, son and heir of the Earl of Lennox. He is proclaimed 'King of Scots'.
1566: March 9	Mary's French secretary, the Italian David Rizzio, is murdered in front of her at Holyrood House, Edinburgh.
1566: June 19	Mary's only child James (later James VI of Scotland and from 1603 James I of England) born in Edinburgh Castle.
1566: ?August	Walsingham takes as his second wife Ursula, widow of Sir Richard Worsley of Appuldurcombe, Isle of Wight. Her two sons are accidentally killed in a gunpowder explosion shortly afterwards.
1567: February 10	Henry, Lord Darnley, syphilitic husband of Mary Queen of Scots, murdered at Kirk o' Field.

1567: May 15	Mary marries James, Earl of Bothwell, according to Protestant rites, at Holyrood House.
1567: June 15	Mary surrenders to the Scottish Protestant 'Lords Associators' at Carberry Hill. Bothwell escapes to Denmark where he dies, insane, eleven years later. Queen of Scots imprisoned in a castle on an island in Loch Leven.
1567: July 24	Mary forced to abdicate in favour of her son. James VI crowned at Stirling five days later. Her half-brother the Earl of Moray becomes Regent of Scotland on 22 August.
1568: May 2	Mary Queen of Scots escapes from Loch Leven and rallies her supporters.
1568: May 13	Mary's forces defeated at the Battle of Langside, near Glasgow, by an army led by the Earl of Moray. Three days later she crosses the Solway Firth and enters England.
1568: August 18	Walsingham employed by Elizabeth's Secretary of State William Cecil on secret business.
1569: November 14	Earls of Northumberland and Westmorland, with 300 armed horsemen, break into Durham Cathedral and destroy English Bibles and prayer books, later marching south. The Northern Rising had begun.
1569	Walsingham writes the propaganda pamphlet *A Discourse touching the Pretended Match between the Duke of Norfolk and the Queen of Scots*.
1570: February 25	Pope Pius V excommunicates Elizabeth by the papal bull *Regnans in Excelsis*, thereby depriving 'the pretended queen' of her throne and absolving her subjects of any allegiance or loyalty to her.
1570: Autumn	Walsingham appointed ambassador in France.
1571: March	Cecil raised to peerage as Lord Burghley.
1571	Ridolphi plot.

1571	Second Treasons Act (13 Elizabeth I cap. 1) of Elizabeth's reign passed, making it treason to 'imagine, invent, devise, or intend the death or destruction, or any bodily harm' to the queen 'or to deprive or depose her' from the 'style, honour or kingly name of the imperial crown of this realm'. Further, it was treason to suggest that Elizabeth was 'a heretic, schismatic, tyrant, infidel or an usurper of the crown'.
1572: January 16	Duke of Norfolk tried by his peers in Westminster Hall.
1572	Burghley appointed Lord Treasurer.
1572: June 2	Duke of Norfolk executed on Tower Hill.
1572: August 24	Massacre of Huguenots in France on St Bartholomew's Day.
1573: April 20	Valentine Dale succeeds Walsingham as ambassador to Paris.
1573: December 20	Walsingham made a Privy Councillor and joint Principal Secretary of State.
1574: May 30	King Charles IX of France dies, aged twenty-four. Succeeded by Henry III.
1577: December 1	Walsingham knighted by Elizabeth at Windsor.
1578: April 22	Walsingham appointed Chancellor of the Order of the Garter, receiving a pension of £100 a year.
1578: June	Walsingham and Lord Cobham sent on a diplomatic mission to the Netherlands.
1579	Walsingham acquires manor of Barnes, Surrey.
1580: July	Death of Walsingham's second daughter, Mary, aged seven.
1581: July	Walsingham involved in negotiating a new treaty with France and in discussions regarding a possible marriage between Elizabeth and Henry, Duc d'Anjou.

1581	Statute against recusants and Catholic missionaries – 23 Elizabeth I cap. 1.
1583: August	Walsingham sent on diplomatic mission to Edinburgh.
1583: September 21	Walsingham's daughter Frances marries Sir Philip Sidney.
1583	Throgmorton plot
1584: January 19	Spanish ambassador Bernardino de Mendoza expelled from England.
1584: July 1	Assassination of Dutch Protestant leader William of Orange at Middleburgh.
1584: July 10	Francis Throgmorton executed at Tyburn for treason.
1584	The 'Bond of Association' drafted to defend Elizabeth against assassination ratified by Parliament.
1584	Parry plot.
1584	Walsingham appointed *Custos Rotulorum* for Hampshire and Recorder of Colchester, Essex.
1585: March 2	Dr William Parry executed for treason in Great Palace Yard, Westminster.
1585: May	Walsingham appointed High Sheriff of Westminster.
1585: August 17	Elizabeth grants Walsingham a lease of customs payable at major English ports.
1586	Walsingham establishes a divinity lectureship at Oxford University.
1586: September 13-14	Anthony Babington and six others tried for high treason and found guilty. All executed on 20 September.
1586: September 15	Other Babington plot conspirators Edward Abington, Charles Pilney, Edward Jones, John Travers, John Charnock, Jerome Bellamy and Robert Gage tried for high treason in Babington plot. Executed on 21 September.

1586: October 11	Elizabeth's commissioners arrive at Fotheringay to try Mary Queen of Scots for high treason.
1586: October 17	Sir Philip Sidney dies from a gangrenous wound at Arnhem in the Low Countries. Walsingham is responsible for his debts. Elizabeth refuses to grant revenues and lands from Babington's and other traitors' estates to Walsingham.
1586: October 25	Trial of Mary Queen of Scots continues in the Star Chamber Court at Westminster. Mary is condemned.
1587: January	'Stafford' plot.
1587: February 1	Elizabeth signs Mary's death warrant.
1587: February 8	Mary Queen of Scots is beheaded at Fotheringay.
1587: July 31	Burial of Mary Queen of Scots at Peterborough. Her body is later moved and reburied in Westminster Abbey by her son, then James I of England.
1588: July–August	Defeat of the Spanish Armada.
1590: ?March	Frances Sidney, Walsingham's daughter, marries Robert Devereux, Second Earl of Essex, in a secret wedding ceremony.
1590: April 6	Death of Walsingham at his home in Seething Lane, London, with debts of £27,000. Buried the following night in Old St Paul's Cathedral.
1598: August 4	Death of Burghley.
1602: June 18	Death of Ursula, widow of Francis Walsingham, at Barn Elms.
1603: March 24	Death of Queen Elizabeth I.

Dramatis Personæ

Details of known spies and agents used by Sir Francis Walsingham can be found in the Appendix: Walsingham's Spy Network.

Agazzari, Alfonso, SJ. First Rector of the English College in Rome until 1586, when he was transferred to the government of Siena.

Alava, Francés de. Spanish ambassador to Paris.

Allen, Dr William, later 'Cardinal of England' (1532–94). Leader of the exiled English Catholics in Europe during Elizabeth's reign. Fled to the Low Countries in 1565. His name headed a list in 1567 of those to be arrested for their 'contempt and obstinacy'. During the following year he founded a college at Douai to instruct English students in the Catholic religion. This college was expelled in 1578 but set up again in Rheims. Allen supported plans to enthrone Philip II in England, with him appointed Papal Legate, Archbishop of Canterbury and Lord Chancellor of a Catholic government. Buried in the Church of the Holy Trinity attached to the Venerable English College in Rome, where a memorial to him remains on the north wall, near the sacristy.

Andrews, Thomas. Sheriff of Northamptonshire, legally responsible for ensuring the execution of Mary Queen of Scots.

Aquaviva, Claudius, SJ (1543–1615). Fifth Superior General of the Society of Jesus from February 1581 until his death.

Arundel, Charles (?1540–87). Second cousin to Thomas Howard, Fourth Duke of Norfolk. English Catholic exile and devotee of Mary Queen of Scots. Fled England in the aftermath of the Throgmorton plot in 1583.

Aston, Roger. Confidential agent of James VI.

Babington, Anthony (1561–86). Catholic conspirator who, as a young man, helped fugitive Catholic missionaries to move about England. His correspondence with Mary Queen of Scots, detailing a conspiracy for a foreign invasion, a Catholic uprising and the assassination of Elizabeth, was the major factor in her subsequent indictment and execution. Executed at Tyburn, 20 September 1586.

Ballard, John, alias Fortescue. Commonly called 'Captain'. Catholic priest and a leading figure in the Babington plot. Executed with Babington.

Beale, Robert (1541–1601). Brother-in-law to Francis Walsingham and his secretary during his ambassadorship in Paris, 1570–3. Clerk to the Privy Council; stood in for Walsingham as Secretary of State during his absences in 1578, 1581 and 1583. Delivered Mary Queen of Scots' execution warrant to Fotheringay.

Beaton, Cardinal James (1517–1603). Archbishop of Glasgow. Mary's ambassador in France.

Bowes, Sir George (1527–80). Provost Marshal of the Earl of Sussex's army, which was sent to suppress the Catholic Northern Rebellion in 1569.

Bromley, Sir Thomas (1530–87). Solicitor-General in 1569. Lord Chancellor of England from 1579 until his death. Presided over trial of Mary Queen of Scots.

Buckhurst, Thomas Sackville, First Lord (1536–1608). Barrister, Privy Councillor and diplomat. Announced sentence of death to Mary Queen of Scots, 1586. Lord Treasurer from 1599 until his death.

Bull. Executioner of Mary Queen of Scots, accompanied at the execution by an assistant. Normally employed at the Tower of London.

Burghley, Baron – *see* **William Cecil.**

Campion, St Edmund (1540–81). Jesuit martyr. Speaker at Elizabeth's state visit to Oxford, 1557. Joined Jesuits 1573 and ordained priest 1578. Chosen for mission to England with Robert Persons, 1580. Arrested at Lyford, Berkshire, on 17 July 1581 and taken to Tower, where he was racked three times. The torture so broke him that he could not raise his right hand to plead 'not guilty' at his trial. Executed at Tyburn, 14 November 1581. Beatified in December 1886 and canonised by Pope Paul VI in 1970. His relics remain in Rome, Prague, London, Oxford and Stoneyhurst.

Carleill or Carlyle, Anne (d.1564). Francis Walsingham's first wife, whom he married in 1562. She was the widow of Alexander, a London wine merchant, by whom she had a son, Christopher.

Carleill or Carlyle, Christopher, Stepson of Francis Walsingham from his first marriage. Served as a soldier in Ireland and the Low Countries and later in the West Indies against the Spaniards. Involved in financing English voyages to colonise North America. Possessed lands producing an annual income of £300 in Ireland.

Castelnau, Michel, Seigneur de la Mauvissière. French ambassador to England 1575–85.

Cecil, William, Baron Burghley (1520–98). Elizabeth's Chief Minister. Lord High Treasuer 1572–98. Organiser of domestic and foreign intelligence network.

Champhuan, Jean de, Sieur du Ruisseau. Mary's chancellor in France.

Charles IX (1550–74). King of France. Second son of Henry II and Catherine de Medici.

Châteauneuf, Claude de l'Aubespine de. French ambassador in England from August 1585.

Cottam, Blessed Thomas (1549–82). Ordained a Catholic priest at Soissons in France. Surrendered to authorities in London in June 1580 and celebrated first Mass in Marshalsea Prison, Southwark. Executed 30 May 1582 at Tyburn. Beatified by Pope Leo XIII, 29 December 1886.

Cumberland, George Clifford, Third Earl of (1558–1605). Naval commander. Named as a commissioner for the execution of Mary Queen of Scots, but took no part in the proceedings. [See also Derby, Pembroke.]

Curle, Elizabeth. Sister of Gilbert Curle. One of Mary Queen of Scots' gentlewomen, present at her execution.

Curle, Gilbert (d.1609). Secretary and cipher clerk to Mary Queen of Scots. Arrested and interrogated by Walsingham's agents in August 1586 and testified that the 'Babington letters' were genuine. Imprisoned for one year.

Davison, William (1541–1608). English Junior Secretary of State and Privy Councillor, 1586–7. Fined and imprisoned in the Tower of London for 'misprision and contempt' over the dispatch of the execution warrant of Mary Queen of Scots. Subsequently Clerk to the Treasury.

Derby, Henry Stanley, Fourth Earl of (1531–93). Sat as commissioner at trial of Mary Queen of Scots but took no part in her execution, although named as a commissioner. Appointed Lord High Steward, 1589. [See also Cumberland, Pembroke].

Douglas, Archibald. Scottish ambassador in England.

Drake, Sir Francis (?1540–96). English naval commander and navigator. Friend of Francis Walsingham.

Drury, Sir Dru (?1531–1617). Gentleman Usher of the Privy Chamber to Elizabeth and later James I. Sir Amyas Paulet's assistant, joint custodian of Mary Queen of Scots at Fotheringay, November 1586 to February 1587.

Englefield, Sir Francis (d.?1596). English Catholic exile. Mary Queen of Scots' agent in Spain. Attainted 1585. Buried at Valladolid in Spain.

Elizabeth I (1533–1603). Queen of England 1558–1603.

Fénelon, Bertrand de Salignac de la Mothe. French ambassador to London 1568–75.

Figliazzi, Giovanni. Florentine diplomat who facilitated intelligence-gathering about the Spanish Armada in Madrid and became a friend to Walsingham.

Fletcher, Richard, Dean of Peterborough (d.1596). Played a prominent role at the execution and funeral of the Scottish queen. Chaplain to Elizabeth, 1583. Bishop of Bristol, 1589; Bishop of Worcester, 1593; and Bishop of London, 1594. Suspended by Elizabeth after his second marriage.

Fontenay, Monsieur de. Brother-in-law of Claude Nau and emissary of Mary Queen of Scots to James VI in 1584.

Francis II (1544–60). King of France 1559–60. First husband of Mary Queen of Scots.

Gray, Patrick, Master of; later Sixth Lord Gray. Confidant of James VI, Scottish ambassador to England 1584–5 and 1586–7. Disgraced in 1587.

Guise, Charles, Cardinal de Lorraine (1525–74). Mary Queen of Scots' uncle. Champion of the Catholic cause against the Huguenots in France.

Guise, Henry, Third Duke of (1550–88). Mary Queen of Scots' cousin. Helped plan the St Bartholomew's Day massacre of Huguenots in Paris and formed the Catholic League. Murdered in 1588.

Guise, Mary of (1515–60). Married James V of Scotland. Mother of Mary Queen of Scots. Regent of Scotland 1554–60.

Hamilton, Lord Claud (?1543–1622). Mary Queen of Scots' agent in Scotland. Commissioned by the Guises to reconcile Mary and her son, James VI, in 1586. Later became insane.

Harborne, William (d.1617). First English ambassador at Constantinople, 1582–8.

Hatton, Sir Christopher (1540–89). Vice-Chamberlain and later Lord Chancellor of England.

Heneage, Sir Thomas (d.1595). Vice-Chamberlain to Elizabeth. Friend of Walsingham.

Henry II (1519–59). King of France 1547–59. Father-in-law of Mary Queen of Scots.

Henry III (1551–89). King of France 1574–89. Brother-in-law of Mary Queen of Scots.

Howard, Charles, Second Baron Howard of Effingham (1536–1624). Lord High Admiral of England.

Howard, Henry, Lord (1540–1614). Younger brother of Thomas Howard, Fourth Duke of Norfolk. Suspected of involvement in Catholic intrigues and imprisoned on several occasions.

Howard, St Philip, Earl of Arundel (1557–95). Eldest son of Thomas Howard, Fourth Duke of Norfolk. Became a Catholic in 1584. Imprisoned after attempting to escape England in 1585. Condemned to death for saying Mass for the success of the Armada but not executed. Died in the Tower of London. Beatified in 1929 by Pope Pius XI and canonised in 1970 by Pope Paul VI.

Hunsdon, George Carey, First Lord (?1524–96). Active in suppressing the Northern Rebellion, 1569. Lord Chamberlain of Queen Elizabeth's household, 1583.

James VI of Scotland, later James I of England (1566–1625). Son of Mary Queen of Scots and Henry Stuart, Lord Darnley. Succeeded Elizabeth to throne of England, 1603.

Jennings, St Edmund (1567–91). Catholic Priest executed at upper end of Holborn by Topcliffe. Canonised by Pope Paul VI, 25 October 1970.

Jones, Edward (d.1590). Received into the English College at Rheims in 1587, ordained the following year and entered England. Arrested in a grocer's shop in Fleet Street in 1590 and executed outside the premises on 6 May 1590.

Keith, William, of Delnies. Scottish ambassador to England 1586–7.

Kennedy, Jane. One of Mary Queen of Scots' gentlewomen, present at her execution.

Kirby, St Luke (?1549–82). Born in Bedale, Yorkshire. Entered Douai College in 1576 and ordained priest two years later. Went to Rome and entered the English College there on 23 April 1579. The following June, he was arrested on arrival at Dover and imprisoned in the Tower of London. Condemned 17 November 1581 and executed 30 May 1582 at Tyburn. Beatified 29 December 1886 and canonised by Pope Paul VI, 25 October 1970.

Leicester, Robert Dudley, Earl of (?1532–88). Supposed by some to have caused the death of his wife, Amy, in 1560. English Privy Councillor. Queen Elizabeth's favourite and her Master of the Horse. Suggested setting up an association for the protection of the queen's person, 1584; commanded the English expedition to support Protestant rebels against the Spanish in the Low Countries, 1585; made absolute governor the following year.

Lewis, Dr Owen. Welsh Catholic exile. Bishop of Cassano, influential in Catholic affairs at Rome – rival to William Allen.

Liggons, Daniel. Mary Queen of Scots' representative in the Low Countries.

Lincluden, Robert Douglas, Provost of. Scottish Privy Councillor.

Lorraine, Charles, Cardinal of. Uncle of Mary Queen of Scots.

Lumley, John, First Baron. English Catholic nobleman, involved in the Ridolphi plot of 1571.

Maitland, William. Scottish Secretary; Chancellor of Scotland from July 1587.

Mayne, St Cuthbert (1544–77). The first Catholic missionary to be executed by Elizabeth's government. Ordained priest at Douai in 1575 and entered England the following year, becoming chaplain to Francis Tregian, disguised as his steward, in his household at Golden in mid-Cornwall. Executed at Launceston, Cornwall, 30 November 1577. Canonised by Pope Paul VI, 25 October 1970.

Medici, Catherine de (1519–89). Queen Mother of France. Married in 1533 to the Duke of Orleans, later King Henry II.

Melville, Andrew. Mary Queen of Scots' steward.

Mendoza, Bernardino de. Spanish ambassador in London 1578–84 and supporter of the cause of the Scottish queen. Implicated in the Throgmorton plot and exiled in January 1584. As Spanish ambassador in Paris from November 1584, he was involved in the Babington plot. Born before 1541, the son of the Count of Corunna, he served as a cavalry captain with Spanish forces in the Low Countries from 1567. He became blind in 1590 and died in the convent of San Bernardo of Madrid in 1604.

Middleton, Anthony (d.1590). Entered the English College at Rheims 9 January 1582 and ordained 30 May 1586. Went into England the same year and was detained in Clerkenwell. Executed in London's Fleet Street, 6 May 1590.

Mildmay, Sir Walter (?1520–89). Chancellor of the Exchequer and brother-in-law to Francis Walsingham.

Morgan, Thomas (1543–c.1606). Cipher clerk to Cardinal James Beaton and professedly one of Mary Queen of Scots' most faithful and diligent servants. Imprisoned in the Bastille in 1584 for plotting against Elizabeth. It is possible that he may have been a double agent for the English government.

Nau, Claude de la Boisseliere (d.1605). Secretary to Mary from 1575. Like Gilbert Curle, he was interrogated in 1586. Freed in September 1587 to return to France.

Norfolk, Thomas Howard, Fourth Duke of (1538–1572). Premier peer and Earl Marshal of England. Norfolk was the favoured marriage candidate for Mary Queen of Scots and became the focus for several Catholic plots against Elizabeth. His alleged involvement in the second Ridolphi plot led to his execution on 2 June 1572.

Northumberland, Blessed Sir Thomas Percy, Seventh Earl of (1528–72). One of the leaders of the abortive Northern Rebellion in 1569. Escaped to Scotland but handed over to the English and beheaded in 1572. Beatified by Pope Leo XIII in May 1895.

Norton, Thomas. Walsingham's first rackmaster.

Paget, Charles (d.1612). Secretary to Cardinal Beaton, Mary's ambassador in Paris, 1572. Her professed servant and agent and close associate of Thomas Morgan. Like Morgan, he may have been a double agent for Walsingham.

Paget, Thomas, Third Lord (d.1590). English Catholic exile from 1583 after the discovery of the Throgmorton plot. Mary Queen of Scots' agent in Spain. Attainted 1587.

Parma, Alexander Farnese, Duke of. Spanish commander in the Low Countries.

Parry, William (d.1585). Conspirator. Secretly became a Catholic around 1579. Accused in 1585 of conspiring to kill Elizabeth and executed.

Paulet, Sir Amyas (?1536–88). Ambassador to France, 1576–9. Custodian of Mary Queen of Scots, April 1585 to February 1587. Appointed Chancellor of the Order of the Garter, 1587.

Pembroke, Henry Herbert, Second Earl of (?1534–1601). Named as a commissioner for the execution of Mary Queen of Scots, but took no part in the proceedings. [See also Derby, Cumberland.]

Persons, Robert (1546–1610). Jesuit missionary. Born in Somerset, the sixth of eleven children of a blacksmith. Fellow of Balliol College, Oxford, but left in 1575 to briefly study medicine at Padua. Received into the Society of Jesus in Rome on 4 July 1575 and ordained in 1578. Rector of the English College in Rome in 1588, from where he organised the Jesuit missions to England. Buried in the church of the Venerable English College, alongside Cardinal Allen, he too has a memorial.

Philip II (1527–98). King of Spain 1556–98 and husband of Elizabeth's half-sister Mary from 1554 until her death in 1558.

Pope Gregory XIII (1502–85). Pontiff 1572–85. Supporter of various plans to overthrow Elizabeth and her Protestant government.

Pope Pius V (1504–72). Pontiff 1566–72. On 25 February 1570, published the bull *Regnans in Excelsis*, thereby excommunicating Elizabeth and depriving this 'pretended' English queen of her throne.

Pope Sixtus V (1521–85). Pontiff, April 1585–90. Published a bull (probably drafted by Cardinal William Allen) in 1588 in support of the Armada.

Ridolphi, Roberto (1531–1612). Florentine banker. Came to London in 1561 and within five years had been tasked to channel the secret funds provided by Pope Pius V to the English Catholics to help overthrow Elizabeth and her government. Agent provocateur in two separate plots. Pius V gratefully made him a Papal Senator and he lived on for another four decades in Florence.

Ross, John Leslie, Bishop of (1527–96). Mary's ambassador to Elizabeth 1569; sent to the Tower in connection with the Ridolphi plot, 1571. Resident in Europe, mainly in France, after 1574.

Sadler, Sir Ralph. Chancellor of the Duchy of Lancaster; custodian of the Scottish queen, August 1584 to April 1585.

Shrewsbury, George Talbot, Sixth Earl of. Custodian of Mary Queen of Scots 1569–84; one of Elizabeth's two commissioners at Mary's execution.

Sidney, Sir Philip (1554–86). Poet and soldier. Married Walsingham's daughter Frances on 21 September 1583. Died in 1586 as a result of wounds sustained in battle in the Low Countries, leaving very substantial debts.

Silva, Diego de Guzman de. Spanish ambassador to London June 1564–8.

Spes, Guerau de. Spanish ambassador to London September 1568 to December 1571 when he was expelled by Elizabeth because of his involvement in the Ridolphi plot.

Stafford, Sir Edward. English ambassador to France.

Stuart, Lady Arbella. Possible contender for the English throne in succession to Queen Elizabeth.

Throgmorton, Francis (1554–84). Member of a large West-Midlands Catholic family who acted as an intermediary between Mary and her agent Thomas Morgan. Throgmorton was executed for his involvement in the plot and the Spanish Ambassador Bernardino de Mendoza sent home.

Topcliffe, Richard (1532–1604). Walsingham's rackmaster and chief torturer. Entered Parliament in 1572 as Member for Beverley; in 1586 he was returned by Old Sarum, a constituency he continued to represent until shortly before his death in 1604.

Walsingham, Frances (1567–1633). Surviving daughter of Francis and Ursula Walsingham. Married Sir Philip Sidney in 1583, then Robert Devereux, Second Earl of Essex, in a secret marriage probably in March 1590. Her third husband was Richard de Burgh, Fourth Earl of Clanrickarde, whom she married in 1603.

Walsingham, Lady Ursula (d.1602). Francis Walsingham's second wife, widow of Sir Richard Worsley of Appuldurcombe on the Isle of Wight, whom she married in 1566.

Westmorland, Charles Neville, Sixth Earl of 1543–1601). One of the leaders of the abortive Northern Rebellion in 1569. Fled to Flanders. Attainted for treason in 1571. Went to Rome 1581. Died at Nieuport, Flanders.

Bibliography

PRIMARY SOURCES

Manuscript Sources

BRITISH LIBRARY

Add. MS 5,520, fol.173 – Pedigree of the Walsingham family.

Add. MS 15,891 – A book of letters received by Sir Christopher Hatton, Vice-Chamberlain to Elizabeth I, probably copied by his secretary Samuel Cox:

> fol.37 – Letter from Walsingham, complaining of his treatment at court, 22 December 1582.

> fol.101 – Letter from Walsingham regarding the queen's opposition to the marriage of his daughter to Sir Philip Sydney, 19 March 1583.

> fol.110 – Letter from Walsingham about his sickness, August 1583.

Add. MS 33,531, fol.151 – Letter from Walsingham to James Douglas, Fourth Earl of Morton, the Regent of Scotland, mentioning his health, April 1575.

Add. MS 48,023 (Yelverton MS 26):

> fols.26–58B – Papers relating to Thomas Norton during his imprisonment in the Tower of London, December 1581 to February 1582.

> fols.26B–27 – Letter from Norton to ?Lord Burghley seeking release from the Tower and the possibility of house arrest, ?5 December 1581.

> fol.33B – Norton's letter to Walsingham asking how he could serve the queen, 23 December 1581.

> fols.42–43B – Norton's letter to Sir Owen Hopton, Lieutenant of the Tower, regarding the queen's safety and his possible house arrest, 6 January 1582.

fol.48B – Norton's letter to Sir Owen Hopton urging that an oath of allegiance be administered to Papists to ensure the safety of the queen, 7 January 1582.

fols.110–111 – 'Names and Dwelling Place[s] of all such Papists at whose houses I have been since my coming into England, which was at midsummer past', a list of priests and recusants in Essex, Suffolk, Norfolk, Derbyshire, Nottinghamshire and Middlesex by Robert Barnard – 'P. H.', undated.

fol.150 – Norfolk's letter of submission to Elizabeth 'after his last committing to the Tower', 10 September 1571.

fols.153–156 – Norfolk's letter to his children, 26 January 1572.

fols.163–164B – 'A form or plan for the ground and order of a petition to be framed to Her Majesty for executing the Duke of Norfolk' by T[homas] N[orton], written before June 1572.

Add. MS 48,027 (Yelverton MS 31):

fols.80–80B – List of executions of queens.

fols.83–125B – Papers relating to the imprisonment, trial and execution of Thomas Howard, Fourth Duke of Norfolk, 1570–2.

fols.222–223B – Considerations for Parliament concerning the queen's safety, 17 November 1586. Endorsed by Walsingham's clerk.

fols.242–247B – Documents relating to Dr William Parry, conspirator, including two accounts of his execution and speech on the scaffold (fols.244–247B), c.1584.

fols.249–251B – Bond of Association for the safety of Queen Elizabeth, 19 October 1584, and oath of adherence to Bond of Association allegedly signed by Mary Queen of Scots at Wingfield, 5 January 1585.

fols.258–262B – Copies of secret correspondence between Anthony Babington and Mary Queen of Scots, 25 June to 3 August 1586. (See also Cotton MS Caligula B v, fols.164–169.)

fols.263–271B – Account of the execution and speeches on the scaffold of Anthony Babington and other plotters, 20 and 21 September 1586.

fols.296–313 – Later copies (?c.1600) of Babington's confession and records of his interrogations, 18 August to 8 September 1586.

fol.313B – Keys to ciphers used by Mary Queen of Scots and Babington.

fols.318–345B – Elizabeth I's instructions to Edward Wotton during his mission to Paris carrying documents detailing the evidence against Mary Queen of Scots, 29 September 1586.

fols.352–352B – Abstract of William Stafford's confession in the alleged plot to assassinate Elizabeth, January 1587.

fols.353–355B – *A Breviate of Babington's Conspiracy 4 August 1586 gathered by Mr Edward Barker, Register of the Court of Delegates and present at the Examinations.*

fols.374–378 – Walsingham's letter to Robert Beale, clerk to the Privy Council, about the proceedings against Mary Queen of Scots and his reply, 21 and 26 September 1586.

fols.390–397B – Discussion paper on the legality of proceedings against Mary Queen of Scots, written by the lawyer Dr John Hammond, undated but mid-1586.

fols.398–403 – Documents regarding the downfall and trial of William Davison, Secretary of State, including a letter from Burghley and Walsingham to Sir Owen Hopton, Lieutenant of the Tower, ordering that Davison be moved 'in a secret manner' to private custody, 23 October 1588.

fols.448–450 – *A True Copy of the Proclamation of the sentence against Mary Queen of Scots*, C. Barker, London, 1586.

fols.451–476 – 'A discourse touching the Just Execution of the Scottish Queen', 1587.

fols.477–484 – 'Notes of the proceedings of the Parliament in the cause of the Queen of Scots', 15 October to 2 December 1586.

fols.489–490B – Letter of William Davison, Secretary of State, to Walsingham reporting conversations with Elizabeth about Mary Queen of Scots, Richmond, 29 October 1586.

fols.492–510 – 'The Copy of the Record of the Proceedings against the Scottish Queen 1587', Latin extracts by Robert Beale, clerk to the Privy Council, from the official record of evidence by the notaries Edward Barker and Thomas Wheeler.

fol.530 – Extract from the will of Mary Queen of Scots with notes by Robert Beale, clerk to the Privy Council, undated.

fols.540–554 – Proceedings against Mary Queen of Scots at Fotheringay and in Star Chamber, 12–15 and 25 October 1586, endorsed: 'This collection was made by Mr Edward Barker, Principal Register of the delegates, who was appointed as a Notary to make a note of that which passed. The notes in the margin were in the Lord Treasurer's hand.'

fols.557B–568 – Documents produced during the Star Chamber hearing against Mary Queen of Scots, 25 October 1586, apparently written by Thomas Egerton, Solicitor-General.

fol.569 – Pencil and ink drawing of the trial of Mary Queen of Scots in the great chamber at Fotheringay, 14–15 October 1586, with figures identified by key in the hand of Robert Beale, clerk to the Privy Council.

fols.570–574 – 'Note of the proceedings at Fotheringay', 14–15 October 1586, with memorandum by Robert Beale, clerk to the Privy Council, on Burghley's attitude to Mary Queen of Scots at fol.574.

fols.579B–580B – 'Matters to charge the Scottish Queen withal', October 1586.

fols.581B–584 – 'Declaration of the late [Babington] Conspiracy by Mr Edward Barker', August 1586.

fols.636–650B – Papers relating to the execution of Mary Queen of Scots, 1587, including a pencil and ink drawing of the execution of Mary Queen of Scots at Fotheringay Castle, 8 February 1587, at fol.650.

fols.651–653 – Petition to Elizabeth to execute the sentence on Mary Queen of Scots by both Houses of Parliament, 12 November 1586.

fols.654–658B – 'A Report of the manner of the execution of the Scottish Queen performed the 8th of February Anno 1586 in the great hall within the castle of Fotheringay, with relation of speeches uttered and actions happening in the said execution, from the delivery of the said Scottish Queen to Mr Thomas Andrews esq., sheriff of the county of Northampton, unto the end of the said execution' by Richard Fletcher, Dean of Peterborough.

fols.666–690B – Accounts of Star Chamber proceedings and sentence against William Davison, Secretary of State, 28 March 1587.

Add. MS 48,029 (Yelverton MS 33):

fols.58–72B – Thomas Norton's *Chain of Treasons*, a collection of Catholic plots compiled after the arrest of Francis Throgmorton in October 1583 but before his execution the following February.

fols.64–65B – Francis Throgmorton's interrogation, October 1583.

fols.85–91 – Examinations of prisoners in the Tower after the defeat of the Spanish Armada, 1589.

fols.131–141B – *A General Discourse of the Pope's Holy Devices* in two books by Walsingham's agent Charles Sledd, a servant in the English College in Rome in 1579.

Add. MS 48,078 (Yelverton MS 85), fols.54–55 – Italian summary of dispatch by Thomas Fenner, flag-captain to Sir Francis Drake, to Walsingham, describing the raid on Cadiz, April 1587.

Add. MS 48,126 (Yelverton MS 141):

fol.103B – List of women and children killed in Paris during the 'Massacre of St Bartholomew', 24 August 1572. Dated 14 September 1573 and endorsed 'Mr Sec. Walsingham'.

fols.107–108B – Information on a league against England made between the Pope, the king of Spain and the Duke of Tuscany involving the deposing of Elizabeth by force, Rome, 23 February 1580.

Add. MS 48,127 (Yelverton MS 142), fols.125–127 – Letter from Stephen Paule to Walsingham regarding Italian and Papal affairs, Venice, 7 August 1587.

Add. MS 48,149 (Yelverton MS 161, Part 1), fols.3B–9B – 'A Treatise of the Office of a Counsellor and Principal Secretary observed by R[obert] B[eale] for Sir Edward Wotton', 1592.

Add. MS 63,742:

fols.78B–79B – Examination of Southworth, priest, by Richard Topcliffe, 1 July 1587.

fols.99–105 – Annual revenues of Spain, c.1584–9.

Cotton MS Caligula B v:

fol.159 – Instrument of an Association for the Preservation of the Person of Queen Elizabeth I, signed at Hampton Court, 19 October 1584.

fols.164–169 – Copies of five letters between Anthony Babington and Mary Queen of Scots, 1586. (See also Add. MS 48,027, fols 258–262B.)

fols.170–174 – Order of proceedings at the arraignment of Mary Queen of Scots at Fotheringay, 6 October 1586.

fols.175B–176 – Account of the execution of Mary Queen of Scots, 8 February 1587.

fol.371 – Commission for and examination of Mary Queen of Scots at Fotheringay (end of document missing), 1586.

Cotton MS Caligula C iii:

fols.57–60 and 166–169 – Information received by William Herle in the Marshalsea Prison, Southwark, April 1571.

fol.96 – Letter in Italian from Roberto Ridolphi to Mary Queen of Scots, Paris, 30 September 1571.

fol.121 – Cecil's account of the alleged treasons committed by Thomas, Fourth Duke of Norfolk, dated January 1571.

fol.217 – Walsingham to Burghley, informing him of a plot against Elizabeth disclosed by his spy from conversations with the Jesuit Darbyshire, Blois, 4 March 1572.

Cotton MS Caligula C iv:

> fol.249 – Henry Cockyn to Burghley supplying intelligence about Mary Queen of Scots' friends in England and seeking his assistance in securing a royal pardon, 20 February 1575.

> fol.261 – Letter from Cockyn to Walsingham describing a Spanish plot to kidnap James VI of Scotland, 18 March 1575.

Cotton MS Caligula C v:

> fols.6–20 – Examination of Henry Cockyn and those named in his confessions, together with the confession of Alexander Hamilton and draft charges, April–May 1575.

> fol.129 – Complaint by Mary Queen of Scots to Walsingham about delays in receiving her letters, Sheffield, 5 September 1579.

> fol.143 – Report of Lawrence Tomson on his discussions with a papal agent in Bologna, 1580.

Cotton MS Caligula C vii:

> fol.106 – Letter from Sir Robert Bowes, English agent in Edinburgh, to Walsingham on the 'danger of some change in Scotland' warning that Brereton (the Jesuit William Holt) and 'another Englishman from Rome' were involved in French attempts to bring the Scots king and the nobility over to the Catholic cause, 4 March 1583.

> fol.115 – Walsingham to Sir Robert Bowes, giving directions about the detention of Father William Holt, 14 March 1583.

> fol.115B – Letter from Walsingham to Sir Robert Bowes, English agent in Edinburgh, regarding the interception of French diplomatic letters on a ship at Gravesend, March 1583.

> fol.119B – Letter from English diplomats in Scotland to Walsingham, warning him of the conspiracy 'between the Pope and the kings of France and Spain to invade this island', 18 March 1583.

> fol.153 – Letter from the spy 'Henry Fagot' to Walsingham with offer to suborn the secretary to the French ambassador in London, ? June 1583, but marked on the reverse, wrongly, as 'April'.

> fol.155 – Letter from the spy 'Henry Fagot' to Walsingham reporting that Throgmorton had dinner with the French ambassador in London.

Cotton MS Caligula C ix:

> fol.2 – Letter from Walsingham to Leicester reporting the outcome of the trial of Mary Queen of Scots at Fotheringay, October 1586.

> fol.212 – Letter from Elizabeth to James VI of Scotland, denying any responsibility for his mother's death, 14 February 1587.

fol.326 – Letter from Mary Queen of Scots to Anthony Babington, 17 July 1586.

fol.378 – Letter from Sir Amyas Paulet to Walsingham, 10 September 1586.

fol.571 – Authorisation from Walsingham to Thomas Phelippes to pay the spy Maliverny Catlyn £5 for his services, 23 December 1586.

fol.606 – Letter from Elizabeth to Sir Amyas Paulet, jailor of Mary Queen of Scots, September 1586.

fol.635 – Burghley's sketch of the arrangements for the courtroom at Fotheringay.

Cotton MS Galba C xi, fol.317 – Letter from Walsingham to Leicester reporting rumours that Drake's force en route to Spain would be recalled, April 1587.

Cotton MS Galba D i, fol.248 – Letter from Walsingham to Leicester, complaining of a seizure and a 'stoppage of water', 14 August 1587.

Cotton MS Galba D ii:

fol.86 – Letter from Walsingham to Leicester about Elizabeth's belief in a possible peace with Spain, 21 September 1587.

fol.178 – Letter from Walsingham to Leicester complaining at the lack of defensive measures against the Armada, 12 November 1587.

Cotton MS Galba E vi:

fol.296 – Letter in Italian from Jacomo Manucci to Walsingham containing intelligence from France, Lyons, 27 November 1574.

fol.309 – Letter from Walsingham to Sir Edward Stafford informing him of the proceedings against Mary Queen of Scots, 27 October 1586.

Cotton MS Julius C iii, fol.297 – Account of a petition presented to King James I by Thomas Phelippes, decipherer, 1622.

Cotton MS Julius F vi:

fol.11 – Questions to be posed to the Duke of Norfolk during interrogation.

fol.21 – Five causes shown against the Queen of Scots, 1572.

fol.26 – Letter from Robert Beale, clerk to the Privy Council, to [?] concerning the trial of Mary Queen of Scots, London, 26 September 1586.

fol.28 – Sir Amyas Paulet to [?] regarding further restraining the Queen of Scots and securing her money, Chartley, 10 September 1586.

fol.30 – Extract of Mary Queen of Scots' grievances and their rebuttal, November 1582 and April 1583.

fol.43 – Paper showing that the proceedings against the Queen of Scots were just and lawful by common and civil law, no date.

fol.53 – Reasons to indicate the ease of the enterprise of invading England, from papers found with Creighton, the Scottish Jesuit, ?1584.

fol.60B – Intelligence on Spanish forces, especially the Armada, extracted from a letter written by J. Conway, Ostend, August 1588.

fol.66 – Letter from 'some English to some Scotch statesmen' showing the impropriety of any resentment by the king of Scotland at the execution of his mother, no date.

fol.70B – Reasons why the king of Scotland 'doth not revenge his mother's death'; also concerning his intended marriage with a Danish princess or Lady Arbella, c.1588.

fol.200B – Arraignment, trial and confession of the Duke of Norfolk, with his confession at his execution, 1571.

fol.254 – A question posed: would it be 'behoveful for Her Majesty to put the Queen of Scots to death or to keep her prisoner?', no date.

Cotton MS Julius F xi, fols.391ff. – *Answer to a slanderous book that was published against the marriage of the Duke of Norfolk and the Scottish Queen,* dated 15 March 1570.

Cotton MS Titus B ii, fol.345 – Letter from Sir Amyas Paulet to Walsingham, offering his sympathies on the death of Walsingham's daughter Mary, 16 July 1580.

Cotton MS Titus B vii, fol.24 – Letter from Walsingham to Leicester bemoaning Elizabeth's indecision over the execution of Mary Queen of Scots and discussing his daughter and her child, 24 December 1586.

Cotton MS Titus C vii:

fol.48 – Summary of Davison's communications with Elizabeth about the case of Mary Queen of Scots, written while he was a prisoner in the Tower, 20 February 1587.

fol.75 – Papers relating to the Spanish Armada, 1587–8.

fol.80 – Instrument for the Association for the Protection of the Queen's Life, 3 November 1584.

fol.97 – List of Spanish stores and equipment at Dunkirk, 1588.

fol.205 – Reports of Spanish shipping in Dutch ports, undated.

Cotton MS Vespasian C viii:

fol.75 – Account of ships' ordnance and stores at Dunkirk, 13 June 1588.

fol.97 – List of crew and equipment under command of Medina Sidonia, 1 May 1588.

fol.205B – Spanish shipping in the Netherlands.

fol.207 – Letter to Walsingham from 'Mr Hunter of Lisbon' describing his imprisonment in that city and the armaments there, 10 February 1589.

Cotton MS Vespasian C xiii, fol.389 – Discourse, in Italian, on the Spanish Armada, addressed to Burghley and Walsingham, undated.

Cotton MS Vespasian C xiv, fols.185 and 215 – Draft epitaphs for Walsingham and Sir Philip Sidney, undated but after April 1590.

Cotton MS Vespasian C xvi, fol.145 – Draft of Mary Queen of Scots' will, in Claude Nau's hand with her corrections, Sheffield, 1577.

Cotton MS Vespasian F vi:

fol.107 – Letter from Walsingham to Burghley about the Duke of Alençon, Paris, 13 July 1572.

fol.261 – Letter from Leicester to Walsingham about his role as a 'councillor' to Elizabeth, 18 January 1573.

Egerton MS 2,074:

fols.5 and 52 – Walsingham to Thomas Wilkes, clerk of the Privy Council, Barn Elms, 21 April and 17 May 1585.

fol.9 – Henry Middlemore and Anthony Wyngfeld to Walsingham, St James's Palace, 22 April 1585.

fol.81 – Memorandum of 'the treasons severally attempted from the ninth year of Her Majesty's reign against her royal state and person by her traitorous subjects on this side and beyond the seas', undated.

fol.108 – Inventory of 'such goods as are left in the Earl of Northumberland's chamber in the Tower', 21 June 1585.

Egerton MS 2,124:

fol.10 – Notes for Sir Christopher Hatton's speech to promote legislation derived from the 'Bond of Association', December 1584.

fol.55 – 'Reasons touching the execution of the Scottish Queen', probably drawn up by Sir Christopher Hatton, undated but probably written December 1586.

Harleian MS 167, fol.39 – Walsingham to Burghley, 23 April 1589.

Harleian MS 286:

fol.56 – Letter from Solomon Aldred to Walsingham, pledging his services as a spy, 15 November 1584.

fol.95 – Letter from the spy Maliverny Catlyn to Walsingham, complaining about shortage of money, December 1586.

fol.97 – Letter from the spy Maliverny Catlyn urging the banishment of imprisoned Catholic priests, undated but after August 1586.

fol.102 – Letter from the spy Maliverny Catlyn to Walsingham, complaining about stage plays in London and the behaviour of actors. No date.

fol.149 – Letter to Walsingham from Thomas Windebank, Clerk of the Signet, 14 September 1588.

fol.266 – Letter from the spy Maliverny Catlyn to Walsingham from Marshalsea Prison, ?May 1586.

Harleian MS 288, fol.218 – Letter to Walsingham from Sir Edward Stafford, English ambassador in Paris, about the demands on his finances, and describing the spy Roger Walton, 10 July 1588.

Harleian MS 290:

fol.81 – Comments by James VI about Walsingham, probably dated 1583.

fol.87 – A summary of events concerning the execution of Mary Queen of Scots sent by William Davison, then a prisoner in the Tower, to Walsingham, written in the hand of Raffe Starkey, 20 February 1587.

fol.88 – Letter from Mary Queen of Scots to Norfolk urging him to escape from house arrest at Howard House, 31 January 1571.

fol.117 – Manuscript copy of A *Discourse touching the pretended Match between the Duke of Norfolk and the Queen of Scots.* Another manuscript copy is in Harleian MS 4,314, fol.120. A printed copy is in Cotton MS Caligula C ii, fols.284–291.

fol.131 – Letter from Robert Beale to Walsingham about Mary Queen of Scots' need of air, Sheffield, 17 November 1581.

fol.213 – An 'intelligencer's' report to Walsingham from France, 1 February 1587.

fols.209–237 – Proceedings against Mr William Davison in the Star Chamber, 28 March 1587.

fol.238 – The queen's secret instructions to Sir Richard Wigmore on his mission to Scotland after the execution of Mary Queen of Scots.

Harleian MS 291, fol.146 – Account of the Scottish hiring of 'Kate', a witch and common scold, to revile Walsingham and the English diplomatic mission at Perth, September 1583.

Harleian MS 296:

fol.46 – Letter in the same hand as 'Pompeo Pellegrini' and signed 'B.

C.', endorsed 'from Mr Standen' on the reverse, Florence, 28 August 1587. Partly in cipher.

fol.48 – Letter from Stephen Paule to Walsingham, Venice, 7 November 1587.

Harleian MS 360, fol.65 – Plan to intern English Catholics in various castles, in Walsingham's handwriting, undated but probably late 1577.

Harleian MS 807, fol.4 – Pedigree of the Walsingham family by Robert Glover, *Somerset Herald*, undated.

Harleian MS 1,174, fol.53 – Another pedigree of the Walsingham family, undated.

Harleian MS 6,991:

>no.9 – Letter from Secretary of State Sir Thomas Smith to Burghley, mentioning the pregnancy of Ursula Walsingham, 7 January 1573.

>no.39 – Letter from Walsingham to Burghley, offering the use of two Italian agents for intelligence work, 20 August 1573

>no.57 – Letter from Walsingham to Burghley about the use of torture to extract information from the London stationer Henry Cockyn, 2 February 1575.

>no.58 – Letter from Walsingham to Burghley about his failure to extract information from the stationer Henry Cockyn, 5 February 1575.

Harleian MS 6,993:

>fol.50 – Letter from Walsingham to Burghley, with details of his illness, 2 July 1583.

>fol.125 – Letter from Walsingham in which he dismisses reports of Spanish preparations for invasion as 'Spanish brag', March 1586.

Harleian MS 6,994:

>fol.76 – Letter from Walsingham to Burghley, urging the return of Drake to harry the Spanish treasure fleets off the Azores, 16 July 1587.

>fol.189 – Letter from Walsingham to Burghley concerning his fever, 27 August 1589.

Harleian MS 9,889 – Letter from Richard Topcliffe to Elizabeth complaining of 'his disgrace' in being imprisoned in the Marshalsea Prison, 1595.

King's MS 119:

>fol.50 – French account of the alleged 'Stafford' plot to assassinate Elizabeth, January 1587.

>fol.80 – Conference between Walsingham and Châteauneuf, the French ambassador in London, about the 'Stafford' plot, 13 April 1587.

Lansdowne MS 31:

> Article 23 – Letter from Thomas Phelippes to Burghley concerning the 'false and base informations' supplied by Lawrence Smith, 1580.

> Article 35 – Letter from Jacomo Manucci to Burghley, seeking reward for his services, 26 January 1580.

Lansdowne MS 39, fol.21 – Letter from Dr William Parry to Burghley about the 'overthrow' of the English seminary at Rheims, 10 May 1583.

Lansdowne MS 43:

> Item 35 – English translation of an Italian letter from Cardinal Como to William Parry with the Pope's blessing, 30 January 1584.

> Item 47 – Parry's confession to Elizabeth in his own handwriting, 14 February 1584.

> Item 50 – Parry's indictment for assaulting and wounding his creditor, Hugh Hare, in his room in the Temple, London, 2 November 1580.

> Item 51 – Evidence against Parry on his arraignment for wounding Hugh Hare, 1580.

> Item 52 – Copy of the warrant for the execution of Parry, March 1585.

Lansdowne MS 49, no.25 – Babington's letter to his associate, Robert Pooley, before his arrest, 4 August 1586.

Lansdowne MS 50, Items 19–21 – Letters between the Earl of Sussex and Lord Burghley about a planned insurrection near Portsmouth, 4 June to 13 June 1586.

Lansdowne MS 51:

> Item 42 – Letter from the Mayor and Aldermen of Exeter to Lord Burghley seeking information on how to act in a hue and cry to retake the Queen of Scots, said to have made her escape, 3 February 1586.

> Item 43 – Letter from the Mayor and Aldermen of Exeter to the Privy Council seeking the truth of reports that London was on fire and that Mary Queen of Scots had escaped, 4 February 1586.

> Item 46 – Robert Wise's account of the execution of Mary Queen of Scots, communicated to Lord Burghley and endorsed by him, 8 February 1586.

> Item 66 – Copy of a long letter to the queen from Anthony Tyrrell, who had denied his Papist beliefs to become a Protestant but was now a Papist again, 1586.

Lansdowne MS 59, Item 74 – Letter from Edward Gage to Burghley asking that Richard Topcliffe's 'manner of making iron with peat may be investigated', written sometime in the 1590s.

Lansdowne MS 64, Item 6 – Confession of Richard Floyd, alias Lloyd, 'an imprisoned seminary priest, taken by Mr Topcliffe and Mr Young', 31 August 1590.

Lansdowne MS 72, Items 39, 40, 49 – Topcliffe papers (letters and reports).

Lansdowne MS 79, Item 93 – George Ellis's letter to Burghley complaining of his treatment by Topcliffe and of his wrongful imprisonment by the Lord Admiral, 1595.

Lansdowne MS 97:

> Items 5 and 6 – Anti-Jesuit documents, describing their 'artful designs and practices', undated.
>
> Item 9 – Articles of inquiry in the examination of Papists, drawn up by Sir Francis Knollys, undated.
>
> Item 10 – Prevarications and pleas of Papists when questioned at the examination, undated.

Lansdowne MS 103, fol.68 – Letter from Lord Burghley to the Tuscan diplomat Count Giovanni Figliazzi in Florence, informing him of Walsingham's death, 2 June 1590.

Lansdowne MS 153, fol.86 – Letter from William Vavasour imprisoned in Newgate to Henry Spiller about his conviction for praemunire and offering a £700 composition to James I, 19 June 1612.

Lansdowne MS 155, fols.84–106B – Thomas Norton's Book of Devices 'for keeping Jesuits and Seminarians from infecting the realm', written before 1585.

Lansdowne MS 167:

> fols.287, 289 – Sir Francis Walsingham's accounts, undated.
>
> fol.294 – Acquittal of debts owed by Walsingham's estate and to him by the crown by the judge Sir Julius Cæsar, 1611.

Lansdowne MS 982 – Vol. XLVIII of Bishop Kennett's collection of biographical memoranda, 1581–1600, fols.162 and 182 – Sir Francis Walsingham.

Lansdowne MS 1,198 – Life of Thomas Sutton, founder of Sutton's Hospital at the Charterhouse, London, undated but written in the seventeenth century.

NATIONAL ARCHIVES (at the Former Public Record Office, Kew, Surrey)

'AO' series – Account rolls of the Auditors of the Imprest and Commissioners of Audit.

'E' series – Documents of the exchequer and related bodies.

'KB' series – Records of the Court of King's Bench.

'PROB/PCC' series – Probate records, Prerogative Court of Canterbury.

'SP' series – State Papers.

AO 1/2,119/2 – Final accounts of Sir Amyas Paulet, custodian, for charges of keeping Mary Queen of Scots at Tutbury and Fotheringay, 1 March 1585 to 4 August 1587.

E 23/4/1 – Henry VIII's will, dated 30 December 1546.

E 101/676/48 – Accounts of Gilbert Dethicke, Garter King at Arms, for the funeral of Mary Queen of Scots, submitted after August 1587.

E 210/10,059 – Assignment of a debt due to Walsingham in payment of a debt due to the queen, 1583.

E 211/163 – Subsidy of poundage. Indenture between the queen and Walsingham, August 1585.

KB 8/42 – Roll and file of Court of Lord High Steward. Charges against Thomas, Duke of Norfolk, for high treason, January 1572.

PROB 11/47 PCC 32 STEVENSON – Will of Anne Walsingham, 28 July 1564. Proved: 28 November 1564.

PROB 11/48 PCC 35 CRYMES and MORRISON – Will of Sir Richard Worsley, of Appuldurcombe, Isle of Wight (first husband of Ursula Walsingham), 9 March 1566.

PROB 11/75 PCC 33 DRURY – Will of Sir Francis Walsingham, 12 December 1589. Proved: 7 December 1590.

PROB 11/100 PCC 55 MONTAGUE – Will of Lady Ursula Walsingham, widow of Sir Francis Walsingham, of Barn Elms, Surrey, 30 January 1602. Proved: 5 July 1602.

SP 12/48/61 – Letter from Walsingham to Cecil, 20 December 1568.

SP 12/141/29 – Account of attempts to convert Catholics in York Cathedral, August 1580.

SP 12/175/110 – 'Secret advertisements touching Mass priests' in the North of England from Walsingham's agent Robert Barnard, December 1584.

SP 12/176/22 – Burghley's proposals for a 'Grand Council' to govern England in the event of the queen's assassination, 1584–5.

SP 12/193/54 – Copy of the forged postscript of Mary Queen of Scots' letter to Anthony Babington, 17 July 1586.

SP 12/198/64 – Instructions to Justices of the Peace on the maintenance and operation of warning beacons, 1587.

SP 46/16, fols.223–224 – Licences granted to Walsingham and others for the export of cloth, 1575–80.

SP 46/17:

> fol.18 – Goldsmith's accounts showing sums owing to Lady Walsingham, August to November 1581.

> fol.166 – Earl of Shrewsbury to Walsingham, seeking favour for the town of Doncaster impoverished by the plague and warning that if the queen's grant of Hextroppe, Hunster Woods and Rossington Park to Nicholas Pudsey takes effect, the queen's mills, etc. in Doncaster will decay for lack of timber, Sheffield Castle, 9 January 1584.

> fol.228 – Conditions for a grant of customs of Plymouth and Fowey, Cornwall, to Walsingham for six years from Michaelmas, 17 August 1585.

SP 46/19/38 – Thomas Phelippes' request to pay his debt to the crown by instalments and to have the aid of the exchequer in recovering his own debts, as his estate is impaired by his imprisonment and loss of office [?1598].

SP 46/34, fols.65–66B – Supplementary Treasury documents, 1586–88: Letter from Walsingham to Mildmay asking that the £829 due from Sir Walter Raleigh and others be accepted as part of his rent for the farm of the customs, 28 May 1586.

SP 46/39, fol.293 – Humble request of Thomas Phelippes concerning his debts to the queen, 1595.

SP 46/40, fol.110 – Stay of process against Thomas Phelippes and his sureties, 5 October 1596.

SP 46/125:

> fol.137 – Jacomo Manucci to Walsingham. He is too ill to come to court but begs that the queen remember Fryman's bill and states that Filippo Corsini will lend Walsingham £400 'if the alderman will be bound', London, 9 June 1584.

> fols.143–143B – Jacomo Manucci to Walsingham. Has information against Filippo Corsini for illegal export of wool. Discusses the difficulties of alien merchants in the wool trade and proposes a conference with the Company of the Staple, London, 10 September 1584.

SP 53/22 and 53/23 – Two books of ciphers and decodes relating to the correspondence of Mary Queen of Scots; blue half-leather volumes both titled *Ciphers – Scotland.*

SP 78/21 – Account of receipts and disbursements during employment of M. de Chateaumartin by Walsingham, July 1590.

SP 84/8/131 – Letter from Sir Philip Sidney to Walsingham, Flushing, 28 June 1586.

NATIONAL LIBRARY OF SCOTLAND, EDINBURGH

Adv. MS 54.1.1. – Last letter of Mary Queen of Scots, to King Henry III of France, Fotheringay, 8 February 1587.

BODLEIAN LIBRARY, OXFORD

Ashmolean MS 1,157, no.87 – Letter from an anonymous correspondent regarding Walsingham's administration of the Duchy of Lancaster, 16 May 1595.

Tanner MS 79, fols.127ff. – Letter (in cipher) from Walsingham to William Harborne, English ambassador to the Turks, Constantinople, 24 June 1587.

GUILDHALL LIBRARY, CITY OF LONDON

Hustings Rolls of the City of London – 13; 131, no.62; 133, nos.24 and 71; 137, no.24; 144, no.16; 192, no.14; 255, no.49.

HATFIELD HOUSE, HERTFORDSHIRE

Manuscripts of Marquis of Salisbury

'**CP**' prefix denotes Cecil Papers.

CP 13/77 – Mary Queen of Scots' bond 'to be an enemy to all those that attempt anything against Queen Elizabeth's life', 5 January 1585.

CP 13/86v–88 – Thomas Morgan to Mary Queen of Scots, 5 January 1585.

CP 15/56 – Warrant for the execution of Mary Queen of Scots, December 1586.

CP 15/79 – 'Note of things to be considered'.

CP 16/17 – Circumstances of the execution of Mary Queen of Scots, bearing Burghley's holograph, 17 February 1587.

CP 90/150 – Letter from Sir Walter Raleigh to Sir Robert Cecil, ?1600.

CP 164/9 – Memo by Sir Francis Walsingham on the execution of Mary Queen of Scots, 2 February 1587.

CP 164/10 – Rough draft of a letter from the Privy Council to Elizabeth on the circumstances surrounding the execution of Mary Queen of Scots, 12 February 1587.

CP 164/15 – Rough draft of a second letter from the Privy Council, 'A writing in the name of all the counsellors that sent Mr Beale to the Earl of Shrewsbury', 12 February 1587.

CP 164/17 – The case of the Queen of Scots' death, bearing Burghley's holograph, 17 February 1587.

CP 164/105 – Letter from the Master of Gray to Archibald Douglas, Scottish ambassador to London, 10 September 1586.

CP 164/109 – Letter from the Provost of Lincluden to Archibald Douglas, Scottish ambassador to London, 26 September 1586.

CP 164/114 – Letter from Burghley to Sir Edward Stafford, ambassador to France, 2 October 1586.

CP 164/140 – Note from Roger Aston, James VI's confidential agent, to Archibald Douglas, the Scottish ambassador to London, 24 October 1586.

CP 165/10 – Elizabeth's warrant for the execution of Mary Queen of Scots, addressed to Sir Amyas Paulet, bearing Burghley's holograph, [blank] December 1586.

CP 165/19 – Reasons against executing Mary Queen of Scots, bearing Burghley's holograph, 1586.

CP 165/20–21 – Description of the execution of Mary Queen of Scots, February 1587.

CP 165/57 – Letter from the Earl of Leicester to Burghley, 9 April 1587.

CP Petitions 2,424 – Suit of Arthur Gregory to James I, seeking recusant lands and fines 'in consideration of my services', no date, probably 1604.

LONGLEAT HOUSE, WARMINSTER, WILTSHIRE

Seymour Papers

SE/Vol. V – Correspondence relating to the clandestine marriage of Lord Beauchamp to Honora, daughter of Sir Richard Rogers of Bryanston, 1581–2.

SURREY HISTORY CENTRE, WOKING, SURREY

Loseley MS LM/1,042/14 – Dispute between the inhabitants of Farnham and their vicar, Daniel Craft, ?1584.

WILTSHIRE AND SWINDON RECORD OFFICE, TROWBRIDGE, WILTSHIRE

947/1,350 – Two accounts of revenues and disbursements of the manors of Bradford and Atworth, property of Sir Francis Walsingham, by Edward Long, Bailiff of Monkton in Broughton Gifford, undated.

PRINTED SOURCES

APC – Acts of the Privy Council, new series:

Vol. VIII, 1571–5, John Roche Dasent (ed.), London, 1894.

Vol. XIV, 1575–7, John Roche Dasent (ed.), London, 1894.

Vol. XV, 1587–8, John Roche Dasent (ed.), London, 1897.

Vol. XVI, 1588, John Roche Dasent (ed.), London, 1897.

Vol. XVII, 1588–9, John Roche Dasent (ed.), London, 1898.

'Bardon Papers' – *The Bardon Papers: Documents Relating to the Imprisonment & Trial of Mary Queen of Scots*, Conyers Read (ed.), Camden 3rd Series, Vol. XVII, London, 1909.

Brown, Joseph, *The Tryal of Thomas Duke of Norfolk by his Peers for High Treason against the Queen [in] 1571*, London, 1709.

Bruce, John (ed.), *Correspondence of Robert Dudley, Earl of Leicester, during his Government of the Low Countries 1585–86*, Camden Society, London, 1844.

'Cal. Scot' – Calendar of Scottish Papers:

Vol. IV, 1571–4, William K. Boyd (ed.), Edinburgh, 1905.

Vol. V, 1574–81, William K. Boyd (ed.), Edinburgh, 1907.

Vol. VI, 1581–3, William K. Boyd (ed.), Edinburgh, 1909.

Vol. VIII, 1585–6, William K. Boyd (ed.), Edinburgh, 1914.

Vol. IX, 1586–8, William K. Boyd (ed.), London, 1915.

'Cal. Spanish' – *Calendar of Letters and State Papers Relating Principally to the Archives of Simancas . . . in the Reign of Elizabeth*, Martin S. Hume (ed.), 4 vols., London, 1892–9.

Camden, William, *Annales in the Historie of the Most Renowned and Victorious Princess Elizabeth, late Queen of England*, 3rd edn., London, 1635.

Corbett, Sir Julian S., *Papers Relating to the Navy during the Spanish War 1585–87*, Naval Record Society, 2 vols., London, 1898.

CRS – Publications of the Catholic Record Society:

Vol. II, *Miscellanea, Letters and Memorials of Father Robert Persons SJ* (1546–84), London, 1906.

Vol. IV, *Miscellanea*, London, 1907.

Vol. V, *Unpublished Documents Relating to the English Martyrs*, John Hungerford Pollen SJ (ed.), London, 1908.

Vol. XXI, *Ven. Philip Howard, Earl of Arundel*, John Hungerford Pollen SJ and William MacMahon SJ (eds.), London, 1919.

Vol. XXXVII, *Liber Ruber Venerabilis Collegii Anglorum de Urbe,* 1579–1630, Wilfred Kelly (ed.), London, 1940.

Vol. XXXIX, *Letters and Memorials of Father Robert Persons SJ* (to 1588), L. Hicks SJ (ed.), London, 1942.

Vol. LIII, *Yelverton MS Miscellanea,* Clare Talbot (ed.), London, 1961, pp.186–245.

CSPF – Calendar State Papers Foreign, Elizabeth:

1569–71, Allan Crosby (ed.), London, 1874.

1572–4, Allan Crosby (ed.), London, 1876.

1577–8, Arthur J. Butler (ed.), London, 1901.

1578–9, Arthur J. Butler (ed.), London, 1903.

1579–80, Arthur J. Butler (ed.), London, 1904.

January–June 1583 and Addenda, Arthur J. Butler and Sophie Crawford Lomas (eds.), London, 1913.

July 1583–July 1584, Sophie Crawford Lomas (ed.), London, 1914.

August 1584–August 1585, Sophie Crawford Lomas (ed.), London, 1916.

CSP Milan – *Calendar of State Papers Existing in Archives of Milan,* Vol. I, Allen B. Hinds (ed.), London, 1912.

CSP Rome – *Calendar of State Papers Relating to English Affairs Preserved Principally at Rome,* Vol. II – Elizabeth 1572–8, J. M. Rigg (ed.), London, 1926.

Digges, Sir Digby, *The Compleat Ambassador – or Two Treaties of the Intended Marriage of Queen Elizabeth . . . Comprised in Letters of Negotiation,* London, 1655.

Fénelon, Bertrand de Salignac de la Mothe, *Correspondance Diplomatique de Bertrand de Salignac de la Mothe Fénelon, Ambassadeur de France en Angleterre, de 1568–75,* A. Teulet (ed.), 7 vols., Paris and London, 1838–40.

Griffin, Ralph, *Visitation of Arms of Kent 1594,* London, 1924.

Harleian Miscellany, William Oldys and Thomas Park (eds.), 9 vols., London, 1808–12.

HMC – Historical Manuscript Commission Reports:

'Cal. Foljambe' – MSS of Francis J. Saville Foljambe of Osberton, London, 1897.

'Finch' – Report on MSS of Allan George Finch of Burley on the Hill, Rutland, Hereford, 1913.

'Rutland' – MSS of the Duke of Rutland preserved at Belvoir House, Vol. I, London, 1888.

'Salisbury' – Report on MSS of the Marquis of Salisbury at Hatfield House, Vol. III, London, 1889; Vol. X, London, 1894.

'Journal' – *Journal of Sir Francis Walsingham from December 1570 to April 1583*, C. T. Martin (ed.), Camden Miscellany, VI, vol. 104 (os), London, 1870.

Labanoff-Rostovsky, Prince Aleksander, *Lettres, Instructions et Mémoires de Marie Stuart published sur les originaux et les manuscrits du State Paper Office Londres*, 7 vols., London, 1844.

Langton, John, *Defeat of the Spanish Armada, Anno 1588*, 2 vols., Naval Record Society, London, 1894.

'Letter Book' – *The Walsingham Letter-Book or Register of Ireland – May 1578– December 1579*, James Hogan and H. McNeill O'Farrell (eds.), Dublin, 1959.

Lodge, Edmund, *Illustrations of British History, Biography and Manners in the Reigns of Henry VIII, Edward VI, Mary, Elizabeth and James I . . . selected from the Manuscripts of the . . . families of Howard, Talbot and Cecil . . .*, 3 vols., London, 1838.

LPFD Henry VIII – Letters and Papers Foreign and Domestic of the Reign of Henry VIII:

Vol. IV, pt.i, J. S. Brewer (ed.), London, 1870.

Vol. IV, pt.ii, J. S. Brewer (ed.), London, 1872.

Vol. IV, pt.iii, J. S. Brewer (ed.), London, 1876.

Vol. V, James Gairdner (ed.), London, 1884.

Murdin, William, *Collection of State Papers Relating to Affairs in the Reign of Queen Elizabeth*, 2 vols., London, 1759.

Naunton, Sir Robert, *Fragmenta Regalia, or Observations on the late Queen Elizabeth, her Times and Favourites*, London, 1641.

Nichols, John, *Progresses and Public Processions of Queen Elizabeth*, 3 vols., London, 1823.

'Paulet' – *Letter Books of Sir Amyas Paulet, Keeper of Mary Queen of Scots*, John Morris (ed.), London, 1874.

'Sadler Papers' – *State Papers and Letters of Sir Ralph Sadler*, Arthur Clifford (ed.), 3 vols., Edinburgh, 1809.

Sharp, Sir Cuthbert, *Memorials of the Rebellion of 1569*, London, 1840.

Smith, Alan (ed.), *The Last Years of Mary, Queen of Scots*, Roxburghe Club, London, 1990.

SPD – Calendar of State Papers Domestic:

Edward VI, Mary & Elizabeth, 1547–80, Robert Lemon (ed.), London, 1856.

Elizabeth, Addenda, 1566–79, Mary Anne Everett Green (ed.), London, 1871.

Elizabeth & James, Addenda, 1580–1625, Mary Anne Everett Green (ed.), London, 1872.

Elizabeth, 1581–90, Robert Lemon (ed.), London, 1865.

James I, 1603–10, Mary Anne Everett Green (ed.), London, 1857.

James I, 1611-18, Mary Anne Everett Green (ed.), London, 1858.

'State Trials' – *State Trials: A Complete Collection of State Trials and Proceedings for High Treason*, 4th edn., 11 vols., London, 1776.

Stow, John, *A Survey of London, 1603*, Charles Kingsford (ed.), 2 vols., Oxford, 1908.

Strype, John, *Annals of the Reformation*, 6 vols., Oxford, 1824.

'Visitations' – *Visitations of Kent in 1574 and 1592 by Robert Cooke, Clarenceux Herald*, W. Bruce Bannerman (ed.), London, 1924.

Watson, Thomas, *An Eglogue upon the Death of the Right Honourable Sir Francis Walsingham*, London, 1590.

SECONDARY SOURCES

Calculations of modern monetary values have been derived from:

McCusker, John, 'Comparing the Purchasing Power of Money in Great Britain from 1264 to any other year including the Present', Economic History Services 2001, http://www.eh.net/hmit/ppowerbp.

Allen, Cardinal Dr William, *A Brief History of the Glorious Martyrdom of Twelve Reverend Priests*, J. H. Pollen (ed.), London, 1908.

Anderson, James, *Collections Relating to the History of Mary Queen of Scots*, 4 vols., Edinburgh, 1727–8.

Baugham, Denver E., 'Sir Philip Sidney and the Matchmakers', *Modern Language Review*, 33 (1938), pp.506–9.

Birch, Thomas, *Memoirs of the Reign of Queen Elizabeth from the year 1581 to her death, in which the secret intrigues of her court and conduct of her favourite Robert, Earl of Essex, are particularly illustrated . . .*, 2 vols., London, 1754.

Bossy, John, *Giordano Bruno and the Embassy Affair*, Yale, 1991.

— *Under the Molehill: An Elizabethan Spy Story*, Yale, 2002.

Brenan, Gerard and Edward Phillips Statham (eds.), *The House of Howard*, 2 vols., London, 1907.

Busse, Daniela, 'Anti-Catholic Polemical Writing on the "Rising in the North" (1569) and the Catholic Reaction', *Recusant History*, 27 (2004), pp.11–30.

Caraman, Philip (trans.) *John Gerard: An Autobiography of an Elizabethan*, London, 1951.

Collier, Jeremy, *Ecclesiastical History of Great Britain, chiefly of England from the first planting of Christianity to the end of the reign of King Charles the Second*, 2 vols., London, 1714.

Collinson, Patrick, *The English Captivity of Mary Queen of Scots*, Sheffield, 1987.

Covington, Sarah, *The Trail of Martyrdom: Persecution and Resistance in Sixteenth-Century England*, Notre Dame, Indiana, 2003.

Dack, Charles, *The Trial, Execution and Death of Mary Queen of Scots*, Northampton, 1889.

Deacon, Richard, *A History of the British Secret Services*, London, 1969.

'DNB1' – *Dictionary of National Biography*, 1st edn., Sir Leslie Stephens and Sir Sidney Lee (eds.), 63 vols., Oxford, 1885–1912.

'DNB2' – *Dictionary of National Biography*, new edn., H. G. G. Matthews and Brian Harrison (eds.), 60 vols., Oxford, 2004.

Dugdale, Sir William, *The History of St Paul's Cathedral in London*, 2nd edn., London, 1716.

Edwards, Francis, *The Marvellous Chance: Thomas Howard, Fourth Duke of Norfolk, and the Ridolphi Plot 1570–72*, London, 1968.

—— *Plots and Plotters in the Reign of Elizabeth I*, Dublin, 2002.

Fell Smith, Charlotte, *John Dee (1527–1608)*, Berwick, Maine, 2004.

Fernandez–Armesto, Felipe, *The Spanish Armada – The Experience of War*, Oxford, 1988.

Fisher, Major Payne, *The Tombs, Monuments and Sepulchral Inscriptions lately visible in St Paul's Cathedral*, London, 1684.

Foley, Henry, *Records of the English Province of the Society of Jesus*, 7 vols., London, 1882.

Fuller, Thomas, *Church History of Great Britain*, London, 1655.

Gallagher, P. and E. Cruickshank (eds.), *God's Obvious Design: A Spanish Armada Symposium at Sligo, 1988*, Bury St Edmunds, 1990.

Graves, Michael, *Profiles in Power: Burghley*, London, 1998.

Guy, John, *My Heart is My Own: The Life of Mary Queen of Scots*, London, 2004.

Harris, John, *History of Kent*, London, 1719.

Hasler, P. W., *History of Parliament 1558–1603*, Vol. III – Members M–Z, London, 1981.

Haynes, Alan, *Invisible Power: Elizabethan Secret Services*, London, 1992.

Houliston, Victor, 'The Fabrication of the Myth of Father Persons', *Recusant History*, 22, ii (1994), pp.141–51.

Howells, T. and T. J. Howells, *Complete Collection of State Trials*, 33 vols., London, 1809–28.

Hutchinson, Robert, *The Last Days of Henry VIII*, London, 2005.

Law, Thomas, *A Historical Sketch of the Conflicts between Jesuits and Seculars in the Reign of Queen Elizabeth*, London and Edinburgh, 1889.

Leader, John, *Mary Queen of Scots in Captivity: A Narrative of Events 1569–84*, Sheffield, 1880.

Lloyd, David, *State Worthies During the Reigns of Henry VIII, Edward VI, Mary, Elizabeth, James I and Charles I*, 2nd edn., 2 vols., London, 1670.

Meyer, Arnold, *England und die Katholische Kirche unter Elisabeth und den Stuarts*, Rome, 1911.

Morris, John SJ (ed.), *The Troubles of Our Catholic Forefathers Related by Themselves*, 3 series, London, 1872–7.

Motley, John, *History of the United Netherlands*, 4 vols., London, 1901.

Nairn, Ian, Nikolaus Pevsner and Bridget Cherry, *Buildings of England – Surrey*, 2nd edn., Harmondsworth, 1971.

Neale, Sir Ernest, 'Proceedings in Parliament Relative to the Sentence on Mary Queen of Scots', *English Historical Review*, XXXV (1920), pp.103–13.

— *Elizabeth I and Her Parliaments 1584–1601*, London, 1957.

— *Essays in Elizabethan History*, Oxford, 1958.

Nicholas, Sir Harris, *Memoirs of the Life and Times of Sir Christopher Hatton*, London, 1848.

— *Life of William Davison*, London, 1823.

Nuttall, Geoffrey, 'The English Martyrs 1535–1680: A Statistical Summary', *Journal of Ecclesiastical History*, 22 (1971), pp.191–7.

Phillips, J. E., *Images of a Queen: Mary Stuart in Sixteenth-Century Literature*, Berkeley, 1964.

Plowden, Alison, *The Elizabethan Secret Service*, Hemel Hempstead, 1991.

Pollen, John H. (ed.), *Mary Queen of Scots and the Babington Plot*, Scottish History Society, Edinburgh, 1922.

Prescott-Jones, R., *Funeral of Mary Queen of Scots*, Privately Printed, Edinburgh, 1890.

Pritchard, Arnold, *Catholic Loyalism in Elizabethan England*, Chapel Hill, North Carolina, 1979.

RCHM – Royal Commission on Historical Monuments, *London*, Vol. V – 'East London', London, 1930.

Read, Conyers, *Life of Sir Francis Walsingham to 1578*, Ph.D. thesis, Harvard, 1908.

— *Mr Secretary Walsingham and the Policy of Queen Elizabeth*, 3 vols., Oxford, 1925.

— 'The Proposal to Assassinate Mary Queen of Scots at Fotheringay', *English Historical Review*, XL (1925), pp.234–5.

— *The Tudors: Personalities and Practical Politics in Sixteenth-Century England*, Oxford, 1936.

— *Mr Secretary Cecil and Queen Elizabeth*, London, 1955.

— *Lord Burghley and Queen Elizabeth*, London, 1960.

Rendle, William, *Old Southwark*, London, 1878.

Rex, Richard, *The Tudors*, Stroud, 2003.

Richings, Mildred G., *Espionage: The Story of the Secret Service of the English Crown*, London, 1934.

Ridley, Jasper, *The Tudor Age*, London, 2002.

Robinson, John Martin, *The Dukes of Norfolk*, Chichester, 1995.

Scot, Mrs Maxwell, *The Tragedy of Fotheringay, Founded on the Journal of Dr Bourgoing, Physician to Mary Queen of Scots*, London, 1895.

Somers, John Baron, *Collection of Scarce and Valuable Tracts*, Sir Walter Scott (ed.), 13 vols., London, 1809–15.

Somerset, Anne, *Elizabeth I*, London, 2002.

Stählin, Carl, *Sir Francis Walsingham und seine Zeit . . . Mit einem Porträt*, 1 vol. (no more published), Heidelberg, 1908.

Steuart, Francis, *Trial of Mary Queen of Scots*, London, 1951.

Stewart, Alan, *Philip Sidney: A Double Life*, London, 2000.

Strong, Roy, *Portraits of Queen Elizabeth I*, Oxford, 1963.

Tanner, J. R., *Tudor Constitutional Documents*, Cambridge, 1951.

VCH – Victoria County History – R. B. Pugh, *Cambridge and the Isle of Ely*, Vol. 4, London 1953.

Wallace, Malcolm, *Life of Sir Philip Sidney*, Cambridge, 1915.

Watson, William, *Historical Account of the Town of Wisbech*, Wisbech, 1827.

Webb, E. A., G. W. Miller and J. Beckwith, *The History of Chislehurst*, London, 1899.

Welwood, James, *Memoirs of the Most Material Transactions in England in the last One Hundred Years Preceding the Revolution in 1688*, London, 1820.

Wernham, R. B., 'The Disgrace of William Davison', *English Historical Review*, XLVI (1931), pp.632–6.

Williams, Neville, *A Tudor Tragedy: Thomas Howard, Duke of Norfolk*, London, 1964.

Worsley, Richard, *The History of the Isle of Wight*, London, 1781.

Index